OMNIVM LVX CIVIVM

BOSTON
PUBLIC
LIBRARY

Y0-ABP-946

PERSON PERCEPTION
IN
CHILDHOOD AND ADOLESCENCE

P211
P229

Person Perception

in

Childhood and Adolescence

W. J. LIVESLEY

D. B. BROMLEY

Department of Psychology
The University of Liverpool

JOHN WILEY & SONS LTD
London · New York · Sydney · Toronto

Copyright © 1973 John Wiley & Sons Ltd.
All Rights Reserved. No part of this publication may be reproduced, stored in a retrieval
system, or transmitted, in any form or by any
means, electronic, mechanical photo-copying,
recording or otherwise, without the prior
written permission of the Copyright owner.

Library of Congress catalog card number
72–8606

ISBN 0 471 54160 5

Made and printed in Great Britain by
The Garden City Press Limited
Letchworth, Hertfordshire SG6 1JS

"BOSTON PUBLIC LIBRARY"

A boy aged 9,11 describes a boy he dislikes:

He smells very much and is very nasty. He has no sense of humour and is very dull. He is always fighting and he is cruel. He does silly things and is very stupid. He has brown hair and cruel eyes. He is sulky and eleven years old and has lots of sisters. I think he is the most horrible boy in the class. He has a croaky voice and always chews his pencil and picks his teeth and I think he is disgusting.

Preface

This book is the culmination of several years of cooperative work between the authors. What can a reader expect to find in it? First and foremost, he can expect to find an account of the development, through childhood and adolescence, of the process variously known as person perception, impression formation or understanding others. This account is interesting in terms of psychological theory and it contains an abundance of empirical data. We are anxious that people who have little or no knowledge of statistics should not be dismayed by the technicalities described and discussed in Chapters 5 and 6. Provided they are prepared to accept the logic of the investigation and the consequential statistical results, their appreciation of the bulk of the empirical findings and of the theoretical framework will not be impaired if they do not fully understand these two chapters. Other readers, however, will not be prepared to take the logic of the investigation on trust; so for their benefit, and because scientific work sets high standards of proof, we have gone to some lengths to describe and justify the statistical and other sorts of methodology used in the main inquiry. Additional statistical information, in the form of analysis of variance tables, can be obtained from the authors on request. We have tried to make the statistical and other methodological sections as simple as possible so that other investigators should have no difficulty in replicating and extending the research we describe. Indeed, we mention a number of possible lines for further inquiry.

What sorts of people can expect to benefit by reading this book? Primarily, of course, people who are, or who expect to become, psychologists or educationalists. Those with little or no prior knowledge of modern psychology will find it difficult, to say the least. But again, we are anxious that people who deal with children or who deal with human relationships, but do not have a professional training in psychology, should make an effort to find out what the book has to say for them. We have in mind here: teachers, counsellors, social workers, and others whose work calls for a 'deep' understanding of the way people come to understand (and misunderstand) themselves and others.

vii

We gave considerable thought to the question of how to present our ideas and findings, and eventually decided that a strictly logical and historical order was the most appropriate. The effect of this decision, however, is that the more interesting findings and discussions are reached only after a detailed consideration of the background literature and research techniques. We appreciate that some readers may wish to go directly to these findings and discussions but feel that some understanding of the background to our thinking and method is necessary.

In our opinion, the book makes a contribution to general psychology —partly on account of its theoretical framework, partly on account of the empirical evidence it contains. In particular, it contributes to: developmental psychology, person perception (understanding others), clinical psychology and personality study, cognitive psychology, social psychology and research methodology. As a psychology textbook, perhaps its special feature is that it brings together a variety of issues in the areas we have just mentioned in ways which we think are basic to the theory and practice of psychology. The book is not a technical monograph—although it might have been written as such. It deals with *persons*, and that is what psychology is all about.

Department of Psychology,   W. J. LIVESLEY
The University of Liverpool   D. B. BROMLEY
                                               April, 1972

Acknowledgements

Our first and foremost acknowledgement goes to the many children and teachers from a number of schools on Merseyside whose cooperation made this study possible. Professor L. S. Hearnshaw, Dr Agnes Crawford, and Dr A. D. Lovie of the Department of Psychology at the University of Liverpool gave support or advice in the early stages of the investigation. Discussions with Mr L. A. Lewis, Principal Clinical Psychologist, Winwick Hospital, Lancashire, helped to clarify our thinking about psychodynamic issues. The Nuffield Foundation provided a grant for the production and testing of a research film. A Medical Research Council grant provided for some secretarial and clerical help during the final stages of the preparation of the manuscript. A number of former students of Liverpool University became interested in person perception and helped in our investigations.

Some brief quotations from the research literature are acknowledged in the usual way by reference to the authors in the text and to published sources in the bibliography.

Mrs D. Southern, Miss C. Georgiou, Miss E. McTear, Miss P. B. Yeomans, Mrs J. Taylor, and Mrs B. J. Fazakerley coped efficiently and pleasantly with our heavy demands on secretarial and clerical services.

We are grateful to Wiley's editorial advisers for help in preparing the manuscript for publication.

We also wish to thank John Livesley's parents for their invaluable help with the many boring and routine clerical tasks that the content analysis entailed.

Finally, and most important of all, we owe an immense debt of gratitude to our wives, Ann and Roma, without whose constant support and unselfishness this book could never have been completed. They have cheerfully tolerated lives organized around our research; Ann has also been a valuable research assistant.

Contents

Contents

CHAPTER 1

Introduction: Perceiving and Thinking about Persons and their Behaviour

I. The Problem of Person Perception (Impression Formation)

The area of psychology concerned with how we 'perceive' or 'cognize' other persons—their intentions, attitudes, traits, emotions, ideas, abilities and purposes, as well as their overt behaviour and physical characteristics—can be referred to variously as 'person perception', 'impression formation', or 'understanding others'.

The problem of how we perceive and understand the behaviour and psychological states of other people has fascinated men throughout the ages. Those of us with an interest in current affairs are constantly being offered ways of making sense of the actions of well-known people. Newspapers and other media present us with character analyses of politicians, businessmen and entertainers, and inform us that they have certain motives, personality traits, weaknesses and talents. We are told that their attitudes and decisions are influenced by various considerations—party loyalty, personal vanity, ethical values or long-range socio-economic aims. In much the same way, historians and biographers try to persuade us to accept their impressions or assessments of characters in history; and again, we are given to understand that the decisions and actions of such people were determined by certain personal qualities, and that their life-histories consisted of specific patterns and sequences of behaviour bound together by the interaction of personality and circumstance.

1

In fiction and biography, writers of all kinds have been fascinated and perplexed as they have tried to portray the subtleties and complexities of individual human behaviour and social relationships. Our impressions of persons in works of fiction are shaped by the way we construe the material presented by the writer, who is free to present all sorts of fictional 'evidence'. He is limited only by considerations of style, ability, length and so on. The fictitious person talks, thinks, acts, reacts, feels, wants; in short, he does all the things that a person in real life might do. In addition, the writer may present his own impressions of the fictional character—making judgments and interpretations and describing him as if he were a real person. He may use secondary characters whose words and actions contribute to the evidence, and help to shape the reader's overall impression of the fictitious person.

Most of all, the problem of understanding others—of being able to predict, explain and manage other people's behaviour—concerns us as ordinary persons in our everyday social interactions, because effective action in personal relationships requires a selective perception of behaviour and a sensitive understanding of the covert psychological processes underlying overt actions. It also requires an appreciation of the emotional and behavioural relationships between one person and another, and the context of circumstances and events in which they are embedded. As regards the related problems of understanding 'self' and 'personal identity', all that needs to be said at this point is that they form important and interesting topics in the psychology of person perception and will be dealt with in due course.

In normal, everyday social activities, we often find ourselves faced with the problem of making sense of the behaviour of another person—like trying to understand why a child engages in unprovoked assault or vandalism, or trying to predict how one's spouse will react to a given situation. In professional circumstances, such as marriage counselling, vocational guidance and selection, and industrial relations, there has to be a *sustained effort* to understand, which requires a willingness to search for evidence and to construct valid inferences about the person with whom one is dealing.

Most of us at one time or another have had our expectations of others either confirmed or refuted; we may have concluded either that our appraisal of the other person was correct, or incorrect as the case may be, or that the experience itself was at fault. The Piagetian processes of assimilation and accommodation are easily exemplified in the way we perceive and interpret the behaviour of other people. As we grow up, we learn to 'form impressions' of other people even without the help of formal education. That is to say, we learn how to perceive and understand their actions and states of mind. We can ignore, for the time being, questions about the validity and accuracy of the 'impressions' we form; most of us are only too well aware of how frequently and badly our understanding of others goes wrong. Usually our interpersonal relationships progress smoothly and efficiently and we can assimilate a wide range of perceptual data about people into reasonably valid and stable schemata which have the function of initiating and guiding our responses in relation to them.

Much of the time, probably most of the time, these systems of ideas and feelings that we have about other individuals operate implicitly, without our reflecting upon them or becoming fully conscious of how they initiate and guide our actions. Rather like well-established habits of learning and thinking, they constitute a kind of cognitive matrix within which our many and varied responses to others are formed, and from which they derive their consistency and organization.

In a similar way, as we grow up, we learn to 'form impressions' of all manner of things in nature—its flora and fauna, the sizes and shapes and weights of things, the actions of light, heat and moisture and so on. The difference, however, is that nowadays children receive systematic formal instruction about the nature of the *physical* world—they are taught geography, biology and natural science; so that, in a sense, their understanding of nature is a great advance upon what their untutored minds would have achieved. Similar instruction is clearly needed in relation to the behavioural, social and psychological aspects of the world in which we live. Only within the last year or two have the social and behavioural sciences been introduced into the curriculum of schools; so obviously we have a long way to go in exploring and eradicating popular misconceptions about *human* nature. Progress is likely to be slow since we must assume that even among the so-called experts—psychologists, social scientists, psychiatrists, educationalists—there exist erroneous preconceptions and ways of thinking that lead to misunderstandings and ignorance about human nature and to the formation of false impressions of individual people.

Apart from any contributions that might be made to the practical problems of understanding other people—for example, in clinical psychology, education and industrial relations—we feel that deep investigations into the processes involved in understanding, and misunderstanding, other people are needed, so that social and behavioural scientists can examine the 'ground rules' of their own discipline. Thus, they can become aware of, and make explicit, the concepts and ways of thinking that underlie their descriptions and explanations of social phenomena and individual behaviour. We feel that at professional and scientific levels of psychological and social work there exists a kind of 'cognitive infrastructure'—a set of implicit assumptions, rules, beliefs and habits of mind—which underlies and gives shape and direction to our ideas about people and society. A simple and familiar example is the persistent 'nature versus nurture' controversy which forces protagonists to disclose the fundamental premises upon which their arguments rest. Issues arising in connection with 'criminal behaviour' provide additional examples. It seems very likely that other controversies and other phenomena which are poorly understood at present, such as marital incompatibility, reputation and the 'self', will become more comprehensible as we uncover the implicit assumptions which lead us to ask the wrong questions (or not to question at all) and to draw the wrong inferences. In much the same way, in dealing with people as individuals our attempts to understand them will sometimes be hindered by implicit false premises analogous to those encountered in the history of science and in legal history.

We have seen that the problems involved in trying to understand others have an implicit interest for historians and biographers, for readers and writers of fiction, and particularly for anyone who, in a professional or semi-professional capacity, is required to make assessments of other people. We have also seen that these problems are absolutely basic to clinical psychology and personality psychology in so far as these disciplines are concerned with the description and explanaation of the behaviour of individual people. Finally, we can briefly mention the implicit interest that some philosophers have in person perception—in particular, those who concern themselves with our knowledge of other minds, such as Ayer (1964), or with persons as objects of perception and as 'individuals', see Strawson (1964), or with the philosophy of behavioural science, such as Turner (1965), or, of course, with the self and personal identity, such as Williams (1964). Ayer, for example, examines the idea that we construe the experiences of other people by analogy with our own states of mind, while Strawson examines the philosophical issues raised by the notion of subjective experience and self-consciousness.

Some interesting areas overlapping psychology and philosophy which have a particular relevance to person perception are dealt with in, for example, Mischel (1969), de Charms (1968) and Peters (1960). Such areas include 'common sense', 'rule-following', and 'personal causation'. In the course of his development, the individual acquires a set of 'mental constructs'—for example: friendly, pompous, reliable. He finds these useful for describing people and predicting their actions in different situations. Similarly, he acquires a set of rules which, when made explicit, are seen to specify the relationships between psychological qualities and the way these qualities are modified by moods and situations. Such rules can be generalized—in the sense that they apply to people in general or to certain broad classes of people. They can also be individualized—in the sense of being tailored to fit a particular person. Hempel (1965) discusses the philosophical and logical problems associated with generalization. Thus, statements such as 'Women always overplay their hand' or 'Scotsmen are careful with money' are generalized rules, whereas statements like 'Miss Name's occupational aspirations exceed her abilities' or 'Miss Name is over-ambitious' are individual rules. It is obvious that both kinds of rule, and the 'mental constructs' previously mentioned, also find expression indirectly—that is, without becoming explicit or formulated in so many words—in the way we attempt to predict and influence people. We are rule-following creatures even if the rules we follow remain unspoken and sometimes change.

Looked at from a social viewpoint, 'interpersonal perception' refers to the reciprocal perspectives of two or more interacting persons. One's 'first impression' of another person seems to play an important part in determining the development of one's subsequent impressions of that person, giving rise to modifications in one's response to him and consequently modifying the other person's reactions to oneself, which in turn affects the formation of further impressions on our part, and so on, until, perhaps, stable mutual impressions are established. Interpersonal perception involves a series of reciprocal perspectives (see Laing, Phillipson and Lee, 1966) whereby A's impression of B is determined in part by his perception of B's perception of A, and by his perception of B's perception of A's perception of B, and so on. The analysis of these processes would constitute a valuable contribution to the psychology of interpersonal relations, but in our opinion such an analysis ought to follow an adequate conceptualization of A's perception of B, that is, an account of the processes linking the stimulus information about B with A's report of his impression. This has not hitherto been achieved, and cannot be achieved without some understanding of the contents and organization of A's impression of B. It is to this aspect of the problem of understanding others that our main attention is directed.

The suitability of the term 'perception' to refer to the process of forming impressions of people has often been questioned, since we experience qualities and properties of the other person which are not immediately given as 'sense impressions' or 'stimulus infomation'; they are arrived at by obscure processes of association and inference based partly on subjective states. Thus we may regard a person as aloof, detached, unresponsive, intelligent, and so on. These qualities are not directly observable but are inferred from our 'experience' of the person in comparison with others. According to Bruner (1957), this tendency to go beyond the information given is a characteristic of most cognitive and perceptual processes not just those involved in person perception. Bruner argues that perception always involves categorization. For example, we perceive a melody as 'bright' or 'rich', or a chair as 'comfortable'. MacLeod (1960), similarly, has argued that 'we can, in fact, establish a meaningful relationship between the perception of persons and the perception of impersonal things and events' (p. 227). This is certainly true if one adopts MacLeod's phenomenological definition of perception as 'the process whereby things, events, and their qualities and relationships become present to the self as here, now and real' (p. 233). According to Newcomb, Turner and Converse (1965), person perception fulfils most of the criteria drawn up by Osgood (1953) for defining perceptual phenomena. Their view is that person perception means *organizing* information about persons and *attributing* properties to them. These properties are perceived as *constant*— although the person's behaviour varies. The perceiver's own psychological characteristics exert a *directing* and *selective* influence on his attention and inference. The information is thus assimilated to a *flexible* framework of ideas.

There is little advantage to be gained by discussing whether the term 'perception' is appropriate to describe the process of impression formation. Some of the considerations that arise when person perception and object perception are compared are dealt with, for example, in Warr and Knapper (1968), de Charms (1968) and Ittelson (1960). The adoption of this convenient term does not imply the acceptance of any explanatory framework nor does it give rise to anything more than vague general hypotheses. The controversy assumes that the term 'perception' is explanatory, or at least descriptive, whereas in fact it merely designates an area of study. The 'inferential' or 'intuitive' character of person perception among adults and older children is obvious; what is not obvious are its developmental origins and sequences in raw experience relating to external (objective) and internal (subjective) phenomena, because hitherto there has been an almost complete lack of interest in the developmental psychology of person perception and behaviour perception.

II. Person Perception, Personality Theory and Clinical Psychology

In recent years, the problem of how we understand other people has become the concern of the psychologist, for, in its broadest sense, 'person perception' is what much of psychology is about. The layman tries to describe and account for other people's actions in commonsense terms, whereas the psychologist, in a more sophisticated, scientific manner, seeks to describe, to control, to predict and to explain human behaviour. One might suppose that the problems of person perception were central to clinical psychology and personality theory, and so they are; but they have not been dealt with in the manner that we think is appropriate.

Until recently, the clinical process of understanding others was handled largely by means of the concepts and methods of psycho-analysis and related psychodynamic schools of thought. The concepts and methods have long been criticized, but the full extent of their in-adequacies, coupled with the undoubtedly revolutionary value of their contributions, has taken a long time to uncover. The particular weakness of these psychodynamic schools has been their failure to reach an accord with the philosophy and methods of science in relation to the study of behaviour and psychological processes—a failure which is exemplified by a dearth of objective evidence regarding the validity of psychodynamic concepts and methods. Surprisingly little effort seems to have been devoted to the examination of the process of psychoanalytic inference or even to the actual content and organization of the analyst's system of ideas about his patient. Farrell (1964), however, has pointed out that psychoanalytic interpretations are sometimes *not* statements expressing a judgment or inference about the patient, but rather asser-tions designed to elicit responses or to persuade or to sensitize the patient to certain ideas and feelings. Smith, Bruner and White (1956) have described and discussed the functions of personal opinions in everyday social interaction; what they have to say applies to the expres-sion of opinions about persons, namely, that such opinions can be instrumental—designed to produce an effect—as well as straightforward statements of belief. The complexities of psychoanalytic inference and explanation, which some would regard as the acme of understanding others, have been dealt with at length by Sherwood (1969), who discusses such topics as puzzlement, explanatory mechanisms, predic-tion, patterns of meaning, and generalization. Sherwood complains, quite justifiably, that there are few detailed psychoanalytic case-histories available for systematic re-examination. In order to be useful, such case-histories would need to include not only the psychoanalytic narrative but also explanatory comments by the analyst on his own observations and inferences.

A completely different approach to what is basically a problem in person perception or understanding others is that of Sarbin, Taft and Bailey (1960) who attempted to deal with clinical inference in terms of cognitive theory. Unfortunately, the inductive and conjectural features of clinical inference seem not to be adequately dealt with, since they concentrate largely on deductive processes in clinical arguments.

In the 1950s, considerable interest was raised by the appearance of a book entitled *Clinical Versus Statistical Prediction* by Meehl (1954). This was a straightforward comparison of the predictive validity of two contrasting methods of personality assessment. No attempt was made to examine the process of inference as such, but the apparent superiority of the apparently objective (psychometric, actuarial) method contributed to the general disenchantment with clinical (subjective, non-quantifiable) procedures.

One branch of psychology which stands to gain much from an examination of its assumptions, preconceptions and procedures is the study of personality and adjustment. Personality study is concerned with the development of concepts and methods for studying individual cases, partly in relation to the clinical diagnosis and treatment of serious abnormalities of behaviour, partly in relation to a wide variety of minor problems of adjustment—in school, at work and in the home. To this end, with historical roots in nineteenth-century psychiatry, psychologists working in the general area of personality have pursued a variety of interrelated aims with varying degrees of imagination and scientific rigour, and with varying degrees of success. Psychoanalysis and related psychodynamic schools of thought represent one main theme in the history of personality study—a theme which emphasizes the importance of family experiences in early childhood as the formative influences in the establishment of basic behavioural dispositions, self-control, and interpersonal relations. It is a theme which offers a number of loosely formulated 'theories of', or 'approaches to', child development and abnormal behaviour, and prescribes a variety of methods for collecting evidence and achieving therapeutic results.

Another theme in the history of personality study is represented by the 'personality assessment' movement, which, encouraged by the success of the intelligence testing movement, attempts to apply quantitative (psychometric) techniques to the measurement of non-intellectual factors in personal adjustment. This theme has given rise to a plethora of psychometric and quasi-psychometric methods—questionnaires, rating scales, checklists, all sorts of projective tests, biographical inventories, repertory grids, and so on. One of the aims of the personality testing movement is the establishment of standardized measures of operationally defined personality characteristics thought to be relevant, for example, to the prediction of academic success, or to the diagnosis of psychiatric disorder. Another aim is the establishment of a definitive set of psychological attributes which will provide a framework of metrical 'personality dimensions'—analogous to a morphological description. The framework is intended to provide common scales by means of which different sorts of people can be compared for the purposes of taxonomy and the study of individual differences, as well as for more immediate practical purposes. Today, personality tests of one sort or another are extensively used in a wide variety of settings such as educational selection, placement and promotion in industry and the Armed Forces, psychiatric diagnosis, and so on. Yet surprisingly little consideration has been given to the assumptions underlying the use of such tests. Several years ago, Meili (1960) made the following remark,

'Somehow, the whole preoccupation with personality tests was based on the notion that we really could perceive and characterize people very well, and that all that was necessary was to find methods with which this perception could be accomplished even faster and safer without having to observe people very long in daily behaviour. We assumed too much.' (pp. 347–8.)

The personality testing movement, however, was too strong and too well entrenched to be much affected by Meili's comment. And it was not until very recently, in the work of W. Mischel (1968), that we find a systematic demotion of many of the concepts and methods of the personality testing movement. Mischel however, fails to consider the study of person perception as a possible way of rebuilding those areas of psychology which he lays waste in the first half of his book. Instead, he prefers the concepts and methods of behaviour modification; but these deal with a rather different set of psychological issues and to that extent do not make a satisfactory alternative to personality study. Furthermore, they depend upon the same preconceptions which we are trying to uncover by research into person perception and behaviour perception.

A third theme in the history of personality study is sometimes called the 'idiographic approach'. It attempts by means of a variety of clinical procedures and philosophical prescriptions to find ways of describing and conceptualizing the individual person. Typical of idiographic procedures are: biographical analysis, the content-analysis of personal documents, and the quasi-judicial case method. The 'quasi-judicial case method' is the term we use to refer to a set of rational and empirical procedures which are extensively but loosely applied in clinical psychology for the study of individual patients—with little realization on the part of clinicians that they bear a strong resemblance to their more rigorous counterparts in legal science. The 'logic' of 'clinical' psychology is the logic of the judicial inquiry—see Bromley (1968). Some of the more elaborate projective tests and personality inventories are also used to provide the empirical basis for an *intuitive* (subjective) appraisal of the person. This so-called idiographic approach differs from psychoanalysis and related schools in so far as it represents a loose congeries of techniques and attitudes largely committed to the problem of 'understanding the person', whereas psychodynamics (while partly idiographic in approach) is a relatively well-defined system of ideas and techniques in widespread use, with a definite (but not undisputed) role in contemporary clinical psychology.

Whichever approach to the study of personality one examines—whether it is psychodynamics, personality testing or idiographic psychology—one eventually sees that it not only sets out to describe human nature in general and individual persons in particular, but it also, necessarily, rests upon a collection of preconceptions, attitudes, and philosophical preferences which tend to be only half-examined or even undisclosed. These psychological foundations constitute the cognitive infrastructure and ground rules for the study of individual behaviour, whether the study is pursued at the level of everyday common sense, or at a more sophisticated level in professional and scientific work in the social and behavioural sciences.

Perhaps the area of clinical psychology which is most closely associated with person perception (impression formation) is that concerned with personal constructs. This work was pioneered by Kelly (1955), see also Bannister and Fransella (1971). The topic of personal constructs will be dealt with in the chapters which review the literature on person perception. At this stage, it is sufficient to say that the psychology of personal constructs is concerned with the ideas and concepts that people use when they attempt to impose patterns of meaning on their experience. That is to say, it is concerned with the way in which human beings 'construe' their world, especially their own behaviour and the behaviour of other people.

Partly as a reaction to the inadequacies of personality study in psychology, the scientific strategy which guides our theoretical efforts and our empirical investigations has a long-range objective, namely, the gradual disclosure or discovery of the cognitive processes underlying our understanding of individual people. The tactical moves intended to implement this strategy, so far, have been as follows. First, we asked a simple and fundamental question, namely 'What are the *contents* of those systems of ideas that we form about other people?' Second, we asked a simple supplementary question, namely 'How are these ideas *organized*?' Next, we considered how we might get over the difficulty presented in trying to study the complex and sophisticated systems of ideas—personality impressions—formed by reasonably intelligent adults. The obvious solution was to study the developmental psychology of person perception by investigating the simpler contents and organization of children's ideas about people—in the manner of Piaget's investigations into their ideas about the physical world. The desirability of obtaining comparable data at different age levels from early childhood to late adolescence (early adulthood) was one reason why we adopted a method which had already been tried with some success, namely, the content-analysis of free descriptions. Our subjects were required to write, in their own words, descriptions of various people whom they knew reasonably well. The contents of these descriptions were then analysed by a procedure known as 'content-analysis', which is well known in social psychology in connection with the study of newspapers, films, political documents, and so on. In previous work and in the course of the pilot inquiries it had become clear that we needed to examine the *organization* as well as the *contents* of personality impressions. Moreover, we were not satisfied with any of the existing methods of listing the contents; hence, we had to develop a purpose-built procedure for dealing with both the contents and the organization of the free descriptions.

The main reason for adopting the method of content-analysis was that it seemed to be the technique most free from methodological preconceptions, and the one most likely to reveal the full range of possibilities for future investigation. Notice, too, that cognitive *processes* can be inferred only through evidence relating to cognitive *products*. We knew from our initial inquiries that the cognitive products known as 'free descriptions' provided a rich mine of information about the processes of person perception; so our main problem was to find ways of extracting it. The wealth of knowledge obtained in the main inquiry, which we describe in the chapters that follow, has not exhausted the mine of information in free descriptions, and from time to time we shall mention further lines of work which look profitable, but have been assigned to future undertakings. However, we felt that it would be a little too single-minded to pursue the content-analysis of free descriptions to the exclusion of *all* other procedures. In Chapter 12, therefore, we have described one or two relatively short and simple investigations which can be regarded as ways of extending our inquiries.

It would be too much to claim that we reached (or even closely approached) the long-range objective of our research strategy. But, with good grounds, we can claim a series of tactical gains which are valuable in their own right apart from being necessary to the main aim of reducing the errors and distortions in our understanding of human nature and of the individual person.

Thus far, then, we have argued that the study of the layman's concepts of personality and his explanations of behaviour, and the manner in which these are acquired, may well aid the behavioural scientist in his search for a satisfactory conceptual framework, especially in those branches of the subject, such as clinical psychology, which deal with the person as such rather than with some isolated aspect of human performance. Of particular interest are those fundamental assumptions and unspoken rules of inference, the discovery of which, as in other sciences, may lead to major revisions in our understanding of *human* nature. We hope to show that the study of person perception is fundamental to personality study and clinical psychology and may well contribute to the conceptual revisions so obviously needed in these areas.

III. The Nature and Scope of Research in Person Perception

Person perception constitutes an area of overlap between different fields of psychology and thus provides opportunities to integrate work in perception, cognition, decision-making, social psychology, developmental psychology and clinical psychology.

Research in person perception is of interest because the impressions we form of others have implications for our interpersonal relations. Our interaction with another person is at least partly determined by our perception of him; and our perception of him has practical implications, since we are likely to see him as someone who can either help us or hinder us in attaining our goals and solving our problems. The manner in which people interact with others is affected by their ability to form realistic and sensitive impressions of others—see Hammond, Wilkins and Todd (1966). Although the relationship between person perception and interpersonal behaviour is unclear, it is apparent that an adequate theory of person perception is a prerequisite for a satisfactory theory of social interaction.

Even more interesting, as we have seen, is the possibility that research in person perception will provide fruitful approaches to the study of personality and adjustment. For example, there are considerable differences between individuals in the way they describe and interpret their social world and form impressions of others. Such differences may well indicate important psychological variables in personal adjustment. The current state of personality theory and assessment is extremely confused—see W. Mischel (1968). Personality has traditionally been considered to consist of internal structures that are hierarchically or dynamically organized; the implication of this approach is that behaviour should be consistent across situations. Mischel (1968) in an extensive review finds little evidence for consistency of behaviour across situations or for its stability over time. One apparent exception is the stability of impressions of self and others. Thus Mischel concludes that, 'the trait categories people attribute to themselves and others may be relatively permanent and may be more enduring than the behaviour to which they refer' (p. 36).

The systematic study of the way we 'apprehend' ourselves—and apprehend other people and behaviour generally—may lead, as we have already suggested, to radical reappraisals of existing behavioural science notions about human nature. A scientific account of human nature must be reflective : it must include notions about how psychologists perceive and understand people; this is an issue which has been discussed by Kelly (1955).

One practical advantage in achieving a detailed understanding of the processes underlying impression formation would be the development of training techniques for improving person perception and hence increasing the effectiveness and sensitivity of interpersonal relationships—see Smith (1966). The popularity of sensitivity training by means of T-groups and encounter groups illustrates the demand for interpersonal understanding, but it is difficult to achieve adequate practical results in the absence of a sound theory of person perception. Many kinds of professional work demand some expertise in the psychological assessment of persons. Such expertise must enable the individual to form useful and valid impressions of another person on the basis of naturally occurring evidence, that is, without recourse to experimental or psychometric procedures because they may be inconvenient, inapplicable, or of doubtful utility and validity. There is no reason why—given the facts, theories and applications described in this book—training in the observation and assessment of people in everyday situations should not form part of the educational curriculum of *any* age group. In fact, there are already in existence some educational materials—in the context of English and liberal studies—which attempt to stimulate children's thinking about normal human behaviour in present-day surroundings. But in our opinion these materials are inadequate and not soundly based, since they do not take into account the kinds of facts we have accumulated which, of course, were not previously known.

IV. Research Trends

Research has followed two main lines of inquiry. The earliest work focused upon the *accuracy* of subjects' judgments of other people's temporary and permanent psychological attributes—see Taft (1955). Later work was concerned with the nature of impressions and the *processes* by which they are reached. Most of this work was concentrated on the processes that mediate judgments of the inner psychological attributes of the stimulus person, although some research dealt with the perception of the more external characteristics of persons, see, for example, Ittelson and Slack (1958).

The research studies described later in this book examine the nature of 'impressions of others' among children, adolescents and adults; they are concerned with psychological *processes*. Consequently, the research work on *accuracy* will not be reviewed in detail. The earlier work on accuracy was reviewed by Bruner and Tagiuri (1954), and Taft (1955); at the time, these were major assessments of the literature. Both were made out of date fairly quickly, however, by a series of papers which levelled severe criticism at the methods used to measure accuracy. By far the most important of these was a paper by Cronbach (1955) in which he pointed out that the most frequently used method of measuring accuracy—by comparing a subject's ratings of a stimulus person's traits with the consensus ratings of experts—was not a straightforward measure of accuracy, but was affected by the manner in which subjects used the rating scales. Later work on accuracy was reviewed by Cline (1964); most of this research was aimed either at developing a satisfactory measure of accuracy or at analysing its nature, in an attempt to discover whether it is a general ability or a set of specific abilities.

While research in *accuracy* declined after Cronbach's methodological critique, work on *processes*—initiated by Asch (1946)—was stimulated by it; this work is reviewed in detail in Chapters 2 and 3. Most of this research concerns adults; there have been relatively few studies of impression formation in children.

One important research question asks, 'What sorts of behavioural and psychological notions can children handle at different ages?' An interesting answer can be obtained by analysing the contents and organization of children's written descriptions of people they know fairly well. The aim, however, is not only to study the nature and content of children's impressions of others, but also to work up to the study of those more complex and subtle processes underlying impression formation in adults, and in psychological assessment at a professional level; in this sense, the present approach is 'developmental'. However, we have already embarked on a study of age differences in person perception in adult life and old age, which will be published in due course. The very early and very late ages present special problems, but we hope eventually to describe the 'lifespan developmental psychology' of person perception.

Previous research into adult thinking about individual persons and human nature generally has made limited progress. Some useful findings have been achieved, however, in attempts to examine the quantitative aspects of trait implications in adults—see Warr and Knapper (1968)—and in the study of personal construct systems—see Bannister and Mair (1968). There has been a reluctance on the part of research workers in person perception to ask how the 'information processing system' arrives at the state found in the mature individual. A developmental approach has proved extremely useful in many areas of research, for example in Piaget's studies of cognitive development and in the study of social behaviour, abnormal behaviour and language; and we have every reason to believe that it has proved fruitful in our studies of impression formation.

It is obviously impossible to deal at length with all the ramifications of the study of person perception, particularly as we shall be adopting the attitude that some of the work in person perception is misdirected or at least premature. The literature surveys we have prepared are not intended to cover all aspects of person perception but only those that are relevant to our investigations.

CHAPTER 2

A Review of Research into the Process of Impression Formation: Part One

I. The Temporal Sequence

Perceptual, cognitive and affective processes all appear to play a part when we form an impression of another person. The temporal sequence can be thought of as involving four phases—adapted from Shrauger (1967). The first is *cue selection*, when, out of all the information available about the other person, the perceiver seems to notice only a part, presumably because it has some sort of personal relevance or significance—not that the perceiver need be aware of the determinants of what he selectively perceives. In the second phase, *interpretative inference*, the perceiver construes the information selected in such a way as to infer general traits and a variety of other personal characteristics. This is followed by a third phase—*extended inference*—in which implications are drawn as to what additional qualities or characteristics the other person might be expected to possess. For example, the perceiver may observe the other person performing a difficult mental task efficiently and effectively and thus regards him as 'intelligent'. For the perceiver, there may be a close link between 'intelligent' and, say, 'considerate', so that this second trait is also assigned to the other person although the perceiver has no direct observational evidence for it. The association is made by the perceiver, but the trait is not necessarily an attribute of the person perceived. Thus, some qualities are assigned to the other person on the basis of information selected, but from them other qualities are derived on the basis of learned probabilities of association. In fact, the trait 'intelligent' is not necessarily applicable to the person, since the interpretation placed upon the information selected may be in error; and in any event, the evidence for it should consist not merely of one isolated instance of intelligent behaviour, but rather of a whole series of intelligent actions showing consistency or design. This idea corresponds to the notion of 'similar facts' in legal evidence in that an isolated fact can be interpreted in various ways, whereas a pattern of facts has the effect of narrowing the range of possible interpretations.

Extended inferences are part of the general process in cognition of 'going beyond the information given' by categorizing and organizing information so that it can be used to predict new information—see Bruner (1957). Thus cues are used as the basis for inferring personal characteristics and these in turn are used to predict further characteristics. Relationships between cues and categories, and between categories themselves, have been referred to as 'implicit' or 'lay' theories of personality—see Bruner and Tagiuri (1954) and Cronbach (1955)—which the perceiver has been obliged to develop in order to construe and predict the behaviour of other people.

The fourth and final stage in impression formation is that of *anticipatory set* or *verbal report*—the former being implicit, the latter explicit, although it is unlikely that all aspects of impressions can be verbalized. This stage is one of organization, in which the characteristics assigned to the other person are grouped and integrated to form a basis for consistent responses to the other person; the characteristics become explicit in the attempt to give a coherent verbal account of his behaviour and personality. This may be further modified in the process of communicating the impression to other people—a kind of 'secondary elaboration'.

All aspects of the process of impression formation are likely to be affected by : (a) the objective stimulus characteristics of the person; (b) the nature of the stimuli to which the perceiver selectively responds, and the order and context in which they are presented; (c) perceiver variables—the perceiver's cognitive abilities and personal characteristics including his moods and expectations; and (d) social interaction—the relationships between the perceiver and the stimulus person, and between perceivers 'sharing' impressions of a stimulus person.

II. The Nature of Impressions

Impressions possess both *content* and *organization*. The contents range from relatively concrete statements about a person's appearance, identity and job to relatively abstract statements about his personality type, and about his personal qualities and potentialities. The perceiver does not merely list descriptive features, he seeks to organize and relate them. Even when the cues are few and diverse, he often strives to see the other person as a 'gestalt', so that any one quality is seen not in isolation but in terms of its contextual relationships with the other qualities the stimulus person is known or assumed to possess—see Asch (1946). The elucidation of the organizing processes in impression formation is one of the main objectives of research.

Asch (1946) demonstrated the organized nature of impressions by presenting subjects with a list of traits such as 'energetic, assured, talkative, cold, ironical, inquisitive, persuasive', said to belong to an actual person, and asking them to give a brief characterization of the person concerned. Subjects did not merely repeat the list of traits or give synonyms; instead, they formed a unified impression of the 'person' and perceived him as possessing a system of interrelated and organized qualities. In our perception of others, there seems to be a tendency to form a 'good figure', and the same 'effort after meaning' that Bartlett (1932) found in his studies of memory. It appears that structure and organizaion are imposed upon the stimulus information by omitting some items and adding new information in order to elimin-ate inconsistencies and omissions.

Luchins (1948) criticized Asch's work on the grounds of the poor control of the conditions and the artificiality of the task. The latter point is an important one since all too often in person perception research subjects are asked to perform tasks which bear little resemblance to their normal and natural mode of perceiving others, and the assump-tion that this makes no difference to what can be inferred about their performance in real life cannot be accepted without further examination.

Asch's conclusions have been supported by experiments dealing with the integration of conflicting information in which subjects were asked to form an impression of another person when presented with con-tradictory information about him. These studies also throw light on the nature of the organizing processes. Gollin (1954), using filmed material, presented adult subjects with information about a young woman. Two scenes suggested she was promiscuous and immoral, the middle scene was neutral, and two scenes suggested that she was kind and considerate. Subjects were asked to record the impression they formed of the woman. Analysis of the descriptions revealed three ways of dealing with disharmonious information : (a) Coherent impressions would include both promiscuity and kindness, and a subject might integrate them by using a superordinate term such as 'happy-go-lucky' or 'easy-going'; (b) Simplified, but unified, impressions would omit reference to one of the qualities and the impression would be organized around the other; (c) Aggregate descriptions would list both qualities but not integrate them. Gollin indicated that 21 per cent of the descriptions were coherent, 49 per cent simplified, and 36 per cent aggregated. In a similar experiment, Haire and Grunes (1950) showed that subjects attempt to resolve conflicting information either by denying the disparate item or by integrating it through the addition of new information.

These experiments support Asch's conclusions. In general, people try to impose the best possible organization on the information given. Sometimes, however, the information is too diverse and contradictory to allow this. Pepitone and Hayden (1955) described to their subjects a man who was a member of a number of exclusive and prestigeful social organizations and at the same time an official of a left-wing political party. Such material strongly contradicts cultural expectations (subjects were American students), and only a minority were able to integrate the information successfully. Most either ignored one sort of information or retained both sorts without relating them. A similar process occurs in everyday life when, for various reasons, we find it difficult to describe and understand some people—possibly because of some disability in ourselves, possibly because they really do behave inconsistently, possibly because they are so reserved and guarded that we can never get sufficient behavioural evidence on which to base a firm impression. When this happens, we may resort to a number of descriptive terms such as 'strange', 'funny', 'peculiar' and 'changeable', which have the effect of excluding the person from normal forms of categorization; it is as if their behaviour were construed as 'not-construable'.

The integrative terms which create bridges or links between disparate items of information may be provided linguistically either by means of qualifying words and phrases which affect the relative importance of each item or by means of logical statements which specify the nature of the relationship (this issue is dealt with in Chapter 10). Alternatively, as Gollin's study demonstrates, the links may be provided by attributing additional qualities which explain or resolve the apparently unrelated traits or contradictions in the other person. The additional traits are presumably arrived at by means of implicit theories of trait attribution which help the perceiver to fill in the gaps in his knowledge of the other person and so integrate conflicting or isolated items of information. Thus the perceiver's ability to organize his impressions of other people seems to depend upon : (a) the number of terms he has for describing people, (b) the extent to which they are organized into clusters, and (c) his verbal and conceptual abilities.

Once impressions have been formed, they are cohesive and tend to resist change, probably because they are influenced by the same processes that stabilize attitudes—selective perception, mutual reinforcement of affective and cognitive components, and avoidance of contradictory information. Asch (1952) asked subjects to form impressions from two trait lists : 'intelligent, industrious, impulsive' and 'critical, stubborn, envious'. When the subjects had recorded their impressions, they were told that all six traits belonged to a single person; they found it difficult to imagine all the traits belonging to the same person. Other subjects who were told at the beginning that all six traits belonged to the same person had no difficulty in forming an impression of him. Despite their apparent stability, impressions are to some extent determined by situational and interpersonal factors—see Chapter 10, sections II and III.

III. Sources of Information about Other People

Impressions can be based upon a wide variety of information about the other person. The following list of cues or stimuli is similar to that of Ichheiser (1949) and of Vernon (1964).

A. Indirect Sources of Information

People frequently form an impression of a person without actually meeting him in a face-to-face situation, basing their impressions upon descriptions of his appearance, behaviour and personality given by people who either know the other person at first hand, or who also received their information from others. Impressions based upon indirect information are usually impoverished in content and organization—see Bromley (1966a). The reliance placed upon indirect information tends to depend upon the credibility of the source—see Rosenbaum and Levin (1968, 1969).

The indirect information the perceiver receives tends to establish an expectancy which affects his perception of the other person and his

••

reaction to him when they first encounter one another. Kelley (1950) showed that this expectancy is easily established. A new lecturer was introduced to a class of students who were told : 'He is 26 years old, a veteran and married. People who know him consider him to be a rather — person, industrious, critical, practical and determined.' The blank was filled with the word 'warm' or 'cold'. After a class discussion the students rated the lecturer on a series of traits. Those who heard him described as 'warm' rated him as more considerate, sociable, informal, popular and humorous. The initial information also affected the subjects' behaviour towards the lecturer. In a class discussion, 56 per cent participated when he was described as warm, but only 32 per cent when described as cold.

Warr and Knapper (1966b) similarly demonstrated that expectancy affects perception. The subjects' tendencies to perceive an actual political figure were assessed by using the Semantic Differential—see Osgood, Suci and Tannenbaum (1957). One week later they were presented with a report of a speech the politician had made, together with an account of the behaviour and attitudes of the politician and his audience. When asked to complete the Semantic Differential scales again indicating their perception of the politician's performance at the meeting, the subjects' responses were positively correlated with the expectancy responses collected previously. The mode of presentation of information of this type also affects the impression formed—see Warr and Knapper (1966a). For a more detailed discussion of the effects of indirect communication see Warr and Knapper (1968).

B. Appearance

Appearance plays an important role in person perception by establishing the identity of the other person and enabling the perceiver to categorize him in terms of age, sex, perhaps social class and a variety of other characteristics. Thus, information about appearance contributes to the formation of conceptions, and misconceptions, about the other person, which the perceiver requires in order to plan his initial interaction with him; the role prescriptions or 'stereotypes' associated with some features of appearance suggests to him how the other person is likely to behave, for example 'racial' characteristics. Stone (1962) reported that most people assume that an individual expresses himself through his appearance, thereby providing valuable information about his values, tastes and attitudes; he may, perhaps, reveal some of his personality traits such as carelessness or fastidiousness, and betray his moods—for example, whether he is gaily or sombrely dressed. Note, however, that this is merely one aspect of implicit theorizing about persons; the validity of such inference is a separate issue. For some individuals, appearance appears to be an important determinant of their acceptance of others.

Specific features of a person's appearance may be used as clues to personal qualities. Secord and his colleagues—see Secord (1958)—have investigated the part played by physiognomic characteristics. Their work indicates that two distinct aspects of the face are important: (a) the structural or physiognomic aspect—for example, length of face, height of brow—and (b) the expressive features brought about by contractions of the facial musculature—for example, type of smile. Their studies also indicate that subjects show considerable agreement in attributing personality traits to faces with particular physiognomic characteristics although some individual and group differences exist.

Some studies have investigated the particular physiognomic cues utilized as a basis for inferring personality traits. Secord and Muthard (1955b) had subjects rate photographs of young women on physiognomic and personality characteristics, from which they were able to identify those attributes of appearance responsible for the impressions. For example, women who had narrow eyes, a relaxed mouth with thick lips and lots of lipstick were seen as more sexually attractive, passionate and feminine than women with thin, straight lips, a compressed mouth and wearing little lipstick; moral character was associated with bright eyes. Similarly, Secord, Dukes and Bevan (1954) demonstrated that men with a dark complexion, coarse oily skin, heavy eyebrows and a straight mouth were perceived as hostile, quick tempered, sly, boorish and conceited. A pleasant expression, regular features and neat appearance are positively correlated with judgments of intelligence—see Cook (1939). Brunswik and Reiter (1937), using schematic drawings, demonstrated a consistent relationship between the structural features of the face and impressions. They also demonstrated that the different structural features interact in forming impressions. Samuels (1939) obtained similar results using Brunswik's schematic drawings. When she used real photographs, however, there was less agreement between subjects, which suggests that physiognomic characteristics other than the ones investigated are important. Samuels also found that women made more uniform judgments than men. This study illustrates the need for research using natural situations, that is, imposing minimum constraints upon subjects in the hope of eliciting key variables which may then be manipulated in more structured experiments.

A number of studies have shown that altering even one feature of a person or his photograph can affect the impression produced—for example, his direction of gaze, see Tankard (1970). Thornton (1943, 1944) reported that ratings of intelligence increased when the stimulus person was wearing spectacles. Manz and Lueck (1968), using drawings, showed that wearing spectacles led to higher ratings of intelligence, industriousness, dependability and honesty, but did not affect judgments of friendliness and led to lower ratings on humour. Argyle and McHenry (1971) reported that this effect depends upon length of exposure. Spectacles affected judgments when the subject was seen briefly, but had no effect when viewed for five minutes. Argyle and McHenry argue that this result casts doubt upon experiments using photographs or brief exposure. It also points, once more, to the need for less artificial conditions, and for studies which examine the sequential changes in cues used and the judgments made during an ongoing interaction. McKeachie (1952), using real subjects rather than photographs, showed that lipstick was a determiner of first impressions. When wearing lipstick, a girl was regarded as significantly more interested in the opposite sex, more frivolous, more placid, less conscientious, and more talkative than when not wearing it. On the other hand, wearing lipstick did not affect the attribution of traits like attentiveness, cooperativeness, cheerfulness, rigidity, secretiveness, imaginativeness, and suspiciousness.

Secord, Stritch and Johnson (1960) found that implicit theories linking psychological qualities and appearance appear to be reversible and are evoked when the stimulus is a personality sketch rather than a photograph of an actual person. Subjects given two brief personality descriptions formed different impressions of the appearance of the people described. It should be possible, therefore, to devise an experimental instrument—along the lines of an identikit—which could be adjusted by subjects to yield a face to fit a verbal description of a personality. Fisher and Cox (1971) reported an investigation in which the features of 'Piderit faces'—outline schematic faces—were systematically varied to determine whether there were typical faces associated with certain social and psychological characteristics.

The effect on impression formation of other aspects of appearance, such as build, has received little attention, despite the interest psychiatrists such as Kretschmer (1936) and psychologists such as Sheldon (1940, 1942) have shown in the relationship between body build, personality and mental illness. Secord and Backman (1964) point out that body build is an important cue to personality impressions although the impression may not be valid. A study by Baer (1964) supports this view by showing consistency among subjects in assigning personality and behavioural traits to full-length photographs of people.

Details of appearance form such an integral part of our impressions of others that, if absent, as in some experiments, subjects often create for themselves an image of the appearance of a person who has been described in terms of traits. It is a common experience, after hearing about someone's personal qualities and then meeting him for the first time, to be surprised because he did not look at all like one had expected. Identity and appearance, together with a few salient personality traits, form the central framework or 'homunculus'—Oldfield (1941)— around which our impressions are organized; our subsequent perceptions are guided by, and develop out of, this initial matrix of impressions. Appearance in general acts as a focus in the formation of first and subsequent impressions, as illustrated by the common requirement that a photograph accompany an application for employment.

C. Expressive Behaviour

Everyday experience suggests that we frequently use the expressive features of a person's behaviour as a guide to his personality and mood. A bouncy walk suggests happiness; slow, dreary movements suggest apathy; quick, jerky movements suggest anxiety; while a frown may suggest doubt, anger or concentration. It is often impossible to specify what expressive cues seem to be operating; they seem to affect the perceiver without his being aware of them. Argyle (1967) has drawn attention to some of the nonverbal cues that initiate and guide social interaction, and provide signs of an individual's moods and attitudes. Eye contact, direction of gaze, physical distance, bodily orientation, and so on, all provide information about the other person and his attitudes towards us—see also Mehrabian (1969). Work on this topic is made difficult by the fact that expressive behaviour is to some extent idiosyncratic and situationally determined, in that one person's social anxiety, say, gets expressed in one particular way, while another person's social anxiety expresses itself differently. Similarly, a frown and a shrug signify one thing for one person and another thing for someone else— depending, of course, on the situation. Thus, while there are undoubtedly common features in expressive behaviour, these are relatively coarse and obvious, whereas subtle individualized understanding is usually called for if interpersonal perception is to be effective.

By far the most expressive region of the human body is the face, and most research has been devoted to what it reveals, although here we are concerned only with what people think it reveals and not with how accurate their judgments are. The facial expression of emotion has received most attention—see Schlosberg (1954), Engen and Levy

(1956), Triandis and Lambert (1958), Engen, Levy and Schlosberg (1957) and Osgood (1966). Buzby (1924) found that the upper parts of the face were more important, whereas Dunlap (1937) considered that the mouth was the most important determinant. It is likely that different aspects of facial expression are important for different inferences, with the lower parts of the face providing cues for the pleasant emotions and the upper parts for anxiety, tension and stress.

The paralinguistic aspects of speech influence judgments of a speaker's personality traits—see Taylor (1934), Fay and Middleton (1936, 1941), Veness and Brierley (1963)—as well as of his values and social class—see Pear (1957). Speech disturbances, that is, errors in articulation and sentence structure, are interpreted as signs of anxiety—see Lalljee (1971). Studies on the identification of emotions and traits from verbal expression have run into the difficulty that the content or meaning of what is said contains cues, although attempts have been made to overcome this—see Kramer (1964).

It seems probable that body movements provide information regarding mood and personality traits. Dittman (1962) has shown that frequency of body movements differentiates moods reliably, and Ekman (1964) demonstrated that subjects are able to match photographs taken during a stress interview with tape-recordings of the interviews more accurately than would be expected by chance. Similarly, Sarbin (1954), using stick figures, showed considerable agreement between subjects in attributing personality characteristics to various postures. Recently, the terms 'proxemics' and 'kinesics' have been coined to refer to the spatial and movement aspects of social interaction—see E. T. Hall (1969) and Birdwhistell (1971).

Tagiuri (1960) investigated the value of movement as a cue to impression formation using line drawings, and films showing moving dots, to represent the path a person was said to take in order to reach a goal. When asked to describe what kind of person would take such a path, subjects were able to do so without difficulty. A person taking a straight path was described as well-reasoned, aggressive, persevering, determined, logical, ambitious, dull, while a person taking a meandering path was regarded as immature, very emotional, stupid, irresponsible, vacillating, gay, sociable, unconcerned, having little sense of direction and curious. Tagiuri's experiment indicates the importance of studying the role of movement in person perception, provided his results apply to the perception of human behaviour in real life. Such experiments might be relevant to the use of metaphor in person perception, for example, in the use of terms such as crooked, direct, straight.

D. Coping Behaviour

In some circumstances, *what* a person does provides the perceiver with more information than *how* he does it. In effect, two distinct sources of information are available since coping or goal-directed behaviour is seen in relation to his expressive behaviour and vice versa. Hypotheses about intentions, moods or traits formulated on the basis of one source of information can be validated against the other, thus providing a check. Usually these two sets of information support each other, but occasionally they conflict—for example, in icy politeness—leaving the perceiver perplexed and uncomfortable.

Behaviour is emitted as a continuous stream of actions—see Barker (1963). To make sense of the stream of behaviour it must be broken down into manageable units. The perceiver must possess appropriate verbal categories to describe it, together with the ability to impute motives and intentions to the other person. We do not necessarily first observe actions and then impute a motive; sometimes we have a prior inclination to attribute intentions, so that the imputed intention affects our subsequent perception of the actions—see From (1960, 1971). The manner in which behaviour is coded and organized and the kind of intention that is imputed to the actor are interdependent in most instances, an exception being when neither circumstances nor the person's previous actions indicate what he is about to do. Even here, intentions are usually assigned before the action is completed, because the action and the situation limit the number of possible interpretations.

Heider (1958), in his analysis of naive or commonsense psychology, argued that the perceiver seeks a sufficient reason for another person's behaviour, and his search for an explanation comes to an end when an intention is assigned to the action. Intentions are assigned rapidly and automatically not only to human behaviour but also to the movement of physical objects—see Heider and Simmel (1944). Assigning intentions to a person, however, is only one of many ways of making sense of his behaviour.

Dickman (1936) investigated the extent to which observers can impose structure and orderliness on the stream of behaviour. He was particularly interested in the way human activity is subdivided and categorized, the nature of the units, and the extent to which different subjects imposed similar structures upon the stream of behaviour. Subjects were shown an 8-minute film and then presented with 144 cards, each card had printed on it a description of one action in the film. They were asked to place the cards into groups so that each group represented an episode or event in the film. The ease with which they understood and completed the task indicated that the concept of behaviour occurring in units was a familiar one. Dickman found statistically significant agreement between subjects with regard to the overall patterning or sequences of breaks and continuities in the stream of behaviour. Yet, despite this overall agreement regarding the beginning and end of a behaviour unit, there was considerable disagreement regarding the number of units in the total sequence. Some subjects divided the film into three units, others into thirty-five units, the median being fourteen. Thus, where subject A saw two units, subject B may have seen only one. Such a result does not necessarily reflect disagreement about what is happening; instead, there may be individual differences in 'behaviour perspective'. When the units are examined, the theme of each unit implies a goal-directed action on the part of the actor. It would seem that the imputation of a goal or intention and the perception of a meaningful unit of behaviour are functionally interdependent. The results of reliability studies using a similar film suggested that the behaviour perspective remains stable, at least over a few weeks. An attempt to replicate Dickman's study uncovered a number of conceptual and methodological problems, and is described in Chapter 12.

If the scale of an observer's perspective is a stable characteristic of his perception of behaviour, this may well have effects on the ease, accuracy and sensitivity of person perception. Dickman reported that subjects adopting broad perspectives found the task easier than those adopting narrow ones. Lyons (1956) found that schizophrenics used much smaller units than did normal subjects to describe the actions of a person engaged in solving one of Maier's problems. In addition, the units they reported were poorly organized into a sequence and lacked the imputation of goals and motives. The correct imputation of intentions to an actor requires the ability to form a perception which is not dominated either by one's own standpoint or by the concrete stimulus situation. This type of abstract thinking is diminished in some schizophrenics; consequently the units they use to describe behaviour are short and concrete. Young children's thinking is also concrete and dominated by the egocentric attitude. Hence they too can be expected to experience difficulties in perceiving and comprehending behaviour and they also may describe it in short, concrete units. The development of the ability to conceptualize behaviour is an important problem, since the perception of behaviour is fundamental to person perception—see Chapter 12. In line with this argument, one could hypothesize that in subnormals, in young adults with diffuse brain damage, and in the mildly deteriorated elderly, there will be poorer perception and comprehension of human behaviour. The research problem is to devise suitable measures of what used to be called 'social intelligence', that is, the ability to adopt the perspective of other people correlated with ing a system for grading the intellectual level of personal impressions and the development of techniques for studying 'behaviour perception' are described and discussed in Chapter 12; thus questions about the nature and measurement of social intelligence can be reopened. In the growth period, social development and intellectual development are closely related, a point demonstrated by Feffer (1959, 1970). In a study of children, Feffer and Gourevitch (1960) showed that the child's ability to adopt the perspective of other people correlated with 'decentring' ability measured by intellectual tests of the type used by Piaget.

Jones and Davies (1965), following Heider's ideas, have analysed some of the processes involved in assigning intentions to persons. The following discussion is based upon their work. Establishing sufficient reason for an action involves the perceiver in an analysis of the action, its effects, situational factors and what is known about the person. Initially, the perceiver has to decide whether the person is causally responsible for the action and its effects, that is, whether the person is the origin of his action or merely the pawn of external agents. This requires an examination of the context to see whether alternative actions were available to him. The perceiver's knowledge of the person affects the attribution of causal responsibility. Subjects tend to perceive the causal locus of an action as internal for high-status people and external for low-status people—see Thibaut and Riecken (1955). Pepitone (1958) cites evidence to demonstrate that the attractiveness of a person depends upon the extent to which he is held to be causally responsible for the consequences of his actions and the extent to which those actions are justified.

An action produces a number of effects. Assigning an intention to an action requires that intended effects be differentiated from those which are accidental, that is, knowledge of the foreseeable consequences of his action has to be imputed to the person—as occurs in legal proceedings. Thus the perceiver must assess the person's ability to produce those effects in that particular situation. If he thinks that the person lacks the necessary skill, he must conclude that he did not foresee the consequences of his behaviour and hence that they were brought about by other factors. The problem becomes more complex for the perceiver when the person fails to produce the expected outcome, for he has then to decide whether the failure was due to lack of skill or deliberate failure, or because the person was really trying to produce a different effect.

The intention imputed to the person does not depend entirely upon an analysis of the action and its effects. The perceiver's knowledge of the person helps to determine the intentions assigned to him. For example, Thibaut and Riecken (1955) showed that better intentions are assigned to an action by a high-status person than the same action performed by a low-status person, and that his action is regarded as more justified. Contextual factors also affect the attribution of causality. When an individual is persuaded to do something by an attractive agent he is seen to be the origin of his action more readily than when the agent is unattractive—see de Charms, Carpenter and Kuperman (1965).

The imputation of intentions is often a precondition to the attribution of permanent and stable characteristics. It is not, however, a necessary precondition, for stable characteristics can be assigned on the basis of expressive behaviour and appearance. The ability to impute intentions represents the attainment of a complex cognitive and social skill. An understanding of the development of this ability would be a valuable contribution to the study of impression formation.

E. Context

Contextual factors affect the perception of a social stimulus in much the same way as 'field' variables affect the perception of physical stimuli; the meaning of a stimulus varies with the situation. Asch (1946) suggested that the meaning of a trait depends upon the other traits a person is thought to possess. Stritch and Secord (1956) showed how the perception of a physiognomic attribute is affected by the other physiognomic attributes the person is seen to possess. Cline (1956), using line drawings, showed that the interpretation of a facial expression was affected by the expression on a second face adjacent to it. Levy (1960) reported a contrast effect in person perception. Target photographs presented in the context of two other photographs were rated in the opposite manner to the contextual photographs if the contextual photographs gave rise to common judgments. Holmes and Berkowitz (1961) reported a similar effect in judgments of pleasantness. A pleasant person seems more pleasant after seeing an unpleasant person.

The context in which behaviour occurs has a considerable effect upon the impression the perceiver forms. It not only guides and constrains the interpretation of the stimulus person's behaviour but also dictates what things the perceiver attends to, or expects, in the other person. The types of interaction and the interaction goals set by the participants determine both the information selected and the use to which it is put—see Jones and Thibaut (1958). Cost-benefit relationships could be expected to play a prominent part in creating contexts for impression formation.

F. The Effects of Order of Presentation

The layman's notion that first impressions are important has been supported by experimental evidence. Asch (1946) presented subjects with a list of discrete traits. A second group of subjects were presented with the same list in reverse order. The two lists gave rise to different impressions presumably because adjectives presented earlier in the series had a greater effect than those presented later. Other experiments using trait lists produced similar results—see Anderson and Barrios (1961), Anderson and Hubert (1963), Anderson and Norman (1964), and Anderson (1965).

Asch suggested that the initial words in a list modify the meaning of later words. For example, the term 'cunning' will give the word 'clever' a meaning which is similar to the word 'shrewd'. Methodological difficulties have hindered experimental examination of this idea. However, Anderson and Lampel (1965) report that the meaning of a personality trait in the context of two other traits was not affected by the context if the subject was instructed to rate the trait itself. If they were told to regard the three traits as belonging to the same person, the meaning of the test trait was displaced towards the contextual traits—see also Wyer and Watson (1969).

An alternative explanation of the primacy effect given by Anderson and Hubert (1963) suggests that instead of a shift in meaning, later items merely carry less weight than the initial items and less attention is paid to them—possibly because of overloading of the subject's information-processing capacity. A study by Anderson (1965) provides some support for the idea that subjects use an averaging process. Triandis and Fishbein (1963) suggest that a summation model is more appropriate. Lovie and Davies (1970) discuss the application of Bayes's Theorem to the problem of combining information about persons. Luchins (1957a) obtained a marked primacy effect by using two blocks of information which described the activities of a teenage boy. One block described him behaving in an extroverted manner, the other in an introverted manner. Despite the strong evidence in favour of primacy effects, slight alterations in the experimental conditions will completely remove them. Luchins (1957b) showed that they could be reduced either by warning the subject not to make snap judgments, or by interpolating a similar warning or an unrelated task, such as an arithmetic test, between the two blocks of information. The interpolated tasks were the most effective; probably because they decreased the likelihood of the two blocks being perceived as a total unit. This interpretation is supported by the work of Asch (1946) cited earlier.

Primacy effects also appear to depend upon the content of the information presented. An outstanding item of information in the material presented will dominate the final judgment regardless of order of presentation or interpolated judgment—see Mink and Briggs (1965).

G. The Effects of Stimulus Variability

Levy (1967) pointed out that impressions are based upon information which is a sample (but not necessarily a large or representative sample) of all the information that exists about the person. The items in information samples are likely to exhibit a certain amount of variation, and such variation may affect impression formation. The effects of extreme variability in the stimulus information have been studied in experiments dealing with the integration of conflicting information. Levy showed that variability in the stimulus person's behaviour reduced the perceiver's confidence in his judgments and reduced the favourability of the impressions formed—see also Wyer (1970).

IV. Conclusion

In conclusion then, it appears that people use a large variety of cues to make inferences about the states of mind and personal qualities of other persons; they seek to combine these inferences in various ways to achieve a unified and organized impression. It seems probable that many cues are normally used to form even relatively simple judgments; so it can be argued that, in many experiments, subjects have been forced to base their judgments on insufficient information—see Tagiuri (1969) —and to record their judgments using unfamiliar judgment categories. We have seen that the interpretation of a cue depends upon the context in which it occurs and the way in which it is presented; a cue presented in a photograph may produce quite different effects from those of the same cue presented by a real person. These considerations point to the need for studies which are more naturalistic. We need to know more about the rules governing inferences made about personal qualities based on cues in natural conditions, and the ways these cues are modified by the presence of additional cues and contextual factors. This leads on naturally to questions about interpretative and extended inference which are dealt with in Chapter 3.

CHAPTER 3

A Review of Research into the Process of Impression Formation: Part Two

I. Interpretative and Extended Inference: The Study of Cognitive Organization

A. The Nature of Cognitive Organization

As we saw in the previous chapter, the initial stage of cue selection is followed by a process of interpretative inference which results in the individual being assigned one or more characteristics ranging from relatively concrete ones, such as age, sex and appearance, to more abstract ones relating to permanent and stable psychological characteristics, such as general habits, motives and traits. These characteristics are then used as the basis for inferring additional qualities. Inference rules are discussed at length in Warr and Knapper (1968). The traits and other concepts used to describe and conceptualize other people

32

constitute the perceiver's interpersonal cognitive system which forms part of his general cognitive system. These traits or elements can be regarded as integrated into a complex structure which tends to be hierarchically organized, adapted, and in equilibrium—see Werner (1948), Kelly (1955), Heider (1958). The individual's interpersonal cognitive organization can also be regarded as a set of implicit rules or assumptions about people in general and about some persons in particular—see T. Mischel (1969) and Peters (1960).

A given element, for example a trait, can be thought of as a member of a cluster of traits linked by conditional probabilities; so that if a trait has been assigned to a person, other traits are, by implication, also assigned to him because of the reciprocal probabilistic associations between them—although they are not necessarily reversible or additive. In this way, the initial categorization of the person, taken in conjunction with the observer's pre-existing cognitive system, is used to generate new information or expectations about him. The relationships between traits can be expressed as correlation coefficients or as conditional probabilities. For example, a person thought of as 'warm' has a high probability of being considered generous, happy, good natured and humorous; he may or may not be thought of as imaginative, and he is unlikely to be thought of as either frivolous or dishonest—see Asch (1946).

B. Cognitive Differentiation

A cognitive system can be described in terms of its degree of differentiation and organization. The term 'cognitive differentiation' refers to both (a) the number of elements a person has available for describing and construing a particular set of objects or events—in this case people and their actions; and (b) the extent to which the individual is able to use these terms differentially and thus to discriminate effectively between the people, or forms of behaviour, he encounters. It is usually assumed, although empirical evidence is lacking, that these two aspects of differentiation are highly correlated—see Crockett (1965).

To say that we 'conceptualize' another person is to say that we form some kind of mental representation of that person—usually a fairly abstract and symbolic representation. The terms a person uses to conceptualize people can be elicited in a number of ways. The simplest method is to apply content analysis to descriptions of other people—see Hastorf, Richardson and Dornbusch (1958), and Beach and Wertheimer (1961). Crockett (1965) outlined a procedure used by Supnick (1964) in which the number of constructs a subject used to describe eight people provided a measure of differentiation. This method is similar to the one adopted in the main investigation to be described in later chapters.

The role construct repertory test—see Kelley (1955)—is an alternative procedure: a list of role titles—such as mother, brother, the person I admire most, a close female friend—are presented to or chosen by the subject, who is then asked to designate actual individuals known to him who fit these role titles. The names of the people designated are presented randomly in triads and the subject is asked to state in what way two of them are alike but different from the third. Thus a subject may decide that two of them are 'intelligent' while the third is 'stupid'. This procedure is repeated until 15 to 25 constructs are elicited—numbers which Kelly claims are sufficient to provide an adequate sampling of the main constructs the subject uses to construe other people.

A number of studies have shown that subjects differ considerably in the types of construct they use. Some favour terms describing external or peripheral features such as appearance, interests, activities and social roles; others favour terms which refer to more central or internal features such as general habits, traits and motivations—see Maher (1957), Bieri, Bradburn and Galinsky (1958), and Fancher (1966). Supnick's study showed that the number of constructs used depends upon the person being described—for example, more constructs are used to describe peers and people liked than to describe older persons or people disliked. This indicates the need for more studies to examine the effects the stimulus person—that is, the person being perceived—has upon the content and organization of impressions.

The use of concrete as opposed to abstract terms to describe others is an important but neglected issue. The abstract approach should lead to better interpersonal predictions and greater interpersonal sensitivity. But, while the use of abstract categories is desirable, it is equally important that they are not applied indiscriminately to large numbers of different people, as are stereotypes for example. The issues raised by the linguistic analysis of words and statements in the psychology of personality and adjustment are difficult and frequently neglected aspects of philosophical psychology. They are taken up later in Chapter 12.

Repertory grids can be used to assess the differential use of traits. Bieri (1955) elicited from his subjects the constructs they used to describe others; he then asked them to say whether or not each construct could be applied to each other person. In this way it was possible to examine the extent to which the constructs were used differentially—see also Bieri, Atkins, Briar, Leaman, Miller and Tripodi (1966). Cronbach (1955, 1958) has suggested that the standard deviation of a subject's ratings of a number of other persons on a trait may be used as a measure of differentiation—see also H. C. Smith (1966).

Although the traits a person assigns to other people are likely to vary with the person being perceived, it is probable that each individual possesses a small number of traits which he uses frequently, and a large number which he uses infrequently. Individual differences in the use of traits are likely to be considerable, but it is probable that some groups of people use similar traits, either because of common personality characteristics, or similar social and cultural backgrounds. Bruner and Tagiuri (1954) pointed out that one of the obvious gaps in the literature of person perception was the absence of information concerning the way *naive* subjects conceptualize and categorize people. They suggested that careful studies should be made of the nature and frequency of use of trait names in different populations. As yet, only a few small studies have been conducted. Sechrest (1962) reported that people who described others as 'friendly', 'nice', 'agreeable', and 'pleasant' tended to be more similar to each other with respect to such factors as socio-economic level, religious beliefs, and family constellations, than were persons who did not use such terms of generalized approval. Sechrest and Jackson (1961) reported that people who used a large number of terms to describe others tended to have relatively complex childhood environments. These studies are interesting and suggest avenues of research, but do not provide systematic data on the frequency with which traits are used. Normative data on the frequency with which traits are used by children of different ages are presented in Chapter 9, section VIII. They constitute a representative pool of items from which adjective checklists and rating scales can be compiled.

C. Cognitive Organization: The Study of Implicit Theories of Personality

We have already seen that an implicit theory enables the perceiver to form expectations about how another person might behave in a new situation. It also directs the growth of his impressions of other people by generating new implications which enlarge his initial impressions, tending to make them more consistent and organized. In terms of gestalt psychology, the implicit theory makes for 'closure' and for a unified impression. When we perceive, or are informed of, some aspects of a person's qualities, we tend to enlarge and round out the image to obtain a sort of 'total impression'; we form expectations about his appearance and his further psychological attributes, and even about details of his past life and future prospects.

The original work on 'implicit theories' and 'cognitive structure' was reported by Asch (1946), although he did not use these terms. He attempted to demonstrate that, in the course of establishing an impression, some personal qualities have more influence than others. Two groups of subjects were presented with a list of discrete traits—intelligent, skilful, industrious, —, determined, practical, cautious. The blank was filled in with either the word 'warm' or the word 'cold'. Subjects were then instructed to write a brief sketch of the person described and to complete an adjective checklist. The free descriptions (brief sketches) showed considerable differences between the 'warm' set and the 'cold' set of traits. In general, the 'warm' impressions were far more favourable and positive. The qualitative differences between the two groups were confirmed in the checklist choices. When the list of traits included 'warm', the person described was regarded as generous, wise, happy, good-natured, humorous, sociable, popular and humane; when the stimulus list included 'cold', he was thought to possess the opposite qualities. Some qualities were not affected by the inclusion of 'warm' or 'cold', for example, reliable, important, good-looking, persistent, serious, restrained, strong and honest. The warm–cold variable affects a considerable number of traits and so transforms the nature of the overall impression; it is what Asch called a 'central' quality.

In a second study, Asch omitted the words 'warm' and 'cold' from the stimulus list and added them to the checklist. The distribution of choices was intermediate between the 'warm' and 'cold' conditions of the first experiment. The inclusion of 'warm–cold' in the checklist permitted the subdivision of the total group into those subjects who judged the person to be warm and those who judged him to be cold. The distribution of the checklist choices in the subgroups were consistent with the choices in the first experiment—indicating a strong tendency to evaluate people. The evaluation then determined the impression formed.

In a further study Asch replaced 'warm' and 'cold' by 'polite' and 'blunt'. The effects produced by the inclusion of 'polite' or 'blunt' were far less than those produced by 'warm' or 'cold'. Asch concluded that 'polite' and 'blunt' were peripheral qualities. He went on to demonstrate that the centrality of 'warm' and 'cold' was not absolute, but depended upon the context in which they occurred. When embedded in lists such as 'obedient, weak, shallow, unambitious, vain' or 'vain, shrewd, unscrupulous, shallow, envious', the terms had little effect. In addition to the effects of context, individual differences occur—a trait regarded as central by one person may be regarded as peripheral by another.

The general findings of Asch have been confirmed by other investigators using much the same procedure—see Mensch and Wishner (1947). Veness and Brierley (1963) also successfully replicated Asch's results. They played a tape recording of a person presenting himself as a veterinarian and describing his activities in terms designed to fit the traits of Asch's stimulus list. Warm and cold were represented by two different tones of voice of the speaker who was actually a speech expert. Kelley (1950), cited previously, obtained similar results in a relatively naturalistic experiment.

The idea of an implicit or 'lay' theory of personality was put forward by Bruner and Tagiuri (1954) and then by Cronbach (1955). Bruner and Tagiuri stressed the importance of studying the kinds of inferences people are led to by the knowledge that another individual has a particular characteristic. Bruner, Shapiro and Tagiuri (1958) studied the trait-to-trait inference network that constitutes one aspect of an individual's implicit theory of personality. Bruner and his colleagues were concerned with systematically relating (a) the inferences made from individual traits taken in isolation to (b) the inferences made from the same traits in combination. Like Asch, they were concerned with the effects that combination has upon impression formation. Subjects were provided with one or more stimulus traits and a list of 59 other traits. They were asked to rate the probability of each trait in the list being present in a person who possessed the stimulus trait(s). The stimulus traits were: 'considerate', 'independent', 'intelligent' and 'inconsiderate'. Taking these four traits one, two and three at a time, without putting 'considerate' and 'inconsiderate' in the same combination, eleven arrangements are possible. Bruner and his colleagues were able to predict the direction of the inference from traits in combination from a knowledge of the direction of inference when the traits making up the combination were in isolation. Thus the effects of traits in combination appear to be merely the sum of their effects in isolation, a finding that runs contrary to Asch's conclusion that person perception is not equally affected by each trait, that is, central traits affect the meaning given to peripheral traits. The results, however, are not really incompatible. Asch's stimulus list contained seven items, Bruner's at the most three. It may well be that as the number of items is increased their different effects become more pronounced. Bruner's list may well have contained traits which were all equal in weight, that is, all central or all peripheral.

Wishner's (1960) studies help to resolve this apparent conflict. Wishner demonstrated that a stimulus trait may be either central or peripheral depending upon the responses the subject is asked to make. Two hundred and fourteen students rated their instructors on a set of traits consisting of Asch's stimulus and checklist traits. Correlations were obtained for each trait with all other traits; the correlation between two traits A and B indicated the extent to which subjects who attributed trait A to a person also attributed trait B. From his matrix of trait-with-trait correlations, Wishner was able to explain and predict Asch's results. Warm and cold were central traits in Asch's list because they were highly correlated with a number of traits in the checklist, such as generosity, sociability, wisdom, happiness, and so on, while the six other traits in the stimulus list were not strongly correlated with the checklist traits. Hence the change from warm to cold had a considerable effect on the checklist choices.

Warm and cold did not correlate with all items in the checklist, however, and hence were central only for certain traits. Blunt and polite correlated with relatively few items in the checklist, so that any change in the traits would not affect judgments. For example, the correlation between happy/not happy and warm/cold was + 0·54, whereas that happy/not happy and blunt/polite was only + 0·20. Wishner demonstrated in further experiments that the centrality of a trait can be manipulated by changing the traits in the checklist.

Wishner's results mean that the concept of central traits must be slightly modified. Traits are central if they have a large number of high correlations with other traits. Wishner's methods allow the identification of such traits and predict the effects they will have when subjects record their impressions using an adjective checklist.

Wishner's reanalysis of Asch's work shows the dangers of placing constraints upon subjects. In everyday life, as in some but not all of Asch's experiments, the perceiver is free to choose the information upon which he bases his judgments, free to choose which terms to use when describing others, and free to integrate this information as he wishes, stressing certain elements, playing others down. Great care is necessary in person perception research if the judgmental situation is to be natural and realistic on the one hand, so that the subject can exhibit his characteristic modes of judging and describing others, and sufficiently structured, on the other hand, to permit replication and interpretation.

In addition to implying associations between characteristics, an 'implicit theory' also implies that a given characteristic has a certain frequency of occurrence in either the general population or in a specific group. Thus, one person may describe people as 'aggressive' much more frequently, that is, perceive 'aggressiveness' more readily, than another person. Furthermore, an implicit theory of personality implies a range and level of intensity of a particular characteristic; for example, it may predispose one to perceive people as being more varied (or less varied) in selfishness or as being on average more (or less) selfish than do others. These effects produce differences between individuals in their perception of others; the effects can be expressed, for example, in terms of their *average* rating and the *spread or dispersion* of their ratings of a number of other persons—see Cronbach (1955, 1958) and H. C. Smith (1966). Gross (1961) demonstrated that such systematic biases do exist but are slight compared with the extent to which stimulus persons affect ratings.

D. Methods of Analysing Cognitive Organization

The existence of trait-to-trait inference networks demonstrates the organized nature of the interpersonal cognitive system. The works of Bruner *et al.* (1958) and Wishner (1960) illustrate that this organization can be examined either (a) by asking a subject to indicate the probability of two traits being attributes of the same person or (b) by computing inter-trait correlations based upon a subject's rating or rankings of a number of other people on a number of traits. Various techniques have been suggested to analyse cognitive organization (structure), most based upon mathematical models, for example, Kelly (1955), Hays (1958), Jackson (1962) and Lay and Jackson (1969), although some phenomenological methods have been suggested—see, for example, Zajonc (1960). Basic to many of the mathematical techniques is the notion that a cognitive system can be analysed in terms of n-dimensional space, the major dimensions of which can be specified by factor analysis—see, for example, Osgood, Suci and Tannenbaum (1957), Kelly (1955) and Cronbach (1958). The assumption that elements within a cognitive system can be treated in this way, rather than in ways appropriate to variables which are discrete and discontinuous, has been questioned—see Bieri *et al.* (1966).

The *Semantic Differential* consists of a set of rating scales defined by bipolar adjectives and was originally devised as a method of studying connotation—see Osgood, Suci and Tannenbaum (1957). For this purpose Osgood obtained ratings of a variety of concepts on a large number of bipolar scales. Factor analysis yielded three main factors—evaluation, potency, and activity. Although the Semantic Differential seems best suited for nomothetic studies, it can be used to study an individual's cognitive structure and has been used to locate 'significant other' persons in the perceiver's cognitive space—see Osgood and Luria (1954). The Semantic Differential can be readily modified to study trait implications by asking subjects to rate a key trait, say 'sincere', on a series of scales each defined by a trait and its opposite, like serious–frivolous, sociable–unsociable. Scales can then be intercorrelated and the resulting matrix factor-analysed. In spite of its popularity the Semantic Differential is not without serious limitations. The method assumes that the distance between the poles is the same for all scales. However, as Jackson (1962) pointed out, this may not be so. Are polite–rude as psychologically distant as loving–hating? The Semantic Differential assumes that they are. Also it is usual to use scales with antonyms arranged as polar opposites. However, a number of Wishner's (1960) results indicate that grammatical antonyms do not necessarily correspond to psychological opposites. For example, the implications of 'unintelligent' are not the exact opposites of the implications of 'intelligent', nor are they the same as those of 'stupid'.

The *Repertory Grid* is similar to the Semantic Differential in that it employs the factor analysis of rating scales—see Kelly (1955). The terms or constructs used by the subject to describe others are elicited by means of the Role Construct Repertory Test described previously. A grid or matrix is then produced; the rows consist of the role titles (persons), and the columns consist of the constructs (characteristics). The subject indicates whether or not each person possesses a particular characteristic. The grid is then factor-analysed to yield the main dimensions that the subject uses to construe his environment. Kelly's scales, like those of Osgood, are dimensional but have only two intervals. Modifications of Kelly's Grid are described by Bannister and Mair (1968).

In personality study, the term 'nomothetic' has been used to refer to general laws and systems of classification; it has been contrasted with the term 'idiographic' which is used to refer to the study of particular instances or individual persons. The terms can be misleading: some general issues were discussed briefly in Chapter 1. The Repertory Grid is regarded as an idiographic procedure, although it can be used in nomothetic studies. It is a flexible instrument which has uses in addition to that of exploring trait implications. It is so flexible that Vernon (1964) finds it almost unmanageable! The mathematical analysis of grids has become considerably more sophisticated since Kelly's original method of analysis—see Bonarious (1965) and Slater (1964).

Cronbach (1958) outlined an approach similar to that of Osgood, Suci and Tannenbaum (1957) and of Kelly (1955). He suggested that two methods be used. In the first, one person's cognitive structure is analysed by asking him to describe a large number of representative others using a multidimensional rating scale, an adjective checklist, or a set of statements for Q-sorting. In the second, a large number of observers are used, each describing one or a few other people. The data obtained in this way can be intercorrelated and factor-analysed or described in terms of the mean and standard deviation of the ratings on each scale. Thus individual and group comparisons can be made.

Hays (1958) provided an alternative to the factor-analytic model by adopting a set-theory approach. Subjects are asked to rate the likelihood of occurrence of a trait in a person given that he possesses a designated trait. For example, 'If a person is intelligent how likely is he to be aggressive?' The subject rates all pairs of traits in this way. Hays's method, like factor analysis, provides measures of the relationships between traits and extracts the basic dimensions of cognitive structure. Hays's method apparently copes easily with the asymmetrical relationships between traits—a problem which creates difficulty for most other mathematical techniques. This problem concerns the fact that the probability of 'sociable' implying 'generous' seems not to be systematically related to the probability of 'generous' implying 'sociable'. Thus a person who is shy has some likelihood of being anxious, whereas the person who is anxious may have a different likelihood of being shy.

The mathematical models of cognitive structure previously mentioned might be expected to yield compatible results. Todd and Rappoport (1964) have shown that Hays's method and factor analysis produce similar descriptions of trait implications but do not show agreement in the way they dimensionalize cognitive structure.

Although Kelly (1955) assumes that the relationship between traits are independent of the persons being judged, cognitive structure seems to be organized so that trait implications take into account both the person rated and situational factors. For example, 'careful with his money' might imply 'miserliness' in a rich person or 'sensible' in a student or newlywed; or 'argumentative' might imply one set of further characteristics when applied to a person as a student, and another set when applied to the same person as a partygoer. Interactions between trait implications and persons judged are avoided in most studies by asking subjects to rate either hypothetical persons—see Bruner et al. (1958)—homogeneous group of real persons—see Wishner (1960)—or merely to indicate the likelihood of two traits being present in the same person. Such methods tend to maximize trait relationships and minimize the effects of stimulus factors. Ideally, trait implications should be examined in a more naturalistic manner with greater attention paid to ecological validity—for example, by asking subjects to judge a large, representative group of stimulus persons on traits which they normally use. Gross (1961) asked subjects to judge a heterogeneous group of 30 stimulus persons aged 20 to 40 years, half male, presented in films lasting 30 seconds. She found that, although there was a response bias in the use of the rating scales, it was small compared with the effects of the stimulus persons and concluded that her results cast doubt upon those theories which assume that 'the judge's unique system of constructs, personifications, or implicit personality theory are central in determining his impressions of others'. This conclusion is a little too strong, because the operation of implicit theories under certain conditions has been conclusively established, but her findings suggest that implicit theories do not play quite as important a role in impression formation as was previously thought; they are not as rigid or as independent of the situation as has been suggested. Actually it makes no sense to argue that the observer's implicit theory of personality is or is not affected by the stimulus person and the stimulus situation. The implicit theory must enable the observer to make sense of the behaviour of other people, that is, enable the observer to assimilate his observations to pre-established cognitive schemata or enable him to accommodate (modify) his pre-established schemata to fit new information. Without stable schemata, the observer could not adjust consistently to the behaviour of other people; without flexible schemata, the observer could not learn or test his ideas against reality. In these respects, the cognitive schemata underlying the perception and understanding of people are no different from other sorts of cognitive schemata, for example those that enable us to deal with motor cars, animals, or foodstuffs.

Koltuv (1962) obtained from each of her subjects traits they normally used and traits they did not use. When asked to rate familiar and unfamiliar persons on these traits, trait intercorrelations were higher for habitually used (familiar) traits and for unfamiliar persons, indicating that implicit theories of trait implications are affected by the stimulus persons. The results obtained by Gross and Koltuv constitute a strong argument in favour of an idiographic rather than a nomothetic approach to the study of implicit personality theories, and point to the importance of studying the effects of different stimulus persons on the contents and organization of impressions—see Supnick (1964).

A better understanding of the cognitive structures underlying person perception might be obtained if procedures were used which involved fewer assumptions than do present methods. For example, bipolar rating scales assume that the psychological distance between the two poles is the same for all trait pairs; ranking partly overcomes this difficulty. Ranking also overcomes the difficulty created by response sets in the use of rating scales; the effects of response sets might be confused with the effects created by implicit theories. Trait implications represented by rank order intercorrelations could be subjected to cluster analysis rather than factor analysis—see Bromley (1966b). The traits used in such studies should be personally relevant to the subjects, i.e., familiar and habitually used in everyday life, otherwise the problems of validation are aggravated.

Zajonc (1960) described a method for investigating: (a) differentiation, (b) complexity, (c) organization and (d) unity of cognitive systems. Zajonc measured these four variables by asking subjects to list the characteristics of a person designated by the experimenter: (a) the number of characteristics listed provided a measure of differentiation; (b) complexity was determined by writing these characteristics separately on cards and asking the subjects to sort them into groups; (c) organization was revealed when subjects were asked whether any of the groups could be subdivided and then whether any of the subdivisions could be further subdivided; (d) degree of unity was determined by asking subjects to imagine that the person changed so that one of the characteristics listed was either absent or no longer true and then to list all the other characteristics that would also change if the first one changed. Subjects were asked to do this for all characteristics. Hinkle (1965) suggested a technique—the Implication Grid—for investigating the hierarchical organization of cognitive systems which is similar to that of Zajonc.

So far, discussion of the mechanisms underlying impression formation has centred on the cognitive aspects of social construing; emotion has received little attention although it clearly plays an important part. We rarely react to people in a non-emotional manner. Liking and disliking are important determinants of social interaction and, as Tagiuri (1958) pointed out, it is important to uncover the determinants of affective responses to others. The perceiver's emotional responses to the other person manifest themselves in the terms he uses to describe them, which therefore reflect both cognitive and affective functions. Evaluation is an important dimension of the connotation of traits and is usually regarded as the major determinant of trait inferences—see Podell (1961). The first factor extracted from the factor analysis of repertory grids is usually evaluative, and it contributes a large part of the total variance. Similarly, Osgood (1962) found such large evaluative factors in the analysis of trait implications that little else could be determined. There appears to be a tendency to use positively evaluated terms more frequently than negatively evaluated terms—the Pollyanna hypothesis formulated by Boucher and Osgood (1969).

Peabody (1967, 1970) claimed that the importance of evaluation has been exaggerated because of a failure to distinguish between the evaluative and descriptive aspects of traits. Peabody selected sets of traits which permitted the separation of these two aspects. Two traits were descriptive of quality X, one of which was positively evaluated, the other negatively evaluated. The other two traits in the set were descriptive of the opposite quality to X, again one was positive, the other negative, for example, timid (−), cautious (+), bold (+), rash (−). Subjects were asked to rate one of these traits on a rating scale defined by two opposing traits, for example cautious was rated on timid–bold. The results indicated that evaluative similarity was always secondary to descriptive similarity. Factor analysis showed that none of the factors were evaluative. Peabody suggests that traits are arranged on an implicit scale, the extremities of which are negatively evaluated. Thus an implicit scale of riskiness would consist of the following traits: timid (−), cautious (+), bold (+), rash (−). The scale is divided according to some criterion. The judgment process consists of two decisions: whether a person is above or below the upper criterion (e.g. 'rash' or 'cautious') and whether he is above or below the lower criterion (e.g. 'bold' or 'timid'). Regions of uncertainty surround these criterion points; and their position and size give rise to considerable individual differences and constitute an implicit theory of the type discussed by Cronbach (1955, 1958).

Research on trait implications not only throws light upon the process of impression formation but also has consequences for the study of personality—see W. Mischel (1968). Many of the dimensions of personality referred to in textbooks and measured by means of tests have been arrived at by factor-analysing the responses of trained judges rating a large number of stimulus persons. Questions arise as to the validity of such factors and the extent to which they are affected by the judges' implicit personality theories. Norman (1963) obtained a stable structure of five factors from interpersonal ratings among different groups of subjects who had known each other for differing lengths of time; the rating scales were based upon Cattell's 'Personality Sphere'. A similar factor structure was obtained when judges rated people with whom they had had no previous relationship—basing their ratings on brief and superficial observations of appearance and manner—see Passini and Norman (1966). These results, showing that stimulus persons appear not to affect trait implications, conflict with the conclusions of Gross (1961). This might result from different traits being used in the different investigations.

The diverse and often conflicting results obtained in studies of implicit theories indicate a need for more adequate methods of studying cognitive structure, for more studies employing the subject's own constructs, and for the development of standard lists of traits that can be used instead of the *ad hoc* collections which investigators tend to use at present.

II. Final Impression: The Stage of Verbal Report

Subjects have been asked to report upon most stages of impression formation, but little attention has been paid to the typical impressions they form. Subjects have rarely been asked to provide verbal descriptions of people they know well. A naturalistic approach of this sort should provide valuable information about the *contents* and *organization* of impressions. Hastorf, Richardson and Dornbusch (1958) advocated the content analysis of free descriptions to yield the major dimensions people use in perceiving and categorizing others. Free descriptions could also provide information about the organization of impressions. We have already seen that an implicit theory of personality fosters organization in an impression, but it is possible that the effect has been exaggerated. Semantic factors probably play an important role in achieving an organized, consistent impression making for effective communication. This unity is achieved through the use of qualifying words and phrases which say something about the frequency with which certain characteristics manifest themselves, the degree to which they are typical of an individual, and the way they are affected by situational factors. Thus certain elements in the impression can be played down, while others can be sharpened or amplified. Similarly, explanatory statements and evidential backing, as well as hypothetical and logical propositions can be used to relate disparate elements in the impression. Unfortunately, although considerable attention has been paid to the study of trait implications the linguistic analysis of impressions has received little attention despite its obvious importance and the contribution it is likely to make to the study of individual differences in person perception. These various aspects of the language of interpersonal impressions will become clearer when we come to deal with their contents and organization.

Some studies of the contents of impressions have already been reviewed, particularly those focusing upon the use of 'internal' versus 'external' terms to describe others—see Maher (1957), Bieri, Bradburn and Galinsky (1958), and Fancher (1966). Warr (1968) draws attention to another difference in judgments; some judgments are 'episodic', describing temporary behavioural qualities, such as 'pleased' or 'angry', while others are 'dispositional', referring to stable and permanent qualities rather than to transient states, for example 'intelligent', 'sociable'. Allport (1961) cited an unpublished study of students' first impressions of a man they saw talking to their lecturer for a few minutes. The contents of the impressions ranged from physical characteristics to personality traits. A more systematic study was conducted by Beach and Wertheimer (1961). Twelve descriptions of people designated by the experimenters were collected from each of 30 female and 36 male students. The free descriptions were divided into statements which were sorted into 13 major content categories grouped under 4 major headings :

1. Objective Information : (a) appearance, (b) background, (c) general information (job, income, etc.).
2. Social Interaction : (d) behaviour towards the subject and (e) his behaviour towards other people, (f) other people's reaction to and acceptance of him, (g) subject's reaction to and acceptance of him.
3. Behavioural Consistencies : (h) temperament, (i) self-concept and emotional adjustment, and (j) morals and values.
4. Performance and Activities : (k) abilities, (l) motivation, and (m) activities and interests.

The striking feature of this study is its indication of the tremendous range of content of the impressions we form of other people. The wide range and variety of free description material has also been found by Hastorf, Richardson and Dornbusch (1958), Richardson Dornbusch and Hastorf (1961) and Bromley (1966a).

So far studies suggest that : (1) people have a small number of categories or terms that they consistently use to describe others—see Hastorf *et al.* (1958); (2) perceivers differ considerably in the categories they use to describe others—a number of sex differences have been reported; Beach and Wertheimer (1961) report that males use more ability terms than females, Sarbin (1954) found that women's first impressions contain fewer role or status categories than men, they use 'inner' traits instead; (3) subjects use different categories to describe different people, although one subject's descriptions of two people tend to be more alike than descriptions of one person obtained from two subjects—see Richardson, Dornbusch and Hastorf (1961): (4) there is also a strong relationship between the categories people use to describe others and those used to describe themselves.

The content analysis of free descriptions provides one of the simplest means of eliciting the terms and categories subjects use to describe and conceptualize other people. By designating the type of person the subject is to describe it is possible to investigate the effects of stimulus person variables on the contents of the descriptions. Such studies are crucial to the analysis of impression formation, because the underlying assumptions are fewer and simpler than those of studies using more elaborate experimental conditions and psychometric instruments, and because such studies provide a convenient method for investigating developmental changes and the naturally occurring phenomena of perceiving and conceptualizing persons. Supnick's (1964) study, cited earlier, illustrates such an approach. Subjects, teenagers and adults, males and females, were asked to describe eight people known to them who fulfilled the following requirements—half must be older than themselves and half must be peers, half male, half female, half people they liked and half people they disliked. They were given three minutes to write each description. The number of constructs used in each description was then analysed. Females produced more constructs than males. More constructs were used to describe people who were liked than those who were disliked and to describe peers as opposed to older people. Significant age by sex-of-other, sex by sex-of-other, sex by age-of-other, sex-of-other by age-of-other interactions were obtained which indicated the effect of varying the stimulus person. These results illustrate the value that analysis of variance might have in the treatment of such data. Note also that the time allowance is probably important in studies of this kind.

III. The Effects of Perceiver Variables on Impression Formation

The types of situation in which perceiver variables—those giving rise to individual differences—are likely to have considerable effect are those created by the presence of ambiguous stimuli and a strong need to form an organized impression, together with a high degree of ego-involvement associated with interpersonal relations. Individual differences have been mentioned elsewhere in this review and therefore will be dealt with briefly. Shrauger and Altrocchi (1964) provide a more detailed review.

The fact that individual differences are present at all stages in impression formation tends to produce research in which investigators select various personality characteristics and then seek some correlate in impression formation. This method produces considerable quantities of data which are difficult to integrate into a theoretical framework. A more satisfactory approach is to identify the various phases and processes of impression formation, and *then* to relate these to individual differences in personality attributes, attitudes, and so on—see Shrauger (1967).

One of the more interesting possibilities in the study of person perception is that it will provide a fresh approach to the study of personality and adjustment, and to the concepts and taxonomies in this area. Any attempt to correlate impression formation processes with an *ad hoc* collection of traits and motives which are themselves frequently arrived at by an unanalysed process of person perception seems to be putting the cart before the horse. Traditionally, judges' ratings of others were assumed to tell us something about the other's personality, whereas we now realize that they tell us something about the judges.

A. Individual Differences in Cognitive Organization

Cognitive systems associated with interpersonal relationships seem to vary in degree of differentiation and organization; so the implications for all stages of impression formation are considerable. Subjects with highly differentiated cognitive systems appear to be more aware of positive and negative attributes in the same person—see Crockett (1965). They are able to integrate conflicting information better than are subjects with less differentiated systems—see Nidorf and Crockett (1965), and Mayo and Crockett (1964). Rosenkrantz and Crockett (1965), however, found no relationship between differentiation and the production of integrated or ambivalent impressions when subjects were presented with conflicting information. However, they found an interaction between differentiation and sex of subject: highly differentiating males produced more integrated impressions than less differentiating males and were less affected by the information presented last.

Leventhal and Singer (1964) found no clear-cut relationship between : (a) the tendency to use trait names in a discriminating way to distinguish between different stimulus persons, and (b) changes in impressions following the receipt of contradictory information or the resolution of such information. More discriminating judges, however, produced less clear impressions after receiving the first block of information and showed more uncertainty. Less discriminating judges responded to external qualities, while more discriminating judges searched for information regarding the other person's inner states.

Bieri (1955) has suggested that the notion of 'cognitive complexity' refers to : (a) the degree to which a system is differentiated, that is, the number of elements it contains, (b) the extent to which these are used differentially, and (c) the degree to which the elements are hierarchically organized. Global indices of 'cognitive complexity', however, are of doubtful value, since they are only slightly correlated with each other. The evidence does not support the idea of a general trait of cognitive complexity—see Vannoy (1965). Miller (1969) suggests that cognitive complexity may be multidimensional. Global indices are inconsistent partly because of differences in the way the concept has been operationally defined. It is still important, however, to examine the various features of cognitive complexity, their interrelationship and their effects, since it is probable that some of these features will be associated with such factors as age, intelligence and education, and may be associated with personality and temperament. Miller and Bieri (1965) report that cognitive complexity was greater for socially 'distant' stimulus persons when they were judged by means of a repertory test.

B. The Effect of Personality Traits and Motives

Since Murray's (1933) early experiment on the effects of fear arousal upon children's perceptions of photographs, a considerable number of attempts have been made to demonstrate that people tend to attribute (project) their own repressed feelings and socially undesirable characteristics to other people. The aim has been to provide a sound empirical basis for the use of projective techniques in personality assessment. Although a number of these studies are relevant to issues in person perception, it is not proposed to review them here—see Kenny (1964).

Authoritarianism is a trait that has received considerable attention—see Jones (1954), Scodel and Friedman (1956), Crockett and Meidinger (1956), Kates (1959), and Lipetz (1960). Authoritarians tend to see other people as similar to themselves, and hence rate stimulus persons higher on authoritarian power and leadership than do non-authoritarians—see for example, Kates (1959). They also appear to use evaluative responses more readily and to make more extreme evaluative responses than do non-authoritarians—see Warr and Sims (1965). High-status persons are usually seen in a more favourable light by authoritarians than by non-authoritarians—see Jones (1954), but authoritarians show more generalized fear, suspicion, and moralistic condemnation of strangers—see Desoto, Kuethe and Wunderlich (1960). The impressions formed by authoritarians tend to be more resistant to change than those formed by non-authoritarians—see Steiner and Johnson (1963). In general, they appear to be less sensitive in their perception of other people, although this possibility has been questioned by Schulberg (1961). When forming impressions, they make more use of external characteristics and cues such as social class than do non-authoritarians—see Wilkins and de Charms (1962).

The tendency to see others as like oneself is true of individuals other than authoritarians. Fensterheim and Tresselt (1953) showed that subjects tend to attribute values dissimilar to their own to people they dislike, but attribute values similar to their own to people they like. There is a tendency for people to asssume that others are similar to themselves. Attempts to measure 'assumed similarity' have had limited success because of methodological shortcomings of the sort that have hindered the development of a satisfactory measure of accuracy—see Cronbach (1958) and Cline (1964). Benedetti and Hill (1960) have argued that the centrality of a trait attributed to another person varies with the strength of the same trait in the perceiver. They reported that their subjects' sociability scores on a questionnaire were significantly related to the impressions they formed of people who were said to be sociable and unsociable.

Neuroticism is an important personality characteristic that may be related to impression formation. Rabin (1962) appeared to find greater differences between maladjusted subjects as compared with normal subjects in their judgments of others. Shrauger and Altrocchi (1964) suggested a curvilinear relationship between adjustment and differentiation, with differentiation increasing from a low level among extremely defensive people (repressors) to a maximum among people with normal insight into self and others, and then decreasing to a low level among people with severe personality disturbance, that is, disrupted defences. Altrocchi (1961) found that, among a group of normals, repressors differentiated less than did sensitizers.

Matkom (1963) reported that maladjusted subjects showed a greater discrepancy between ratings of 'real' versus 'apparent' personality than did well-adjusted subjects, and that there was a large difference between maladjusted and well-adjusted subjects in their ratings of 'real' personality, which perhaps reflects the maladjusted subjects' suspiciousness of people. Given both positive and negative information about the stimulus person, maladjusted subjects were most confident in their judgments of 'apparent' personality. When rating 'real' personality, however, maladjusted subjects were more confident than well-adjusted subjects in their ratings only when the information was negative—indicating that they expected people to have unfavourable qualities.

Impression formation is a reflexive process. That is to say, a person can form an impression of himself, and even contemplate the impression he has of himself, that is, his self-concept. The impression a person has of himself can be expected to influence his perception of others. Research on the self-concept, however, has not yet progressed far enough for us to understand much about this topic—see Wylie (1961) and Gergen (1971). It seems somewhat premature therefore to discuss the relationships between concepts of self and concepts of others. Some provisional results are discussed in Chapter 12.

IV. The Effects of Social Interaction on Impression Formation

The existence of a definite psychological relationship between one person and another is likely to affect the impressions formed. For example one interpersonal relationship that is likely to have a great effect is the degree of liking. Liking exerts a considerable influence on the traits we assign to other people (see Lott, Lott, Reed and Crow, 1970, and Fensterheim and Tresselt, 1953). Subjects tend to assign fewer favourable traits to people they dislike—see Pastore (1960a, 1960b)—and liking helps to determine the frequency with which we interact with the other person, and this in turn determines the variety of behaviour we encounter. Tagiuri (1958) drew attention to the need to uncover the determinants of liking and disliking and outlined a procedure for recording feelings of liking and disliking in groups—see also Tagiuri (1957).

The nature of the social interaction is important because it determines not only what the perceiver looks for in the other person but also what types of behaviour the other person exhibits and how much of his real self he shows. If the interaction is routine or superficial or merely ritual in character, the participants may not expect to meet again, and may not form any impression of the other as a 'person'. The perceiver responds to cues for which prescribed patterns of behaviour are appropriate; and for this purpose information about status and role will usually be sufficient. In such a formal situation, the other person usually puts on a socially desirable front or adopts a socially prescribed role; in either case he will not reveal his inner personal states or fundamental characteristics to any marked extent. This has the effect of reducing the perceiver's confidence in the impression he forms—see Jones, Davies and Gergen (1961). Role-taking prescribes what the other person reveals, and the perceiver's role in such interaction prescribes what things he attends to—see Jones and de Charms (1958).

Impressions are affected by status relationships in the interaction. High-status persons are more likely to be seen as the origin of their actions than are low-status persons, even when these actions are compliant—see Thibaut and Riecken (1955). The higher the status of a person the greater the tendency to see his actions as justified, even when they are aversive (negative), provided they are relevant to his status; there is also a stronger tendency to assign good intentions to his actions—see Pepitone (1958).

V. Implications

The lengthy but far from exhaustive review of the literature in Chapters 2 and 3 has indicated that, despite a considerable amount of work in person perception, well-established findings are few, and theory construction has been carried out only on a small scale. While acknowledging that there has been relatively little progress in understanding impression formation, it can be argued that some investigators seem to have assumed that the processes and variables in person perception were fairly obvious and that all that was required was a kind of rigorous experimental proof. This assumption could lead such investigators to experimentally manipulate what they consider to be key variables only to find that their results cannot be corroborated by the findings of simpler and more naturalistic studies. The fact is that the processes and variables in person perception are obscure and complicated, to say the least, and we have scarcely begun to appreciate how fundamental the problem is. Further research in person perception seems to require less emphasis on variables chosen for ease of experimental manipulation, and more emphasis on issues related to fundamental concepts and problems, such as the content and organization of naturally occurring impressions. Studies of this sort should help us to formulate the basic problems, and to decide what sorts of theories can be constructed and what sorts of evidence is relevant to those theories—see Bromley (1970). To begin with at least, these further studies should employ methods of presenting the stimulus information which are familiar to or at least natural for subjects, and they should use equally natural methods for obtaining response data. In other words : (a) the subject should not be artificially constrained by inappropriate conditions, (b) the subject should be free to select whatever stimulus information he finds relevant, and (c) the subject should be able to respond in such a way as to permit the investigator to generalize his findings to natural, everyday conditions of life.

The complex nature of person perception suggests that developmental studies might be usefully employed, so that evidence about its relatively simple forms may be studied first. The subtlety of the skills and the complexities of the processes of person perception in normal adults makes it a difficult problem to study, but it should be possible to understand the simpler forms of impression formation in young children and to trace some of the developmental phases leading eventually to complex adult forms and to professional levels of understanding.

It may be further argued that the role of implicit theories of personality in determining the contents of impressions seems to have been exaggerated, while the role of the stimulus person has been underestimated. It is important to study the properties of *experimental subjects* on the one hand and the properties of *stimulus persons* on the other. As we shall see, both sorts of variables give rise to main effects and interaction effects in impression formation.

CHAPTER 4

Person Perception in Children: Past Literature and Present Orientation

I. Research Problems

The developmental psychology of person perception is a comparatively unworked area. There has been no systematic analysis of children's concepts of human behaviour and personality comparable to the study of their concepts of the physical world or of space, number and causality. This is a little surprising considering its importance. The impressions children form of people who have some psychological significance for them are likely to set a pattern for the development of their characteristic styles of social interaction, as well as contributing to their frames of reference for judging people. The practical techniques and theoretical ideas suitable for such a study have been available for several years. Some of the methods used to investigate impression formation in adults could be adapted for use with children, in conjunction with methods used to study other aspects of concept formation in children, for example, morals and games—see Piaget (1932). On the theoretical side, the developmental psychology of Piaget and Werner, and the cognitive psychology of Bruner, could provide a general conceptual orientation for research into the growth of the child's understanding of human nature.

Perhaps one reason for neglecting the developmental psychology of

53

children's thinking about 'human nature' is that even at the professional scientific level we lack an agreed and stable framework of ideas about human personality and the organization of behaviour. In other words, although there may be disputes about matters of detail—as there are about philosophical presuppositions with regard to number, space, causality and the physical world—nevertheless there is broad agreement about these issues which provides a stable frame of reference against which developmental levels can be measured; it also provides a target towards which a child's education and training can be directed. While there is fairly broad agreement about the nature of the physical and biological aspects of nature, there is, at present, no such broad agreement about human nature. The same principle—of agreement between competent adult observers—applies in a different way to the moral education of children in a given culture. But as far as psychological (and perhaps political or sociological) concepts are concerned, there is much less agreement, and much more confusion about the meaning and validity of such concepts. Thus the study of the development of the child's concepts of human personality and human behaviour generates a paradox for psychology that is not generated for other sciences by developmental studies of their concepts. The paradox is that by unravelling the developmental processes of 'understanding others', and by revealing some of the fundamental errors and confusions, we may expect to improve upon professional and scientific concepts of human nature. The argument is that the problems we encounter as scientists in trying to understand human behaviour are partly objective, in that they have to do with the complexities of the facts themselves, and partly subjective, in that they have to do with the way we try to conceptualize these facts. In this respect, of course, psychologists are in the same position as other sorts of scientist. But, as it is literally true that the psychologist as a scientist is trying to understand himself, it seems likely that he will have to pay even more attention to the epistemology of his subject than will, say, the natural scientist. The study of the developmental processes of 'understanding others' may prove to be a prerequisite for a satisfactory epistemology of psychology, that is, for a satisfactory account of the conceptual groundwork of our knowledge of human psychology and behaviour—its assumptions, primitive notions, modes of argument, and so on.

The first research problem with which we are concerned is how to systematically observe and record the way children perceive and conceptualize people. That is, how to obtain evidence about the concepts of human personality and behaviour that children form at different stages of development, and how to elicit representative samples of the statements they use to describe people. The second problem is how to develop procedures for describing—that is, classifying and systematizing—the contents and organization of impressions formed by children and adults. The third problem is how to explain any developmental changes that might be found.

Studies of these related problems are of value because the impressions children form will probably help to determine not only their immediate social interactions, but also their long-term strategies of adjustment and interpersonal relations. In addition, developmental studies may throw light upon the process of impression formation in adults. The processes involved in person perception are many and complex and, in the adult at least, the skills involved are well established, functioning so rapidly and automatically that they are difficult to analyse. In children, the skills are being acquired and are likely to be much simpler and less well organized, and hence easier to describe and analyse. It may well be that person perception can best be understood in terms of its development, just as other aspects of adult personality, such as strategies of adjustment or social attitudes, can be more thoroughly understood in developmental terms. The analysis of concept formation in children has enriched our understanding of concept formation in adults, and we have already implied that there is every reason to expect that the analysis of person perception in children will enrich our understanding of adult concepts of human nature.

II. A Review of Research into Person Perception in Children

A. Children's Perceptions of their Parents

A number of studies have examined the child's perception of his parents (see Dubin and Dubin, 1965), but they have been largely concerned with the types of judgment children make of their parents rather than with the *processes* that mediate such judgments.

From an early age, children learn to describe mother and father in different terms and to distinguish between their respective roles. By the age of 4 years they have formed a fairly clear-cut concept of 'mother' as the person who does household chores and takes care of children—see Mott (1954). Kagan (1961), using rating scales to record impressions, found that children aged 6 to 8 years described 'father' as stronger, larger, darker, dirtier, more angular, and more dangerous than 'mother'. Similarly, Kagan and Lemkin (1960) reported that children saw 'mother' as nicer, more nurturant, and more likely to give presents than 'father', who was seen as more fear arousing, more competent, and more punitive. Emmerich (1961) reported that children saw 'father' as more powerful than 'mother', and that adults were regarded as more powerful than children. Older children, however, tend to see the same-sex parent as less benevolent and more frustrating than the opposite-sex parent, while older girls tend to see 'mother' as the boss more than do younger girls—see Kagan (1956). In adolescence, there is still a tendency to see 'mother' as more expressive and 'father' as more instrumental (Dahlen 1970). Siegelman (1965), in a factor-analytic study of Bronfenbrenner's questionnaire for assessing children's perceptions of their parents, found three factors underlying judgments, which he labelled : loving, punishing and demanding.

The tendency to see 'father' as more punitive and more powerful than 'mother' is affected, presumably, by the personality of the child and by the family situation. Rabkin (1964) found that schizophrenic boys saw their mothers as more dominant and more punitive than their fathers, who were seen as passive and feminine. Neurotic boys on the other hand saw significantly more nurturance in their parents' behaviour than did normal boys, although their father was still perceived as the dominant figure. Boys with behaviour disorders saw their fathers as more punitive and their mothers as nicer than did other groups. Vogel and Lauterbach (1963) reported that disturbed adolescent boys tended to have more idealized views of their mother's behaviour and more hostile views of their father's behaviour than did normal boys. Kagan (1958) reported that the fantasy stories of aggressive boys contained more parent-child hostility and less dependency than those of non-aggressive boys.

The studies convey comparatively little information about the nature of impression formation in children, but they do provide an interesting picture of children's perceptions of their parents. Unfortunately, however, the methods used were somewhat artificial and severe constraints were placed upon the child's responses because of the use of rating scales (see Kagan, 1961), and because of the use of structured questions or structured response alternatives to pictorial stimuli—see Emmerich (1961), and Kagan and Lemkin (1964). Free response methods analysed by means of content analysis would have been more satisfactory given our present limited knowledge about the child's understanding of human nature.

B. Children's Free Descriptions of Others

Watts (1944), who was interested in the part language plays in mental development, carried out one of the earliest and most comprehensive studies of children's concepts of personality and the descriptive terminology they use to describe people. He claimed that descriptions pass through a series of stages as children become more aware of the range of differences between people and the complexities of the individual person, and as they acquire more words to refer to them.

On the basis of non-systematic observation, Watts concluded that until the age of $6\frac{1}{2}$–7, children usually limited their descriptions to appearance, unless some oddity of gait or gesture caught their attention and provoked comment. If the child went beyond what he saw and tried to describe the individual's personality, he usually divided people into two classes—those that pleased him and those that did not. He described the former as 'kind', 'good', or 'nice', and the latter as 'unkind', 'bad', or 'horrid'. From the age of 7 onwards children made marked progress in describing the more obvious qualities of people. They differentiated between the various meanings of 'nice', 'kind' and 'good', and their opposites. Using a sentence completion test, Watts demonstrated that 'nice' differentiated into 'well-mannered', 'polite', 'courteous' and 'agreeable'; 'good' differentiated into 'honest', 'truthful', 'unselfish' and 'steadfast'; and 'kind' differentiated into 'generous', 'sympathetic', 'helpful', and 'good natured'.

Watts did not give any detailed information about the nature and organization of the descriptions produced by children aged 7 to 11 years but he did indicate that at first descriptions were univalent (that is, either positive or negative in emotional tone) and organized around a single salient trait and its immediate implications. The next step consisted of thinking of people as possessing a cluster of similarly evaluated traits. At the age of 11 years, 75 per cent of descriptions were of this type, at 12 years 65 per cent, and at 13 years the number fell to 50 per cent. Thus, up to the age of 11 years, children's descriptions were univalent and did not refer to people as possessing *both* good and bad qualities. This finding was supported by the results of a test in which subjects were asked whether a person could possess two qualities at the same time, one quality being positively and the other negatively evaluated—for example, faithful and stupid, grumpy and generous, affectionate and dishonest. Responses showed that few children under the age of 11 years realized that the same person could possess both positively and negatively evaluated attributes, and less than 50 per cent of children aged 13 and 14 years understood that these combinations were possible. Boys did better on this test than did girls. Thus, a late normal stage in the development of concepts of other people is to realize that others can possess both desirable and undesirable features, and to be able to reconcile these in a unified impression.

Watts's studies constitute an interesting and valuable qualitative description of general developmental changes in the nature of impressions. Unfortunately, however, Watts provided no information about his subjects. He did not give the number of subjects used in the study or the numbers of descriptions each subject provided. He did not provide details of the instructions he gave to his subjects or any information about procedure. No information was given about the number of descriptions in each age group which fell within the four categories he outlined. As a result, generalization from his conclusions is virtually impossible.

Richardson, Dornbusch and Hastorf (1961) used content analysis in a quantitative manner to account for children's free descriptions of other children, and to account for the effects upon the content categories employed of group differences such as sex, race, physical handicap, and rural or urban home. In a free interview situation, 736 children were asked to describe themselves and three other children known to them. In addition, they were asked to make up stories about six children, with and without physical handicap, portrayed in line drawings. The procedure was repeated in a second interview to determine the consistency of category usage. Some of the categories employed in the analysis were developed inductively following inspection of the data, others were developed deductively from general theoretical considerations. The free descriptions were divided into units, referring to one thought or fact about the person described. Each unit was (a) first coded into one of 69 first-order categories, such as age, religion, physical aggression, trust, humour, mental abilities or manners, and (b) second, recoded into nine second-order categories which were more abstract than the first-order categories; examples of these are positive evaluation, negative evaluation, morality, role-taking and achievement motivation. It was possible, therefore, to assign statements to more than one category. Richardson and his colleagues showed that these categories were also suitable for analysing free descriptions obtained from adults.

Richardson and colleagues did not report their findings in detail but rather indicated some of the general results they obtained. The contents of the children's descriptions were not determined entirely by their frame of reference or cognitive structure, because the person described—the stimulus person—had a considerable effect; this was shown by content differences between descriptions for different sorts of stimulus person. When two subjects described two different children, the category overlap was 38 per cent indicating that cultural influences have a considerable effect upon the terms used to describe others, and that children show considerable uniformity in the terms they use. When two subjects described the same child, the overlap increased to 45 per cent, which suggests, obviously, that the stimulus person constitutes a common factor affecting the contents of the impressions. It should be borne in mind, however, that two children forming impressions of one and the same person do not experience identical samples of that person's behaviour. This is an aspect of person perception in interpersonal relationships that we deal with elsewhere. When one subject described two children the overlap was 57 per cent; this indicates that the perceiver's cognitive structure acts as an important determinant of the contents of his impressions. But again, the subject may not experience equivalent samples of the behaviour of the two other children. Dornbusch, Hastorf, Richardson, Muzzy and Vreeland (1965) reported similar results. This method of assessing commonality between descriptions from the overlap among categories may overestimate the actual agreement between two descriptions—the terms used in each might be quite different and yet both could be included in the same category.

Richardson and colleagues showed that the categories used are affected by the sociometric status of the person described; for example, children talked more about interaction with high-status as compared with low-status children, and showed more positive feeling towards high-status children. Low-status children used more aggressive statements than did high-status children.

Physical handicap affected the use of categories: physically handicapped children used categories related to involvement with peers less frequently that did non-handicapped children, but they made greater use of categories describing relationships with adults.

Richardson et al. (1961) did not report any details of coding reliability. Dornbusch et al. (1965), however, using the 69 first-order categories referred to above, reported 86·4 per cent agreement between two coders. The criterion was that if one interviewer coded any idea in a specific category, then the other interviewer coded it in an identical category more than 17 times out of 20. They did not give details of how reliably the descriptions could be decomposed into units.

Yarrow and Campbell (1963) investigated person perception in 267 boys and girls, white and negro, aged from 8 to 13 years while they were at summer camp. Groups of 8 children, originally strangers, were placed together in cabins. Children's impressions of the cabin member they knew best were elicited in interviews at the beginning and end of the two weeks at camp. For 20 of the 32 cabins studied, systematic behaviour observations were made at the beginning, middle and end of camp.

The free descriptions were divided into units, a unit being defined as a 'discrete action, or a single characteristic or evaluation'. The units were then assigned to one of seventeen content categories. In a check on coding reliability two coders agreed upon 77 per cent of a sample of 185 units. The reliability with which descriptions were divided into units was not reported.

On average, the children used 11 units per description with a range of 1 to 27. The content analysis showed that the children gave broad evaluations—85 per cent of the descriptions contained units of this type, and that these judgments were elaborated mainly with details of the other child's interpersonal behaviour, for example 'shares things', 'friendly' or 'bossy'. Qualities not associated with interaction, such as details of abilities, physique and identity, featured in only half the reports; physical appearance was the most frequent of these. The most frequent 'interaction' categories were those dealing with sociability, conformity, verbal sociability, physical play and affiliation. This probably reflected the strong affiliative needs aroused by a new social situation.

When the content categories were collapsed into four major dimensions of interaction—aggression, affiliation, assertion, submission—46 per cent of the subjects concentrated their description on only one dimension, only 2 per cent used all four; 31 per cent of the subjects were able to see opposing tendencies in the other person.

Considerable similarity was found in the contents of descriptions obtained at the beginning and end of camp. In general, however, there was an increase in interaction statements and a decrease in non-interaction statements. Within the interaction content categories, there was a decreased use of the affiliative dimension and an increased use of dimensions referring to aggressive and dominating behaviour. Bromley (1966a), also found serial changes in students' impressions of lecturers as they came into increased contact with them. A detailed investigation of such serial changes in the content and organization of impressions in both adults and children would add considerably to our understanding of impression formation.

Age trends in the use of categories did not occur except for the dimensions of aggression and domination which were used more frequently by the older subjects. However, descriptions given by the older children were better organized and more complex.

Sex differences in the use of categories occurred, with girls stressing nurturant qualities such as 'shares things' and 'comforts me', while boys made greater use of categories relating to non-conforming behaviour and withdrawal, such as 'stubborn'. Sex differences in the complexity of descriptions were not found.

By examining the behavioural records of the children in camp,

Yarrow and Campbell were able to compare the descriptions of active children with those of more withdrawn children, and those of friendly with those of hostile children. They found that active and friendly children gave the most complex descriptions, and that friendly children were more likely than hostile children to make inferential statements. They also found that disliked children were described in a much more systematic manner than liked children, who in turn were described more systematically than neutrally evaluated children.

Yarrow and Campbell were surprised to find rather small developmental trends. They suggested that this might be because interpersonal perceptual skills develop earlier in life, or because the more specific age differences were not detected by the content analysis; for example, the actual terms used to describe an action may be quite different at different age levels although they would be classified in the same content category. This last suggestion seems very likely; a more valuable system of classification, from the point of view of assessing age trends, may well be one which describes statements in terms of their 'abstractness' rather than their 'meaning'. Such a system would classify statements according to whether they refer to specific patterns of behaviour or to more abstract and generalized personal qualities such as traits. When such a system is used to analyse free descriptions considerable developmental trends are revealed. As might be expected, abstract or psychological terms are used more frequently by older children because of growth in intelligence and experience—see Livesley and Bromley (1967), Livesley (1969), Haycock (1969), Scarlett, Press and Crockett (1971), and McHenry (1971). In addition, the age range and age sampling of the Yarrow and Campbell study may well have been inadequate—the age range of subjects, 8 to 13 years, could constitute a period of relatively slow growth in interpersonal skills and concepts.

Livesley and Bromley (1967) described an exploratory investigation in which 90 children aged 8, 9 and 11 years were asked to provide written descriptions of a man, a woman, a boy and a girl known to them. Age and sex differences were found in the descriptive categories used. Younger children tended to describe people in terms of their physical characteristics, and specific habits and actions, while older children referred more often to stable dispositions. Girls tended to use more personality terms than boys. Children used more personality terms to describe other children than to describe adults. McHenry (1971) obtained similar age differences, and found that the stimulus person affects the contents of free descriptions.

Scarlett, Press and Crockett (1971), using Werner's terminology, proposed that development should lead to: (a) increased differentiation which would be revealed as an increase in the number of constructs used to describe another person, and (b) to increased integration reflected in the use of abstract constructs. These hypotheses were tested using a procedure similar to that used by Supnick (1964) and in our investigation to be described later.

In an interview lasting 10 to 20 minutes, three groups of boys, mean ages 6,9 years, 9,2 years and 10,9 years, described a boy liked, a boy disliked, and girl liked, and a girl disliked. Their constructs were classified into four categories : (a) concrete constructs in which the subject did not differentiate between himself and the other person; for example, 'We play together'; (b) egocentric-concrete constructs in which the object of the sentence was the subject himself; for example, 'He hits me'; (c) non-egocentric-concrete constructs that referred to concrete behaviour on the part of the other person; for example, 'He hits people all the time'; and (d) abstract constructs that referred to personal qualities; for example, 'He is kind.' These four categories were considered to be arranged in developmental sequence from egocentric to non-egocentric and from concrete to abstract.

The number of constructs used increased with age and there was a developmental shift from predominantly egocentric and concrete constructs to non-egocentric and abstract constructs. Stimulus person variables affected the use of constructs. More constructs were used to describe boys than to describe girls. The youngest subjects, mean age 6,9 years, used more constructs to describe boys than to describe girls, but there was no difference between the number of constructs used to describe liked boys and the number used to describe disliked boys. Subjects of mean age 9,2 years used more constructs to describe liked boys than to describe disliked boys, as did the older subjects, mean age 10,9 years. These older subjects also used more constructs to describe liked females than disliked females.

C. Children's Use of Personal Constructs

Adaptations of the Role Construct Repertory Test—see Kelly (1955)—have been used to study the terms children use to describe others, and results tend to support the conclusions reached by analysing free descriptions. Brierley (1966), for example, used this test and a sentence completion test to study children's personal constructs. Individual interviews were given to 270 children aged 7, 10 and 13 years, half boys, from working-class and middle-class schools. The constructs elicited were classified into six categories; kinship, social role, appearance, behaviour, personality and literal. Marked age and sex differences were obtained. Younger children used constructs referring to 'appearance' most frequently, followed by 'social role' and 'behaviour' constructs. Ten-year-old children used 'behavioural' constructs most frequently followed by 'social role' and 'appearance' constructs. The 13-year-old subject used 'behavioural' constructs most frequently, closely followed by 'personality' constructs. Considerable age differences in the number of personality constructs used were obtained. Girls used personality constructs more frequently than did boys, with working-class girls using the most.

Little (1968) also reported a content analysis of children's responses to a version of the Role Construct Repertory Test. Eighty-six children, half males, aged from 10 to 18 years, were divided into three groups —pre-adolescent (mean age 11,10), adolescent (mean age 13,7), and post-adolescent (mean age 16,8). Subjects were given four sheets of paper; at the top of each were three role titles—for example, 'A boy in your room', 'A girl in your room', 'Last year's teacher'. They were asked to write down the names of people who fitted the role titles, and then instructed to write down a way in which two of the three named persons were alike and different from the third. Subjects were allowed 2 minutes for each page during which time they were asked to write down as many constructs as possible.

The responses were coded into three categories : psychological (for example, friendly, unfriendly), role (for example, both teachers, not a teacher) and physical (for example, short, tall). Inter-rater reliability was high with $r = +0.91$ for two independent raters. Marked increases with age were found in the number of psychological and role constructs while physical constructs reached a peak in the adolescent group. No significant age or sex differences were obtained in the proportion of psychological constructs used. Significant sex differences, however, were found in the proportion of role constructs used, with males using a higher proportion than females, especially in the pre-adolescent group. A significant sex difference was also found in the proportion of physical constructs used, with girls using more than boys, especially in the pre-adolescent group. In adolescence, both sexes used predominantly physical constructs, which presumably reflects the adolescents' concern for the image they wish to present to others. The post-adolescent group used role and psychological constructs the most.

D. Children's Ability to Organize Information

Studies by Watts (1944) and Yarrow and Campbell (1963) indicate that as children grow older their impressions become more complex and better organized. In previous chapters it was suggested that the ability to produce an organized impression depends upon the ability to create links between the items of information in the impression, either (a) by generating new convergent items of information about the person through the use of an implicit theory of personality, or (b) by using qualifying words and phrases which bind together the component parts of the impression; for example, logical propositions may specify the relationship between the items and thus 'explain' or 'organize' the main contents of the impression—see Bromley (1968). Both processes depend upon the ability to work out connections and implications and to use abstract, psychological constructs to conceptualize persons.

Gollin (1958) used a procedure similar to that used in his earlier study on adults—see Gollin (1954)—when he investigated children's ability to make inferences following the receipt of conflicting information about a person. A total of 712 subjects from three age groups (mean ages, 10,7 13,6 and 16,6 years) were shown a film, lasting approximately $3\frac{1}{2}$ minutes, of the activities of an 11-year-old boy. Two of the scenes showed him behaving in a socially desirable manner—preventing an older boy from spoiling a game some younger children were playing, and helping a small boy who had fallen off his tricycle. The other two scenes showed him behaving in a socially undesirable manner—tearing up some books two other children had been reading, and breaking a 'soapbox' car two boys were making. Subjects were asked to write down what they thought of the boy and what they had seen him do.

Subjects' responses were scored according to whether or not they used inferences and concepts in their reports. An 'inference' was credited to the subject if he attempted to go beyond the information presented and describe some underlying motive or situation which accounted for one of the actions in the film. Subjects were credited with a 'concept' if they attempted to relate and integrate the conflicting features in the other person's behaviour.

The results showed a marked increase with age in the use of both inferences and concepts. Girls used concepts and inferences more frequently than did boys, and subjects from the upper socio-economic classes used them more frequently than did children from lower classes. When the subjects were divided into two groups on the basis of their intelligence quotients, the high intelligence group used more concepts and inferences than did the low intelligence group. The results show quite clearly that the ability to relate and organize information about other people increases with age, and the results are thus consistent with the observations of Yarrow and Campbell (1963).

E. Conclusions

Studies by Watts (1944) and Brierley (1966) indicate that younger children are more concerned with the readily observable external features of persons, and learn to recognize them at an early age. Levy-Schoen (1964) reported that young children were more interested in the 'object' qualities of people than in their 'psychological' qualities. Studies in the development of prejudice support this conclusion. Clark and Clark (1947) reported that the majority of 3-year-old negro children could distinguish accurately between negro and white dolls. Kogan, Stevens and Shelton (1961) showed that 4-year-old children could accurately rank photographs of people according to age.

The ability of younger children to differentiate between persons is not limited to judgments of appearance. Children aged 4 years and over can differentiate between parental roles—see Mott (1954), Kagan (1961), and Emmerich (1961)—and between adult and child roles—see Emmerich (1961). Hartley and Hardesty (1964), using pictures and open-ended questions, asked children aged 8 to 11 years to describe male and female activities, and found that their subjects had a clear-cut understanding of sex roles. Jahoda (1959) employed a pictorial test to assess the ability of subjects to perceive social class differences and found a marked increase in this ability, probably because of intellectual growth between the ages of 6 and 10 years.

Young children seem to be able to differentiate between liked and disliked persons—see Watts (1944)—and their concepts for describing people appear to have their early origins in moral concepts. Free description studies—see Watts (1944)—indicate that children's psychological vocabulary, particularly their trait vocabulary, begins to develop around the ages of 7 and 8 years and increases rapidly. Yarrow and Campbell (1963) found no significant age differences among children aged 8 to 13 years in their use of person perception categories, probably because of the system of content categories they used. Their study supports Watts's contention that psychological vocabulary develops relatively early. Further confirmation is found in studies using free descriptions—see Livesley and Bromley (1967), Livesley (1969), McHenry (1971), Scarlett, Press and Crockett (1971).

Responses to the Role Construct Repertory Test, however, suggest that it is not until adolescence that personality terms are used frequently—see Brierley (1966). It may be that this test underestimates the size of children's psychological vocabulary because of the difficulty young children experience with this method.

The results of studies of person perception in children have shown that the child's cognitive system becomes increasingly differentiated with age, which probably means that it becomes increasingly organized (structured) as probability relationships develop between constructs. No direct studies of this problem have been conducted. Crockett (1965) suggests that abstract psychological constructs can be considered to be superordinate constructs that subsume and go beyond the concrete constructs and are inferred from them. He takes the increased use of abstract concepts to be evidence for increasing hierarchical organization. The free description studies of Watts (1944), Yarrow and Campbell (1963) and Livesley and Bromley (1967) showed that descriptions become increasingly complex with age, which again suggests that the cognitive system is becoming increasingly structured. Similarly, Gollin (1958) found a marked increase with age in the ability to make inferences; Hallworth, Davies and Gamston (1965) found that a factor analysis of adolescents' ratings of peers on 14 traits yielded five factors, suggesting the existence of a stable, shared frame of reference—see also Morrison and Hallworth (1966). Fiedler and Hoffman (1962) reported that the Semantic Differential judgments of subjects aged 12 to 17 years became increasingly critical with age and that older subjects differentiated more between stimulus persons than did younger subjects.

The problem of the effects of individual differences on the development of person perception has received even less attention than other problems in this area, and those studies that have been conducted have yielded conflicting results. Brierley (1966) reported that girls used more personality constructs than boys, with working-class girls using more than middle-class girls. Little (1968) found no significant sex differences in the use of personality constructs; but he found that boys used more role constructs than girls. Goodenough (1955) reported that pre-school-age girls were more interested in people than were boys, in that they drew people and mentioned people more frequently than did boys. Livesley and Bromley (1967) reported that girls use more personality terms than do boys. According to Watts (1944), boys were more aware than girls that desirable and undesirable qualities could be present in the same person. Gollin (1958), however, found that girls and more intelligent children were able to integrate conflicting information through the use of inference statements than were boys and children of low intelligence. Fiedler and Hoffman (1962) reported that girls differentiate more than boys.

These studies indicate that more detailed investigations are required of children's concepts and of the words they use in understanding and describing others. The richness and variety of the data produced by free descriptions strongly suggests that this would be a profitable research method, especially in exploratory studies of the developmental psychology of person perception.

III. Research Methods

The comparative lack of progress in the study of person perception is probably due to the complexity of the phenomena and inadequate formulation of the problem. Reports by Cronbach (1955, 1958) illustrate how attempts at quantification in the absence of a thorough conceptual analysis yield results which seem to have meaning only as measurement artefacts and response sets. Nevertheless, some investigators prefer such apparently inappropriate methods as rating scales and adjective checklists compiled with little regard for their relevance to the natural processes of making judgments about people and attributing characteristics to them.

Research may also have been retarded by the use of the name 'person perception'. Whether the processes involved in impression formation are the same as, or somehow different from, those involved in the perception of the physical world is a comparatively unimportant point; scarcely worth considering at present, since the term 'person perception' serves merely to designate a research topic, and not to define the nature of a process. Yet research has undoubtedly been influenced by the connotation of the word 'perception'. Experimenters have tried to emulate research in object perception by conducting highly structured experiments in which both stimuli and responses are under close laboratory control. Subjects have been asked to form judgments using information they do not normally use, and their responses have been determined not by typical psychological processes, but by the constraints of the situation as, for example, in experiments by Asch (1946) on trait centrality. Subjects have rarely been provided with relatively unstructured situations and allowed to select the information they think relevant, or to respond in their usual manner. Such a 'naturalistic' approach may seem to run counter to current attitudes and methods in psychology, but, in the absence of developed theories about the way we perceive and understand others, it is an obvious approach and a legitimate one from a philosophy of science point of view. The use of fairly natural and unstructured situations minimizes the risk of our being misled by false assumptions or experimental artefacts, and it allows us to identify the key variables which can be studied subsequently under more closely controlled conditions.

Ideally, the first step involves natural observation in everyday situations, and although this is satisfactory as an exploratory procedure at the commonsense level, it serves only to whet the appetite of the scientist. A useful development was suggested by Hastorf, Richardson and Dornbusch (1958), who argued that it makes little sense to gather precise quantitative data about personality impressions when the problem of the relevance of the categories for the perceiver has been ignored. They suggested that it is more important 'to study the qualities of a person's experience of others in terms of the verbal categories he uses in reporting that experience' (p. 56). This involves studying person perception in the simplest and least artificial way possible—for example, by eliciting from subjects free descriptions of people known to them. These descriptions, which may be either written or oral, can then be analysed for content and organization (structure).

Our present work derives in part from, but goes some way beyond, what might be termed the 'natural history' of person perception. Samples of the subject's verbal behaviour are collected as he gives his impressions of people he knows. Little attempt is made to manipulate this behaviour other than by designating the stimulus person to be described. The procedure yields large amounts of information and may well provide a more valid and productive procedure for person perception research than the more structured approaches referred to earlier.

The 'free description' method has a number of advantages: (1) The subject himself has a great deal of choice in selecting the information upon which he bases his impression, and he is free to respond as he thinks fit, thereby acting in a relatively natural fashion. (2) Factors such as anxiety, aggression, duplicity, embarrassment, lack of skill in communication, and so on, may influence the description but to a lesser extent than in natural situations, thus revealing the cognitive processes more clearly. (3) Leaving the subject as free as possible to respond in his own way reduces the effects of bias caused by the experimenter's own assumptions about person perception, that is by his implicit theories of personality. (4) The freely written descriptions can be analysed to provide information about a person's usual methods of categorizing others, the sorts of category commonly used, and their frequency of usage in different populations. These data are of interest not only in their own right for the light they throw on person perception, but also because they can be used in the development of relevant psychometric measures for use in more closely controlled experimental studies. (5) Free descriptions could provide information about the way impressions are affected by factors such as the primacy effect, implicit personality theory, superordinate traits, and qualifying words and phrases. Thus the psycholinguistic aspects of impressions can be examined in some detail.

The use of the free description method appears promising in connection with the study of the final stage of impression formation—the stage of verbal report—since it solves a number of problems and provides information about the contents and organization of impressions. But the method is not without its difficulties. One drawback is that it depends upon the verbal skills of the subject, and upon his ability to formulate and communicate judgments which may normally be nonverbal or implicit. But then it is very likely that the types of judgment made, and the way the subject categorizes others, depends to a large extent upon his verbal skills and vocabulary. In many instances, the more articulate person appears to make more complex judgments about, and perhaps finer discriminations between, the people he meets. Although no great reliance can be placed on studies of 'accuracy', at least they indicate that the more intelligent judges are slightly more accurate—see Bruner and Tagiuri (1954). It should be borne in mind, however, that many aspects of impression formation cannot be reported upon, possibly because the notions are preverbal, or automatic and implicit, so that the subject is not fully aware that he is using them. Such nonverbal or preverbal impressions may greatly affect the subject's response to a stimulus person. Nevertheless, even though free descriptions provide only partial information, and need to be supplemented by other techniques, the information so obtained warrants intensive study; such study may clear the ground for deeper investigations into implicit preverbal impression formation.

Another drawback is that the elements in each description have to be categorized, and the danger is that the experimenter may impose his own idiosyncratic and invalid system of ideas upon the data. The method, however, assumes that content items can be assigned to categories with a reasonably high degree of reliability and with good agreement between judges. Thus, if the descriptions are decomposed into component parts, the identity of each part can be subjected to some test of 'public verification'. Or it might prove possible, for example, to write an algorithm or a computer program (see Stone et al., 1966) which would carry out an automatic content analysis. Such a method, although time consuming, would at least have the effect of making the experimenter's personal preconceptions explicit. In the present investigation, a provisional scheme has been developed, so that the contents of descriptions from subjects of all ages, including adults, can be classified and counted in a way which is open to 'public' examination. It remains to be seen whether a computer can be programmed to handle the content analysis of free descriptions of persons. At first glance, the problems of specifying an adequate range of grammatical forms or a sufficient vocabulary of terms seem insuperable. It is interesting to observe, however, that the content categories adopted have much in common with those arrived at independently by other investigators, for example by Richardson, Dornbusch and Hastorf (1961), and by Beach and Wertheimer (1961).

It may not be possible to achieve a 'universal' system of classification which completely eliminates the effects of experimenter variables; and in some circumstances experimenters will want to adopt, for their own special purposes, a particular system. Even so, the 'public verifiability' of the system cannot be legitimately evaded, in the sense that every experimenter has the burden of proving that his system is sufficiently reliable and valid for his purpose.

The problem of reliability is that of developing a set of well-defined categories with explicit rules for categorizing. Beach and Wertheimer (1961) analysed the contents of free descriptions into thirteen categories and quoted phi-coefficients between three judges ranging from 0·00 to +0·95 with means of +0·56, +0·62 and +0·57. The intra-judge reliabilities ranged from +0·57 to +0·94 with a mean of +0·75. Although a mean inter-judge reliability of +0·58 leaves much to be desired, the study does suggest that the contents of free descriptions can be reliably analysed if care is taken in selecting the categories and in defining them adequately. Support for this conclusion is provided by Dornbusch, Hastorf, Richardson, Muzzy and Vreeland (1965) who obtained 86·4 per cent agreement between two independent judges, and by Yarrow and Campbell (1963) who obtained 77 per cent agreement.

The free description method appears to be particularly suitable for preliminary studies in the development of person perception. Minimal constraints are placed upon the child, thus reducing the effects of the experimenter's own preconceptions—a particularly important point in work with children. The method also overcomes difficulties arising from children's small vocabulary and limited comprehension and is easily understood. It has much in common with familiar classroom exercises, and the preceding instructions create little difficulty. In this sense, the method has considerable advantages over the Role Construct Repertory Test which has been used in studies with children—see Brierley (1966) and Little (1968). In a similar sense, the method could be regarded as superior to ratings, Q-sorts, checklists and other tests derived from the psychometrics of personality study in adults.

The present studies are based on the assumption that a developmental approach will ultimately contribute to the conceptualization of person perception in adults, and on the further assumption that developmental stages may be usefully distinguished with regard to both qualitative and quantitative differences. As a relatively naturalistic approach, the present studies are similar to the clinical or quasi-experimental approaches characteristic of, say, Bruner or Piaget, but different from the psychometric approach in that less attention is paid initially to the somewhat arbitrary operational definition and scaling of supposedly important psychological variables. Instead, the present studies are directed towards the collection of descriptive data from representative samples of subjects; the underlying preconceptions seem to be minimal, and the whole enterprise exploratory. The definition and isolation of key variables are the end results rather than the starting points of the exercise, as in much of the work of Piaget (1932) and Barker (1963). The independent variables of age, sex, intelligence and stimulus person have been selected because of our prior theoretical expectations; some of the dependent variables—measurements of the contents and organization of impressions—have been similarly selected, but others have been examined as a consequence of subsequent thinking on our part.

To a large extent the present study is mapping new territory; hence, when parameters are estimated, when statistical tests are made, and when *ex post facto* explanations are put forward, they should be regarded as tentative and subject to corroboration by further investigations. As will be seen shortly, however, some predictions can be made on the basis of cognitive theory and previous research, so that many of the statistical analyses are concerned directly with testing hypotheses. As implied by what has gone before, the adoption of a developmental approach emphasizes the fundamental requirement of systematic description as an integral part of scientific investigation. We were concerned to achieve the least distortion of naturally occurring psychological phenomena by avoiding possibly artificial and irrelevant conditions, and by ensuring that subjects could respond in a manner not very different from the way they behave in normal circumstances.

The approach, therefore, is closely related to that suggested by Hastorf *et al.* (1958). Since the research strategy has advantages both in developmental psychology and in the study of person perception, there are good reasons for adopting it in the present study. It is to be hoped, of course, that following the establishment of a firm groundwork of facts based on methods calling for minimum assumptions, the way will be clear for the construction and application of technically superior psychometric instruments designed to measure the processes of person perception in ways that are not merely reliable, but also valid, relevant, practicable and based on a well-articulated theory of interpersonal perception.

CHAPTER 5

Experimental Design and Pilot Studies

I. Experimental Design

A. Between-Subject Variables

1. Chronological Age. The investigations to be described were pursued by means of multivariate methods, since developmental research is of limited value if its findings are restricted to quantitative statements about chronological age differences. For example, developmental changes may vary under different environmental conditions such as enrichment or impoverishment. Age differences may interact with other individual differences such as intelligence, interests, and personality, and rates of development may differ as between one group and another—males and females, for example, or different social classes.

It cannot be assumed that the descriptions of different types of person will be equally rich in content and organization, and it seems unlikely that developmental changes in impression formation will be the same for descriptions of each sort of stimulus person. For example, children seem to describe other children more easily than they describe adults, and they make inferences more readily when describing children. Thus, in order to relate chronological age differences to other variables, two sets of variables are necessary: (a) *between-subject variables* established by selecting subjects from different populations, and (b) *within-subject variables* established by asking subjects to describe different sorts of person.

2. *Sex.* Sex differences in person perception have been observed repeatedly in adults. Bruner and Tagiuri (1954) and Allport (1961), in their reviews, concluded that women tend to be slightly more accurate then men. The existence of sex differences in the process of impression formation has been reported by Samuels (1939), Sarbin (1954), and Secord and Muthard (1955a). Gollin (1958) found that girls were better than boys when integrating conflicting information, because of their superiority in drawing inferences. Watts (1944), by contrast, found that boys were more aware than girls that people could possess both positively and negatively evaluated qualities. Brierley (1966) reported that girls used more psychological constructs than boys when responding to the Role Construct Repertory Test and a sentence completion test. It seems fairly clear that girls use more personality terms to describe people than do boys, yet it is not clear whether this difference emerges at a particular age or whether it is true of all age groups. The question is: Do girls start to use personality terms before boys? If so, do they maintain or even increase their lead? In view of these differences and their associated problems, sex is one of the more obvious variables to include in a study of this kind.

3. *Intelligence.* Gollin (1958) reported that intelligence had a significant effect upon a subject's ability to integrate conflicting information. In view of this, and the fact that the subjects face a verbal task, it is necessary to control for intelligence.

Other between-subject variables can be expected to have effects upon impression formation, particularly those associated with family structure, social class and personal characteristics. It would be extremely interesting to explore the effects of these and other variables, but there are limits to the scope of any one investigation. In any event, we are engaged in a developmental study of a fundamental sort, and at present we are concerned only with the isolation and description of age trends for key variables. Thus, it is logical to analyse the main development trends first, and to relate them to the standard variables of intelligence and sex.

B. Within-Subject Variables: Age, Sex, and Like/Dislike of the Stimulus Person

Supnick (1964) reported that subjects do not describe all types of stimulus person in the same way. Gross (1961), similarly, reported that the effects of an implicit theory of personality on trait ratings of different persons were small as compared with the effects of different kinds of stimulus person. Studies of this type show that when observing variations in the contents and organization of impressions, it is desirable to explore the interactions between (1) different sorts of stimulus person and (2) different sorts of experimental subject. If the experimental subjects' pool of acquaintances is not adequately sampled by asking him to describe a variety of people, interesting aspects of impression formation may be missed. In work with children, however, only a small sample of stimulus persons can be drawn, otherwise the testing procedure takes too long and the children become bored.

In the present series of investigations, three within-subject (stimulus person) variables were selected—*age of the other person* (man and woman versus boy and girl), *sex of other person* (man and boy versus woman and girl), and *affective relationship* with other person (like versus dislike). These were felt to provide a fairly representative sample of people in the child's social world. Note, however, that the stimulus persons were real not imaginary. The like/dislike variable was selected in view of the stress that the many investigators have placed upon evaluation as a major determinant of judgments of others and of the content of impressions—see Asch (1946), Podell (1961), Watts (1944) and Lott, Lott, Reed and Crow (1970).

C. Hypotheses about Differences between Subjects

As mentioned previously, we regard the present inquiries as fundamental and exploratory, in that the isolation of key variables is the goal rather than the starting point. Consequently, *ex post facto* explanations are needed to account for some results, and naturally these cannot be accepted with complete confidence in the absence of corroborative evidence. In other instances, however, theoretical considerations and previous research have enabled us to formulate prior hypotheses which can be tested against relevant data.

1. Chronological Age. It is generally assumed that older children are less dominated by the stimulus situation, that is better able to 'go beyond the information given' than are young children—see Bruner (1957) and Bruner, Olver, Greenfield *et al.* (1966). Thus, we can predict that young children will describe other people in terms of external characteristics, that is simple surface characteristics, while the main development with age will consist of an increasing ability to make more abstract judgments requiring inference and to describe others in terms of internal or psychological qualities, that is depth characteristics.

Werner (1957) defined development as 'an orthogenetic principle which states that whenever development occurs it proceeds from a state of relative globality and lack of differentiation to a state of increasing differentiation, articulation and hierarchical organization (p. 106, quoted from Baldwin, 1967, p. 499). Applying this definition to the cognitive system underlying interpersonal perception gives rise to two general hypotheses : (1) younger children will describe people in global, diffuse terms which will differentiate into more precise and exact trait names; (2) this process of differentiation will be paralleled by a simultaneous process of integration and hierarchical organization as probability relations develop between traits—although these will not be examined directly in this study. Werner's notions, of course, do not provide a theory of development in the strict sense of implying testable hypotheses, but they do provide a kind of meta-psychological orientation which directs the investigators' attention to some of the organizing features in impression formation which can be expected to give rise to more consistent and coherent descriptions among older children.

Two further issues related to chonological age should be mentioned at this point, although we are not yet in a position to describe any research findings relevant to them. The first issue is that human development can be regarded as a process of change continuing throughout the entire lifespan. There are important developments in person perception during the main growth period—these will be described presently, but there may be changes during the adult years too—in middle age or later life for example. Moreover, we need to investigate both the very earliest aspects of person perception—in very young, pre-school children, and even in children not yet able to talk—and the changes, if any, in very late life. These remarks give some indication of the natural expansion of our long-range research programme. The second issue is that, as has been amply demonstrated in gerontological research in humans, there are serious objections to the use of only one sort of research design. By far the best approach to any examination of human development and ageing is one which combines the longi-tudinal and cross-sectional methods of comparing observations. The present study, however, is limited to cross-sectional comparisons.

2. *Sex.* On the basis of studies previously mentioned, it is hypothesized that girls will use more personality terms to describe others than will boys, partly because they tend to be more verbally fluent and possess a larger vocabulary, and partly because they may be more concerned with interpersonal behaviour.

3. *Intelligence.* Gollin (1958) showed that the ability to make inferences from information about persons was associated with intelligence. Thus, it is predicted that children of higher intelligence will use more 'central' terms—that is terms referring to personality and psychological processes —to describe others, and use a higher proportion of such terms than children of lower intelligence, thus correcting for differences in the length of descriptions. It is also predicted that the descriptions written by children of higher intelligence will contain more terms for organizing the impressions than will those of children of lower intelligence.

D. Hypotheses about Differences between Stimulus Persons

There should be considerable within-subject differences in all aspects of impression formation arising from variations in the frequency of interaction between the subject and different stimulus persons, and from variations in the degree of similarity between the subject and the stimulus persons. It is predicted that subjects will describe in greater detail those persons they see more frequently, if only because they are likely to be better informed about such persons and to see them as personally more relevant than others they know less well. It can be taken for granted that children normally see peers and people they like more frequently than adults and people they dislike. Note, however, that in the present investigations subjects were asked not to describe members of their own family. Subjects should describe in greatest detail those people most like themselves, that is, other liked children of the same sex; this outcome should be particularly obvious in the case of younger children whose impressions of others will be greatly influenced by their relatively simple and egocentric manner of apprehending the world. These considerations give rise to the following specific predictions.

1. Age of Stimulus Person. Children first begin to show inferential activity when describing other children, and therefore use more central (psychological or personality) terms to describe children than to describe adults.

2. Sex of Stimulus Person. Children produce longer descriptions and use more psychological or personality statements to describe people of the same sex than to describe people of the opposite sex.

3. Like/Dislike of Stimulus Person. Supnick (1964) found that her subjects used more terms to describe people they liked than to describe people they disliked. A similar result is anticipated in this study, although there are no definite grounds for such a prediction except perhaps the following : the effects of assumed similarity, the greater availability of terms describing desirable as compared with undesirable qualities, and the fact that children, and adults too for that matter, prefer to use socially desirable terms rather than socially undesirable terms to describe people—see Yarrow and Campbell (1963) and Bromley (1966a). Dislike or aversion gives rise to withdrawal and a reduction in interaction with, and information about, the disliked person; so the subject has limited knowledge of the personal qualities and circumstances of the person he dislikes. Liking produces the opposite effects. Thus, the descriptions of liked persons will be longer than descriptions of disliked persons; it is also predicted that they will contain more 'central' terms, since a liked person will probably disclose more of himself, and the subject will have more and better evidence for making inferences about his fundamental attributes.

E. Content Analysis

1. Units of Analysis. Explicit verbal impressions can be regarded as containing *elements*, that is individual items of information about the person, such as 'intelligent' and 'used to be a teacher', and as having *organization*, that is the observer tries to organize or 'structure' the elements in order to make the overall impression consistent and coherent, especially if he has to communicate it to others. The organizing aspects of impressions will be seen to consist, in part, of qualifying words and phrases, such as 'because' and 'only when with close friends will he . . .', which add meaning to the total set of elements by relating them to each other and by presenting them as an organized system of ideas.

The main aim of the present study is to describe, by means of the content analysis of children's descriptions, the basic elements in verbal impressions and the main ways of organizing them. It is concerned almost exclusively with the cognitive properties of impressions, since written descriptions cannot reveal the full extent of the affective and motivational aspects of person perception. Nevertheless, it should be borne in mind that the elements in impressions, and the way these elements are organized, not only fulfil the *cognitive* function of apprehending the other person, thus giving rise to varying degrees of understanding, prediction and control, but also fulfil an *affective* and *motivational* function, in that they provide opportunities for the expression of the subject's feelings about and intentions towards the other person, as well as providing an outlet for generalized feelings of hostility, defence, aggression and anxiety. Having said this, we can reaffirm that affective and motivational features are found in written descriptions of others and probably provide useful leads into the psychodynamics and sociodynamics of person perception; but we have not yet explored these aspects of interpersonal perception—see Hall and van de Castle (1966), Holsti (1969) and Gottschalk and Gleser (1969).

Content analysis is fairly straightforward, although time consuming. The first step is to divide the material into elements which are of psychological interest and can be reliably distinguished. The second step is to develop a taxonomic system, that is a way of classifying these elements. Ideally, the system of classificaion should be both exhaustive and exclusive; exhaustive in the sense that all the elements can be subsumed under one or other of the categories, and exclusive in the sense that every element can be placed in one and only one category. In practice, systems of classification in content analysis are often made exhaustive only by introducing 'remainder' or 'residual' categories for those items which cannot be subsumed under the other categories, and reliability is far from perfect. An exhaustive system can be attained by having either a large number of narrow categories or a few broad categories. Naturally, broad categories are less likely to be psychologically interesting or statistically discriminating, while narrow categories are more likely to be unreliable and to give rise to low frequencies of occurrence. Exclusiveness is difficult to achieve in practice, in that some elements seem to have the characteristics of more than one class. This problem can be dealt with by assigning such items to the most appropriate category and, if necessary, adjusting the definition of the categories.

Although the taxonomy of elements in verbal descriptions of stimulus persons seems to create a problem for research using content analysis methods, the problem is more apparent than real for a number of reasons. In the first place, many elements are ambiguous because the written descriptions are of limited length and the respondent has not disclosed the full meaning of each element. Subsequent interrogation would undoubtedly clarify the membership characteristics of any particular element, for example, by providing contextual clues or by making two or more elements of it. In the second place, in everyday life we are adept at assimilating information about people, even without consciously classifying the items of information that are presented to us. Furthermore, as the bulk of the information in an impression forms a single coherent picture, any item of information which is ambiguous when considered in isolation tends to be assimilated to the impression as a whole, which forms a 'gestalt', and therefore tends to make a similar contribution whichever meaning it is taken to have.

The reliability with which items of information can be identified and assigned to categories needs to be checked both between different judges, and within the same judge on different occasions.

The units commonly employed in the content analysis of verbal material are words, sentences and themes. Since the intention in the present studies is to analyse the types of ideas children use, and the terms or phrases they employ in describing people, the individual word is not the appropriate element or unit. One advantage of using the individual word as a unit is that it can be objectively defined, as can the sentence. Sentences, however, often contain a number of ideas. For these reasons, the basic unit we have preferred, in spite of its subjectivity, is the 'statement' or 'idea', which may be defined as a fact or item of information referring directly or indirectly, to the stimulus person. Although these sorts of elements lack the objectivity of the other two sorts, they seem to be the ones most suited to these studies. Their statistical value depends upon the extent to which they can be unambiguously classified, that is, upon the degree of intra- and inter-scorer reliability. Their psychological value depends upon the extent to which they can be fitted into a fruitful theory of interpersonal perception, that is upon their 'relational fertility'.

We must not lose sight of the fact that our main concern is to describe and explain the contents and organization of children's *experiences* (impressions) of other persons. That is to say, we are attempting to study the cognitive *processes* underlying impression formation by examining their associated *products,* namely, the written descriptions. Evidence about the reliability of our measure is therefore very relevant. The validity or accuracy of the descriptions, on the other hand, is a very different issue, and one that has arisen previously in research into person perception. While it is obvious that the issue of validity and accuracy in impression formation cannot be evaded indefinitely, it is also obvious that it cannot even be raised effectively until these other, more fundamental, issues have been settled.

2. *Four Phases of Content Analysis.* The phases of content analysis to be carried out are described in detail and justified in later sections. For the moment, it is sufficient to say that four phases are applied to the elements or units making up the impressions. They are as follows:

Phase one : central versus peripheral statements. This analysis focuses upon a dimension which appears to be particularly relevant to a developmental study—the use of abstract and general statements as opposed to concrete and particular statements. This is a familiar dimension in cognition, and seems to correspond to the use of psychological as opposed to non-psychological terms. We shall refer to them as 'central' versus 'peripheral' terms. The point is that some subjects can go beyond observational evidence and make inferences, that is they can construct conceptual classes and rules.

Phase two : item classification. The first phase reveals only one aspect of impression formation. It is supplemented by this more detailed analysis which describes—by means of thirty-three content categories— all the different sorts of ideas found in children's descriptions.

Phase three : personality traits. The analysis examines children's use trait names by compiling age differences in psychological vocabulary.

Phase four : organization and qualification. The final phase in the content analysis employs a further nine categories to describe the way in which the elements in a personality impression are qualified and organized.

F. Statistical Method

Once the data have been analysed for content, tests of statistical significance can be applied to the appropriate hypotheses. As the study involves six variables, and one of them—the age variable—has more than two levels, a thorough analysis of the effects of these variables on even one phase of the content analysis, for example the proportion of central statements per description, would require many nonparametric tests; and, unless the necessary restrictions were introduced, a number of apparently significant effects would arise entirely by chance. Although the effect of a given independent variable on each of the thirty-three content analysis categories can be statistically tested in isolation, there is no way of detecting spurious statistical effects. This is a serious problem with a content analysis as large as the one proposed in this research, and there appears to be no easy solution. It is apparent, however, that the difficulties created by piecemeal analysis, together with the lower statistical power of nonparametric tests, indicate that parametric procedures are more appropriate. An investigation with six variables lends itself most readily to an analysis of variance design; this overcomes the difficulties involved in testing for individual effects and it enables interaction effects to be studied. Consequently, the investigation was designed as a six-factor factorial experiment—age, sex and intelligence of the subject—with repeated measures on three factors—age, sex and like/dislike of the stimulus person. The effects of the six variables are analysed by means of a model outlined by Winer (1962).

1. A Technical Note of Explanation. The basic statistical method we have used is analysis of variance (ANOVA). The term 'variance' refers to the way in which observations or measurements are distributed about an average value. In technical terminology, 'variance' refers to the mean of the sum of the squares of the deviations from the mean of a set of measurements. The general purpose of an ANOVA design is to distinguish between (a) the systematic variance associated with the effects of the experimental variables and their interactions, and (b) the variance arising from error factors in the subjects and the measurements.

Each of 320 experimental subjects wrote one self-description and eight descriptions of other stimulus persons; the ANOVA design, therefore, used 'repeated measurements' obtained from the same subjects. The use of 'repeated measures' is a way of combining observations from the same subjects, rather than using different subjects for each measure. This procedure reduces variations arising from differences between subjects, and therefore makes it more likely that true effects will be detected.

We were interested in testing whether the systematic variance associated with differences in sex (male versus female) or age (eight age levels) or intelligence (higher versus lower) was large enough—in comparison with the unavoidable error variance—to warrant the assertion of a statistically significant difference for a given measure of impression formation.

It is usual to reject the null hypothesis (that there is no difference) by reference to what are called 'levels of significance'. Thus, if the observed value of the statistic lies at the extreme tail of the sampling distribution for the statistic, then it is argued that the observed difference is probably genuine because such a value rarely occurs by chance, that is, it has a probability of less than the accepted values of 0·05 or 0·01. For example, if the variance associated with a measurement difference between boys and girls was not significantly larger than the accompanying error variance, then the null hypotheses would not be rejected, and boys and girls would be regarded as equivalent with respect to that particular comparison measure.

Although the above-mentioned levels of significance are effective in minimizing one sort of error, they leave open the risk of accepting a null hypothesis which is really false. For example, a small but real difference between boys and girls in a measure of trait usage might not be detected because the significance level is too extreme. The risk of this kind of error can be reduced by increasing the size of the various subsamples or by reducing measurement errors. Unfortunately, the administrative problems encountered in psychological research generally oblige the research worker to use sample sizes smaller than he would wish, and he often has no firm prior idea of the size of the effects he wishes to detect. This is the situation in the present investigation. However, some of the differences actually observed and found to be statistically significant were so small as to be of little or no importance, psychologically speaking; so it seems that the statistical tests were powerful enough to detect any psychologically interesting effects.

We have not presented the 'power' of the various statistical tests, in other words we have not calculated the probabilities that substantial differences have not been detected. Some indication of the psychological value of the results, however, can be obtained by calculating the correlation ratio (η), which is derived from ANOVA.

Thus, factorial ANOVA is a statistical method for analysing the effects of several main factors and their interactions. It is possible, for example, to account for the main effects associated with Age, Sex and Intelligence. When the main effects have been accounted for, there may still be considerable variance associated with interactions between the main variables, and it is possible, for example, to test whether Brighter Girls perform differently from Brighter Boys, or whether descriptions of Disliked Girls are different in form and content from descriptions of

Liked Men, or whether Boys write differently about Males as compared with Girls writing about Females.

The total variation for measures of any dependent variables can be partitioned into (a) variation *between* subjects, and (b) variation *within* subjects. The variation *between* subjects can be partitioned into : (i) variation within subgroups, and (ii) variation between subgroups; the variation *within* subjects can be partitioned into (i) variation between treatments (stimulus persons), and (ii) residual variation.

Figure 1 illustrates the ANOVA design. There were 320 subjects altogether : ten subjects in each cell of the 8×4 matrix; thus $N = 320 = 10$ (Subjects) $\times 2$ (Sex groups) $\times 2$ (Intelligence groups) $\times 8$ (Age groups). Each subject wrote descriptions of eight stimulus persons and one self-description.

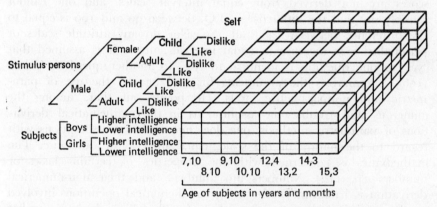

Figure 1. Schematic relationships between subject variables and stimulus person variables in the analysis of variance design of the main investigation

2. *General Discussion.* The primary purpose of the repeated measure design is to control for the effects of individual differences. It was thought undesirable to use separate samples of subjects to describe each stimulus person, since the differences in 'stimulus person' effects are probably small compared with the average differences between samples. On the other hand, the disadvantages of the design are that repeated measurements of the same subject can (and undoubtedly do) give rise to practice effects, fatigue and boredom. The experimental design assumes that the sequence in which subjects perform the tasks is randomized, so that such effects are not removed but merely averaged out over treatment effects, and this does not constitute a serious disadvantage in this study.

A more crucial question concerns the validity of analysis of variance techniques when they are applied to content analysis data. The use of parametric statistics, such as analysis of variance, involves a number of assumptions. The least important of these is normality of distribution, for the F-test has been shown to be extremely robust in conditions of non-normality. It is sensitive, perhaps even oversensitive, however, to heterogeneity of variance. The variances can be stabilized, however, by means of a square root transform (when frequency data are numerically small) or an arcsin transform (when proportions are involved)—see Winer (1962, pp. 220–1) and Edwards (1965, pp. 130–1).

There is also the argument that analysis of variance can be applied only to measurements derived from equal-interval scales. There are relatively few scales of this type in psychology. Even intelligence scores are not derived from equal interval scales, and one cannot sensibly say that the difference in I.Q. between 90 and 100 is equal to the difference between 130 and 140. Nor do any attitude scales or personality tests measure in equal intervals, unless it is assumed that 'yes' to one question is identical to 'yes' to another question. Cohen (1965) summarizes the arguments for and against the use of parametric and nonparametric tests. He points out that, 'among the numerous and troublesome assumptions in the mathematical derivations of parametric methods, one does *not* find any assumptions with regard to the nature of the scale, equal interval or otherwise. The mathematics is concerned with the properties of certain classes of numbers' (p. 112). Numbers are numbers, and their non-numerical derivation is irrelevant as far as the mathematical operations involved in the statistical test are concerned, for 'numbers don't remember where they came from'—see Lord (1953). Cohen quotes Burke (1953, p. 74) who states that 'the statistical technique begins and ends with the numbers and with statements about them. The psychological interpretations that the experimenter imposes upon his data takes cognizance of the origin of the numbers, but this is irrelevant for the statistical test as such.' The question is *not* whether a series of mathematical operations can be logically carried out on a set of data, but rather whether it is *psychologically meaningful* to do so, that is, whether the results of the statistical analysis can be translated into meaningful psychological statements.

Analysis of variance is frequently used in this study where the data are suitable, and where such treatment appears to be psychologically meaningful. For example, the number of central statements in each description is analysed as a six-factor experiment. Analyses of this type are used to test a variety of hypotheses, such as 'The number of central statements used increases with age.' For the purpose of these analyses, it is assumed that any one central statement, or trait, is equivalent to any other. This assumption is legitimate provided the statements made on the basis of the analysis refer only to the *number* of statements used. It may well be that 'number of central statements' deals with only one aspect of the data, and that other aspects of 'central statements' are important. If so, then the set of central statements can be further analysed. Thus, such considerations do not affect the legitimacy of the statistical procedure, they merely show that statistical considerations should not impose unnecessary restriction on the kinds of content analysis carried out, or on the sorts of psychological hypotheses tested.

II. Pilot Studies

Several small pilot investigations were conducted to explore the following problems :

1. Is the free description technique a feasible method for studying children's impressions of others?
2. Does it make any difference whether descriptions are reported orally or in writing?
3. What are the effects of different types of test instructions?

In the first study, eight children, four boys and four girls, four aged 8 and four aged 11 years, were tested individually and asked to describe people known to them. The interviews were tape-recorded. When asked to think of a child in their class and then describe him, the children merely gave an account of the child's appearance, that is, they described his physical build, his facial features, the clothes he wore, and so on. Few references were made to his personality traits or other psychological attributes. When asked to say what they *thought* about the person concerned, however, and when asked to describe *what sort* of person he was, the subjects, especially the older ones, used a number of personality and psychological terms. It became apparent in these interviews that the task instructions were crucial, since the contents of children's descriptions were readily adapted to the type of instructions given.

These preliminary interviews suggested that a more informative procedure would be to create a 'negative set' by telling the subject in detail what he was *not* expected to do, that is, to tell him *not* to describe the other person in terms of his appearance but rather describe *what sort of person* he is. As the aim of the main inquiry is to explore the way children conceptualize personality, such instructions are justified. The instructions allow children to formulate their impressions in their own words, and they are unlikely to lead children to use terms they do not normally use. The revised instructions—described in detail in the next chapter—make greater demands on children's powers of verbal expression and push them closer to the limits of their understanding of others, thus revealing more about cognitive development than would be achieved by instructions eliciting superficial and routine verbal responses, or by instructions which lead or prompt them into artificial (unnatural) forms of response, for example, ratings or checklists.

The next step was to explore the effects of the revised instructions in a group-testing situation in which the children were asked to write their descriptions rather than tape-record them. Three groups of subjects, aged approximately 8, 9 and 11 years, were tested in their usual classroom. Each child was given four sheets of paper and asked to write his name on each of them. They then wrote, 'A man I know', 'A woman I know', 'A boy I know' or 'A girl I know' at the top of each page. The children shuffled the four sheets of paper to ensure that the descriptions were written in a random order. They were then given the instructions outlined above and encouraged to ask questions if they did not fully understand what they had to do. No time limits were imposed. There were marked differences between the three age groups. The younger children made comparatively little reference to the personality and behaviour of the people they described. Instead, they focused upon more peripheral qualities, and, despite instructions to the contrary, described the other person's appearance, thus demonstrating the considerable extent to which young children's impressions of others are dominated by relatively concrete and superficial, aspects of external appearance. In addition, they gave many details about his identity; where he lived, his age, what school he went to, and even his telephone number! When personal or central qualities were described, they tended to be routine habits rather than personality traits or dispositions. Descriptions by older children were more complex, and greater emphasis was placed upon inner qualities; trait names were used with greater frequency, and relatively little reference was made to appearance and identity.

A quantitative analysis was carried out on these exploratory data. Ten sets of descriptions were selected at random from each age group, five from boys, five from girls. Thus thirty sets of descriptions, 120 in all, were examined. Before a detailed analysis was carried out, however, most of the thirty children were interviewed and questioned about the people they had described to see whether additional information, particularly about the other's personality, could be elicited. Surprisingly little additional information was obtained, and this was usually either incidental information, for example, statements about things the person had done, or repetitions, in a slightly different form, of statements the child had already made—almost as if the child felt obliged to say something. It was assumed therefore that the written descriptions adequately revealed the child's impressions and that the small amount of additional information obtainable by interviewing the children did not justify lengthy individual testing. A developmental study requires large numbers of subjects in each age group in order to detect reliable trends and differences; individual testing may be necessary to study the nuances of impression formation, but it was not thought to be necessary to isolate main effects such as those associated with age, sex, intelligence, and type of stimulus person, or their interactions.

For the purposes of content analysis, the descriptions were divided into 'units'. Each unit or element was a statement or idea broadly defined as one item of information referring directly or indirectly to the other person. These elements were first assigned to one of two types of statement—peripheral or central. Peripheral statements referred to appearance, identity (for example, age, sex, residence, school), social roles, possessions, details of family, and so on. Central statements included references to personal qualities and general habits.

The number of central or psychological statements was analysed in a four-factor design with repeated measures on two of these factors. The four factors were: age and sex of the subject, and age and sex of the stimulus person (repeated for two stimulus persons each). Significant age and sex differences were found in the number of central statements used to describe other people. Older children used more of these terms than did younger children and girls used more than boys. Of the two within-subject factors, only 'age of the stimulus person' was significant—the children used more central statements to describe children than they used to describe adults. A significant interaction term was observed between 'age of subject' and 'age of the stimulus person'—there was a greater difference between descriptions of children and descriptions of adults in 11-year-olds than in 8-year-olds. Another significant interaction term was observed between 'age of subject' and 'sex of stimulus person'; 8-year-old children used significantly more central statements to describe males than to describe females, but no such difference was found in the older age groups. Perhaps surprisingly, there was no significant interaction between 'sex of subject' and 'sex of stimulus person.'

The following conclusions are based on the results of the pilot studies:

1. The freely written descriptions yield useful data for research into impression formation; the procedure is suitable for children and can be administered in a standard form over a wide age range.
2. The method allows children to report their experiences of other people in ways which are familiar to them. It does not impose unnatural conditions in the form of unusual terms of reference or unusual modes of response.
3. Freely written descriptions obtained by means of group testing are as satisfactory as oral descriptions obtained by means of individual testing, bearing in mind the purpose of the main study which is to isolate and examine major effects associated with chronological age, sex differences, differences in intelligence and different types of stimulus person.
4. The contents of free descriptions are affected quite considerably by the form of instructions given. Inducing a 'negative set' seems to minimize the more obvious and less interesting contents of the descriptions, and so more fully reveal the child's ability to form impressions of other people.

The results of those preliminary investigations proved to be sufficiently interesting to warrant the much larger investigation using similar procedures for collecting and analysing the written descriptions of stimulus persons. We were confident that the results of the main study would make a contribution to the developmental psychology of person perception, and perhaps provide a basis for some definition statements about the relationships between person perception and the study of personality.

CHAPTER 6

Main Investigation: Experimental Design, Subjects, and Analysis of Statement Fluency

I. Experimental Design

The method of content analysis, the variables, hypotheses and experimental design of the investigation were referred to in the previous chapter. Briefly, six independent variables were selected: three between-subject variables—Age, Sex and Intelligence—and three within-subject (stimulus person) variables—Age, Sex and Like/Dislike. The dependent variables include the number of statements per description, and the various types of statement (categories) used by the subjects. The hypotheses refer to: (a) the main effects of the Age, Sex and Intelligence of the Subjects, and of the Age, Sex and Like/Dislike of the Stimulus Person, on the contents and organization of the written descriptions; and to (b) the interaction effects between two or more of these main variables.

89

The study was designed as a six-factor factorial experiment with repeated measures on three factors, the stimulus person factors, so that the data, where suitable, could be examined by means of analysis of variance. A major aim of the inquiry, however, was to collect data for standardization purposes, and the numerical results have provisional value as descriptive statistics relating to norms of performance. In addition, the systematic ordering of the data by means of an analysis of variance design permits a number of statistical hypotheses to be tested and the appropriate inferences to be drawn. In some instances the hypotheses were formed prior to (and formed part of) the design of the investigation; in other instances, the hypotheses were developed in the course of the main investigation, but still prior to the analysis of the results; in yet other instances, the hypotheses were formulated *ex post facto,* that is after the data had been examined, and so stand in need of further internal or external corroboration.

II. Subjects

A. Selection

The method of investigation and considerations of administrative convenience limited the age groups that could be studied to those between 7 and 15. Several primary and secondary schools on Merseyside agreed to participate in the investigation. Subjects aged 7 to 11 years were obtained from two Church of England Primary Schools serving similar communities. Older subjects were obtained from three schools. All male subjects, that is both higher and lower verbal intelligence groups, were obtained from a boys' comprehensive school which drew pupils from an area similar to that of each primary school, but probably contained a greater proportion of working-class children. A comparable group of older female subjects was selected from two schools : a girls' comprehensive school provided the lower verbal intelligence group. It was not possible to obtain girls of higher verbal intelligence from this school, for, although it was comprehensive, children of superior intelligence usually chose to go to a nearby grammar school. The girls of higher ability were selected from a grammar school in an adjacent area. The girls' schools drew pupils from an area similar to that of the boys' schools and hence contained more working-class children than did the primary schools.

The primary schools were single-stream intake with about forty children per class. All four classes in each school were tested. All the secondary schools were streamed. The upper streams of the boys' comprehensive school and the girls' grammar school were selected for testing in order to provide subjects for the higher intelligence groups. The two comprehensive schools provided children with IQ.s in the upper middle range by using information from record cards which was not made available as research data. As children were placed in classes on the basis of I.Q., the procedure adopted was for the school to select the classes which best fitted the investigators' criteria.

Altogether, twenty-four classes totalling approximately 500 children were tested. When the study was planned, it was decided that 320 subjects were to be used : forty in each age group with equal numbers in each sex and intelligence group. Subjects whose written descriptions were to be analysed were selected according to a number of criteria. The first was age : an attempt was made to ensure that the mean age and range of ages for the different sex and intelligence groups were comparable. The second criterion was verbal intelligence. In addition to selecting within a restricted range of I.Q.—see above—an attempt was made to establish two comparable levels of ability—'higher' and 'lower'—for each age and sex group. But, on account of the considerable difference in chronological age between the younger and older children, different tests of verbal ability had to be administered and the scores assimilated to a common frame of reference—see section C below. Where two or more subjects were equally suitable according to these criteria, but only one was required for inclusion in the study, random selection was used. Children selected for inclusion in the study were assigned to their respective subgroups before the written exercise was administered. But it was convenient to give the exercise to all pupils in a class and then to discard unwanted reports.

B. Chronological Age

A total of 320 schoolchildren ranging in age from 7,4 to 15,9 served as subjects. Half were males. The children were divided into eight age groups with forty subjects in each group. In addition, the sample was arranged so as to give two intelligence groups, with equal numbers in each group. Chronological ages, to the nearest month, are shown in Table 1; the age difference between adjacent groups is approximately 1 year, except for groups 4 and 5 where the difference is 18 months. This is because the testing was cond[...] [...]rent times of the year. The four younger groups were tested [...] January, the older groups in May and June. Differer[...] the lower and higher intelligence groups are not sh[...]ible, except in age group 8. In this age group, [...]oys were on average 4 months older than the [...] versus

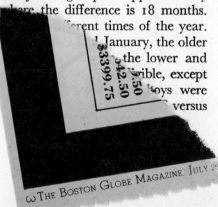

ω THE BOSTON GLOBE MAGAZINE. JULY 25.

Table 1. Age, sex and intelligence of the main sample

Age group	1	2	3	4	5	6	7	8
Mean ages								
Male	7,10	8,10	9,9	10,10	12,5	13,3	14,3	15,4
Female	7,10	8,10	9,10	10,10	12,3	13,2	14,2	15,1
Both	7,10	8,10	9,10	10,10	12,4	13,2	14,3	15,3
Range	7,4 to 8,4	8,5 to 9,3	9,4 to 10,3	10,4 to 11,3	11,9 to 12,10	12,11 to 13,9	13,10 to 14,9	14,10 to 15,9
Mean ($\bar{x}$) and standard deviation (s) of verbal intelligence								
Schonell essential intelligence test I.Q.								
Male $\bar{x}$	126·6	119·8	125·4	123·8				
Male s	15·1	15·5	14·3	9·7				
Female $\bar{x}$	126·7	119·6	125·4	123·3				
Female s	11·7	14·1	11·9	9·8				
Both $\bar{x}$	126·7	119·7	125·4	123·6				
Both s	13·5	14·8	13·1	9·4				
Verbal intelligence: Mill Hill Vocabulary raw score								
Male $\bar{x}$				33·5	38·3	41·7	44·4	43·2
Male s				5·5	4·0	7·8	5·6	11·4
Female $\bar{x}$				34·4	38·4	41·4	44·1	40·2
Female s				5·7	4·7	4·8	6·1	9·7
Both $\bar{x}$				34·0	38·3	41·6	44·3	41·7
Both s				5·7	4·4	7·1	5·9	12·4
Higher intelligence subgroups								
Male $\bar{x}$	138·8	133·0	137·4	36·9	41·4	48·9	49·4	53·1
Male s	9·4	9·1	9·0	4·4	2·9	3·4	2·6	2·5
Female $\bar{x}$	134·6	131·5	135·5	36·4	41·4	45·6	48·8	49·7
Female s	8·9	7·5	6·8	5·2	2·9	2·9	4·9	4·3
Both $\bar{x}$	136·7	132·3	136·5	36·6	41·4	47·3	49·1	51·4
Both s	8·9	8·3	8·2	5·1	2·9	3·6	3·9	4·0
Lower intelligence subgroups								
Male $\bar{x}$	114·4	106·6	113·3	30·1	35·1	34·4	39·4	33·3
Male s	8·3	7·4	4·8	4·9	3·6	5·8	2·5	6·7
Female $\bar{x}$	118·7	107·7	115·3	32·4	35·3	37·2	39·4	30·7
Female s	5·7	7·6	8·8	5·4	4·2	2·5	3·2	4·7
Both $\bar{x}$	116·0	107·2	114·3	31·3	35·2	35·8	39·4	32·0
Both s	7·4	7·2	7·2	5·2	3·9	4·7	2·9	5·9

15,2, respectively); the higher intelligence girls were on average 5 months older than the lower intelligence girls (15,4 versus 14,11, respectively). The differences occur because children of lower ability tend to leave school as soon as they are 15 years, while brighter children tend to stay on to sit the Ordinary level examination for the General Certificate of Education.

C. Verbal Intelligence

The subjects were divided into groups of higher and lower ability on the basis of tests given before the free description exercise. The assessment of the children's intelligence was not altogether satisfactory for a number of reasons. There was no single group test suitable for administration to children aged from 7 to 15 years. In addition, the time that secondary schools were prepared to make available for testing purposes was fairly limited, since the children were preparing for examinations of various kinds. In the case of one group, the total time the school was able to allow for testing was approximately $2\frac{1}{2}$ hours. The free description exercise alone requires about 2 hours to complete for children aged 12 years and upwards. Hence, the time available for intelligence testing was very short. Precise information about intelligence was not really necessary, however, since sufficient information was available to establish age and sex groups of higher and lower ability. The Mill Hill Vocabulary Scale (see Raven, 1948) was used to estimate the verbal ability of the secondary school children. The Schonell Essential Intelligence Test (see Schonell and Adams, 1940–9) was used to estimate the verbal ability of the the four youngest age groups ranging in age from 7,4 years to 11,3 years. The means and standard deviations of the I.Q.s of the four younger age groups and details of the Mill Hill Vocabulary Scale scores of the five older age groups are shown in Table 1. Note that the scoring procedure for the Schonell Essential Intelligence Test incorporates an adjustment for chronological age and therefore gives a measure of I.Q., that is intellectual brightness, rather than of Mental Age. The Mill Hill vocabulary scores, however, are not adjusted for age, as shown in Table 1.

The Mill Hill Vocabulary Scale provides a reasonably valid and reliable estimate of verbal ability. Raven (1958) obtained a correlation of +0.93 between vocabulary test score and Terman-Merrill mental age for a representative group of 150 schoolchildren. Raven (1960) reported a correlation of +0.57 between the Mill Hill Vocabulary Scale and the Progressive Matrices Score for children aged 12 to 14 years. Thus, while acknowledging that a better estimate of intelligence, particularly of nonverbal ability, would have been more satisfactory, administrative limitations made it necessary to use the Mill Hill Vocabulary Scale for the purpose of separating subjects into groups of higher and lower ability. It should be borne in mind, however, that the schools had already divided the subjects into groups on the basis of intelligence tests, and, in every instance, the Mill Hill scores agreed with the school's classification. As recommended by Raven (1958), the Mill Hill Junior form was used for children up to the age of 14 years. Children over this age were given the Senior form in addition to the Junior.

Children in the fourth age group, mean age 10,10, were given *both* the Schonell Essential Intelligence Test and the Mill Hill Vocabulary Scale. As part of the attempt to assimilate the two rather different tests of verbal ability to a common frame of reference for distinguishing children of higher and lower ability, the Mill Hill Vocabulary raw score was correlated with Mental Age obtained from the Schonell Test. A rank order correlation of $+0.59$ was obtained ($N=40$, $p<0.001$) equal to an estimated product-moment correlation of $+0.61$. While the degree of assocation leaves a lot to be desired, it does provide grounds for supposing that the Mill Hill Vocabulary Scale provides an estimate of the verbal intelligence of the older subjects—comparable with that provided by the Schonell Essential Intelligence Test. Furthermore, for this fourth age level, the higher and lower intelligence groups, selected on the basis of their Schonell scores, were also significantly different in their scores on the Mill Hill Vocabulary Scale.

There was no overlap between the Mill Hill scores of the higher and lower intelligence groups, and it seems reasonable to assume that they are significantly different in verbal intelligence. But are the different age groups of comparable intelligence? The mean Schonell I.Q. at the fourth age level (mean age 10,10) is not significantly different from the mean Schonell I.Q.s at the three lower age levels. The mean Mill Hill score of subjects at the fourth age level is thirty-four, which, if regarded as a single subject's score, is equivalent to a percentile of approximately seventy-five. The mean Mill Hill scores for the fifth, sixth and seventh age levels are similarly equivalent to percentiles of between seventy and seventy-five. Only subjects at the eighth and oldest age level differ from this pattern—because the lower ability group have exceptionally low Mill Hill scores. Thus, it appears that, with the exception of the oldest group, all age groups have comparable levels of verbal intelligence relative to their chronological age. The lower intelligence group of the eighth age level (mean age 15,3) performed at a much lower level than expected. Their Mill Hill scores reversed the upward trend of the scores with age. This may have been because they were in fact less intelligent than younger subjects in comparable groups; but this is unlikely, as the classes tested were equivalent to the classes at a lower age level. In addition, the boys and girls were obtained from two different schools, so that they were in a sense independent samples, and it seems improbable that this age group was less 'intelligent' in both schools. A more likely explanation is that the lower average score arises from motivational factors. All twenty subjects in this group were due to leave school at the end of the term in which they were tested. Indeed, testing took place towards the end of term (in June) and subjects gave the impression that they were rather bored with school and anxious to leave. The Mill Hill Vocabulary Scale and the impression formation exercise were looked upon as just another school exercise to be completed in the easiest and quickest possible way, whereas other subjects appeared to find the task interesting. All attemps by the investigator to arouse more enthusiasm failed. It is assumed that motivation in the higher intelligence group did not diminish. It is interesting to observe that the discrepancy between the mean scores of the higher and lower intelligence groups increases with age. Unfortunately, the metric limitations of the Mill Hill Vocabulary Scale do not permit any clear-cut explanation of this phenomenon.

III. Procedure

A. Materials

The subjects were asked to describe eight people known to them—a man, woman, boy and girl they liked, and a man, woman, boy and girl they disliked. The children carried out the exercises in their usual classroom. Each child was provided with a ten-page booklet. The front page asked for details of the subject's name, age, sex, school, date of birth and date of testing. The second page was the same for all children and they were asked to write an impression of themselves as a person, that is to describe the sort of person they thought they were. The other eight pages were arranged in random order and at the top of each was printed a role description, for example 'A boy I know very well and like is . . .' The random order of pages distributed the effects of fatigue and practice over all stimulus persons. The children were asked to write in the name of someone they knew who fitted this description and then to describe him. They were asked to name the person they were describing to ensure that they described a real person rather than an imaginary one. The main purpose of the self-description was to provide a 'buffer item'. The analyses of the contents and organization of these self-descriptions are presented separately in a later chapter.

The subjects were required to write at least fifty words; the size of the page (foolscap) provided an upper limit on the amount written. Thus, constraints were deliberately imposed on verbal fluency. On each page, there were twenty-one lines for the child to write on; these lines ran two-thirds of the way across the page. The right-hand side contained six columns to be used for coding purposes; subjects were instructed not to write in these columns. Two examples of the sorts of description written by children are shown below.

Transcription of an original description of a person as written by a boy aged 15.

A man I know fairly well and dislike. Name or initials : J.Y.

The main reason I dislike this man is because he is so methodical and boring. He is school teacher and when he enters the room he always says the same thing and does the same actions. The lesson always runs like clockwork, and you always know what the home-work is going to be, and that the following lesson the homework will be gone over and you will write up your corrections. This means the lessons are very boring and you hate the subject that the man is teaching.

Transcription of an original description of a person as written by a girl aged 12.

A girl I know fairly well and like. Name or initials : E.T.

E.T. is my best friend but she is in London now, in London she used to live by me, and she go to the same school with me, evey every morning we got the bus together, and we play together. she is a very nice girl but she ise a bite crippled, because when she was very little, she fell over in the road, but she go to see the doctor, the doctor said her li lift leg is broken, her Mother was very as upset, but a few years later, she can walk, e but not very fast, her sister goes to a same school as she. and we all are f very good friends. but now I can't see her, because is she is in London, but we always write the letters to each other.

B. Instructions

The pilot studies had indicated that the length and contents of descriptions were affected by the type of instructions given. Lengthy instructions were necessary, and the best type seemed to consist of giving the children a negative set; that is, they were told in detail what the investigator did *not* want them to write about. The instructions were broadly as follows :

> Look at the description of a person at the top of the page. Now think of someone you know who fits the description. I want you to describe the person as carefully as you can. I don't want you to tell me how tall they are, or whether they are fat or thin, whether they have brown eyes or blue eyes, dark hair or fair hair. I don't want you to tell me what sort of clothes they wear. Instead, I want you to describe what sort of person they are. I want you to tell me what you think about them and what they are like.

The length of these instructions varied with the age of the subjects. Younger subjects were given more examples and asked to repeat what they *were not* expected to describe, and finally to repeat what they *were* asked to write about. At no time was a positive example given. In the case of the youngest group, the instructions took at least ten minutes to give. Subjects were also told to complete the booklet in the order in which the pages occurred and not to miss out any page. Subjects were not allowed to describe any member of their family.

The written reports, including the self-description, took between 2 and 4 hours to complete, depending upon age and ability. No time constraints were imposed as these might have given rise to an underestimation of the younger child's performance. Testing sessions lasted just under 1 hour and occurred at weekly intervals until the booklets were completed. Subjects were reminded of the instructions at the beginning of each session and half-way through each session.

One of the major criticisms levelled at many earlier studies of person perception—for example those involving ratings, trait lists or pictures—was that they were 'artificial', in that they forced subjects to respond in unfamiliar ways to unnatural stimulus information. It cannot be argued that the present study is similarly 'artificial' to anything like the same extent, because the children were not required to do something that was outside the range of their normal experience—daily life requires them occasionally to formulate verbal impressions of themselves and others, and their schoolwork requires them to put their ideas into writing. It would not be unusual for children to have written similar material for an essay or story in ordinary class work. This argument is confirmed by the experience of the investigators with teachers to whom we have talked, many of whom readily seize upon the method as a useful educational exercise.

Although the instructions make great demands upon the child's descriptive powers and push him to the limits of his ability to conceptualize others, they leave him free to respond normally in selecting the information upon which he bases his impressions and in organizing it as he wishes. The instructions have the effect of maximizing the more interesting and subtle aspects of impression formation, for example the 'psychological' contents of descriptions and the 'organizational' features. The pilot inquiries had shown that such instructions were necessary to prevent the children from making simple, obvious, and stereotyped responses by describing people in terms of obvious external physical characteristics, thus leading to an underestimation of their ability to perceive and conceptualize psychological characteristics.

IV. Statement Fluency: The Number of Ideas or Elements in Each Description

A. Unit of Analysis: Definition and Reliability

For the purposes of this analysis of fluency, each written description was dissected into its component statements. A 'statement' was defined as one element or idea referring directly or indirectly to the stimulus person, or to some other person since some of the descriptions contained statements which did not refer to the stimulus person.

The validity and usefulness of statements as basic units in content analysis rests in part upon the extent to which written materials can be reliably coded as facts or ideas, since statements lack the objectivity of such units as words and sentences. Most content analyses of free descriptions have neglected to examine statement coding reliabilities (see Beach and Wertheimer, 1961; Richardson, Dornbusch and Hastorf, 1961; Yarrow and Campbell, 1963; and Dornbusch et al., 1965) but the importance placed upon the idea of the 'statement' as the basic unit of analysis makes it necessary to study the extent to which agreement exists between independent judges.

Each of sixty-four descriptions (2·5 per cent of the total) was divided into statements by the investigator (E) and four other judges, W, X, Y and Z, who were all psychology honours students. The sixty-four descriptions were not selected in a completely random manner. Instead, eight descriptions were selected from each age group; within each age group four descriptions were selected from each sex group and within each sex group two were selected from each intelligence group. In addition, the eight descriptions selected from each age group were chosen so that one description of each type of stimulus person was obtained. Within these limits the actual descriptions were randomly selected.

Agreement between judges was determined by counting the number of statements that each judge assigned to each description and computing product-moment correlations between judges' scores. The results indicated that reliability was high; the correlations between judges ranged from $+0.89$ to $+0.98$. An eighteen-month interval between successive codings resulted in a repeat reliability (a correlation for the same judge on two occasions) of $+0.94$.

This method of assessing reliability, of course, takes into account only the overall number of facts or ideas discriminated; it does not test the extent to which the *same* facts or ideas are identified.

It also seems reasonable to ask to what extent the subjects were reliable —or consistent—in the way they described other people. This is a difficult question, however, and it cannot be conclusively answered within the framework of the present investigations. The children were asked to describe a series of different sorts of people rather than a number of people of the same sort. Hence, one would not expect to find consistency—in terms of similar contents and organization—between the various descriptions. It is also likely that performance on the task of writing descriptions of similar people would be greatly affected by practice. Measures repeated over long intervals of time, say three or six months, would be affected by changes in developmental status. However, there is no prior reason for supposing that the process of person perception is less reliable than any other kind of complex mental function. The effect of intra-subject unreliability would be to make it more difficult to demonstrate statistically significant trends and differences.

B. Method

Fluency—the number of statements per description—was analysed as a six-factor experiment with repeated measures on three factors. The data were not transformed.

We have adopted the useful convention that whenever statistically significant differences are reported in the form of F ratios, details of degree of relationship are also reported. This procedure has been adopted because authors often report significant differences, and go to great lengths to explain them, when the size of the effect, that is the degree of association between the dependent and independent variables, is negligible. In the case of analysis of variance, where the test of significance is the F test, the corresponding measure of association is the correlation ratio (η). Cohen (1965) suggested that ϵ, an unbiased estimate of η,

Table 2. Mean number of statements per description used by various groups of subjects to describe different types of stimulus person

Panel A — by age group of subjects

	All	7,10	8,10	9,10	10,10	12,4	13,2	14,3	15,3
Mean age of groups in years and months	9,0	7,10	8,10	9,10	10,10	12,4	13,2	14,3	15,3
Subjects									
All	9.0	7.4	9.1	9.1	8.7	9.4	9.6	9.7	8.9
Boys	8.6	7.7	8.4	9.1	8.9	8.4	8.6	9.2	8.4
Girls	9.4	7.2	9.8	9.1	8.5	10.4	10.6	10.2	9.4
Higher intelligence	8.9	6.8	9.4	8.9	9.1	8.5	9.3	9.6	9.3
Lower intelligence	9.1	8.0	8.8	9.3	8.3	10.3	9.9	9.8	8.5
Stimulus person									
Male	9.5	7.7	9.6	9.3	9.1	10.2	10.3	10.1	9.6
Female	8.4	7.1	8.6	8.9	8.3	8.6	8.6	9.0	8.2
Adult	8.5	7.2	8.4	8.4	8.4	9.0	9.2	9.3	8.3
Child	9.5	7.6	9.8	9.8	9.0	9.7	10.0	10.1	9.6
Liked	9.1	7.5	9.1	9.2	8.6	9.6	9.7	10.1	9.1
Disliked	8.9	7.3	9.1	9.0	8.8	9.2	9.5	9.3	8.7

Panel B — by intelligence, sex, age and liking

	Subjects		Sex		Age		Liking	
	Higher intelligence	Lower intelligence	Male	Female	Adult	Child	Liked	Disliked
Subjects								
All	8.9	9.1	9.5	8.4	8.5	9.5	9.1	8.9
Boys	8.7	8.5	9.0	8.1	8.1	9.2	8.7	8.7
Girls	9.1	9.8	10.1	8.8	8.9	9.9	9.5	9.4
Higher intelligence	—	—	9.5	8.3	8.4	9.3	9.7	9.7
Lower intelligence	—	—	9.6	8.6	8.6	9.6	9.2	9.2
Stimulus person								
Male	9.4	9.7	—	—	—	—	—	—
Female	8.3	8.6	—	—	—	—	—	—
Adult	—	—	—	—	—	—	—	—
Child	—	—	—	—	—	—	—	—

Panel C — Stimulus person (liked and disliked adults and children)

	Adult		Child	
	Liked	Disliked	Liked	Disliked
Subjects				
Boys	8.2	8.0	9.3	8.9
Girls	9.2	8.7	9.8	9.9
All	8.7	8.3	9.6	9.4

could be computed by subtracting unity from the value of the F ratio, using the following formula :

$$\varepsilon = \frac{df_b \ (F - 1)}{df_b F + df_w}$$

where df_b is the number of degrees of freedom associated with the numerator of the F ratio, and df_w is the number of degrees of freedom associated with the denominator.

C. Analysis of Results

1. Between-subject Variables. On average, the children produced nine statements per description. Significant age differences were found in the mean number of statements ($p < 0.01$; $\varepsilon = 0.38$) with younger children tending to use fewer than older children—see Table 2. Note that in the tables figures have been rounded to one decimal place. As chronological age was a major variable, differences between the means of each age group were examined in some detail. Multiple comparisons between the age means were made using Duncan's New Multiple Range Test—see Edwards (1965). The results showed that the mean for the youngest age group (mean age 7,10) was significantly less than the means for all other age groups, while the mean of age level four (mean age 10,10) was significantly less than the means of age levels six and seven (mean ages 13,3 and 14,3 respectively). In other words, the age trend in statement fluency was relatively small and irregular—a not unexpected finding since the constraints on word fluency imposed by the test instructions would naturally also reduce differences in statement fluency.

The nature of the relationship between chronological age and statement fluency was examined by means of trend analysis—see Winer (1962) and Edwards (1965). The linear component of the overall trend was highly significant ($F = 22.1$ with 1 and 288 d.f.; $p < 0.01$). Thus the means show a linear upward trend with age. The quadratic component was also significant ($F = 16.63$ with 1 and 288 d.f.; $p < 0.01$) indicating a significant curvature in the age trend. The results displayed graphically in Figure 2 are difficult to interpret. Unless produced by some obscure experimental artefact, the age trends for boys and girls shows remarkably parallel fluctuations with boys retarded one year as compared with girls. The simplest interpretation is that the age trends are slightly curvilinear and decelerating but overlaid by systematic reductions in output at about age 10 or 11 and at age 15 years.

Significant sex differences were observed. Girls used more statements than boys ($p < 0.01$; $\varepsilon = 0.25$). As Table 2 and Figure 2 show, however,

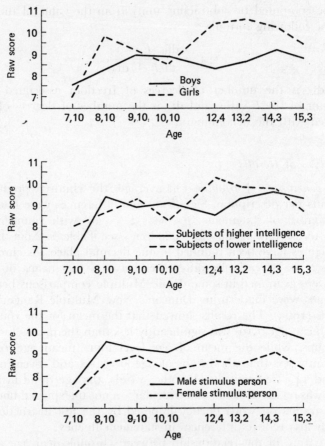

Figure 2. Age trends and interactions for the mean number of statements per description (raw scores)

Upper: Boy and girl subjects (all stimulus persons)
Middle: Subjects of higher and lower intelligence (all stimulus persons)
Lower: Male and female stimulus persons (all subjects)

sex differences were not independent of age; the 'Age × Sex' interaction was significant ($p < 0.01$; $\varepsilon = 0.25$). Boys in the youngest age group (mean age 7,10) produced slightly more statements than did girls. In the older age groups, girls produced slightly more than boys, the difference increased with age.

The difference between the intelligence groups was not significant, although the 'Age × Intelligence' interaction was significant ($p < 0.01$; $\varepsilon = 0.24$)—see Table 2 and Figure 2. Surprisingly, the lower intelligence children in the youngest age group produced more statements than those of higher intelligence. The greatest difference between the intelligence groups occurred in early adolescence with the higher intelligence groups being the most fluent.

The 'Sex × Intelligence' interaction was also significant ($p < 0.5$; $\varepsilon = 0.13$)—see Table 2. The difference between boys and girls was greatest in the lower intelligence group, with intelligence having the greatest effect in the case of girls. The girls of lower intelligence, surprisingly, produced on average even more facts and ideas than did girls of higher intelligence, but, like the 'Age × Intelligence' interaction just mentioned, it does not imply any qualitatively superior performance in person perception.

2. Within-subject variables. Significant stimulus person effects were obtained. One of the most interesting of these was the effect of the Sex of the Stimulus Person : more statements were used to describe males than females (9.54 against 8.45; $p < 0.01$; $\varepsilon = 0.58$). The differences between the means for the two levels of this factor depended upon age of subject, since the 'Age × Sex of Stimulus Person' interaction was significant ($p < 0.01$; $\varepsilon = 0.21$)—see Table 2 and Figure 2. The differences increased with the age of the subject. Sex of the subject also had a significant effect on the number of statements used to describe males and females ($p < 0.05$; $\varepsilon = 0.12$); the difference was greater in the case of girls—see Table 2.

As predicted, more statements were used to describe children than to describe adults (9.48 against 8.51; $p < 0.01$; $\varepsilon = 0.55$) and to describe liked as opposed to disliked persons (9.13 against 8.86; $p < 0.01$; $\varepsilon = 0.19$). A significant third-order interaction was obtained between 'Sex of Subject × Age of Stimulus Person × Like/Dislike' ($p < 0.05$; $\varepsilon = 0.14$). In the case of boys, liking had the greatest effect upon their descriptions of children, whereas in the case of girls, the greatest effect was on their descriptions of adults. Boys used fewer statements to describe disliked persons than to describe liked persons regardless of whether describing adults or children. Girls behaved in a similar manner when describing adults but not when describing children; they used slightly more terms to describe disliked children than liked children—see Table 2.

3. Discussion of Results. One of the more interesting features of this analysis is that the degrees of association between independent and dependent variables are greater for within-subject (stimulus person) variables than for between-subject variables. This is surprising considering the considerable age range involved. Some of the within-subject effects were a little unexpected, for example, it was not anticipated that subjects would use more statements to describe males than females. Such a result cannot be explained on the basis of frequency of interaction with the stimulus person, for the difference between the mean number of statements to describe males and females was greatest in girls, and it seems unlikely that girls spend more time with the opposite sex than with their own sex. One tentative explanation is that the male has a higher 'value' or 'interest' in our society than has the female. We live in a male-dominated society. Consequently, at most ages, males may tend to be more interested in their own sex than in girls, whereas girls, at most ages, are more interested in the opposite sex. This idea is supported by the significant 'Age of Subject × Sex of Stimulus Person' interaction which suggests that cultural factors exert a strong influence in that the difference between the mean number of statements used to describe males and females increases with age. An additional factor that might account for these results is that males are more active, more diverse in personal qualities and behaviour, adopt a greater variety of social roles, and may be referred to by a greater number of appropriate terms—it is in these respects that they act, on average, as more interesting and 'attention getting' stimulus persons than do females. An alternative explanation is that subjects were influenced by the sex of the investigator (male). But, as the subjects were familiar with both male and female adults (teachers) in the classroom situation, this explanation is not especially convincing.

The effects of the Age of the Stimulus Person can be accounted for on the basis of frequency of interaction and degree of similarity between subject and stimulus person. Children have much more contact with other children than with adults; indeed, young children know surprisingly few adults outside their immediate family circle apart from their teachers. The effects of Like/Dislike can be similarly accounted for : dislike tends to give rise to decreased contact with the other person, hence one comes into contact with fewer aspects of his behaviour and personality. When describing liked persons the child is also helped by his ability to understand himself and by his knowledge of himself, since there is a tendency to see liked persons as similar to oneself—see Fensterheim and Tresselt (1953).

This analysis clearly shows the importance of statistical interactions between the main variables, previously mentioned in Chapter 3, since the number of terms used to describe other people varies with the characteristics of subjects and with the type of stimulus person described. But do the contents of the descriptions also change? It is to this problem that we now turn.

CHAPTER 7

Content Analysis I: Peripheral versus Central Statements

I. Preview

This chapter contains details of an investigation of the use of psychological (central) statements as opposed to non-psychological (peripheral) statements. Reliability studies show that statements can be assigned to these two categories with a high degree of inter- and intra-judge agreement. Analysis of variance is used to test hypotheses regarding (a) the *number* of central and (b) the *proportion* of central statements in each description. A significant increase with age is found in both of these measures. Girls use significantly more central statements than do boys, but do not use a higher proportion of these statements, thus indicating that girls are not more psychologically developed than boys, but simply more verbally fluent. Intelligence has a significant effect upon both the number and the proportion of central statements used. As for within-subject (stimulus person) factors, Sex of Stimulus Person and Age of Stimulus Person have significant effects on both the number and proportion of central statements; the effect of Like/Dislike is, in both cases, non-significant. More central statements are used to describe males than to describe females; but the number of central statements used to describe females constitutes a higher proportion of the total number of statements used than those describing males. A greater number of and a higher proportion of central statements are used to describe children than to describe adults. Several significant interaction effects are described.

II. Rationale, Definitions and Reliability

The various aspects of written descriptions call for different applications of the method of content analysis, since each analysis deals with a different facet of the material. The first analysis is rather gross: statements are categorized and contrasted as either psychological (central) or non-psychological (peripheral). This rather crude method of categorizing children's statements is employed in this study for two reasons. Firstly, this dimension has been used a number of times in content analyses of responses to versions of the Role Construct Repertory Test (see Kelly, 1955); it has revealed considerable individual differences in the personal constructs of adults (see Maher, 1957; Bieri et al., 1958, and Fancher, 1966) and children (see Little, 1968). It is used in the present investigation in order to relate research employing free descriptions to previous studies. Secondly, the 'central versus peripheral' contrast is analogous to that of 'abstract versus concrete' in cognitive psychology, and seems to be associated with levels of conceptual competence in interpersonal relationships. If a person uses concrete or peripheral terms to describe people, he is probably at a disadvantage, because effective and sensitive social interaction depends upon being able to discern regularities in the superficially diverse actions of a person and to take contextual (situational) factors into account when forming expectations about an individual's actions. To do this, moreover, the perceiver must employ central (dispositional) terms, since peripheral qualities have little or no generality and are poor predictive cues. It is of interest to chart the development of this social skill (the acquisition of dispositional concepts) in order to discover to what extent the rate of acquisition is associated with variables such as sex and intelligence, and whether it varies with different sorts of stimulus person.

Peripheral statements refer to the external qualities of a person and to his surroundings; they include the following:

Appearance—descriptions of physique, facial features, clothing.
General information and identity—name, age, sex, residence.
Routine habits and activities.

Actual incidents.
Possessions.
Life history—specific details.
Likes and dislikes.
Social roles, such as school teacher or postman.
Kinship and social relationships.

Central statements are more abstract and generalized and refer to inner, psychological qualities; they include the following:

Personality traits, such as generous, kind or helpful.
General habits, for example, hits people, always tells us off.
Motives, needs and values, for example, wants to succeed in life.
Attitude and orientation, for example, very religious.

The reliability with which the contents of the written descriptions could be categorized as either central or peripheral was examined by two methods. The first required judges to read all the descriptions and note the different kinds of statement used. In all, 989 different kinds of statement were found. These were printed on separate cards, and sorted by the principal investigator into peripheral and central categories. The cards were then given to two independent judges—a final-year psychology honours student and a postgraduate student—to sort independently. There was 95·2 per cent and 98·3 per cent agreement between the investigator's sorting and those of the two independent judges, and 94·2 per cent agreement between the two independent judges themselves. The overall agreement between the three judges was 93·8 per cent. Agreement assessed by means of phi-coefficients yielded correlations of +0·90 and +0·96 between the investigator and the two independent judges. The correlation coefficient between the two independent judges was +0·88.

The second method of assessing reliability was for the investigator and four independent judges (all psychology honours students) to analyse the contents of the 64 descriptions which were used to investigate the reliability of statement coding—see Chapter 6. The number of central statements in each description was counted. Interjudge reliability was assessed using product-moment correlations. The results indicated high reliability, and the correlations ranged from +0·77 to +0·93. With an interval between codings of 18 months, intra-judge reliability was +0·86. Note, however, that in this second method of estimating reliability, the measures refer to the overall numbers of each category of statement, and not to the extent to which judges agree in categorizing the *same statements*.

These results indicated a satisfactory level of reliability and are similar to those reported in other studies. Maher (1957) reported interjudge reliabilities ranging from 91·1 per cent to 99·0 per cent, Little (1968) obtained a correlation of + 0·91 for two independent judges.

III. The Number and Proportion of Central Statements per Description

A. Methodological Note

The results we shall describe support many hypotheses about the relationships between the independent variables and two dependent variables: the number and the proportion of central statements. Before discussing these effects in greater detail it is necessary to consider an important issue raised by this analysis. The issue is whether the observed effects appear only because of overall differences in fluency. For example, does the increase with age in the number of central statements used merely reflect an overall increase with age in the total number of statements written? Or is a change in attitude and orientation taking place as the child grows older? While it is interesting to analyse differences in fluency (overall fluency and number of central statements), it is important to investigate possible changes in attitude and orientation. Such a change in perceiving and conceptualizing others could be reflected not only by an increase in the *number* of central statements but also in the *proportion* of central statements per description. For example, one would expect older children to be more aware of the inner personal aspects of individual behaviour and to be more likely to have the 'psychological' concepts and vocabulary needed to form an impression of a person. Their descriptions, therefore, should contain not only *more* central statements but also a *higher proportion* of them. This possibility is examined by comparing the *proportion* of central statements with the *absolute number*. In general, the results are the same for both, and only in isolated instances are they discussed separately. The proportions were calculated as follows:

$$\text{Proportion} = \frac{\text{Number of central statements}}{\text{Number of statements}}.$$

B. Hypotheses

The broad, general hypotheses underlying this study were outlined in Chapter 5. Applying them to the present analysis gave rise to the following predictions.

1. Between-subject Variables

Chronological age: the mean number and the mean proportion of central statements per description should increase with age, since age is associated with higher levels of mental ability and experience, and the use of central statements implies inferential activity and the ability to form a perception and categorization which is not dominated by particular features of the concrete, here-and-now, stimulus situation.

Sex: sex differences in person perception have not been clarified by previous studies, and the present study was designed to shed light on this issue; on the basis of research on adults (see Sarbin, 1954, and Supnick, 1964) and on children (see Brierley, 1966, and Little, 1968), girls could be expected to use more central statements than boys.

Intelligence: subjects in the higher intelligence group should use more central statements than those in the lower intelligence group because of their superior grasp of abstract and general rules.

2. Within-subject Variables. It was suggested in Chapter 5, on the basis of previous findings and psychological knowledge, that the ability to describe people in inferential terms depends not only upon characteristics of the subject but also upon the degree of similarity between the subject and the stimulus person, and upon their frequency of interaction. These general hypotheses gave rise to the following predictions.

Sex of other: children should use more central statements to describe people of the same sex, that is, a significant 'Sex of Subject × Sex of Stimulus Person' interaction should be observed; a nonsignificant difference, however, was predicted between the mean number of statements used to describe males and the mean number of statements used to describe females.

Age of other: more central statements should be used to describe children than to describe adults. In addition, the difference between the mean number of statements used to describe adults and the mean number of statements used to describe children should decrease with age as subjects became more aware of adult roles and behaviour in preparation for adopting them in late adolescence—that is, a significant 'Age of Subject × Age of Stimulus Person' interaction should be observed.

Liking for other: significantly more statements should be used to describe liked than to describe disliked persons.

C. Method and Results

The number and proportion of central statements in each description were examined in separate six-factor repeated measures analyses of

variance. The number of central statements per description were in general small, therefore a transformation was necessary in order to stabilize variances. A square root transformation was applied to the *number* of central statements. The actual transformation employed was:
$\sqrt{X} + \sqrt{(X+1)}$—see Winer (1962) and Edwards (1965). The *proportion* of central statements was transformed by means of an angular transformation, namely, $2 \arcsin \sqrt{p}$, where p is the proportion of central statements in the description.

Note that when the results of an analysis of transformed data are described, the summary tables preserve the untransformed data, so that their value as developmental norms will be more readily appreciated. The graphs of the statistically significant interactions are based on the transformed data used in the statistical analysis. It should be borne in mind that graphs based on transformed data would not have the same configuration as those based on the untransformed data in the summary table. The main results of this analysis were mentioned in the preview to this chapter. The fine details of these results are presented in the next two subsections. Readers who are not interested in these technicalities can omit these sections and go directly to the discussion in section IV.

1. Between-subject Variables. As predicted, the effect of age on the mean number and mean proportion of central statements per description was significant ($p < 0.01$ in both cases). The calculated correlation ratios (ε) were 0.58 and 0.53 respectively. As Table 3 indicates, the relationship with age was somewhat erratic, but in general the mean number of central statements per description increased with age. The linear component in the overall trend was significant ($F = 81.76$ with 1 and 288 d.f.; $p < 0.01$). The quadratic component was also significant ($F = 22.35$ with 1 and 288 d.f.; $p < 0.01$) indicating that a significant curvature occurs in the trend of the overall age means.

Multiple comparisons between the age means, using Duncan's New Multiple Range Test, shed further light on the relationship between age and the mean number of central statements. The mean for the youngest age group was significantly less than all other means; the mean of the sixth age group (mean age 13,3) was significantly higher than the means of all the younger age groups, but not significantly different from the means of the two older age groups. The frequency of use of central statements increased considerably between the ages of 7 and 8 years, and had more or less levelled off by the age of 13 years.

Similar results were found for the proportion of central statements. The trend showed significant linear and quadratic components giving $F = 61.46$ (linear) and 14.07 (quadratic) with 1 and 288 d.f., in each case

Table 3. Mean number (and mean proportion in brackets) of central statements per description used by various groups of subjects to describe different types of stimulus person

Mean age of groups in years and months	All	7,10	8,10	9,10	10,10	12,4	13,2	14,3	15,3
Subjects									
All	3·7 (0·40)	1·6 (0·22)	3·9 (0·43)	3·2 (0·36)	3·9 (0·44)	3·3 (0·35)	4·7 (0·48)	4·6 (0·47)	4·1 (0·46)
Boys	3·4 (0·39)	1·6 (0·21)	3·7 (0·45)	3·0 (0·34)	3·8 (0·41)	3·0 (0·34)	3·8 (0·44)	4·0 (0·43)	4·3 (0·51)
Girls	4·0 (0·41)	1·7 (0·24)	4·2 (0·42)	3·4 (0·38)	4·0 (0·47)	3·6 (0·36)	5·6 (0·52)	5·2 (0·51)	3·9 (0·41)
Higher intelligence	3·9 (0·43)	1·4 (0·21)	4·1 (0·42)	3·5 (0·39)	4·3 (0·47)	3·0 (0·36)	5·0 (0·52)	5·1 (0·53)	4·9 (0·53)
Lower intelligence	3·4 (0·37)	1·9 (0·23)	3·8 (0·44)	3·0 (0·33)	3·5 (0·41)	3·6 (0·34)	4·3 (0·44)	4·1 (0·41)	3·3 (0·39)
Stimulus person									
Male	3·8 (0·39)	1·3 (0·17)	3·8 (0·39)	3·1 (0·33)	4·0 (0·43)	3·4 (0·33)	5·1 (0·49)	5·3 (0·51)	4·7 (0·48)
Female	3·5 (0·41)	2·0 (0·27)	4·0 (0·47)	3·4 (0·39)	3·8 (0·45)	3·2 (0·37)	4·2 (0·48)	3·9 (0·43)	3·5 (0·43)
Adult	3·3 (0·38)	1·2 (0·17)	3·5 (0·41)	2·6 (0·32)	3·5 (0·47)	3·1 (0·34)	4·5 (0·48)	4·5 (0·47)	3·8 (0·45)
Child	4·0 (0·42)	2·1 (0·27)	4·4 (0·45)	3·8 (0·40)	4·4 (0·47)	3·6 (0·36)	4·8 (0·48)	4·8 (0·47)	4·4 (0·47)
Liked	3·7 (0·40)	1·6 (0·22)	3·8 (0·42)	3·2 (0·35)	4·0 (0·45)	3·4 (0·35)	4·6 (0·48)	4·8 (0·46)	4·1 (0·45)
Disliked	3·7 (0·37)	1·9 (0·23)	4·0 (0·44)	3·3 (0·36)	3·8 (0·43)	3·6 (0·35)	4·7 (0·49)	4·4 (0·48)	4·1 (0·47)

Breakdown: Stimulus person × Subjects

Stimulus person	Subjects — Higher intelligence	Subjects — Lower intelligence	Sex — Male	Sex — Female	Age — Adult	Age — Child	Liking — Liked	Liking — Disliked
Male	3·8 (0·39)	3·6 (0·36)	—	—	3·7 (0·40)	4·0 (0·42)	3·8 (0·39)	3·7 (0·40)
Female	3·5 (0·41)	3·3 (0·39)	—	—	3·4 (0·42)	3·7 (0·43)	3·5 (0·39)	3·3 (0·39)
Adult	3·3 (0·38)	3·1 (0·36)	3·5 (0·41)	3·6 (0·41)	—	—	3·4 (0·38)	3·4 (0·37)
Child	4·0 (0·42)	3·8 (0·39)	4·3 (0·43)	3·8 (0·40)	—	—	3·9 (0·42)	4·0 (0·43)

Breakdown: Subjects × Stimulus person

Subjects	Stimulus person — All	Stimulus person — Adult	Stimulus person — Child
Male			
Higher intelligence	3·7 (0·42)	3·4 (0·40)	4·1 (0·44)
Lower intelligence	3·1 (0·36)	2·7 (0·34)	3·3 (0·38)
Female			
Higher intelligence	4·1 (0·44)	3·7 (0·41)	4·5 (0·47)
Lower intelligence	3·8 (0·39)	3·5 (0·38)	4·1 (0·40)

$p<$0·01. Multiple comparisons between the age means using Duncan's procedure, showed that the proportion of central statements increased considerably between the ages of 7,10 and 8,10 (22 per cent and 43 per cent, respectively). This is, of course, an important developmental finding. The proportion of central statements in the descriptions of 7-year-old children was significantly less than all other age groups. Surprisingly, however, 8-year-old children did not differ significantly from the older age groups, that is the 13-, 14- and 15-year-old groups. Twelve-year-old children used a smaller proportion of central statements than did 8- and 10-year-old children. The proportion of central statements did not vary significantly between the three older age groups. Unless the proportion of central statements is too crude a measure of development in person perception, the findings indicate that an important growth phase occurs *below* the age of 8 years.

As predicted, girls used significantly more central terms than did boys (3·95 against 3·41; $p<$0·01; ε =0·20), but these did not constitute a significantly higher proportion of the total number of statements. Subjects of higher intelligence used significantly more central terms than did subjects of lower intelligence (3·92 against 3·43; $p<$0·01; ε =0·15), and a higher proportion of such statements (43 per cent against 37 per cents; $p<$0·01; ε =0·18). The effects of age and intelligence on the number of central statements were not independent: the 'Age × Intelligence' interaction was significant ($p<$0·05; ε =0·15). The difference between the intelligence groups increased with age, as shown in Table 3 and Figure 3.

2. *Within-subject Variables.* Predictions regarding the main effects of the within-subject variables were supported only in the case of Age of Stimulus Person. The predicted effects of Like/Dislike for the other person were not obtained: subjects did not use significantly more central statements to describe liked persons than disliked persons. The effects of Sex of Stimulus Person were significant ($p<$0·05; ε =0·13): more central statements were used to describe males than females (3·84 against 3·51). This effect was not predicted; a nonsignificant difference had been expected. The size of this difference depended upon Age of Subject and Sex of Subject. The 'Age × Sex of Stimulus Person' interaction was significant ($p<$0·01; ε =0·38), though only in the adolescent groups were there substantial differences—see Table 3 and Figure 3. The difference in the mean number of central statements used to describe males and females was affected by Sex of Subject ($p<$0·01; ε =0·30), as shown in Table 3 and Figure 5. Although some interaction between these variables was expected, the outcome was not quite as hypothesized. It was predicted, on the basis of frequency of interaction and degree of similarity

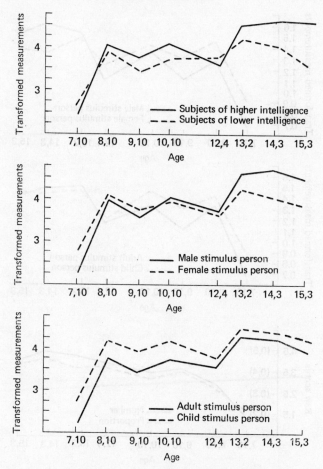

Figure 3. Age trends and interactions for the mean number of central statements per description (transformed measurements)
Upper: Subjects of higher and lower intelligence (all stimulus persons)
Middle: Male and female stimulus persons (all subjects)
Lower: Adult and child stimulus persons (all subjects)

between subject and stimulus person, that more central statements would be used to describe people of the same sex than of the opposite sex. The opposite tendency was found, however, this being most pronounced in girls, indicating perhaps that girls are more interested in the opposite sex than are boys.

Although a greater number of central statements were used to describe males than females, those used to describe females constituted a higher

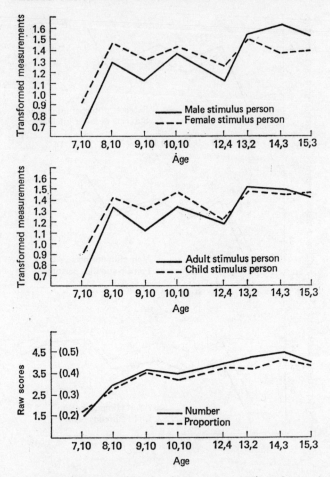

Figure 4. Age trends and interactions for the mean proportion of central statements
per description

Upper: Male and female stimulus persons (all subjects)
Middle: Adult and child stimulus persons (all subjects)
Lower: Smoothed age trends for the mean number and mean proportion for all
subjects and all stimulus persons

proportion of the total number of statements (41 per cent against 39 per
cent; $p < 0.05$; $\varepsilon = 0.13$).

The repeated measures ANOVA design appears to have been successful in revealing a number of effects which are statistically significant but
of no great psychological importance (as indicated by small percentage
differences and low correlation ratios).

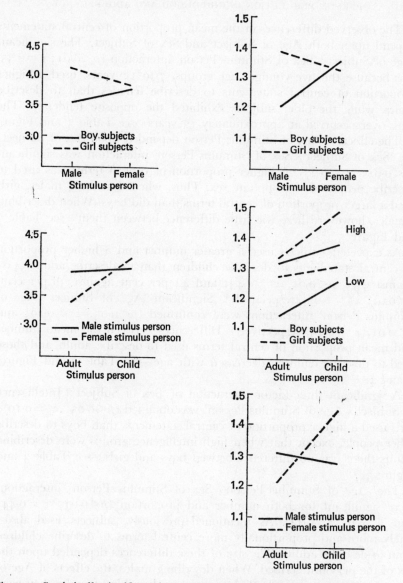

Figure 5. Statistically significant interactions (transformed measurements)
  Left: Mean number of central statements per description
          Upper: Sex of subject × sex of stimulus person
          Lower: Sex of stimulus person × age of stimulus person
  Right: Mean proportion of central statements per description
          Upper: Sex of subject × sex of stimulus person
          Middle: Sex and intelligence of subject × age of stimulus person
          Lower: Sex of stimulus person × age of stimulus person

The observed differences in the mean proportion of central statements depend upon both Age of Subject and Sex of Subject. The significant 'Age of Subject × Sex of Stimulus Person' interaction ($p<0.01$; $\varepsilon = 0.35$) was because the five younger age groups, 7 to 12 years, used a higher proportion of central statements to describe females than to describe males, while the older subjects exhibited the opposite tendency. The cross-over occurred at approximately 13 years—see Table 3 and Figure 4. The effects of Sex of Stimulus Person depended upon Sex of Subject; the 'Sex of Subject × Sex of Stimulus Person' interaction was significant ($p<0.01$; $\varepsilon = 0.27$). A higher proportion of central terms was used to describe people of the opposite sex. Thus, when describing males, girls used a larger proportion of central terms than did boys. When describing females, however, there was little difference between them—see Table 3 and Figure 5.

As expected, subjects used a greater number and a higher proportion of central statements to describe children than to describe adults (4·03 against 3·33, $p<0.01$, $\varepsilon = 0.43$; and 42 per cent against 38 per cent, $p<0.01$, $\varepsilon = 0.25$, respectively). Significant 'Age of Subject × Age of Stimulus Person' interactions were confirmed ($p<0.05$, $\varepsilon = 0.19$; and $p<0.01$, $\varepsilon = 0.23$, respectively). Differences between the mean number and mean proportion of central terms used to describe adults and those used to describe children decreased with age—see Table 3 and Figures 3 and 4.

A significant three-factor interaction of 'Sex of Subject × Intelligence of Subject × Age of Stimulus Person' was obtained ($p<0.05$; $\varepsilon = 0.10$): girls used a higher proportion of central statements than boys to describe other people, except that when high intelligence groups were describing adults there was no difference betwen boys and girls—see Table 3 and Figure 5.

The 'Age of Stimulus Person × Sex of Stimulus Person' interactions were significant for both number and proportion ($p<0.01$, $\varepsilon = 0.44$; and $p<0.01$, $\varepsilon = 0.44$). As mentioned previously, subjects used absolutely more and proportionally more central terms to describe children than to describe adults. The size of these differences depended upon the sex of the person described. When describing males, the effects of Age of Stimulus Person were only slight, but when describing females they were considerable—see Table 3 and Figure 5.

The 'Age of Stimulus Person × Sex of Stimulus Person' interaction was significant ($p<0.01$, $\varepsilon = 0.44$). The difference between the mean proportions of central statements used to describe adults and children depended upon Sex of Stimulus Person the difference was greatest for female stimulus persons. In the case of male stimulus persons, the mean number and mean proportion were slightly higher for adults than for children. Thus, Age of Stimulus Person had little effect for descriptions of males. In the case of adult stimulus persons, a greater number and a higher proportion of central statements were used to describe males than females; whereas the opposite was the case for child stimulus persons. The Sex of Stimulus Person had greater effect when adults were described. The interaction between 'Age of Subject × Intelligence of Subject × Sex of Stimulus Person × Age of Stimulus Person' was significant ($p < 0.01$; $\varepsilon = 0.22$) in the case of the proportion of central statements, but it was difficult to interpret, like the following higher order interactions: 'Age of Subject × Age of Stimulus Person × Like/Dislike' ($p < 0.05$; $\varepsilon = 0.16$), and 'Age of Subject × Intelligence of Subject × Age of Stimulus Person × Like/Dislike' ($p < 0.05$; $\varepsilon = 0.17$) The first of these might mean that older subjects generally use a relatively higher proportion of central statements to describe liked adults; the second might mean that older, more intelligent children used an even higher proportion of central statements to describe liked adults.

In the analysis of the number of central statements, two of the four-factor interactions were significant: 'Age of Subject × Sex of Subject × Age of Stimulus Person × Like/Dislike' ($p < 0.05$; $\varepsilon = 0.19$) and 'Age of Subject × Intelligence of Subject × Age of Stimulus Person × Like/Dislike' ($p < 0.05$; $\varepsilon = 0.18$). It could be, for example, in the first case, that older girls write more central statements about girls they like, whereas younger boys write more about men they dislike. In the second case, older more intelligent children write more central statements about adults they like whereas younger less intelligent children write more about children they dislike. Interpretation of these interactions is difficult. Although the degree of association between the variables is small, it should be noted that it is as large as some of the main effects reported, for example, the effects of Intelligence of Subject and Sex of Stimulus Person.

IV. Discussion

The analyses of the number and proportion of central statements yielded mostly consistent results. Chronological age was a significant factor in both analyses; and the degrees of association between this factor and the dependent variables were higher than for any other factor or combination of factors. Further analysis is needed of this observed developmental change, since chronological age is merely a convenient index of a host of interrelated organismic and environmental variables. Relationships between age and both the number and the proportion of central statements were remarkably similar. When running averages were used to smooth the graphs—see Figure 4—both sets of data approximated to negatively accelerated growth curves typical of psychological development. The age changes cannot be explained by an increase in verbal fluency, since the proportion of central statements increased in a similar manner to their frequency of use. They probably indicate a change in attitude and orientation—a shift from one level of development to another. The fact that growth appeared to be rapid between seven and eight years, and slow thereafter, suggests that there may be some connection with a transition from egocentric to socialized thinking, since a number of studies of the Piagetian type have found marked changes in the quality or conceptual level of intellectual performance at these ages. It is recognized, of course, that longitudinal studies of changes *within* subjects would improve our understanding of the developmental processes. A reduction in egocentrism makes way for the development of socialized and operational thinking and for the acquisition of the inferential skills necessary for the use of abstract and generalized psychological terms which enable the subject to form impressions in terms of inner, dispositional constants rather than in terms of outwardly observable and varying appearances and actions.

The growth curves in Figure 4 show a slight decrease in the 10-year-old group—on unsmoothed curves this occurs in the 12-year-old subjects. It is not clear whether this was produced by sampling errors or imperfect reliability or by other circumstances. For example, it could reflect a temporary setback in the acquisition of the social skills involved in perceiving and conceptualizing others caused by a reorganization of the interpersonal cognitive system required in the interests of greater flexibility, consistency and predictability. However, such speculation is profitless in the absence of corroborative studies, particularly when the observed fluctuations might be attributed simply to error factors.

Girls used significantly more central statements than did boys but not a significantly higher proportion. This suggests that girls are no more psychologically advanced than boys, but simply more fluent. The increased fluency, however, might reflect a greater interest in persons and may well have implications for their interpersonal relationships, since it implies that they are more aware of psychological qualities and of the variety of such qualities that people possess. On the other hand, the observed sex difference may simply reflect the more general fact that girls are verbally more fluent than boys.

Intelligence had a significant effect on the use of central statements: the higher intelligence group used more central statements and a higher proportion of such statements than did the lower intelligence group. This was almost certainly because the more intelligent subjects possessed superior inferential skills and a better grasp of abstract and generalized rules. These abilities enabled them to form impressions which were not as dominated by concrete and particular stimuli as those of less intelligent subjects, and enabled them to process and integrate information more efficiently so as to discern some of the more important central regulating factors in the behaviour of individuals. None of the interactions involving the between-subject (stimulus person) factors were significant in both analyses. The 'Age of Subject × Intelligence of Subject' interaction, however, was significant in the analysis of statement fluency (see Chapter Six) and the difference in the number of central statements associated with difference in the two levels of intelligence increased with age.

In the case of the within-subject factors, Sex of Stimulus Person and Age of Stimulus Person had consistently significant effects. The effects of Like/Dislike were not significant in either analysis, despite the fact that previous analyses had shown that descriptions of liked persons were significantly longer than those of disliked persons. The absence of effects due to Like/Dislike were not really surprising, although a number of studies have demonstrated that evaluation affects all aspects of impression formation. It appears that, as far as personality terms are concerned, the effects of Like/Dislike are qualitative rather than quantitative, and are limited to affecting the *kinds* of statement made rather than their number or proportion. A person is usually liked or disliked for his personality and behaviour rather than because of his peripheral qualities. Hence, central qualities figure equally in descriptions of liked and disliked persons, the dislike is expressed by the choice of statements. Normally, we tend to form an impression of a disliked person in terms of socially undesirable qualities accompanied by negative evalutions.

More central statements were used to describe males than to describe females, but those used to describe females constituted a higher proportion of the total than those applied to males. The larger number of central and peripheral statements in descriptions of males may be ascribed to the greater prestige of males in our society and to the greater diversity of activities they engage in and qualities they possess. In general, men are more active than women and engage in a wider range of activities and interests, and hence possess more social roles. Similarly, boys are more active than girls and usually show greater variety in the games they play and in the things that interest them. In addition, the greater freedom and independence given to men and boys means that their actual behavioural environment is greater than that of women and girls, that is, their activities are located in a greater number of settings, and are therefore more interesting and noticeable. Males also tend to express their abilities and personal qualities in a more obvious manner than do females, for example, males tend to be more aggressive than females and express their aggression in a more directly observable way.

The suggestion that our culture is male oriented and that males are more 'valued' and 'interesting' is supported by the consistently significant 'Age of Subject × Sex of Stimulus Person' interaction, although it is not until adolescence that this evaluation manifests itself. Thus social learning appears to be an important factor. The pre-adolescent subjects used more central statements and a higher proportion of central statements to describe females than to describe males—perhaps because they based their evaluations upon their relationships with their mothers and female schol teachers. Young children are certainly brought up in a predominantly female environment, and it is not until late in their primary-school careers or early adolescence that they become aware of the attitudes and values that are prevalent in adult society. Thus, frequency of interaction seems to be a particularly important determinant of the contents of impressions in young children.

Differences between descriptions of male and female stimulus persons may have been accentuated by the onset of adolescence with its attendant interest in the opposite sex. As puberty occurs earlier in girls than in boys, girls' descriptions are affected earlier, thus increasing the difference between descriptions of males and females. The significant 'Sex of Subject × Sex of Stimulus Person' interaction showed that boys use about the same number of central statements to describe males as to describe females, suggesting that boys are not selectively attentive to their own sex. Girls, however, used more central statements to describe males than to describe females. The proportion of central statements in girls' descriptions was little affected by the sex of the stimulus person, while boys used a greater proportion of central statements to describe females than to describe males. This suggests that subjects found it relatively difficult to describe females, especially women, in terms of peripheral qualities, possibly because women are less diverse in their activities and possess fewer social roles than men. The activities they pursue are so mundane and so familiar that they are not considered worthy of mention, for example, household tasks. In general, it seems that the interaction between 'Age of Subject, Sex of Subject and Sex of Stimulus Person' is complicated, to say the least, and seems to be related to factors such as child-rearing practices, sex roles and status.

The age of the stimulus person had a significant effect in both analyses; greater use was made of central statements when describing children than when describing adults. It was hypothesized that the size of this difference would decrease with age as older subjects changed their reference groups in preparation for the adoption of an adult role. In fact, the opposite effect was observed in connection with the number of central statements, probably because subjects interpreted 'a boy you know . . .' or 'a girl you know . . .' to mean someone their own age; they therefore described peers. The hypothesized effect, however, was obtained in conection with the proportion of central statements; the differences between the proportions used to describe children and adults became negligible at about 13 years. This seemed to be due not so much to a growing understanding of adults and a change of reference group, but rather to an increased understanding of personality. Thus, less reference was made to peripheral qualities, and this had the effect of increasing the relative proportion of central statements in the description.

In the analyses of the number and proportion of central statements, the effects of Age of Stimulus Person depended upon Sex of Stimulus Person. When males were being described, Age of Stimulus Person had little effect. When females were being described, however, it had considerable effect—greater use was made of central statements when describing girls than when describing women. It may be that, at least under the experimental conditions established, there was an optimum length of description and that this normally occurred when describing children. It also occurred when describing men because of the relative ease with which males can be described (as compared with females), thus partially offsetting the greater difficulty of describing adults.

These results indicate that to contrast central and peripheral qualities is a useful way of conceptualizing the development of person perception. One major developmental trend is an increase in the use of central statements. Initially, these statements are assigned to persons similar to the self, that is, to children, and later to dissimilar persons, that is, to adults. Thus, development proceeds by the assimilation of new experiences to an initially 'self-centred' frame of reference, and by the gradual accommodation of this frame of reference to the facts of social life. The child's cognitive system extends in scope and level with new experiences so as to incorporate ideas and facts associated with people different from himself. In this manner, the child's perception of himself facilitates his perception and comprehension of others, and vice versa. One apparent exception to this rule is that children seem to find it easier to describe the 'preferred' sex rather than the same sex.

CHAPTER 8

Content Analysis II : Varieties of Statements

I. Preview

The content analyses described in the previous chapter revealed some interesting if complicated results, and demonstrated the relevance of the contrast between central and peripheral (abstract and concrete) characteristics in impression formation. Such a crude classification of the contents of written impressions, however, does not describe in sufficient detail the complexities and subtleties of children's descriptions. In the present section, therefore, the varieties of statement children make about other people are described in detail.

II. Content Categories

One of the problems associated with content analysis is the development of a set of categories which are free from experimenter bias. A number of attempts have been made to develop a suitable set of categories—see Beach and Wertheimer (1961), Richardson *et al.* (1961), Yarrow and Campbell (1963) and Brierley (1966). These were not adopted since they employed too few categories to describe the varieties of statements found in the present study. The procedure for analysing the contents of the impressions was to identify statements having a similar form and content. The statements were put onto cards, each card containing several statements of the same sort. The cards were then sorted in an attempt to establish an exhaustive and exclusive system which would be psychologically meaningful and statistically manageable. Nine hundred and eighty-nine different kinds of statements were identified and thirty-three different categories were required in order to catalogue them. They are listed and defined in Table 4. The following four examples illustrate the procedure; the last of these is a content analysis of all eight descriptions obtained from a single subject.

Table 4. Definitions and examples of content analysis categories

I. Objective Information

1. Appearance	References to external qualities, that is, physical build, facial appearance, clothing, and so on, including approvals, 'He is tall', 'She is pretty', 'He has blue eyes', 'He has fair hair'.
2. General information and identity	The person's name, age, sex, nationality, religion, residence, school and physical environment, for example, 'He lives at . . .', 'He is a catholic', 'He goes to our school', 'She will be 10 years old on Wednesday'.
3. Routine habits and activities	Daily and weekly routine, for example, 'He goes to work at 8 o'clock', 'She goes skating every Thursday', 'He gets up at 6 o'clock and makes the fire'.
4. Actual incidents	Statements about specific actions, things done and said, events the other person has been involved in or the places he has visited, for example, 'He went to France for his holidays', 'He painted his house last week', 'She told me that she dislikes a woman who talks behind people's backs'.
5. Possessions	The person's property and possessions, for example, 'He has a pet rabbit', 'He owns a car', 'He has a new bicycle'.

II. Contemporary and Historical Circumstances

6. Life history	Historical circumstances, childhood experiences, background, origin, for example, 'He was brought up wrong, 'He comes from Leeds', 'He was not well educated'.
7. Contemporary social circumstances	Contemporary constraints and opportunities in his environment, pressures exerted on him, for example, 'His father won't let him play out', 'His parents are very rich', 'His mother won't let him climb trees', 'He always has lots of money to spend'.

Table 4. — *Continued*

8. Physical condition	Health, physical fitness and strength, for example, 'He is strong', 'He is often ill', 'He has a bad leg'.

III. *Personal Characteristics and Behavioural Consistencies*

9. General personality attributes	Personality traits and temperament, for example, 'friendly', 'conceited', 'selfish', 'kind', 'moody', 'bad tempered', 'gentle', 'changeable'.
10. Specific behavioural consistencies	General habits, characteristic reactions to others of a specific nature, reaction to blame, stress, failure, and so on, for example, 'grumbles', 'can't take a joke', 'shouts', 'plays nice', 'groans a lot'.
11. Motivation and arousal	Aspirations, aims, ambitions, wants, needs, goal directedness of behaviour, motivation in tasks undertaken, for example, 'His ambition is to go to grammar school', 'He wants to go in the Army'.
12. Orientation	Expectations, wishes, fears, self reproaches; how the person sees the situation; how he feels things are going; feelings of hope, anxiety, neglect; for example, 'She is always crying because she is fat', 'She does not like war and gets very afraid when anyone mentions it', 'He is only of average ability but that does not worry him'.
13. Expressive behaviour	Specific personal habits and mannerisms, characteristic gait, speech characteristics, for example, 'He twitches his moustache', 'Walks funny', 'He has a funny voice', 'She speaks with a squeaky voice'.

IV. *Aptitudes and Achievements*

14. Intellectual aptitudes and abilities	Mental skills and intellectual capacity, scholastic ability, scholastic achievements and failures, for example, 'intelligent', 'clever', 'good at sums'.
15. Achievements and skills	Physical skills, successes, failures, disabilities, for example, 'He is a good footballer', 'She is good at cooking', 'She wins a lot of house points'.

V. *Interests and Preferences*

16. Preferences and aversions	Likes and dislikes (both persons and things), for example, 'He likes sweets', 'He likes watching television', 'He does not like school', 'He is very fond of ice-cream'.
17. Interests and hobbies	General interests and hobbies, including play activities, for example, 'His hobby is collecting stamps', 'He enjoys walks in the country', 'He is very interested in ships'.

VI. *Attitudes and Beliefs*

18. Beliefs, attitudes and values	Standards, values and ideals that the person accepts and conforms to, for example, 'She is very religious', 'He does not believe in war'.
19. Stimulus person's opinions and attitudes towards himself	The person's self-evaluation and opinion of himself, for example, 'She thinks she is very beautiful', 'He thinks he is better than everyone else', 'She thinks she's a hard knock'.

Table 4.—*Continued*

VII. Evaluations

20. Evaluations — The subject's evaluations of the stimulus person. Social desirability or undesirability of behaviour, manners, outright evaluations, including abusive statements, for example, 'good', 'nice', 'nasty', 'horrible', 'rude', 'cheeky', 'polite', 'clean', 'dirty'.

VIII. Social Factors

21. Social roles — Group and organizational membership, occupational role, for example, 'He is a teacher', 'She is a member of the tennis club', 'He is a cub'.

22. Reputation — What people in general think of the person, for example, 'He is popular', 'Other people like him'.

23. Friendships and playmates — The person's friends, acquaintances and playmates, including details of the number of friends he has, for example, 'He plays with . . .', 'Her best friend is . . .', 'He has lots of friends'.

24. Effect upon, and relations with, others — The consequences and effects the person's behaviour has upon other people and the consequences for himself, for example, 'He makes us miss our playtime', 'At parties he just mopes around with a face like a "wet Echo" and puts a big black cloud over everybody', 'He makes people feel embarrassed', 'She makes everyone feel happy'.

25. Other people's behaviour towards the stimulus person — The specific reactions of other people to the person described, for example, 'Karen dislikes her', 'Other people hit him', 'Cathy said she did not like her', 'My brother says he is not too bad as a friend'.

(Note the distinction between this category and category 22—reputation. This category refers either to a single person's response towards the stimulus person or to the specific reactions of some other people. Category 22 refers to the overall opinion and nonspecific behaviour of people in general in relation to the stimulus person.)

26. Relations with the opposite sex — Attitudes towards and relations with opposite sex, for example, 'Her boyfriend is . . .', 'He is not interested in girls', 'He is very sexy'.

IX. Subject-Other Relations

27. Mutual interaction — Interactions between the subject and the stimulus person; the things they do or have done together, length of acquaintanceship, frequency of interaction, for example, 'I see her at the weekend', 'We play together after school', 'He knows our family well', 'I have always known him'.

28. Subject's opinion of, and behaviour towards, the stimulus person — General pronouncements about the person, for example, 'I like him', 'He is my best friend'.

X. Comparison against Standards

29. Comparison with self — Comparisons between the person and the subject, for example, 'He is smaller than me', 'He is not as clever as me'.

30. Comparison with others — Comparisons between the person and other people or an ideal, for example, 'He is the tallest in the class', 'He is more clever than his sister'.

Table 4. — *Continued*

XI. *Family and Kinship*

31. Family and kinship	The person's family and relations, the number of children he has, descriptions of a relative, for example, 'He has three children', 'His son is called Peter', 'His wife is horrible', 'She has three brothers', 'Her brother is in my class'.

XII. *Illustration, Corroboration and Explanation*

32. Collateral facts and ideas	Specific statements in support of a previous assertion, illustrations of personal qualities, explanations of behaviour, for example, '[She is quite lonely] because her daughter is now in London and she is alone', '[She treats her best friend very badly] when she has a party she doesn't invite her', '[If he sees something he likes he takes it] for example, if he feels like a drink he would take a bottle of milk from anyone's front door and think nothing of it'.

XIII. *Residue*

33. Irrelevant and unclassifiable facts and ideas	Irrelevant information—usually about someone unrelated to the other—or statements which cannot be placed in any other category.

A boy aged 7,4 years describes a girl he likes:

Statement	Category
She is shy	9. General Personality Attribute
She is blonde and	1. Appearance
she likes working.	16. Preferences and Aversions
She likes playing.	16. Preferences and Aversions
She was born in Liverpool.	6. Life History
She is small.	1. Appearance
She is active.	9. General Personality Attribute
She does not get hot.	8. Physical Condition
She is kind and	9. General Personality Attribute
does not need much sleep.	8. Physical Condition

A girl aged 15,5 years describes a women she dislikes:

Statement	Category
This lady is one of my neighbours.	2. General Information and Identity
I dislike her because she talks about things which are none of her business anyway behind people's backs.	28. Subject's Opinion 10. Specific Behavioural Consistencies

Statement	Category
She is fairly old and	2. General Information and Identity
lives with her son	31. Family and Kinship
who suffers a great deal with nerves.	33. Irrelevant and Unclassifiable
She is always out shopping	9. Routine Habits and Activities
and she keeps people talking for hours.	10. Specific Behavioural Consistencies
She knows all the local gossip	32. Collateral Fact (collateral to the second statement)
and told me the other day that she dislikes a woman who lives near-by because she talks about everybody behind their backs!	4. Actual Incident
(This is the only reason why I dislike her)	32. Collateral Fact (collateral to the second statement)
as she is quite friendly.	9. General Personality Attribute

As can be clearly seen from the second example, the present content analysis deals with only a limited aspect of the description—the elements. Other aspects of the description—those concerned with the way the description is organized and qualified—are dealt with in an additional content analysis in Chapter 10.

A girl aged 15,6 years describes a man she dislikes:

Statement	Category
He is rather a horrible man	20. Evaluation
who is ruled by his wife and mother-in-law.	7. Contemporary Social Circumstances
He does not care about his appearance	13. Expressive Behaviour
and just goes about in his slippers with his trousers tucked into his socks, with a cigarette dangling out of his mouth.	32. Collateral Facts and Ideas
He shouts and hits his children	10. Specific Behavioural Consistencies
and does not care what he says.	10. Specific Behavioural Consistencies

Any residual uncertainty regarding the classification of statements could, in theory, be eliminated by asking questions of the subject as to the meaning of doubtful statements. Research is under way to examine this possibility. The point is that some degree of unreliability arises because of lack of information; there is no intrinsic uncertainty.

A girl aged 9,8 years describes eight stimulus persons:

A man she likes

Statement	Category
Mr Emery is a man I know very well.	2. General Information and Identity
He owns a sweet shop in the middle of our road.	2. General Information and Identity
And when I go in he sometimes gives me sweets that are broken and ones he can't sell.	10. Specific Behavioural Consistencies
He has written my name on the wall of his sweet shop.	4. Actual Incident
And he says I am his girl friend but he has got four children and a wife.	27. Mutual Interaction 31. Family and Kinship

A woman she likes

Statement	Category
Mrs Hall has got three children, Joan, Sydney and baby Patrica.	31. Family and Kinship
This Christmas we are going to stay with them for a couple of days.	27. Mutual Interaction
She works as a night sister in a hospital.	21. Social Role
We call her Auntie Enid, but she is not a real auntie, just a friend of my mother's.	27. Mutual Interaction
Last year, for Christmas, she sent mummy a box of chocolates, daddy some Scotch matches, Ann an under-skirt, Mathew a Fish and Fishing book and me an Enid Blyton book.	4. Actual Incident

A boy she likes

Statement	*Category*
Sidney Hall is a sort of cousin of mine	2. General Information and Identity
He likes watching television and riding his bicycle.	16. Preferences and Aversions.
	16. Preferences and Aversions.
He lives in Liverpool.	2. General Information and Identity
His behaviour is sometimes good and sometimes it is bad.	20. Evaluation
	20. Evaluation
He likes watching television	33. Irrelevant and Unclassifiable (repetition)
and eating sweets.	16. Preferences and Aversions
He has got favourite television programmes but I don't know what they are.	16. Preferences and Aversions
He is three years older than me but he will soon be four years older than me.	29. Comparison with Self
He goes to school on the train	3. Routine Habits and Activities
and he is quite good at his school work.	14. Intellectual Abilities and Achievements

A man she dislikes

Statement	*Category*
Mr Evans is a man who lives in our road.	2. General Information and Identity
He lives three houses up from us, Flat 60, number twenty-two.	2. General Information and Identity
Whenever my brother and I are playing football we are always very careful to see that the ball does not go into his garden.	33. Irrelevant and Unclassifiable
If it does I hold the gate while my brother creeps into the garden and gets it.	33. Irrelevant and Unclassifiable
The reason I hold the gate is so that it does not bang, because if it did	33. Irrelevant and Unclassifiable
he would come out and tell us off.	21. Mutual Interaction

A woman she dislikes

Statement	Category
Mrs Townsend is a lady who lives down our road.	2. General Information and Identity
She is always telling us off for climbing over the wall but we shouldn't really climb over it because it was not put there for that reason.	10. Specific Behavioural Consistencies
Mrs Townsend rides a bicycle but she is getting quite fat now and if she gets any fatter she will probably fall off.	3. Routine Habits and Activities 1. Appearance
She always shouts hello but she	10. Specific Behavioural Consistencies
does not know that I dislike her.	12. Orientation

A boy she dislikes

Statement	Category
David Calder is a boy I know.	2. General Information and Identity
He goes to this school	2. General Information and Identity
but he is not in our class.	2. General Information and Identity
His behaviour is very bad,	20. Evaluation
and he is always saying cheeky things to people.	10. Specific Behavioural Consistencies
He fights people of any age	10. Specific Behavioural Consistencies
and he likes getting into trouble for it.	16. Preferences and Aversions
He is always being told off by his teachers and other people.	25. Other People's Behaviour towards the Stimulus Person
He has got one sister who is younger than him,	31. Family and Kinship
and she is cheeky too,	33. Irrelevant and Unclassifiable
but she does not like being told off for being cheeky.	33. Irrelevant and Unclassifiable

A girl she dislikes

Statement	Category
Joan Hall is Sidney's sister	2. General Information and Identity
but she is not as nice as I thought she was.	20. Evaluation
She came over to stay with us for a few weeks,	27. Mutual Interaction
and she was always buying sweets for everybody	10. Specific Behavioural Consistencies
and she was always boasting about things she had done	10. Specific Behavioural Consistencies
but we didn't believe her.	26. Subject's Opinion and Behaviour towards the Stimulus Person
She said that she had climbed on some scaffolding and waited for someone to rescue her.	4. Actual Incident

A girl she likes

Statement	Category
Stephanie Green likes dancing.	16. Preferences and Aversions
She goes to dancing lessons once or twice a week.	3. Routine Habits and Activities
She likes watching television	16. Preferences and Aversions
and playing out.	16. Preferences and Aversions
She is a very good runner	15. Achievements and Skills
and she is also good at jumping.	15. Achievements and Skills
Her behaviour is good nearly all the time.	20. Evaluation
Her hair is just below her waist,	1. Appearance
and she keeps it in a pony tail.	1. Appearance
She plays the recorder	15. Achievements and Skills
and is good at her school work.	14. Intellectual Aptitudes and Abilities
Stephanie is good at the recorder but is in a group below but she could not help that as she was	33. Irrelevant and Unclassifiable
away when we took our test to get into a higher group.	4. Actual Incident

III. Coding Reliability

As we have seen, the value of a set of content categories depends upon the extent to which statements can be assigned to them with high inter-judge and intra-judge reliability. Inter-judge reliability was assessed by comparing three judges' categorization of the 989 statements used in the development of the system. The three judges were the principal investigator, a postgraduate psychology student, and a final-year psychology honours student. There was 85·8 per cent and 92·4 per cent agreement between the investigator and each of the other judges and 84·3 per cent agreement between the other two judges. Overall agreement between the three categorizations was 82·6 per cent. No doubt, practice and discussion between judges would lead to improvements on these figures.

Intra-judge reliability was assessed by comparing two separate codings by the principal investigator of the sixty-four descriptions used to assess the reliability of coding statements—see Chapter 6. There was 81·8 per cent agreement when the interval between codings was two years. This figure is less than those given above because the descriptions had to be divided into statements before they could be categorized; so unreliability in dividing into statements was added to unreliability in categorizing into types of statement. Nevertheless, these studies indicate that written impressions can be coded into statements and categorized with a satisfactory degree of reliabiliy and consistency. It should be noted that the effect of unreliability is to reduce the likelihood of detecting significant differences and associations. Those that are detected are so, as it were, *in spite of* imperfect reliability.

IV. Results

The effects of the between-subject variables (Age, Sex and Intelligence of Subject) and within-subject variables (Sex, Age and Like/Dislike of the Stimulus Person) upon frequency of usage of the categories were examined by nonparametric methods. These were used because the distributions of some of the categories were skewed on account of low frequencies of occurrence. In the case of the between-subject variables, the frequencies of usage of each catgeory were summed across all eight stimulus persons and the scores so obtained dichotomized at the median; the resulting contingency tables were analysed by means of a χ^2 test. The scores in each category were also expressed as a proportion of the total number of statements used, thus controlling for individual differencies in fluency. The proportions were dichotomized at the median and the resulting contingency tables were again examined by means of a χ^2 test.

The effects of the within-subject variables were examined using the Friedman two-way analysis of variance for ranks—see Siegel (1956). The frequencies for each category were summed across the four stimulus persons for each level of the variable and each total frequency was expressed as a proportion of the total number of statements applied to the four stimulus persons, thus controlling for fluency.

The analysis of the effects of the six main variables on each of the thirty-three content categories involved a total of 297 individual nonparametric tests. There is a danger, therefore, that a number of differences might be accepted as significant when they are in fact due to chance. In order to reduce this error to a minimum, a more stringent level of significance was specified before the analyses were attempted. Only those findings which were significant at the 0·01 level or less were accepted. This does mean, of course, that a number of null hypotheses will be accepted when they are in fact false; this type of error, however, seems preferable to the former.

A. Between-subject Variables

1. Effects of Age of Subject. Table 5 gives the results of analyses using a χ^2 test to examine the effects of age on the frequency and proportion of each category. Chronological age had a significant effect on twenty of the thirty-three content categories. In the case of those categories where frequency of usage varied significantly with age, the proportion was also significant and vice versa. The frequency of occurrence of each category for each age group is given in Table 6. Table 7 shows the proportion of statements occurring in each category. As can be seen from Table 6, the 320 subjects used a total of 23 026 statements to describe 2560 persons. The most frequently used category was Specific Behavioural Consistencies (10), and the most infrequently used category, apart from Irrelevant and Unclassifiable Facts and Ideas (33), was Life History (6). The relationships between category usage and age are summarized below. Some categories decrease in frequency with age, some increase in frequency with age, and in others the relationship tends to be curvilinear.

Categories showing a decrease with age:

2. General Information and Identity
3. Routine Habits and Activities
5. Possessions

31. Family and Kinship
33. Irrelevant and Unclassifiable Facts and Ideas

Categories showing an increase with age:

9. General Personality Attributes
10. Specific Behavioural Consistencies
18. Beliefs, Attitudes and Values
19. Stimulus Person's Attitudes towards Himself
22. Reputation
24. Effects upon, and Relations with, Others
25. Other People's Behaviour towards the Stimulus Person
26. Relations with Opposite Sex
28. Subject's Opinion of, and Behaviour towards, the Stimulus Person
30. Comparison with Others
32. Collateral Facts and Ideas

Categories showing a curvilinear relationship:

7. Contemporary Social Circumstances
13. Expressive Behaviour
16. Preferences and Aversions
20. Evaluations

There was a decrease with age in the use of categories containing statements about General Information and Identity (2), Routine Habits and Activities (3), Possessions (5), Family and Kinship (31), and Irrelevant and Unclassifiable (33). The first four of these describe some of the more peripheral or obvious aspects of the person; they account for 33·6 per cent of statements made by 7-year-old children, but only for 9·2 per cent of those made by 14-year-olds, and 10·0 per cent of those made by 15-year-olds. In each case approximately half of each percentage is accounted for by category 2 (General Information and Identity), that is by statements referring to name, age, sex, residence and so on. The greatest change in categories 2, 3, 5 and 31 occurred between the ages of 7 and 8 years, since they account for only 17·2 per cent of statements in 8-year-olds—approximately half that of 7-year-olds.

Another category that is used with decreasing frequency as age increases is 33 (Irrelevant and Unclassifiable Facts and Ideas). This category comprises mainly statements that relate to people, objects, or events not connected with the stimulus person. These statements constitute 2·7 per cent of the total in 7-year-olds but only 0·5 and 0·9 per cent, respectively, in 14- and 15-year-old subjects.

Table 5. Effects of age of subject on the frequency and proportion of different kinds of statement used to describe all stimulus persons

Section	Contents Category	Chi-squared values for: Frequency	Proportion
I. Objective information	1. Appearance	9·26	11·62
	2. General information and identity	28·19 †	34·40 †
	3. Routine habits and activities	37·82 †	37·82 †
	4. Actual incidents	8·00	8·20
	5. Possessions	35·69 †	35·69 †
II. Contemporary and historical circumstances	6. Life history	9·71	9·71
	7. Contemporary social circumstances	62·16 †	62·16 †
	8. Physical condition	10·86	10·86
III. Personal characteristics and behavioural consistencies	9. General personality attributes	64·43 †	54·80 †
	10. Specific behavioural consistencies	61·19 †	51·89 †
	11. Motivation and arousal	16·58	16·58
	12. Orientation	17·37	17·37
	13. Expressive behaviour	32·08 †	28·80 †
IV. Aptitudes and achievements	14. Intellectual aptitudes and abilities	17·82	17·82
	15. Achievements and skills	16·38	16·38
V. Interests and preferences	16. Preferences and aversions	28·21 †	29·56 †
	17. Interests and hobbies	16·63	16·63
VI. Attitudes and beliefs	18. Beliefs, attitudes and values	79·60 †	79·60 †
	19. Stimulus person's opinions and attitudes towards himself	63·58 †	63·58 †
VII. Evaluations	20. Evaluations	21·20 *	24·13 *
VIII. Social factors	21. Social roles	8·07	8·07
	22. Reputation	19·71 *	19·71 *
	23. Friendships and playmates	10·83	10·83
	24. Effects upon, and relations with, others	33·07 †	33·07 †
	25. Other people's behaviour towards the stimulus person	19·20 *	19·20 *
	26. Relations with opposite sex	26·61 †	26·61 †
IX. Subject—other relations	27. Mutual interaction	14·48	11·09
	28. Subject's opinion of, and behaviour towards, the stimulus person	27·11 †	24·40 *
X. Comparisons against standards	29. Comparison with self	17·28	17·28
	30. Comparison with others	23·52 *	23·52 *
XI. Family and kinship	31. Family and kinship	31·74 †	38·29 †
XII. Illustration, corroboration and explanation	32. Collateral facts and ideas	44·80 †	44·80 †
XIII. Residue	33. Irrelevant and unclassifiable facts and ideas	28·66 †	28·66 †

(* $p < 0.01$ and † $p < 0.001$ with 7 d. f.)

Table 6. Frequency of occurrence of each content category for all stimulus persons at each age level

Content category	7,10	8,10	9,10	10,10	12,4	13,2	14,3	15,3	Total
1. Appearance	307	107	236	153	223	153	198	127	1504
2. General information and identity	361	227	270	188	297	226	159	194	1922
3. Routine habits and activities	35	30	31	14	12	11	5	6	144
4. Actual incidents	96	97	135	127	144	146	106	123	974
5. Possessions	140	65	103	53	54	24	26	20	485
6. Life history	12	7	6	6	6	11	16	8	72
7. Contemporary social circumstances	18	11	6	4	11	12	20	24	106
8. Physical condition	15	12	12	14	15	21	19	9	117
9. General personality attributes	104	330	299	419	340	512	545	438	2987
10. Specific behavioural consistencies	150	479	306	393	428	592	532	577	3457
11. Motivation and arousal	5	9	8	4	15	10	13	21	85
12. Orientation	2	5	3	11	7	14	16	18	76
13. Expressive behaviour	18	57	79	105	66	73	68	59	525
14. Intellectual aptitudes and abilities	63	91	91	59	21	36	40	28	429
15. Achievements and skills	34	98	99	92	44	31	29	28	455
16. Preferences and aversions	60	143	168	167	109	105	71	79	902
17. Interests and hobbies	19	39	62	49	46	41	33	34	323
18. Beliefs, attitudes and values	0	2	1	3	18	18	38	42	122
19. Stimulus person's opinions and attitudes towards himself	1	9	18	11	37	27	72	40	215
20. Evaluations	186	285	244	254	175	236	234	142	1756
21. Social roles	54	66	72	41	68	26	36	45	408
22. Reputation	9	19	15	17	37	40	43	33	212
23. Friendships and playmates	29	45	31	22	18	24	22	24	215
24. Effect upon, and relations with, others	2	13	23	15	20	41	31	38	184
25. Other people's behaviour towards the stimulus person	4	32	17	10	17	24	19	22	145
26. Relations with opposite sex	1	15	11	12	39	34	32	18	162
27. Mutual interactions	200	128	160	173	253	197	174	258	1543
28. Subject's opinion of, and behaviour towards, the stimulus person	89	178	120	175	233	154	248	193	1390
29. Comparison with self	19	7	16	12	17	26	32	20	149
30. Comparison with others	2	14	25	25	26	28	25	19	164
31. Family and kinship	261	180	181	106	136	103	96	66	1129
32. Collateral facts and ideas	11	41	26	26	48	63	99	70	384
33. Irrelevant and unclassifiable facts and ideas	64	78	39	22	27	14	16	25	285
Total	2371	2919	2913	2782	3007	3073	3113	2848	23 026

Table 7. Percentage frequency of occurrence of each content category for all stimulus persons at each age level

Content category	Age								Mean
	7,10	8,10	9,10	10,10	12,4	13,2	14,3	15,3	
1. Appearance	12·95	3·67	8·10	5·50	7·42	4·98	6·36	4·46	6·81
2. General information and identity	15·23	7·78	9·27	6·76	9·88	7·35	5·11	6·81	8·52
3. Routine habits and activities	1·48	1·03	1·06	0·50	0·40	0·36	0·16	0·21	0·65
4. Actual incidents	4·05	3·32	4·63	4·57	4·79	4·75	3·41	4·32	4·23
5. Possessions	5·90	2·23	3·54	1·91	1·80	0·78	0·84	0·70	2·21
6. Life history	0·51	0·24	0·21	0·22	0·20	0·36	0·51	0·28	0·32
7. Contemporary social circumstances	0·76	0·38	0·21	0·14	0·37	0·39	0·64	0·84	0·47
8. Physical condition	0·63	0·41	0·41	0·50	0·50	0·68	0·61	0·32	0·51
9. General personality attributes	4·39	11·31	10·26	15·06	11·31	16·66	17·51	15·38	12·74
10. Specific behavioural consistencies	6·33	16·40	10·50	14·13	14·23	19·26	17·09	20·26	14·78
11. Motivation and arousal	0·21	0·31	0·27	0·14	0·50	0·33	0·42	0·74	0·37
12. Orientation	0·08	0·17	0·10	0·40	0·24	0·46	0·51	0·63	0·32
13. Expressive behaviour	0·76	1·95	2·71	3·77	2·19	2·38	2·18	2·07	2·18
14. Intellectual aptitudes and abilities	2·66	3·12	3·12	2·12	0·70	1·17	1·28	0·98	1·89
15. Achievements and skills	1·43	3·36	3·40	3·31	1·46	1·01	0·93	0·98	1·99
16. Preferences and aversions	2·11	4·90	5·77	6·00	3·62	3·42	2·28	2·77	3·86
17. Interests and hobbies	0·80	1·34	2·13	1·76	1·53	1·33	1·06	1·19	1·39
18. Beliefs, attitudes and values	0·00	0·07	0·03	0·11	0·60	0·59	1·22	1·47	0·51
19. Stimulus person's opinions and attitudes towards himself	0·04	0·31	0·62	0·40	1·23	0·88	2·31	1·40	0·90
20. Evaluations	7·84	9·76	8·74	9·13	5·82	7·68	7·52	4·99	7·69
21. Social roles	2·28	2·26	2·47	1·47	2·26	0·85	1·16	1·58	1·79
22. Reputation	0·38	0·65	0·51	0·61	1·23	1·30	1·38	1·16	0·90
23. Friendships and playmates	1·22	1·54	1·06	0·79	0·60	0·78	0·71	0·84	0·94
24. Effect upon, and relations with, others	0·84	0·45	0·79	0·54	0·67	1·33	0·99	1·33	0·87

Table 7. — *Continued*

Content category	Age								Mean
	7,10	8,10	9,10	10,10	12,4	13,2	14,3	15,3	
25. Other people's behaviour towards the stimulus person	0·17	1·10	0·58	0·36	0·57	0·78	0·61	0·77	0·62
26. Relations with opposite sex	0·04	0·51	0·38	0·43	1·30	1·11	1·03	0·63	0·68
27. Mutual interactions	8·44	4·39	5·49	6·22	8·41	6·41	5·59	9·06	6·75
28. Subject's opinion of, and behaviour towards, the stimulus person	3·75	6·10	4·12	6·29	7·75	5·01	7·97	6·78	5·97
29. Comparison with self	0·80	0·24	0·55	0·43	0·57	0·85	1·03	0·70	0·65
30. Comparison with others	0·08	0·48	0·86	0·90	0·86	0·91	0·61	0·67	0·67
31. Family and kinship	11·01	6·17	6·21	3·81	4·52	3·35	3·08	2·32	5·06
32. Collateral facts and ideas	0·46	1·40	0·89	0·93	1·60	2·05	3·18	2·46	1·62
33. Irrelevant and unclassifiable facts and ideas	2·70	2·67	1·33	0·79	0·90	0·46	0·51	0·88	1·28
Total	100·33	100·02	100·32	100·00	100·03	100·01	99·80	99·98	100·14

There was increased use with age of those categories relating to Personal Characteristics (9), Behaviour Consistencies (10), Attitudes and Beliefs (18), Social Relationships (19, 22, 24, 25, 26, 28), Comparisons with Others (30) and Collateral Facts and Ideas (32). The analyses of central statements presented in Chapter 7 revealed a marked increase with age in the use of 'central', that is psychological, statements. The present analysis shows that in 7-year-old children, categories 9 and 10 comprise 11·8 per cent of the total, this increased to 30·1 per cent in 8-year-olds and 39·1 per cent in 15-year-olds.

Closer examination of General Personality Attributes (9) and Specific Behavioural Consistencies (10) sheds light on the development of 'psychological' construing since the majority of 'central' statements are accounted for by these two categories. Category 9 accounts for 4·4 per cent of statements in 7-year-olds, 11·3 per cent in 8-year-olds, 17·5 per cent in 14-year-olds, and 15·4 per cent in 15-year-olds. The corresponding percentages for category 10 are 16·4, 6·3, 17·0, and 20·3. This was the most frequent category overall. Thus the bulk of 'psychological' or 'central' statements consisted of traits, general habits and specific interpersonal responses. Items in category 11 (Motivation and Arousal) and category 12 (Orientation) were largely absent from the descriptions, especially from those of the younger subjects; they constituted only 0·3 per cent in 7-year-olds, and 1·4 per cent in 15-year-olds. The use of these categories did not increase significantly with age as was expected, although the chi-squared values approached the significance level specified and could be regarded as significant at the 0·02 level.

The increased psychological sophistication of the older subjects was reflected by their interest in the stimulus person's attitudes and beliefs about persons and things, and about himself. The two categories dealing with attitudinal statements—category 18 (Beliefs, Attitudes and Values) and 19 (Stimulus Person's Attitudes towards Himself)—constituted 0·04 per cent of all statements made by 7-year-olds and 3·5 and 2·9 per cent of those made by 14- and 15-year-olds, respectively. It was only in adolescence that these categories were used relatively frequently—reflecting perhaps the adolescent's concern with religious and political values and his search for a relevant value system. Category 19 (Stimulus Person's Attitude towards Himself) was used more frequently to describe disliked than to describe liked persons. Some statements in this category —for example, 'He thinks he is clever'—are intentionally sarcastic, others may be subtle methods of making derogatory comments about the other person while at the same time avoiding culpability for doing so by assigning the causal locus of the statement to the other person rather than to the self. Such statements can serve an 'expressive' function in revealing the writer's feelings and opinions in a more socially desirable manner than would be the case with outright derogatory statements—see Smith et al. (1956) for an account of the psychodynamics of opinion expression.

Increased age brings increased concern with the other person's social relationships. Young children, of course, were interested in the stimulus person's family and his friends and playmates, but the statements they made were limited to specifying the number of persons in his family or who his friends were, whereas older children were more concerned with the nature of the stimulus person's relationships with other people, with other people's opinion of him, and with their reactions towards him. Thus, there was an increase with age in the use of category 22 (Reputation), category 24 (Effect upon, and Relations with, Others), category 25 (Other People's Behaviour towards the Stimulus Person) and category 26 (Relations with the Opposite Sex). These categories account for 1·4 per cent of statements in 7-year-olds and 4·0 and 3·9 per cent in 14- and 15-year-olds, respectively. The use of these categories by older subjects shows a marked change from the egocentric attitude of younger children whose main interest was in the other person's behaviour towards the subjects themselves rather than his effects upon others and other people's opinions of him. It reveals a growing realization that the other person's social relationships and reputation are important, both in themselves and because they provide evidence relevant to understanding his personal qualities. Thus, the older child is prepared to draw upon other people's experiences in his assessment. Statements about Relations with the Opposite Sex, category 26, which were made most frequently by adolescents, seem to reflect a change in interests and orientation, and demonstrate the effects of motivation on the contents of impressions.

Older subjects not only referred more often to other people's behaviour and attitudes towards the stimulus person but also referred more often to Subject's Opinion of, and Behaviour towards, the Stimulus Person (category 28). This suggests that there was at least a limited comprehension of the reciprocity which characterizes interpersonal relationships— a growing realization that the behaviour of another person is partly determined by the behaviour of the observer. This development indicates that the older children understand (or have a practical grasp of) some of the laws and processes governing social interaction. The use of category 28 also suggests that there was some concern for objectivity in communication—a need on the part of the older subjects to make their own position and viewpoint clear.

The superior cognitive skills of the older subjects were reflected in their increased use of category 30 (Comparison with Others) and category 32 (Collateral Facts and Ideas). The comparisons made by the younger subjects frequently involved peripheral attributes, for example, 'He is the tallest in our class', whereas those made by older subjects usually concerned more central qualities, for example, 'She does not appreciate a joke as much as most people.' The use of illustrative, corroborative and explanatory material to account for or strengthen other assertions showed —as did the use of category 28 (Subject's Opinion of, and Behaviour towards, the Stimulus Person) that the older subjects recognized, if only implicitly, that their descriptions were personal viewpoints liable to differ from those of other observers. Thus, attempts were made to justify their conclusions and to illustrate and support their statements. The ability to make statements like some of those in categories 28, 30 and 32 reveals that, among older children, thinking has become reflexive, that is they can reflect upon the products of their own cognitive processes.

The third set of categories shows a curvilinear relationship with age. These are: category 7 (Contemporary Social Circumstances), category 13 (Expressive Behaviour) and category 16 (Preferences and Aversions).

Category 7 was used relatively infrequently by all age groups. In 7-year-olds, statements in this category constituted 0·76 per cent of the total, decreasing to 0·14 per cent in 10-year-olds and then increasing to 0·84 per cent in 15-year-olds. These changes are explained by a change in the types of statement made by children of different ages. The contemporary social circumstances referred to by young children were usually relatively concrete statements often specifying limits or constraints placed upon the person, for example, 'He has to stay in at playtime', 'His mother won't let him go on the shore'. Those made by older children were more subtle, describing current circumstances which have implications for adjustment and the expression of personal qualities, for example, 'He is very generous although he can't really afford to be', 'She is more or less ruled by her mother.' Statements of the first type are not directly relevant to the other's personality (although they help to account for his behaviour), hence they are used less frequently as the child's concept of personality develops, while the latter type of statement is directly relevant and hence used with increasing frequency, since, in general, older children exhibit an increasing awareness of the importance of psychological (central) processes.

Category 13 (Expressive Behaviour) and category 16 (Preferences and Aversions) show the opposite type of relationship with age to that of category 7. They were used relatively infrequently in 7-year-olds, 0·76 and 2·1 per cent for categories 13 and 16 respectively. Frequency of usage then increased to 3·8 and 6·0 per cent respectively at the age of 10 and then decreased to 2·1 and 2·8 per cent respectively at the age of 15. These age changes are possibly explained in terms of a shift, with increasing age, from cues which are merely salient (and not very useful) to cues which (though not very salient) are more useful in understanding the person and predicting his behaviour. The external or peripheral cues which figure so prominently in the descriptions of 7-year-olds are poor predictors; they are gradually discarded as the child overcomes the limitations of his egocentrism and learns which cues are more useful. Among the more noticeable and readily communicated features of a person, apart from his appearance and identity, are his likes and dislikes and the mannerisms and peculiarities of gait and speech. These attract attention because they are fairly obvious and seem to express personal qualities. Hence, in the earlier phases of psychological development, they are used with increasing frequency. Like appearance and identity, however, these cues are also relatively poor guides to understanding the other person. Hence, they get referred to less often as more satisfactory guides become available in association with increased intelligence, experience and the development of 'psychological' concepts and vocabulary.

Evaluations, category 20, figure in the descriptions of most subjects: 7·7 per cent of the total number of statements were outright evaluations. The use of evaluations showed a statistically significant relationship with age, although the relationship was somewhat erratic. Evaluations accounted for 7·8 per cent of statements made by 7-year-olds and 9·8 per cent of those made by 8-year-olds. Such statements then decreased to 5·8 per cent in 12-year-old children. Thereafter, the proportions increased to 7·7 per cent in 13-year-olds and 7·5 per cent in 14-year-olds, only to decrease to 5·0 per cent in 15-year-olds. The number of evaluations made by each age group was relatively constant except that they occurred less frequently in 7-, 12- and 15-year-old subjects. Even a *post hoc* explanation of such an age trend is difficult to formulate, but assuming the relationship is reliable, it might be the case that the increasing use of evaluations in the younger age groups reflects an increasing sensitivity to personal qualities. The increased frequency of evaluative statements in young adolescents, on the other hand, may reflect a growing concern with morality.

A number of categories showed no significant relationship with age but were used relatively frequently by all age groups. Category 1 (Appearance) was used by all age groups, in spite of instructions to avoid such information, and constituted 6·8 per cent of all statements. It was used most frequently by the 7-year-old subjects and accounted for 13·0 per cent of all statements in that age group. Category 4 (Actual Incidents) accounted for 4·2 per cent of all statements and was used equally by all groups. The two categories dealing with Aptitudes and Achievements, categories 14 and 15 respectively, accounted for 3·9 per cent of all statements. Although the frequency of use of these categories did not show a significant overall relationship with age, they seemed to be used more frequently by younger subjects than by older subjects. In the four younger age groups (7 to 10 years), these two categories accounted for 5·6 per cent of all statements, but in the four older groups (12 to 15 years), for only 2·1 per cent. Category 14 (Intellectual Aptitudes and Abilities) was used significantly more frequently by the 7- to 10-year-old subjects than by the 12- to 15-year-olds ($\chi^2 = 9.83$, d.f. = 1, $p < 0.01$). In the case of category 15 (Achievements and Skills) a similar relationship held ($\chi^2 = 7.03$, d.f. = 1, $p < 0.01$).

References to Social Roles, category 21, accounted for only 1·8 per cent of all statements. References to Mutual Interactions (between subject and stimulus person), category 27, occurred relatively frequently and accounted for 6·8 per cent of all statements. Items in this category usually referred to the things they did together and to their frequency of interaction, but in older subjects more reference was made to how well they got on together and what situations produced disharmony.

We should like to remind readers that without the 'negative set' induced by the test instructions, statements about Appearance (category 1) would have swamped the more subtle low frequency statements.

2. Effects of Sex of Subject. The sex of the subjects had few effects as regards the frequency of use of the different categories of statement. Table 8 indicates that only four categories showed significant sex differences. Girls used significantly more General Personality Attributes (category 9); they made more references to the Stimulus Person's Opinions and Attitudes towards Himself (category 19) than did boys; they also used more Evaluations (category 20) and were more interested in Family and Kinship relations (category 31). Girls, however, were more fluent than boys—see Chapter 6—so that some of these effects could be attributed to increased fluency. When differences in fluency were eliminated by using proportions rather than raw frequencies, significant differences were found only in categories 19 and 20. It was suggested previously that making statements about the Stimulus Person's Opinions and Attitudes towards Himself (category 19) could be a subtle way of expressing an unfavourable attitude. Thus it might be that girls are more likely to express indirect verbal hostility towards a person than are boys. On the other hand, it might be that girls are, on average, more aware than are boys of inner-personal factors such as the self-concept.

3. Effects of Intelligence. None of the categories showed significant differences in raw frequencies between the two intelligence groups—see Table 8. When fluency differences were allowed for, however, it was found that the 'higher' intelligence group made a higher proportion of statements about General Personality Attributes (category 9) as compared with the 'lower' intelligence group who made a greater proportion of statements about Appearance (category 1) and Family and Kinship (category 31). These findings suggest that it requires a higher level of intelligence to form impressions about personality attributes, that is, that such concepts are more abstract and cognitively complex than concepts relating to appearance and family.

B. Within-subject Variables

The results of a Friedman two-way analysis of variance method applied to within-subject differences in the proportion of statements in each category are shown in Table 8.

Table 8. Effects of sex of subject, intelligence of subject, and stimulus person variables on the frequency and proportion of statements in thirty-three content categories

Content category	Chi-squared values				Friedman values		
	Sex		Intelligence		Sex of stimulus person	Age of stimulus person	Like/dislike of stimulus person
	Frequency	Proportion	Frequency	Proportion			
1. Appearance	0·05	0·01	6·06	7·81*	0·80	2·11	7·81*
2. General information and identity	1·56	0·05	1·04	0·05	1·13	42·78†	2·81
3. Routine habits and activities	0·38	0·38	4·81	4·81	0·00	2·45	0·25
4. Actual incidents	0·00	0·50	4·06	5·00	1·38	22·58†	33·15†
5. Possessions	0·61	0·61	2·11	2·11	0·11	30·01	0·61
6. Life history	0·53	0·53	3·61	3·61	0·53	0·45	0·08
7. Contemporary social circumstances	1·26	1·26	0·39	0·39	0·53	0·08	0·38
8. Physical condition	2·23	2·23	0·00	0·00	1·25	0·53	3·05
9. General personality attributes	9·81*	6·05	5·00	9·80*	5·51	0·00	8·13*
10. Specific behavioural consistencies	2·13	1·01	1·02	5·51	1·13	1·80	23·65†
11. Motivation and arousal	1·43	1·43	2·39	2·39	0·03	2·81	0·01
12. Orientation	0·55	0·55	2·66	2·66	0·45	0·20	0·00
13. Expressive behaviour	1·87	0·11	0·45	0·31	0·50	0·20	0·01
14. Intellectual aptitudes and abilities	0·20	0·20	1·76	1·76	0·25	48·83†	15·31†
15. Achievements and skills	0·63	0·63	2·51	2·51	3·00	7·20*	24·75†
16. Preferences and aversions	0·32	0·00	0·01	0·00	4·28	14·88†	35·11†
17. Interests and hobbies	1·02	1·02	2·13	2·13	7·50*	3·61	24·20†
18. Beliefs, attitudes and values	0·02	0·02	4·94	4·94	0·11	1·13	0·70
19. Simulus person's opinions of, and attitudes towards, himself	8·42*	8·42*	0·66	0·66	0·03	5·51	37·13†
20. Evaluations	16·20†	17·11†	6·05	5·51	1·01	25·31†	0·01
21. Social roles	0·34	0·34	0·34	0·34	19·50†	73·15†	7·50*
22. Reputation	5·37	5·37	0·05	0·05	0·45	0·61	3·83
23. Friendships and playmates	0·05	0·05	0·05	0·05	0·20	7·81*	2·45
24. Effects upon, and relations with, others	2·97	2·97	2·97	2·97	0·01	2·28	19·50†
25. Other people's behaviour towards the stimulus person	1·75	1·75	1·75	1·75	0·11	3·83	3·20
26. Relations with opposite sex	0·13	0·13	0·13	0·13	0·05	16·65†	1·65
27. Mutual interactions	4·54	4·51	5·55	3·61	0·20	0·13	30·01†

Table 8. —*Continued*

Content category	Chi-squared values				Friedman values		
	Sex		Intelligence		Sex of stimulus person	Age of stimulus person	Like/ dislike of stimulus person
	Fre- quency	Pro- portion	Fre- quency	Pro- portion			
28. Subject's opinion of, and behaviour towards, the stimulus person	1·51	0·45	1·01	0·80	4·75	0·38	24·75†
29. Comparison with self	4·14	4·14	0·36	0·36	0·00	11·63†	8·78*
30. Comparison with others	0·67	0·67	0·34	0·34	0·00	2·99	0·11
31. Family and kinship	7·85*	4·51	2·83	7·81*	7·81	52·81†	4·05
32. Collateral facts and ideas	0·46	0·46	6·17	6·17	0·31	0·45	33·15†
33. Irrelevant and unclassifiable facts and ideas	0·66	0·66	3·05	3·05	0·90	1·80	0·38

$* p < 0.01$ $† p < 0.001$ with 1 d.f.

1. Effect of the Sex of the Stimulus Person. With fluency held constant, the sex of the stimulus person had a significant effect on only three of the thirty-three categories. The proportion of statements referring to Interests and Hobbies (category 17) was higher for male stimulus persons than for females. Category 21 (Social Roles) was also used more frequently to describe males than females; however, more reference was made to Family and Kinship (category 31) in describing female stimulus persons.

2. Effect of the Age of the Stimulus Person. The age of the stimulus person had a significant effect on the proportion of statements in twelve of the thirty-three categories. Five categories referred more to adults than to children :

2. General Information and Identity
4. Actual Incidents
5. Possessions
21. Social Roles
31. Family and Kinship

These are exactly the kind of things one would expect to be prominent in children's impressions of adults.

Seven categories referred more to children than to adults :

14. Intellectual Aptitudes and Abilities
15. Achievements and Skills
16. Preferences and Aversions
20. Evaluations
23. Friendships and Playmates
26. Relations with Opposite Sex
29. Comparison with Self

These, by contrast, reveal the salient features in children's impressions of children, and the result seems to support the expectations of common sense.

3. Effect of Like/Dislike of the Stimulus Person. Like/dislike had a significant effect on fifteen content categories. Eight were used more often to describe liked than disliked persons :

9. General Personality Attributes
14. Intellectual Aptitudes and Abilities
15. Achievements and Skills
16. Preferences and Aversions
17. Interests and Hobbies
21. Social Roles
27. Mutual Interactions
29. Comparison with Self

Seven were used more often to describe disliked than liked persons :

1. Appearance
4. Actual Incidents
10. Specific Behavioural Consistencies
19. Stimulus Person's Opinions of, and Attitudes towards, Himself
24. Effects upon, and Relations with, Others
28. Subject's Opinion of, and Behaviour towards, other Stimulus Person
32. Collateral Facts and Ideas

Thus, whereas the children's impressions of liked others refer to favourable, or at least neutral, topics, those of disliked others seem to contain a relatively large proportion of justificatory and evidential material; and, again, this is what one would expect.

V. Discussion

A. *Age Differences and Cognitive Development*

The relatively large developmental trends obtained in the present investigations were not obtained in all other studies. Yarrow and Campbell (1963), for instance, found no age difference in the use of their categories, perhaps because they studied a more limited age range : 8 to 13 years. Relatively little change over this age range was observed in the present study. A contributory factor can be found in the content categories used by Yarrow and Campbell. In general, their categories referred to varieties of interpersonal behaviour exhibited by the other person, for example, aggression, submission, conformity, and so on, rather than to the conceptual categories into which statements can be sorted, for example, habits, traits, and so on. Apparently, the varieties of behaviour recognized by children change little with age, whereas the conceptual categories which enable children to construe the behaviour of others do change.

Age changes in the use of categories reveal that the number of dimensions along which the child can conceptualize other persons grows throughout childhood, and this produces an improvement in the ability to differentiate between different people with regard to the same characteristic, and between different characteristics in the same person. The greatest increase in differentiation was observed between the ages of 7 and 8 years; thereafter, the rate of change was generally much slower. Frequently, the differences between the 7- and 8-year-old groups were greater than the differences between 8- and 15-year-olds. This is perhaps the most important finding of all; it suggests that the eighth year is a critical period in the developmental psychology of person perception. This apparent growth spurt is paralleled by similar trends in other areas of cognitive development.

The strategy used to construe the behaviour of persons varies with age. In general, two broad strategies are suggested : (a) under the age of 7 or 8 years, children adopt a relatively concrete approach, focusing upon 'overt' rather than 'covert' qualities. Consequently, descriptions by 7-year-old children consist mainly of statements about appearance, identity, possessions and family. Older children, on the other hand, adopt a more abstract approach. They focus upon 'covert' qualities—striving to discover consistencies and regularities in overt behaviour, and using concepts referring to various inner personal factors such as dispositions, values and beliefs.

The change of strategy in impression formation between the ages of

7 and 8 years is probably a consequence of the child largely relinquishing his egocentrism and developing operational modes of thinking. As he becomes capable of inferential thought, he integrates events separated in time and finds underlying regularities, similarities and consistencies in the other person's behaviour. He thus forms a concept of the other person which is not dominated by the immediate and concrete stimulus situation. To some extent, he can 'take the role' of the other person, and see things from his viewpoint. Beyond the age of 8 years, however, impression formation, as revealed by the present content analysis, changes remarkably little. It may be that for some time after a change of cognitive strategy has occurred in impression formation, further growth serves merely to consolidate the new strategy. As will be seen in Chapter 10, however, the *organization* of impressions does change considerably in older children, as a second phase in development.

The development in children of a cognitive strategy which enables them to impose a 'pattern of meaning' on the behaviour of other people can be seen in terms of Kelly's (1955) concept of man the scientist—construing, anticipating and influencing events in his environment. Thus cognitive development can be regarded as stimulated by the search for useful predictors of events. The problem facing the young child is how to establish a set of constructs that have descriptive and predictive potential when applied to the behaviour of persons. The development of this system of conceptual constructs is stimulated and facilitated by the acquisition of reflexive thought. When thought becomes reflexive, ideas and experiences are examined to rule out inconsistencies. Consequently, predictions are compared with the actual outcomes, and those categorizations which give rise to confirmed predictions tend to be adopted, and those which do not tend to be rejected. The system develops by a continual process of validation and invalidation of its elements; the use of a construct is reinforced by the fulfilment of a prediction derived from it. In person perception, categorizing a person in terms of psychological, as opposed to physical, qualities enables the perceiver to exercise greater predictive control. And, as in other kinds of cognition, abstract and general forms of reasoning are usually more economical and more successful than concrete and particular forms, although there is some risk of loss of contact with the facts, for example in the failure to anchor an abstraction firmly to empirical data, which results in the abstract statement becoming less open to rebuttal and therefore less meaningful. It should be noted that even at a professional level, one not infrequently finds people using psychologically meaningless (empty or misleading) concepts—a great many Freudian and Jungian concepts, for example, lack satisfactory empirical grounds, and some terms associated with projective testing are similar in this respect.

The finding that statements referring to behavioural consistencies and personality traits are used with increasing frequency at later ages, whereas statements dealing with appearance, identity, family and possessions (which are poor predictive cues) are used decreasingly with age, illustrates the shift from a concrete/particular to an abstract/general mode of cognizing others. Of course, the reflexive and inferential nature of thought that makes the acquisition of a 'psychological' vocabulary possible does not develop independently of the perception of persons. Piaget (see Flavell, 1963) stressed that the emergence of operational thought depends upon repeated interpersonal interactions in which the child is forced by arguments and disagreements to see things from the viewpoint of the other person. In this way, he gradually comes to share with others a common frame of reference—a common grammar and vocabulary for dealing with persons and their behaviour—which provides the basis for consensual validation or public verifiability.

If central or psychological terms are used by younger children, they probably refer to specific qualities as exemplified by statements in category 10 rather than to General Personality Attributes (category 9). Heider (1958) argued that the basic goal of the perceiver is to comprehend the structure of behaviour. The perceiver, in fact, using whatever concepts are at his disposal, imposes a pattern of meaning on the behaviour of the other person and feels that he has identified the underlying structural properties or invariants. These can, of course, be described at different levels of abstraction and generalization. Each level involves the classification of a number of behavioural episodes into a common category. Within the limits imposed by the child's inferential skills, the conceptual level adopted for dealing with a particular situation is, presumably, the one that enables him to act effectively and to predict accurately. It is assumed, therefore, that items in category 10 (Specific Behavioural Consistencies) are used more frequently than items in category 9 (General Personality Attributes) because they are at a lower level of abstraction. They make less demand on the younger child's cognitive capacity, but nevertheless permit him to act effectively. Even when trait names are used by young children, they are usually simple terms closely tied to behaviour, for example, 'kind', 'bad tempered', 'clever'. In younger subjects, the present continuous tense is often used to refer to behavioural tendencies, for example 'He steals', or 'He lies.' These are among the simplest invariances one can apply to human behaviour.

Later in development, these habits are integrated into more abstract invariances, for example 'honest' or 'trustworthy'. Such adjectival terms are arrived at by attributing a common quality to a number of behavioural forms, thus rendering them equivalent in this respect. Hence, they come to function as economical descriptive terms which reduce the work required of memory, simplify cognitive processes, and permit limited predictions. In the early stages, these terms refer to concrete behavioural sequences; it is only later that they become further abstracted and assigned the causal role of internal dispositions or traits with considerable forecasting potential. It is sometimes argued that there are dangers in such hypostatization, unless one continues to distinguish carefully between reasons and causes for behaviour, and between words and things.

The strategy employing central or psychological concepts consisted mainly of using items in category 9 (General Personality Attributes) and category 10 (Specific Behavioural Consistencies). Items in categories 11 (Motivation) and 12 (Orientation) were largely absent, especially from descriptions by younger children. The explanation for this is probably fairly simple. Motivation and orientation are covert psychological processes which can be comprehended only by an observer who can separate cause from effect and distinguish between observation and inference, and who is concerned to find organization and meaning in his experience of others. Young children lack these abilities and can do little more than report what they observe. An additional reason for the relative absence of motivational statements lies in the lack of an adequate vocabulary such as exists for traits. Motivational concepts therefore are either fewer or of a higher order of abstraction or complexity. In general, the layman seems much less interested in motives than does the psychologist. Motivational processes are not easy to discern and statements about them have limited predictive value. For these reasons, adults use motivational statements infrequently except to refer to familiar short-term needs, such as hunger or thirst, or perhaps to enduring motives which are readily inferred, such as ambition and curiosity—these sorts of motivation may even be regarded as personality traits, like 'ambitious' and 'inquiring mind'.

Young children categorize people into those they like and those they do not like and apply vague generalized evaluations to them, such as nice, not nice, nasty, good, horrid. These moralistic judgments appear to be the origins of many of the personality terms used later in childhood, such as well-mannered, polite, likable, honest, selfish. In 7-year-old children, statements in category 20 (Evaluations) occurred more frequently than statements in either category 9 (General Personality Attributes) or category 10 (Specific Behavioural Consistencies). The importance placed upon evaluations by all groups of subjects ties in closely with studies of person perception in adults, especially with studies of trait implications. In fact, the percentage of statements in category 20 underestimates the role of evaluations, since many items coded into categories 9 and 10 were strongly evaluative. The instruction to subjects to describe liked and disliked persons (rather than neutral ones) may have increased the incidence of evaluations because it would be easier and more natural to pass judgment on these more extreme cases. Nevertheless, it seems probable that such statements are used frequently in everyday judgments.

Some of the categories are of interest without being significantly related to age. One of the more important of these is category 1 (Appearance) which was prominent in descriptions from many subjects in spite of the experimenter's instructions to the contrary. The percentage of appearance statements declined with age, but the trend was not statistically significant because there were considerable differences between individual subjects in the use of this category. Appearance plays an important role in most people's impressions, as described in Chapter 2; it serves to introduce and identify the person described and acts as a sort of central core around which other parts of the impression are organized. And this is in spite of the fact that appearance is largely unrelated to psychological qualities. Category 21 (Social Roles) was used surprisingly infrequently. The suggestion by Little (1968) that role constructs constitute a kind of transitional stage in development between peripheral and central constructs was not supported. Most descriptions were contemporary conceptualizations of personality, and little or no reference was made to previous qualities the stimulus person had exhibited or or to other biographical facts, as in Life History (category 6). In general, no great concern was shown in the historical determinants of current behaviour; causal analysis was limited to explanations in terms of contemporary factors. This finding is interesting in so far as it reveals that commonsense lay impressions of persons conform more closely to judicial standards of explanation than to clinical (psychodynamic) standards which seem to stress remote functional and historical links in psychological development.

B. Sex and Intelligence of Subjects

The between-subject variables of sex and intelligence had surprisingly little effect on the kinds of statement made. As stated in Chapter 7, girls made greater use of central statements than did boys mainly because they made significantly greater use of category 9 (General Personality

Attributes). They did not use category 10 Specific Behavioural Consistencies) more than did boys. Consequently, the girls' descriptions reached a higher level of abstraction and generalization than did those of the boys. This might imply that girls are more interested in people and have a better understanding of human behaviour. This suggestion is supported by the fact that girls made more reference to Family and Kinship (category 31) than did boys. The girls' descriptions contained more Evaluations (category 20) and more references to the Stimulus Person's Opinions of, and Attitudes towards, Himself (category 19). Presumably, the greater interest and value placed upon persons by girls, as compared with boys, evokes a strong tendency to make evaluative judgments about people and to use their impressions as a vehicle for the expression of their feelings towards them. As suggested earlier, derogatory opinions in category 19 often represent subtle ways of expressing resentment and hostility. The effect of intelligence on the proportions of statements in the different categories was also small. The superior cognitive skills of the 'higher' intelligence group enabled them to make greater use of abstract judgments, for example, statements in category 9 rather than the more literal statements appropriate to category 10.

C. Stimulus Person Effects

By contrast with inter-subject differences, and as hypothesized in Chapter 5, the effects of the stimulus person variables were considerable. In general, these can be accounted for by reference to the degree of similarity between the observer and the stimulus person, and to the frequency with which they interact. Thus, children appeared to find it easier to describe peers and liked persons than to describe adults and disliked persons, and their descriptions usually showed greater knowledge and understanding of the former. These factors, however, do not explain the observed differences between descriptions of male and female stimulus persons. The suggestion advanced in Chapter 7, to the effect that males are more active, more interesting and more highly valued than females, seems adequate to account for the differences found in the present analysis.

The descriptions of male stimulus persons were shown to be longer than those of female ones, and to contain more central statements. This effect was produced by a slight tendency for subjects to use *all* the categories more frequently when describing males. That is to say, descriptions of male stimulus persons did not emphasize some categories at the expense of others, except for category 17 (Interests and Hobbies) and category 21

(Social Roles), and this merely reflects the social facts. Category 31 (Family and Kinship) was used more frequently when describing female stimulus persons and reflects either the development of sex role expectations (whereby females are more closely associated with home and family than are males) or perhaps lack of other salient information.

The age of the stimulus person had widespread effects on the extent to which the different categories were used. Descriptions of adults were more factual than descriptions of children; they contained more frequent references to General Information and Identity, Actual Incidents, Possessions, Social Roles, and Family and Kinship. This kind of result gives indirect support to the validity of the whole experimental procedure, in that where the external facts are independently verifiable, or not in dispute, as in the case of adult-child differences, the correspondence between written impressions and actual facts increases one's confidence that other aspects of the written impressions, which are not independently verifiable and are in dispute, are equally valid. Thus, the children have formed the impression, correctly, that adults engage in more pursuits, own more things, and occupy a greater number of positions in society than do children. In addition, adult behaviour is often complex and outside the subjects' own personal experience; so they cannot make sense of it as they can make sense of another child's behaviour.

Impressions formed of children were much less stereotyped than those formed of adults, and they showed better discrimination made possible by more frequent interaction and closer similarity between subjects and other children. Subjects were not allowed to describe members of their family. Of course, the relative ease with which children were described in central terms may have been because of more frequent interaction with, rather than because of greater similarity between, the subjects and other children. Bromley (1966a) showed that the incidence of central terms increases with increased contact between subjects and the stimulus person. As the children were asked to describe persons they knew fairly well, it seems probable that both factors—familiarity and similarity— were operating. Comparisons between self and other were most often made when describing children, with the self-concept probably serving as an anchorage point for judgments about others. Hastorf et al. (1958) suggest that there is undoubtedly a close relationship between perception of oneself and the perception of others—see Chapter 12.

Evaluations were used most frequently when describing children, probably because evaluation is an important determinant of behaviour towards peers. Children are often unable to avoid encountering adults, whether they like them or not, since their encounters are frequently initiated by adults and adults place constraints upon them over which children have little control. Interactions with peers are a different matter, for children have more choice about which children they will play with, so that evaluation becomes important. The effects of close and frequent contact with children were revealed by the subjects' considerable knowledge of the stimulus children's friendships and playmates, and their likes and dislikes.

Ability and achievement seem to be important values for children, living as they do in a competitive world where physical and mental skills are important indices of status. As we have already demonstrated (p. 142) this is true particularly of children aged between 7 and 10 years. This period was designated by Erikson (1950) as the age of industry, it is the age in which children acquire many new skills and are obliged to compare their aptitudes and achievements with those of their peers. Judgments of this type (categories 14 and 15) occurred more frequently in descriptions of peers than in descriptions of adults, thus demonstrating a close link between ego-development and person perception.

Like/dislike had a greater effect than any other variable except Age of Subject on the extent to which categories were used. Although descriptions of liked persons did not contain more central statements than did descriptions of disliked persons, there were significant differences in the types of statement used. In general, descriptions of liked persons were more abstract since they contained more Personality Attributes (category 9) and less reference to Specific Behavioural Consistencies (category 10). Descriptions of liked persons also showed greater interest and knowledge than did descriptions of disliked persons. Subjects were more familiar with the liked person's Preferences and Aversions (category 16), his Interests (category 17), and his Social Roles (category 21). Details of Mutual (subject-other) Interaction (category 27) were also given most frequently when describing liked persons, presumably because liking affects frequency of interaction—we actively seek out those we like and avoid those we dislike. Comparisons with Self (category 29) and references to Abilities and Achievements (categories 14 and 15) were also made more frequently when describing liked persons. Subjects usually found it much easier to give positive instances than negative instances; so they found it easy to mention abilities and achievements but relatively difficult to describe disabilities and failures. They also found it easier to describe similarities to the self than differences from the self, this helps to explain why Comparisons with Self were made more frequently when describing children than when describing adults. Consequently, statements about abilities, which have a high value for children, are applied mainly to liked persons.

Descriptions of disliked persons indicated a general lack of interest and were relatively factual. Greater use was made of Appearance (category 1) and Actual Incidents (category 4). Although Evaluations (category 20) were applied equally to liked and disliked persons, descriptions of disliked persons contained more statements about the Subject's Opinion of, and Behaviour towards, the Stimulus Person (category 28). Also, more reference was made to the disliked Stimulus Person's Opinions of, and Attitudes towards, Himself (category 19) and these often seem to operate as disguised derogatory statements. Many subjects found it necessary to corroborate and justify their dislike for the stimulus person; they did so by making use of Collateral Facts and Ideas (category 32).

We have shown that children conceptualize others along many dimensions, and the use of these dimensions is affected as much by stimulus person variables as by subject variables. The effects of different sorts of stimulus person on the contents of impressions constitute some of the more interesting results of this study. They support the argument advanced in Chapters 3 and 5 that more attention should be paid to stimulus person variables and their interaction with subject variables.

We have attempted to separate out effects attributable to the subjects' characteristics from effects attributable to the stimulus persons' characteristics. We have observed systematic effects for both sorts of characteristic. In many respects, the children's performances revealed that the contents and organization of their 'cognitive maps' of other people conformed to a common pattern. Children were sensitive to similar traits, behavioural themes and modes of interacting. They gradually acquire a common grammar and vocabulary to describe persons and their behaviour. These common interests, concepts and words can be explained, no doubt, in terms of a broad similarity of genetic morphology, and a broad similarity of environment—a common culture, a common educational process and, of course, a common pattern of psychobiological development.

CHAPTER 9

Content Analysis III: Children's Use of Trait Names

I. Preview

This chapter contains details of repeated measures analysis of variance of both the number and the proportion of traits used in each description.

Significant age differences and sex differences were found for both measures; within-subject differences attributable to the age and sex of the stimulus persons were also found, together with a number of significant interaction effects. The increase in the use of traits among the older age groups strongly indicates an increase in trait vocabulary. Girls use more traits per description than do boys, for two reasons: (a) their greater trait vocabulary, and (b) their more frequent use of each trait. There are qualitative as well as quantitative aspects to consider in children's use of trait names.

II. Rationale for the Analysis of Trait Names

The descriptive unit that has received most attention in both personality study and person perception research is the 'trait'. There are good reasons for this, and the content analysis in Chapter 8 demonstrated that general and specific traits were used more frequently than any other descriptive category. A trait is a psychological concept which enables an observer to impose a meaningful and an economical construction on a person's behaviour and, if it is a valid assessment, to predict or influence that person's actions. Crandall (1970) has shown that the judged importance of traits is related to their usefulness for anticipating actual behaviour and for inferring other traits. A large number of trait names exist in the English language. Allport and Odbert (1936) listed over 18 000 of them—see also Allport (1937, 1961). With the exception of Cattell (1965), remarkably little effort seems to have been made to follow up the possibilities inherent in this pioneering document; and even at the present time the philosophy and psychology of the language of personality and adjustment remain incredibly neglected topics.

In view of the important role played by traits in impression formation, the analyses of their use presented in Chapter 8 are insufficient in themselves. They demonstrated age and sex differences in the frequency of use of traits, but they did not completely describe the incidence of traits in impressions, for traits were included in more than one content category: Intellectual Aptitudes and Abilities (category 4), Evaluations (category 20) and General Personality Attributes (category 9), all of which contained terms, that is names and phrases, which are normally thought of as 'traits'. The analyses in the previous chapter, moreover, did not deal with interactions between the main variables. To remedy these shortcomings, the use of traits is examined in the present chapter by means of the repeated measures analysis of variance method used previously in Chapters 6 and 7.

III. Analysis of the Number and Proportion of Traits Used in Each Description

A. Hypotheses

The hypotheses tested by this analysis are similar to those examined in the analysis of central statements described in Chapter 7. Briefly, they are as follows:

1. Age of Subject. There should be a significant increase with age in the number and proportion of traits per description because of the increase in inferential and abstract thinking as children grow up.

2. Sex of Subject. There should be a significantly greater use of traits per description by girls as compared with boys, because girls are more aware of psychological (central) factors in human behaviour than are boys.

3. Intelligence of Subject. There should be a significantly greater use of traits per description by the higher intelligence group as compared with the lower intelligence group because of the association between intelligence and the verbal and inferential abilities required in impression formation.

4. Sex of Stimulus Person. There should be a nonsignificant difference between male and female stimulus persons in the mean number and proportion of traits per description if the sexes are equally preferred. There should be a significant 'Sex of Subject × Sex of Stimulus Person' interaction—with subjects using more traits to describe same-sex persons than opposite-sex persons—because the use of traits is facilitated by a high degree of similarity between subject and stimulus person and by a greater frequency of interaction.

5. Age of Stimulus Person. There should be a significantly greater use of traits when describing children than when describing adults, because of the greater similarity between subject and peer and their greater frequency of interaction. There should be a significant 'Age of Subject × Age of Stimulus Person' interaction—with the effect of age of stimulus person decreasing with age of subject—because subject/peer interaction gradually develops into subject/adult interaction.

6. Like/Dislike of Stimulus Person. There should be a significantly greater use of traits in describing liked as compared with disliked persons, because liking and interaction are correlated.

B. Method

The number and proportion of trait names per description were examined in separate six-factor experiments with repeated measures on three factors. The observed frequencies were numerically small—ranging from 0 to 12; so, in order to stabilize variance, a square-root transformation was carried out; the actual formula was: $\sqrt{X} + \sqrt{(X-1)}$ (see Winer, 1962, and Edwards, 1965).

A method is needed to examine whether the significant effects described in the previous section (particularly age and sex differences) are attributable to the greater fluency of older children and girls, or to a difference in attitude and orientation. In the analysis of central statements, this problem was solved by expressing the number of central statements per description as a proportion, and then reanalysing the data. The same method was adopted in this instance, that is the number of traits (or trait phrases) in each description was expressed as a proportion of the total number of statements in that description. These proportions were then adjusted by an angular transformation: $2 \arcsin \sqrt{p}$ (see Winer, 1962).

For the present purposes, a trait was defined simply and objectively in terms of the Allport and Odbert (1936) list of trait names. That is to say, terms corresponding to any listed by Allport and Odbert were scored as traits. Consequently, coding reliability studies are omitted.

C. Results

The results are summarized in Table 9 and Figures 6 and 7. As before, results described in the summary table are based upon raw data, whereas results described in figures are based upon transformed data. This procedure conveys the maximum amount of information. The main results of this analysis were briefly mentioned in the preview to this chapter. The fine details of these results are presented in the next two subsections. Readers who are not interested in these technicalities can omit these sections and go directly to section IV.

1. Between-Subject Variables. As predicted, the effect of age was significant for both number and proportion ($p < 0.01$; $\varepsilon = 0.42$, and $p < 0.01$; $\varepsilon = 0.38$ respectively). The overall age means, for the number

Table 9. Mean number (and mean proportion in brackets) of traits per description used by various groups of subjects to describe different types of stimulus person

Mean age in groups in years and months	All	7,10	8,10	9,10	10,10	12,4	13,2	14,3	15,3
Subjects									
All	1·88 (0·20)	0·91 (0·12)	1·93 (0·20)	1·78 (0·19)	2·18 (0·24)	1·59 (0·16)	2·36 (0·24)	2·42 (0·24)	1·86 (0·20)
Boys	1·61 (0·18)	0·78 (0·10)	1·71 (0·20)	1·64 (0·18)	2·08 (0·22)	1·08 (0·12)	1·69 (0·19)	2·00 (0·21)	1·92 (0·22)
Girls	2·14 (0·22)	1·04 (0·15)	2·16 (0·21)	1·91 (0·21)	2·29 (0·26)	2·09 (0·21)	3·02 (0·28)	2·85 (0·27)	1·79 (0·18)
Higher intelligence	1·95 (0·21)	0·78 (0·11)	2·16 (0·22)	1·76 (0·19)	2·21 (0·24)	1·55 (0·18)	2·45 (0·25)	2·51 (0·25)	2·17 (0·22)
Lower intelligence	1·80 (0·19)	1·03 (0·13)	1·71 (0·19)	1·80 (0·19)	2·16 (0·25)	1·62 (0·15)	2·26 (0·22)	2·26 (0·23)	1·54 (0·18)
Stimulus person									
Male	2·16 (0·22)	0·84 (0·11)	2·01 (0·20)	1·84 (0·19)	2·40 (0·26)	1·87 (0·18)	2·82 (0·27)	3·06 (0·29)	2·41 (0·25)
Female	1·60 (0·18)	0·98 (0·13)	1·86 (0·21)	1·71 (0·19)	1·97 (0·23)	1·31 (0·15)	1·89 (0·20)	1·79 (0·19)	1·30 (0·16)
Adult	1·65 (0·18)	0·71 (0·14)	1·65 (0·18)	1·43 (0·17)	1·92 (0·26)	1·43 (0·15)	2·10 (0·21)	2·32 (0·24)	1·66 (0·19)
Child	2·10 (0·22)	1·10 (0·14)	2·21 (0·23)	2·13 (0·22)	2·44 (0·26)	1·74 (0·17)	2·61 (0·26)	2·53 (0·24)	2·05 (0·21)
Liked	1·86 (0·20)	0·83 (0·11)	1·84 (0·20)	1·65 (0·17)	2·29 (0·25)	1·59 (0·16)	2·38 (0·24)	2·48 (0·24)	1·86 (0·20)
Disliked	1·89 (0·21)	0·98 (0·13)	2·02 (0·21)	1·91 (0·21)	2·08 (0·23)	1·58 (0·17)	2·33 (0·23)	2·37 (0·25)	1·86 (0·21)

	Higher intelligence	Lower intelligence	Sex		Age		Liking	
			Male	Female	Adult	Child	Liked	Disliked
Subjects								
All	1·95 (0·21)	1·80 (0·19)	2·16 (0·22)	1·60 (0·18)	1·65 (0·18)	2·10 (0·22)	1·86 (0·20)	1·89 (0·20)
Boys	1·70 (0·19)	1·52 (0·17)	1·76 (0·18)	1·47 (0·17)	1·37 (0·16)	1·85 (0·20)	1·59 (0·17)	1·64 (0·18)
Girls	2·20 (0·23)	2·09 (0·21)	2·56 (0·25)	1·73 (0·18)	1·92 (0·21)	2·34 (0·23)	2·14 (0·22)	2·15 (0·23)
Higher intelligence	—	—	2·28 (0·23)	1·61 (0·18)	1·73 (0·19)	2·17 (0·23)	1·91 (0·19)	1·98 (0·22)
Lower intelligence	—	—	2·03 (0·20)	1·58 (0·18)	1·58 (0·18)	2·03 (0·21)	1·81 (0·19)	1·80 (0·19)
Stimulus person								
Male	—	—	—	—	2·01 (0·21)	2·31 (0·22)	2·14 (0·21)	2·17 (0·22)
Female	—	—	—	—	1·30 (0·16)	1·90 (0·21)	1·59 (0·18)	1·60 (0·19)
Adult	—	—	—	—	—	—	1·68 (0·18)	1·62 (0·18)
Child	—	—	—	—	—	—	2·04 (0·21)	2·16 (0·23)

	All	Age		Liking	
Subjects		Adult	Child	Liked	Disliked
Boys					
Higher intelligence	1·70 (0·19)	1·48 (0·17)	1·93 (0·20)	1·72 (0·18)	1·68 (0·19)
Lower intelligence	1·52 (0·17)	1·26 (0·15)	1·79 (0·20)	1·46 (0·16)	1·59 (0·18)
Both	1·61 (0·18)	1·37 (0·16)	1·86 (0·20)	1·59 (0·17)	1·64 (0·18)
Girls					
Higher intelligence	2·20 (0·23)	1·97 (0·21)	2·42 (0·25)	2·11 (0·22)	2·28 (0·25)
Lower intelligence	2·09 (0·21)	1·91 (0·20)	2·28 (0·22)	2·17 (0·22)	2·01 (0·21)
Both	2·14 (0·22)	1·94 (0·21)	2·35 (0·23)	2·14 (0·22)	2·15 (0·23)

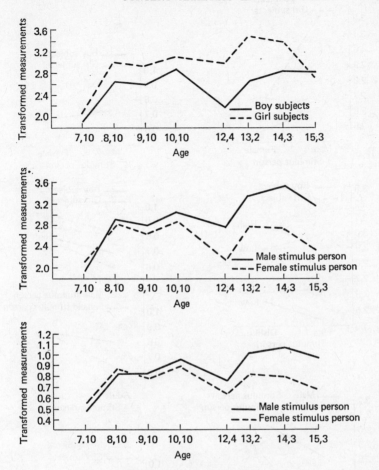

Figure 6. Age trends and interactions for the mean number of and mean proportion
of traits per description (transformed measurements)
Upper: Mean number—boy and girl subjects (all stimulus persons)
Middle: Mean number—male and female stimulus persons (all subjects)
Lower: Mean proportion—male and female stimulus persons (all subjects)

and proportion of traits per description showed significant linear
trends ($F = 25.7$ with 1 and 288 degrees of freedom, p<0·01 and
$F = 16.6$ $p<0.01$ respectively). In addition, there were significant curva-
tures in the trends of the means; the quadratic components were significant for both ($F = 14.9$ and $F = 26.9$ respectively, and 1 and 288 degrees
of freedom; $p<0.01$). In line with earlier findings, there was a considerable increase in the use of traits between 7 and 8 years. Comparisons

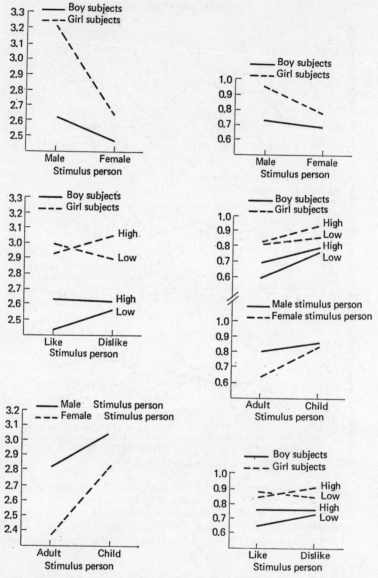

Figure 7. Statistically significant interactions (transformed measurements)
Left: Mean number of traits per description
        Upper: sex of subject × sex of stimulus person
        Middle: sex and intelligence of subject × like/dislike of stimulus person
        Lower: sex of stimulus person × age of stimulus person
Right: Mean proportion of traits per description
        Upper: sex of subject × sex of stimulus person
        Middle: (top) sex and intelligence of subject × age of stimulus person
        Middle: (bottom) sex of stimulus person × age of stimulus person
        Lower: sex and intelligence of subject × like/dislike of stimulus person

between the age means using Duncan's New Multiple Range Test (see Edwards, 1965) showed that the mean for the 7-year-old group was significantly lower than all other age means. After the age of 8 years, however, there was only a slight increase in the use of traits up to a maximum at 14 years, but the difference between the 8-year-old group and 14-year-old group was not significant. Nine-year-old children used significantly fewer traits than 14-year-old children, while the 12-year-old group used significantly fewer and a lower proportion of traits than the 10-, 13- and 14-year-old groups. The significant decrease in the use of traits in 12-year-old subjects is consistent with the decrease in the use of central statements described in Chapter 7. It is unclear whether this represents a sampling artefact or some other factor. There is, then, a short period of rapid development in the use of traits in the lower age groups followed by a longer, slower period of growth.

As predicted, girls used significantly more and a higher proportion of traits per description than did boys (2·14 against 1·61, $p < 0.01$, $\varepsilon = 0.26$; and 22·2 per cent against 17·9 per cent, $p < 0.01$, $\varepsilon = 0.24$, respectively). The difference in the frequency of use of traits depended upon the age of the subjects: 'Age × Sex' interaction was significant ($p < 0.05$, $\varepsilon = 0.16$). The difference between the means of the number of traits used by the two sexes increased with age, except in the oldest group where girls appeared to use slightly fewer traits than did boys, possibly because of sampling error—see Table 9 and Figure 6.

The observed differences are not as small as might appear, since the *total* number of statements per description was nine.

2. *Within-subjects Variables.* Of the within-subject variables, only Age of Stimulus Person had the effect predicted; Like/dislike had a non-significant effect on the use of traits, while Sex of Stimulus Person had unexpected significant effects. Subjects used more traits to describe males than to describe females (2·6 against 1·60, $p < 0.01$, $\varepsilon = 0.43$) and these formed a higher proportion of the total description (22 per cent against 18 per cent, $p < 0.01$, $\varepsilon = 0.30$). In both cases the difference depended upon Age of Subject ($p < 0.01$, $\varepsilon = 3.38$ and $p < 0.01$, $\varepsilon = 0.34$). As with central statements generally, younger children made slightly greater use of traits to describe females than to describe males, this probably reflects the greater importance of female others in early childhood. Development soon reverses this interpersonal orientation, since the difference between the mean number and mean proportion of traits used to describe males and females increased with age—see Table 9 and Figure 6. The differences between the mean number and the mean proportion of traits describing males and the mean number and mean

proportion describing females depended also upon Sex of Subject ($p < 0.01$, $\varepsilon = 0.24$; $p < 0.01$, $\varepsilon = 0.20$, respectively), being greatest for girls—see Table 9 and Figure 7.

Age of Stimulus Person had a significant effect in that subjects used significantly more traits and a higher proportion of traits to describe children than to describe adults (2.10 against 1.65, $p < 0.01$, $\varepsilon = 0.45$, and 22 per cent against 18 per cent, $p < 0.01$, $\varepsilon = 0.34$). As in previous analyses, the association between the dependent variables and the independent variables was high. The predicted 'Age of Subject × Age of Stimulus Person' interactions were not significant because most subjects, regardless of age, described a peer when asked to describe either a boy or girl.

A significant 'Sex of Subject × Intelligence × Age of Stimulus Person' interaction was obtained for the proportion of traits per description ($p < 0.05$, $\varepsilon = 0.10$). The differences between the intelligence groups depended upon interaction with Sex of Subject and the types of person being described. When adults were described, there was comparatively little difference between the intelligence groups in the case of girls; but in the case of boys, the higher intelligence group used a greater proportion of traits than did the lower intelligence group. This situation was reversed when children were described; so that there was little difference between the two intelligence groups in boys, but there was a marked difference in girls—the more intelligent girls used a higher proportion of traits than did the less intelligent girls—see Table 9 and Figure 7. No explanation for this effect is readily available.

The number and proportion of traits used in descriptions of adults and children depended upon whether they were male or female. The 'Age of Stimulus Person × Sex of Stimulus Person' interaction was significant in both cases ($p < 0.01$, $\varepsilon = 0.23$ and $p < 0.01$, $\varepsilon = 0.26$). Not surprisingly, the corresponding interaction term was significant in the earlier analysis of central statements. Although traits were used more frequently in descriptions of children than of adults, and formed a greater proportion of the total description, these differences were greatest when females were described; the least use of traits was made in descriptions of female adults—see Table 9 and Figure 7.

Although the main effects of Like/dislike were not significant, the 'Sex of Subject × Intelligence × Like/dislike' interaction was significant in both analyses ($p < 0.05$, $\varepsilon = 0.14$). In general, the mean number and mean proportion of traits per description was higher for the higher intelligence boys and girls than for the same-sex lower intelligence equivalents, except that intelligence had no effect when girls described persons they liked.

In addition, the higher intelligence girls and the lower intelligence boys used more traits and a higher proportion of traits to describe disliked persons, while the lower intelligence girls and the higher intelligence boys showed the opposite tendencies; they used more traits and a higher proportion of traits to describe liked persons—see Table 9 and Figure 7. It is difficult to find a convincing explanation for these statistically significant findings.

IV. First Discussion

The foregoing analyses of the use of traits in descriptions of persons produced a consistent, if somewhat complex, pattern of results which ties in well with earlier analyses of central statements. The two analyses are not independent, however, since 'traits' form part of the class of 'central statements'. And one would expect 'traits' to be correlated with some parts of the class of 'central statements' but not with others. The ability to conceptualize others in terms of traits showed a similar relationship to age as did the use of central statements, thus indicating that, as children grow up, they use more abstract types of central statement. Throughout the age range, girls used traits more frequently than did boys, and traits constituted a higher proportion of the contents of their impressions. Consequently, descriptions by girls were more abstract and generalized than those of boys and referred to a greater number of personal qualities.

The use of traits, unlike some other dependent variables, was not affected by intelligence. This is surprising, since the use of traits as cognitive categories and rules would seem to depend upon the acquisition of a complex skill enabling subjects to go beyond the information given to draw appropriate inferences and conclusions. Had this result been positive, it might have been worthwhile to resurrect at this point the once important, but long defunct, issue of 'social intelligence', that is to consider whether, after all, there might be something distinctive about the ability to handle 'psychological' facts, concepts and relationships. The negative result is confusing because of the previous finding that subjects in the higher intelligence group used significantly more central statements than subjects in the lower intelligence group. Presumably, the higher intelligence group made greater use of the more specific types of central statement while using approximately the same number of traits as the lower intelligence group. The higher intelligence group, apparently, were able to form well-balanced impressions combining generalized descriptive terms, which are *broadly* predictive, with more specific terms, which are more *narrowly* predictive. Bromley (1968) has pointed out the necessity of distinguishing between the 'general force of application' of a trait name—corresponding broadly to its dictionary definition—and the 'criteria for using' a trait name—corresponding to its behavioural definition, which depends a great deal upon the context in which the statement is made.

Partly for the reason mentioned above, the effects of the within-subject variables on the use of traits were similar to their effects on the use of central statements. More traits, and a higher proportion of traits, were used to describe males and children than to describe females and adults. In general, the differences between the two levels of each of these factors increased with Age of Subject. In the case of Sex of Other, the younger subjects used more traits to describe females—perhaps because their upbringing takes place largely in the care and control of females. Older subjects, on the other hand, used more traits to describe males, perhaps because they had become aware of the extent to which males are the 'preferred' sex in our society. Traits were used least to describe adult females, perhaps because, being adult, they were less similar to the subjects than were other children and, being female, the subjects were less interested in them. The other stimulus person variable, Like/dislike, had no effect on the use of traits.

Developmental changes in person perception are associated with the processes of socialization, for example, with the acquisition of attitudes, values and beliefs, and with changes in interpersonal relationships. The question now arises as to whether age and sex differences in the use of traits can be explained by older children and girls having a larger vocabulary of traits than younger children and boys, or by their using a given trait more frequently, or both, since these two possibilities are not mutually exclusive. One suitable way of studying the growth of the trait vocabulary, and of comparing different populations, is to construct a vocabulary test of trait names. Before this can be done, however, information of the type provided by this investigation is required, so that the test will contain a representative set of traits. Another way of studying the growth of the trait vocabulary would be to select terms at random from the Allport and Odbert list (assuming it correctly defines the population of trait names). But this procedure would not be very satisfactory unless the test contained a sufficiently large sample of items, and unless information was available about frequency of usage. The data provided by the present study could be used to construct a satisfactory test of trait vocabulary. A child's vocabulary of traits can be examined by analysing the number of *different* traits he uses to describe the eight stimulus persons. Although this number is not a measure of how many traits a child *knows*, nevertheless it provides an estimate of the number of traits he *uses* to describe others. There is probably a correlation between the size of a child's trait vocabulary and the extent to which he can apply them differentially. This is a research possibility that can wait upon the development of the psychometric instruments mentioned above. Other problems include that of estimating the frequency of use of traits in written and spoken English, and those of determining the effects of context and levels of meaning.

V. The Size of the Trait Vocabulary

A. Method

The number of different traits used by subjects to describe all eight stimulus persons was examined for differences in Age, Sex and Intelligence as an $8 \times 2 \times 2$ factorial experiment using the method described by Edwards (1965). As in previous analyses, a trait was defined objectively as one listed in the Allport and Odbert catalogue of trait names.

B. Results

The mean number of different traits used by each group of subjects is given in Table 10. The age effect was significant ($p < 0.01$): children in the age group 7,10 used an average of 5.2 *different* traits in their descriptions. This index number doubled over the next year and increased up to the age of 14,3, when on average 15.4 traits were used, except for a marked decline in the group aged 12,4. The decrease in trait vocabulary in this group is parallel with the decrease previously found in all types of fluency and occurs mainly in boys.

Girls used a larger number of *different* traits than boys (12.7 against 10.0, $p < 0.01$). The higher intelligence children used 12.1 traits as compared with 10.6 for the lower intelligence group ($p < 0.05$). The sex difference is particularly interesting because, although the girls had a larger trait vocabulary than did the boys, it will be remembered that the two groups had been equated for verbal ability by means of the Mill Hill Vocabulary Test or the Schonell Essential (verbal) Intelligence Test. The analysis suggests that girls may develop a somewhat specialized vocabulary in response to their concern with the interpersonal environment, and there are other reasons for supposing that they have a different orientation towards people than do boys. The number of *different* traits used by the subjects to describe eight people was, in some cases, impressively large: the overall mean was 11.4; the highest mean for any subgroup was 19.2 (for girls of higher intelligence aged 13,2); the highest individual score was 35. The richness and variety of the descriptive terminology was, in many ways, surprising; it would be interesting to investigate the sources and uses of these terms, for the systematic treatment of the child's understanding of human behaviour could add a new dimension to the educational curriculum.

Table 10. Mean number of different traits used to describe all stimulus persons by subjects differing in age, sex and intelligence

Sex	Intelligence	Age								All
		7,10	8,10	9,10	10,10	12,4	13,2	14,3	15,3	
Male	Higher	4·70	10·80	10·00	12·40	6·30	12·10	14·50	14·70	10·69
	Lower	4·80	8·40	7·50	12·30	8·50	10·70	12·10	9·50	9·23
Female	Higher	4·00	12·90	11·80	14·90	13·20	19·20	18·70	12·90	13·45
	Lower	7·40	10·10	11·40	12·70	12·20	16·60	16·20	10·20	12·10
Both		5·23	10·55	10·18	13·08	10·05	14·65	15·38	11·83	11·37

VI. The Differential Use of Traits

A. Method

We have suggested that the more frequent use of traits by girls could be attributed either to their larger vocabulary or to their more frequent use of each trait, or to both of these factors. The second of these possibilities could be investigated by computing the average frequency of use of each trait for each subject. Instead, the method employed was that of the type/token ratio—obtained by dividing the number of *different* traits used by each subject by the total frequency with which traits were used by him. This ratio is actually the reciprocal of the mean frequency of use of each trait, and it can be regarded as an index of 'psychological' differentiation, since it provides a measure of the extent to which the subject applied different traits to different stimulus persons. A maximum index of one (unity) would show that the subject had used each trait once only, and hence had discriminated perfectly between the individuals he was describing. The type/token ratio was computed for each subject, and the data were analysed for differences in Age, Sex and Intelligence using the same analysis of variance model as in the previous analysis. As the data were expressed as proportions, they were subjected to the angular transformation: $2 \arcsin \sqrt{p}$ described earlier. An index of, say, 10/20 (10 different traits, and 20 trait statements altogether) means that, on average, the subject used each trait twice. This would indicate that the subject was not discriminating perfectly between the eight stimulus persons, but rather attributing some of the same traits to different persons.

B. Results

The mean frequencies of trait usage over eight stimulus persons by different groups of subjects are given in Table 11. Older subjects tended to

Table 11. Mean frequency of use of traits used to describe all stimulus persons by subjects differing in age, sex and intelligence

Sex	Intelligence	Age								All
		7,10	8,10	9,10	10,10	12,4	13,2	14,3	15,3	
Male	Higher	5·80	15·10	13·80	16·00	7·20	13·80	17·30	18·90	13·49
	Lower	6·40	11·40	12·20	17·80	10·80	13·00	14·40	11·60	12·20
Female	Higher	6·00	18·70	14·50	18·80	17·30	25·40	24·00	15·30	17·50
	Lower	9·70	16·20	16·30	17·60	15·20	23·20	22·70	11·90	16·60
Both		6·98	15·35	14·20	17·55	12·63	18·85	19·60	14·43	14·95

use traits more differentially than did younger subjects ($p < 0.05$) and boys used traits more differentially than did girls ($p < 0.01$). Intelligence had no significant effect.

VII. Second Discussion

The type/token ratio was higher for boys than for girls for all age levels, which means that, on average, girls used each trait more frequently than did boys. Thus, girls appear to be more fluent and have a larger vocabulary of traits, but they use these traits in a less discriminating way than do boys. On the other hand, it may be that trait names which are more salient in the young child's vocabulary (very probably corresponding to the trait names which occur more frequently in common usage among children) are the very ones which enable him to discriminate between (or to categorize) stimulus persons, whereas the less salient trait names (those which occur less frequently and perhaps usually appear as secondary attributes) are more affected by context—that is, by local 'criteria for use', by the stimulus person's primary attributes, and the observer's purpose and frame of reference; so, although the *same* trait name is applied to different persons, its meaning may be *different* for each. We reach the conclusion that, perhaps, girls only *appear* to be less discriminating than boys in the use of trait names because our methods of content analysis are not sensitive to those effects of context which give a deeper meaning to the subjects' statements than is apparent from their surface characteristics.

A question which can be asked, but remains unanswered as far as the present study is concerned, is whether the apparently larger trait vocabulary but poorer differentiation of girls is an isolated effect or merely a reflection of a more general difference between the sexes in verbal fluency and vocabulary size. The two groups were not significantly different on their Mill Hill scores, but then, in all likelihood, the Mill Hill test was constructed so as to minimize sex differences, this test, however, does not indicate how frequently the subject uses the words he knows. A somewhat different measure was used to assess trait vocabulary, namely, the number of different traits used to describe eight people. While the *total number of words known* probably correlates highly with the *number of different words used*, marked sex differences could occur with, say, girls (as compared with boys) using a higher proportion of the words they know. It would be interesting to test whether the girls used a larger number of different words of all types than did the boys. This task requires extensive computerization because, altogether, 178 539 words would have to be sorted and counted. The free descriptions, moreover, contain rather specialized samples of children's vocabularies—samples which are, nevertheless, interesting in their own right.

A more satisfactory answer to the question of sex differences in the use of traits might be achieved by means of a general vocabulary test plus a trait vocabulary test. In this manner, it might be possible to see whether the observed sex differences in use of traits could be accounted for by greater verbal facility on the part of girls or, more specifically, by their greater 'psychological' orientation. The latter explanation would be supported by finding that girls matched with boys of equal general vocabulary nevertheless performed significantly better on a test of 'psychological' vocabulary or trait names.

Regardless of the outcome of this proposed exercise, a number of advantages must accrue to subjects having a large vocabulary of traits. If a subject has more traits available for describing people, he can discriminate better among the persons he meets, and he will be more aware of subtleties and complexities in the behaviour of a stimulus person. Thus, a girl's larger trait vocabulary must undoubtedly facilitate her interpersonal behaviour. Against this facilitation, however, must be weighed the disadvantage of using each item more frequently. Unless our result is some sort of experimental artefact, the two sorts of sex difference would tend to counterbalance each other as far as differentiating among persons is concerned. Nevertheless, as we have already argued, the more complex and more diverse impressions formed by girls must have some inter-personal consequences, and they probably reflect the greater weight that females place upon interpersonal relations, plus the cultural pressures exerted upon them to develop interpersonal skills. Society encourages the average girl to do what she seems predisposed to do, that is, to take an interest in human activities and her preferred toys and play activities show this orientation. The average boy, on the other hand, is encouraged, and seems predisposed, to take an interest in the non human aspects of his environment and his preferred toys and play activities reflect his orientation. For both sexes, the effect is to direct the child's development along socially approved lines.

The analyses described in this chapter have all been quantitative and, for the purpose of these analyses, all traits have been regarded as identi-cal. This has been both convenient and useful, for it has produced interesting results and a variety of hypotheses for future research. Such analyses, however, are not sufficient in themselves. If the full implications of the data are to be drawn out, then *qualitative* analyses are required to show what types of traits are associated with the independent var-iables. This issue is dealt with in the next section.

VIII. The Development of a Vocabulary of Traits

One important characteristic distinguishing children of different ages was the use of trait names. There was growth in trait vocabulary through-out the age range studied, but especially between 7 and 10 years. Table 12 gives details of the numbers of subjects in each age and sex group who used a given trait. Only traits used by more than 1 per cent of the sample, that is four or more children, are included. A list of infrequent traits, that is those used by three or fewer children, is given in Table 13. In drawing up these lists, only a moderate effort has been made to group equivalent or related terms; the reader is free to combine and resort the trait statements into a smaller, more manageable set. The list provides a genuine count of the incidence of trait names in common use among children represented by the sample. Apart from providing normative data for educational and psychometric purposes, such as we have suggested, the list could be used in an investigation of transitional probabilities (associative links) between traits, thus giving some insight into the social

Table 12. Numbers of subjects in each age and sex group using trait statements.
Only terms used by more than 1 per cent of the sample are included

	Age																Total	Percent-age
	7,10		8,10		9,10		10,10		12,4		13,2		14,3		15,3			
	Boys	Girls	Boys	Girls	Boys	Girls	Boys	Girls	Boys	Girls	Boys	Girls	Boys	Girls	Boys	Girls		
Mood and temperament: temper and irritability																		
Good tempered, not/never bad tempered, no temper, hardly ever loses temper	1	–	2	3	3	2	3	3	1	3	3	2	1	5	3	–	35	10·9
Bad tempered, not good tempered, terrible temper, loses temper, has temper	2	1	6	5	1	7	8	10	4	4	5	7	2	9	3	2	76	23·7
Quick, hot, violent temper, flies into temper/mood, gets mad	–	2	3	–	–	2	3	3	–	2	–	3	2	3	–	1	25	7·8
Temperamental, moody, bad moods	–	1	1	2	1	1	1	1	1	2	2	8	5	3	2	1	31	9·7
Not/never moody, always in good mood	1	–	–	–	1	–	–	2	–	–	–	1	1	–	–	1	6	1·9
Sulks, sulky	–	–	–	1	1	1	2	–	–	1	1	1	1	–	1	2	11	3·4
Angry	–	–	5	1	–	1	2	3	2	1	2	–	–	1	–	–	18	5·6
Not angry, never angry	–	–	1	–	1	–	1	–	1	1	–	–	1	1	2	–	7	2·2
Cross	1	2	6	6	3	–	3	7	–	–	2	–	1	1	1	–	41	12·8
Not/never cross, rarely cross	–	–	2	–	3	–	3	2	1	–	3	–	–	–	1	–	12	3·7
Narky	–	–	–	–	–	–	–	–	1	1	1	–	2	–	–	–	4	1·3
Mood and temperament: happiness																		
Happy, never sad	2	–	2	1	1	1	2	1	3	–	4	1	7	6	3	7	41	12·8
Sad, not happy, unhappy	1	–	1	–	–	1	1	–	1	–	1	–	–	–	2	–	6	1·9
Jolly	3	–	1	–	1	1	2	–	2	1	1	–	2	2	3	–	18	5·6
Cheerful	–	–	–	1	1	–	2	2	1	–	1	–	4	2	5	3	27	8·4
Generosity																		
Generous, not mean	–	–	–	1	2	–	4	4	3	10	5	8	3	7	5	6	66	20·6
Not generous, mean, skinny, miser, stingy	–	1	2	1	3	–	6	6	4	2	1	5	1	5	4	1	46	14·4

Table 12—continued

	7,10 Boys	7,10 Girls	8,10 Boys	8,10 Girls	9,10 Boys	9,10 Girls	10,10 Boys	10,10 Girls	12,4 Boys	12,4 Girls	13,2 Boys	13,2 Girls	14,3 Boys	14,3 Girls	15,3 Boys	15,3 Girls	Total	Percentage
Kind, kindhearted	7	10	10	14	7	11	10	11	14	11	11	7	17	11	11	12	173	54.1
Not kind, unkind, not kindhearted	—	3	1	1	1	2	—	2	—	1	—	1	2	2	1	1	19	5.9
Shares	—	—	1	1	1	1	—	1	1	—	1	1	2	2	2	1	11	3.4
Selfish	—	—	4	1	1	1	2	1	2	2	6	—	2	2	1	1	23	7.2
Not/never selfish, unselfish	—	—	3	3	—	1	1	1	1	1	1	2	—	—	1	1	12	3.7
Greedy	—	—	2	2	—	1	—	—	—	—	1	1	—	1	1	1	8	2.5

Humour

	7,10 Boys	7,10 Girls	8,10 Boys	8,10 Girls	9,10 Boys	9,10 Girls	10,10 Boys	10,10 Girls	12,4 Boys	12,4 Girls	13,2 Boys	13,2 Girls	14,3 Boys	14,3 Girls	15,3 Boys	15,3 Girls	Total	Percentage
Funny	3	3	6	6	2	5	5	6	2	2	3	3	4	4	1	1	56	17.5
Humorous, sense of humour	1	—	1	2	5	3	4	5	1	4	4	4	7	7	6	1	49	15.3
Not humorous, no sense of humour	—	—	—	—	3	—	3	—	1	—	—	3	1	1	1	1	12	3.7
Good fun, full of fun, lots of fun	—	—	—	—	—	2	1	3	—	2	—	4	1	1	2	1	17	5.3
Comical, laughable, hilarious	—	—	—	1	—	—	—	—	—	—	—	1	—	—	1	—	4	1.3

Conceit

	7,10 Boys	7,10 Girls	8,10 Boys	8,10 Girls	9,10 Boys	9,10 Girls	10,10 Boys	10,10 Girls	12,4 Boys	12,4 Girls	13,2 Boys	13,2 Girls	14,3 Boys	14,3 Girls	15,3 Boys	15,3 Girls	Total	Percentage
Shows off	—	—	4	4	3	4	5	5	7	4	3	8	4	5	8	—	64	20.0
Not show off	—	—	1	1	—	1	2	2	—	—	1	1	—	1	1	—	6	1.9
Big headed, too big for boots	—	1	1	—	1	1	2	2	3	4	1	4	5	4	6	4	38	11.9
Boasts, boastful, boaster, brags	—	—	2	3	4	3	—	1	2	4	4	4	3	2	5	1	38	11.9
Not boast, not boastful, not brag	—	—	—	—	1	1	1	1	1	—	—	2	2	2	3	1	13	4.1
Conceited	—	—	—	—	—	1	—	1	1	2	2	1	2	2	—	2	8	2.5

Sociability

	7,10 Boys	7,10 Girls	8,10 Boys	8,10 Girls	9,10 Boys	9,10 Girls	10,10 Boys	10,10 Girls	12,4 Boys	12,4 Girls	13,2 Boys	13,2 Girls	14,3 Boys	14,3 Girls	15,3 Boys	15,3 Girls	Total	Percentage
Sociable, mixes well, gets on well with people	—	—	—	—	—	—	—	—	1	1	1	2	—	4	4	1	10	3.1
Friendly	1	—	5	1	2	5	3	1	2	3	7	2	4	5	8	6	54	16.9
Not/un/friendly	—	1	1	1	—	1	—	—	1	1	1	—	1	1	3	1	10	3.1

Table 12—*continued*

	Age																	
	7,10		8,10		9,10		10,10		12,4		13,2		14,3		15,3		Total	Percentage
	Boys	Girls	Boys	Girls	Boys	Girls	Boys	Girls	Boys	Girls	Boys	Girls	Boys	Girls	Boys	Girls		
Talkativeness																		
Talks too much, talkative, chatterbox	3	–	3	3	3	4	2	4	–	2	2	4	3	2	5	1	41	12·8
Silent, quiet	–	1	3	2	–	1	2	4	2	2	4	5	2	1	1	2	30	9·4
Control over others																		
Strict	–	1	–	2	2	–	2	1	2	1	–	–	–	2	1	1	15	4·7
Stern	1	–	2	1	–	1	1	1	3	–	1	1	2	2	–	–	11	3·4
Rationality																		
Sensible	–	–	1	3	–	–	1	1	1	1	1	1	2	3	–	2	17	5·3
Not sensible, not much sense	–	–	2	–	–	–	2	–	–	–	1	1	1	1	1	–	7	2·2
Serious	–	–	–	–	–	–	1	–	–	–	1	1	1	2	1	1	6	1·9
Modesty																		
Modest	–	–	–	–	–	–	1	–	1	–	1	–	–	–	3	–	5	1·6
Shy	1	–	–	–	–	–	3	1	4	1	5	1	3	6	4	4	32	10·0
Not shy	–	–	–	–	–	–	1	1	1	–	1	1	2	2	2	–	9	2·8
Quality of relationships with others																		
Considerate, thoughtful, thinks of others	–	–	2	–	–	1	2	1	1	1	1	5	2	3	3	3	25	7·8
Inconsiderate, not considerate, thoughtless	–	–	1	–	–	–	–	–	1	–	–	–	–	–	–	–	6	1·9
Understanding	–	–	1	–	1	–	1	3	1	3	4	5	5	4	1	3	27	8·4
Helpful, helps people, always willing to help	1	–	2	1	6	4	6	1	4	7	9	1	8	10	6	6	76	23·7
Not helpful, never helpful	1	–	–	–	–	–	1	–	1	–	1	1	–	–	1	1	7	2·2
Patient, never impatient	–	–	–	–	–	1	–	–	1	–	2	–	2	–	–	3	9	2·8
Impatient, never patient	–	–	–	–	–	–	1	1	–	1	–	2	2	–	2	1	5	1·6
Good friend	–	–	–	–	–	–	2	1	1	2	2	6	–	2	2	1	19	5·9

Table 12—*continued*

	Age																	
	7,10		8,10		9,10		10,10		12,4		13,2		14,3		15,3		Total	Percentage
	Boys	Girls	Boys	Girls	Boys	Girls	Boys	Girls	Boys	Girls	Boys	Girls	Boys	Girls	Boys	Girls		
Loyal	—	—	—	—	—	—	—	—	—	—	—	—	2	—	1	1	4	1·3
Bossy, bosses people, bossyboots	5	5	4	10	6	7	5	10	3	7	7	13	10	7	2	1	76	23·7
Not bossy	—	—	3	1	—	3	1	5	—	1	—	—	—	—	2	1	6	1·9
Gentle, not rough	—	—	—	2	1	3	2	5	2	—	1	1	—	—	2	—	15	4·7
Rough, not gentle	—	1	—	1	1	3	3	5	1	2	1	1	—	—	2	—	19	5·9
Bully, bullies	1	1	—	1	—	1	2	2	—	4	—	1	3	—	4	1	29	9·1
Sympathetic, comforting	—	—	—	—	1	2	2	1	—	—	1	—	1	5	1	2	9	2·8
Spiteful	—	—	—	—	—	—	—	2	1	—	1	1	1	—	—	1	13	4·1
Cruel	—	—	2	—	4	—	—	2	1	—	—	2	1	—	2	—	13	4·1
Jealous	—	—	—	—	—	—	—	2	—	—	2	2	—	3	4	—	13	4·1
Sly	—	—	—	1	—	1	—	—	1	—	2	—	1	—	3	—	7	2·2
Loving, loving heart	—	—	—	—	—	—	—	2	—	—	—	—	1	—	—	—	5	1·6
Nosy, nosyparker, busybody	—	2	1	—	—	3	1	2	2	2	6	3	1	—	2	5	31	9·7
Evaluations																		
Nice	12	16	16	17	13	13	15	15	2	11	13	13	10	7	4	11	186	58·1
Not nice	3	5	2	8	2	9	4	4	2	2	3	3	1	1	1	1	34	10·6
Good	5	12	10	12	10	9	10	3	4	5	4	2	2	2	2	1	92	28·7
Bad	6	4	4	7	5	3	2	3	2	1	4	4	—	2	1	1	40	12·5
Nasty	1	1	1	3	2	3	2	2	—	2	1	1	3	2	1	1	29	9·1
Horrible, horrid	2	5	7	8	6	8	6	10	—	8	4	2	5	4	—	2	75	23·4
Terrible	—	—	—	—	1	—	3	2	1	1	—	1	—	1	1	—	9	2·8
Evil, wicked	—	—	—	—	—	—	1	2	1	—	—	—	—	—	1	—	9	2·8
Fab, gear, great, fantastic, smashing	—	—	—	—	—	—	—	—	—	6	—	—	2	—	4	—	17	5·3
All right	—	1	—	—	3	3	1	4	—	—	4	—	3	—	1	—	16	5·0
Pleasant	—	—	—	—	1	1	1	1	—	1	4	1	2	1	5	—	18	5·6
Sweet	—	—	—	—	—	—	—	1	1	—	1	—	1	—	—	—	5	1·6
Lovely	—	—	—	—	—	—	—	—	—	2	—	—	—	—	—	—	4	1·3
Perfect	—	—	—	—	—	—	—	—	—	—	2	2	—	—	—	1	4	1·3
Good natured	—	—	—	—	—	—	1	—	1	2	—	1	4	—	—	1	13	4·1

Table 12—*continued*

	7,10		8,10		9,10		10,10		12,4		13,2		14,3		15,3		Total	Percentage
	Boys	Girls	Boys	Girls	Boys	Girls	Boys	Girls	Boys	Girls	Boys	Girls	Boys	Girls	Boys	Girls		
Dirty minded	—	—	—	—	—	—	—	—	—	—	1	—	3	1	—	—	5	1·6
Nice personality/character	—	—	—	—	—	—	1	5	—	5	5	1	5	3	1	3	25	7·8
Good personality	—	—	—	—	—	—	—	—	1	3	3	—	2	2	—	4	13	4·1
Horrible/no/rotten/personality	—	—	—	—	1	—	1	1	2	3	2	2	2	—	1	2	14	4·4
Great/wonderful/terrific personality	—	—	—	—	—	—	—	—	—	3	2	—	3	3	1	6	17	5·3
Silly	5	5	1	7	4	4	2	2	3	—	3	2	1	—	1	—	39	12·2
Stupid	2	1	—	1	3	3	2	2	1	1	3	1	1	—	—	1	27	8·4
Daft	1	—	—	—	1	—	3	3	2	1	—	—	1	—	—	—	12	3·7
Clean	—	2	—	—	2	—	3	1	1	—	2	1	3	—	—	—	14	4·4
Dirty	—	2	—	—	1	1	1	—	2	—	2	1	2	—	—	1	15	4·7
Tidy	—	1	—	—	1	2	2	1	3	2	2	2	3	1	2	1	23	7·2
Untidy	2	—	1	1	—	1	1	—	2	1	—	2	—	1	1	—	10	3·1
Old fashioned, not fashionable	—	—	—	—	—	—	—	—	1	—	1	—	1	—	1	—	6	1·9
Modern, mod, with it	—	—	1	—	1	1	—	—	—	1	—	1	2	—	1	—	6	1·9
Snob, snobbish, posh	1	—	—	—	1	—	1	—	3	3	8	1	2	2	2	—	23	7·2
Not snobbish	—	—	—	—	—	—	—	—	3	—	1	—	2	—	—	1	5	1·6
Nuisance	—	1	1	—	—	1	1	1	2	—	1	—	2	—	1	—	10	3·1
Naughty	6	9	6	—	3	7	2	3	—	3	1	1	2	1	1	—	48	15·0
Well behaved, not naughty	2	3	2	—	3	—	2	3	1	1	1	—	6	1	—	1	27	8·4
Disobedient	—	—	—	—	—	—	2	1	1	—	1	—	1	—	—	—	6	1·9
Polite	—	1	—	3	2	2	2	2	2	1	2	2	5	—	—	—	26	8·1
Not polite, impolite	—	1	—	1	1	1	2	—	1	—	—	2	1	—	—	—	6	1·9
Rude	3	—	3	3	3	5	3	4	3	1	2	4	2	1	—	1	35	10·9
Cheeky	—	—	—	6	2	2	1	1	2	1	4	4	6	2	—	2	35	10·9
Good manners, well mannered	—	1	2	3	—	1	5	5	1	1	7	4	5	1	2	1	36	11·3
Bad/no/horrible manners	1	4	—	1	4	—	1	2	—	—	1	1	2	2	2	1	24	7·5
Intellectual ability																		
Clever	3	1	2	3	2	4	3	4	2	1	7	1	3	3	2	3	44	13·7
Not clever	2	—	1	2	1	2	2	3	1	1	1	1	2	2	1	—	20	6·3
Intelligent	—	—	—	—	1	—	1	1	1	—	4	—	3	3	2	1	18	5·6

Table 12—*continued*

	Age																	
	7,10		8,10		9,10		10,10		12,4		13,2		14,3		15,3		Total	Percentage
	Boys	Girls	Boys	Girls	Boys	Girls	Boys	Girls	Boys	Girls	Boys	Girls	Boys	Girls	Boys	Girls		
Not intelligent												1	2		1	2	6	1·9
Brainy, bright			3	3								1				1	8	2·5
Not brainy, not bright			2			1		2	1		1			1			8	2·5
Good at school work, good scholar	2	2	2						1		1						8	2·5
Miscellaneous																		
Honest, truthful		2					2			1	4		2	2			11	3·4
Fussy, fusspot	2		4	2	4	1	1	1	2		2		1			1	19	5·9
Ungrateful, never grateful				1		1							1		2	1	5	1·6
Stubborn		1					1				1		2				7	2·2
Argumentative, argues	1											1				2	5	1·6
Calm, placid, easygoing							2	1					2	4	2	2	14	4·4
Proud		1							2				2				4	1·3
Lively, active, energetic	2	1		1	1		2		1	1	5	2	3	1	3	4	28	8·7
Outspoken, frank							1	1				4	1				8	2·5
Spoilt				1					2			1					4	1·3
Moans, complains									4	1	3		2				10	3·1
Does not moan				1			1		1			1			1		4	1·3
Tomboy			2	1	1	2					2		1			1	7	2·2
Strange, peculiar			1	1	1		1	1	1		1		1		1		8	2·5
Mad, nuts	1					1		1	1		2		1		2		8	2·5
Scruffy	1	1					2	2	1		2		1		1		10	3·1
Clumsy		1	1				2	2	1		1	1	3		1		7	2·2
Good sport			1			1			2		1		1	3	1		13	4·1
Bad sport, spoilsport									1		1		1		1		5	1·6
Childish, babyish	1		2	1	3	1	2	1	1		1		3	1	3		17	5·3
Lazy, idle	2	1	3	2	3	1	1	1	1	1	2		3	1	3	2	28	8·7
Good worker, works hard		1		4	3	1		1			3	1	2		3	3	23	7·2
Forgetful, absentminded			1	1		1	1				1				1		4	1·3
Playful							1				1		3		1		4	1·3

The last two columns give the total number and percentage of subjects using each trait.

Table 13. Trait statements used by less than 1 per cent of the sample

abrupt	gay	not sociable
adorable		not stubborn
affectionate	hard	not sulky
aggressive	hateful	not tender
agreeable	heartless	not talkative
amiable	hopeless	
average	hospitable	optimistic
	hypocrite	ordinary
bashful		
biased	ignorant	perfectionist
bold	impish	pompous
	insensitive	punctual
callous	insincere	
carefree	interfering	reliable
careless		reserved
charming		respectable
cissy	jovial	responsible
common	joyful	restless
confident		
contented	lovable	sarcastic
coward	loyal	self-conscious
cunning		sexy
	malicious	shrewd
	meddlesome	smug
daring	meditative	squeamish
decent	menace	stoic
depressed	mischievous	superstitious
destructive	miserable	suspicious
determined	moral	surly
detestable	morbid	
deceitful		tactless
despicable	nervous	tender
dishonest	normal	touchy
domineering	not bigheaded	
dozy	not a bully	unpleasant
	not care for others	unreasonable
efficient	not cheerful	unscrupulous
	not cissy	unsociable
false	not conceited	
fierce	not energetic	vain
filthy	not funny	vile
firm	not fussy	vulgar
foolish	not greedy	
	not loyal	warmhearted
gorgeous	not playful	weed

psychology of norms governing interpersonal perception, as well as giving an objective method of sorting or clustering the items. Further research possibilities would be to study developmental changes in trait clustering, and to test whether traits in common use at the adult level are clustered (in terms of commonly held associative bonds) in a fashion similar to that claimed by Cattell (1965) on the basis of his factor-analytic treatment of trait ratings.

Well over 300 different traits were used. The most frequently used terms were 'kind' and 'nice', the former being used by over half the subjects. As can be seen from Tables 12 and 13 and Figure 8, the data accord with Zipf's Law (see Zipf, 1949, and Osgood, 1953) in that a large number of subjects used a few frequently occurring salient traits, whereas a rapidly diminishing number of subjects used many infrequently occurring traits.

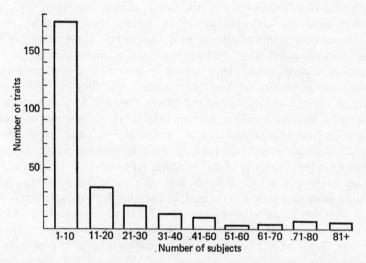

Figure 8. Number of traits used by different numbers of subjects

As one might expect, trait names become more precise and take on a more adult meaning as the child grows older (see also Baldwin and Baldwin, 1970). Those used by 7-year-olds are vague, global and diffuse, as well as being strongly evaluative, for example, kind, nice, not nice, good, bad, horrible, funny. Some of the less frequently used terms, however, seem to reflect socializing pressures, for example, rude, no manners and naughty; others reflect current value systems, for example, clever, lazy and good at work. As the child gets older, these global nonspecific terms seem to differentiate, becoming more precise and more abstract. Thus, the terms used more frequently by 14- and 15-year-olds were, for example : bad tempered, cheerful, generous, kind, humorous, boastful, sociable, shy, considerate, jealous, sensible and calm. When evaluations were made by older subjects, only 'nice' was used with approximately the same frequency as in 7-year-olds. In general, evaluations made by older subjects refer to the stimulus person's impact on other people, for example : good personality, pleasant and great personality. Terms like 'great personality' and 'wonderful personality' serve a more expressive function than do terms such as 'nice' and 'good', since they indicate the greater intensity of the subject's emotional involvement with the person described, and this enhances their information value.

As the vague, global, nonspecific concepts become differentiated into more precise and more discrete terms, it seems likely that each of the new terms will retain part of the meaning and affect of the original. Thus kind, Not kind—one of the main dimensions used by young children—seems to differentiate into : mean, shares, selfish, greedy, generous, friendly, sympathetic, helpful, and so on. These terms are more precise than the word 'kind' and are restricted to more specific attributes and actions. Consequently, they are more informative and more accurate (as regards assessment and predictions); but they do not lose the associated affect and meaning of the parent concept. It may well be that a process of successive differentiation into more specific terms provides the basis for the implicit theories of personality—of trait implications—that play such an important part in adult impression formation. Since the new terms retain some of the meaning and affect of the parent term, it seems likely that terms derived from the same parent term will be associated with that parent term and, in varying degrees, with each other, thus giving rise to associative networks. Naturally, associative links will become diversified (strengthened or weakened) as experience increases (otherwise there would be no reason to differentiate). We suggest that the associative probabilities between the differentiated term and its parent should be greater for terms which differentiate earlier in development than for terms which differentiate later. In the case of kind/not kind, the association between 'kind' and 'generous' might be expected to be greater than between 'kind' and 'sympathetic', since 'generous' appears earlier in development than does 'sympathetic'. In this, and in other ways, a careful study of trait differentiation might contribute significantly to our understanding of trait implications.

Traits can be loosely classified into groups—see Table 12. Those used by young children fall into relatively few groups : temperament, ability, humour, generosity and evaluations; and this gives their descriptions a stereotyped quality. These various groups of personal qualities are the ones which are most readily expressed and recognized in overt behaviour; therefore, they make less demand on the child's capacity for psychological inference. As children grow older, they become interested in other kinds of personal qualities which are less obvious—for example, conceitedness, sociability, control over others, rationality, modesty and interpersonal relationships. The younger child can handle only a limited number of traits (dimensions of personality) partly because of limitations imposed by selective attention and short-term memory, partly because of inexperience and conceptual immaturity. As he grows older, however, these limitations are reduced and he becomes capable of dealing with many facets and complexities of human nature.

To our way of thinking, one important finding is that the traits used by subjects in their written descriptions differ considerably from those used by psychologists to construct adjective checklists, rating scales and other so-called objective measures in the study of personality assessment, person perception and the self-concept. This again raises the problem, mentioned in earlier chapters, of whether the measures employed are appropriate to the subject's normal ways of behaving. The trait lists in Tables 12 and 13 can be used to construct psychometric tests for use in more systematic and controlled studies of impression formation—see also Chapter 12. Another important finding is that, although studies of person perception have mainly focused on problems associated with the use of traits, traits make up only about 20 per cent of the total contents of a normal description of a person written by an older child. Traits are important, perhaps the most important, parts of such a description, but it is unfortunate, to say the least, that so little attention has been paid to the other 80 per cent of our normal, or basic, conceptual framework for understanding people. It can scarcely be denied that these other components are important in impression formation and in interpersonal behaviour. But, more important, our argument is that the neglect of these other components has produced serious errors (methodological and conceptual, if not factual) in the study of personality and adjustment.

Sex differences in the grouping of traits were slight : girls tended to be a little more sensitive to the stimulus person's interpersonal qualities than were boys, and made slightly more use of such terms as understanding, comforting, thoughtful, patient, gentle, rough and jealous. Girls also used a greater variety of outright evaluations, so that terms such as 'good personality' and 'great personality' were used almost exclusively by girls. This again might reflect their apparently greater emotional investment in people, as compared with things.

It has been pointed out by a number of writers, but especially

Asch (1958), that metaphor plays an important part in person perception. Many of the terms used to describe persons are also applied to physical objects; for example, warm, hard, straight. Asch pointed out that the existence of dualistic terms such as these is not limited to English, and that some languages unrelated to English also possess them. We may feel or experience the 'behaviour' of persons and things as similar and use the same term to describe it—for example, children, machines, texts and climbs can all be 'difficult'. Similarly, when we say a thing is 'stupid' we mean its design is not appropriate for its intended use, and when we say a person is 'stupid' we mean his behaviour is not appropriate to the situation. Thus, many of the terms used to describe persons and mental processes may have their origins in terms used to describe physical events (see Sarbin, 1968), but one can also argue precisely the opposite point of view—see Krech and Crutchfield (1948) pp. 9-11. Little seems to be known about the historical origins of trait names. Metaphorical, that is, dual terms were used by only one or two older subjects. Indeed, metaphor was used very infrequently. The terms young children apply to persons seem to be completely different from those they apply to objects, except that a few generalized evaluations—such as 'nice' and 'good'—are applied to all 'behaviour' that produces a pleasant effect.

It would have been surprising had dual terms been used by young children to describe persons, since dual terms refer to complex and relatively covert personal qualities. That there are common features in person perception and object perception is not disputed (see Warr and Knapper, 1968) but it could be the perception of persons that is primary rather than the perception of objects. This point of view would go a long way to explain the psychological basis of animism—we are psychologists first and physicists second! Adults encourage children to adopt animistic accounts of natural events, and even knowledgeable adults find it appropriate to use animistic terms to refer to the 'behaviour' of complex devices such as cars and computers. Judging by the tremendous interest value of the human face, infants seem to find persons more interesting than things and, as we have just said, children readily assign such human qualities as intention and consciousness to inanimate objects.

Metaphorical terms were not entirely absent from the present study; for example, sweet, modern, brainy, calm and spoilt were used. Nevertheless, the relative lack of metaphorical terms does raise two minor issues. The first is whether such metaphorical terms as 'straight', 'difficult', or 'warm' require an abstract level of understanding which appears only late in childhood. The second issue is whether the period of adolescence not covered in the present investigations, that is from 15 to 20 years, is marked by a 'growth spurt' of the sort that would quickly incorporate metaphorical terms into the language of impression formation. Adolescent growth is commonly associated with changes in language style, at least in Western societies. Adolescents and young adults commonly adopt an argot largely limited to their own age group, just as other relatively specialized human groups develop their own jargon and slang. It may be that terms like 'switched on' and 'hung up' (probably already out of date!) are the sorts of metaphorical terms to which we have just referred. In so far as they reflect mere passing fashions and fulfil a largely expressive (affective) role in interpersonal communication, such adolescent metaphors are probably of limited interest in the study of the language of impression formation. Consideration of them would probably add little to our knowledge of the origins and functions of animism and metaphor in cognitive development, and they can probably be dealt with more effectively in the context of social and expressive behaviour.

CHAPTER 10

Impression Formation and Change

I. Preview

The process of impression formation and change cannot be accounted for entirely in terms of cognition, although at present the cognitive processes are the ones most readily investigated. A full account of the process of impression formation would entail an examination of the differences between individuals, the relevant social psychological processes, and the associated conditions of learning. A theory of impression formation and change, moreover, needs to be sufficiently comprehensive to incorporate evidence pertaining not only to cognition but also to emotion and motivation. At present, much of the evidence is based on common knowledge, and is dealt with in terms of analogies with psychological processes other than impression formation. Some indication of the complex cognitive and psychodynamic processes underlying impression formation is obtained by analysing the way in which cognitive organization is imposed on the multifarious items of information. Changes in cognitive organization dominate the later years of development—from adolescence to young adulthood.

II. The Background to a Theory of Impression Formation and Change

It will not have gone unnoticed by the reader that there is more to a personality impression—presented in the form of a written description—than is revealed by a list of its informational contents, no matter how exhaustive and detailed such a list might be. The contents, in other words, are *organized*. But how is the information organized, and what does an analysis of this organization imply about the psychodynamics of impression formation and developmental changes in person perception?

The question is best approached by regarding the impression one has of another person as a subjective map (schema, programme or plan) which guides one's behaviour in relation to the stimulus person. Looked at in its simplest terms, the impression is the way we represent the person to ourselves. It acquires its contents and organization through a complex process of learning which is, of course, determined by our innate capacities and dispositions, and by our particular experiences and circumstances.

It is too soon to say whether 'learning about persons' is a special kind of learning. There seems to be no *prima facie* evidence for it, and we have already seen that little or nothing is gained by regarding 'person perception' as a special kind of perception. On the other hand, ethologists working with animals have demonstrated the operation of some highly specific perceptual and learning mechanisms, so we would be wise to leave that isue open for the time being.

Whatever processes underlie the *formation* of an impression, the *function* of the impression seems to be to enable the subject to orient himself to, and to adjust his own behaviour in relation to, the stimulus person. This statement is important because it implies that our impressions of others are basically subjective and personal—an issue that has been well worked over by Kelly and others. Looked at in this way, impression formation is instrumental. That is to say, it is a mechanism which subserves psychological adjustment (adaptation)—especially interpersonal adjustment.

If it is to be an efficient psychological mechanism of adjustment, impression formation—like other cognitive functions—must enable us to learn, that is to accommodate to the realities of life; and it must enable us to understand or influence, that is to assimilate the stimulus person's behaviour and circumstances. In practice, these two criteria are not always adequately met, in that, as already explained, we sometimes persist in holding erroneous ideas about other people which lead us to fail in our attempts to predict or influence their behaviour; similarly, we are sometimes unable to understand why other people behave as they do, and we are left feeling puzzled. Given adequate psychological resources and adequate opportunities for learning, however, we are continually comparing our expectations of others with actual outcomes, and readjusting our image of the other person so as to correct for such discrepancies—rather like an explorer tries to map new territory. The fault with this analysis is that it over-intellectualizes the process of impression formation, since it is obvious that our impressions of others are not entirely based on empirical evidence and logical reasoning. On the contrary, our impressions are often quite irrational, laden with feeling and motivational states, apart from being personal and subjective.

If we combine categories 27, 28 and 29 (Mutual Interaction, Subject's Opinion of and Behaviour towards the Stimulus Person, and Comparison with Self, respectively) we find that they make up something like 13 per cent of the total contents of a description of a person (see Table 7). This gives us an estimate of the extent to which our impressions of others are based on personal factors. Information relating to more objective information is contained in categories 1 to 5, and averages about 22 per cent of the total. Thus, as one might expect, our impressions of others are partly subjective and partly objective. We also have information, not presented in this book, which shows that when a group of subjects are describing the *same* person (with whom they are about equally well acquainted) they agree with each other in some respects but differ considerably in others. This result emerged from our research work into the social psychology of reputation. The studies carried out with the film, and described later, also revealed a considerable consensus of opinion—as judged by the distribution of ratings—about the stimulus person in the film. Again, as one might expect, our impressions of others are partly personal (or idiosyncratic) and partly social (or shared).

We could expect to find, too, that, on average, a person's impression of himself would be partly objective, partly subjective, and partly idiosyncratic, partly shared. There is, therefore, a sort of triadic relationship between the person, his self-concept and his reputation; they form an interlocking system of psychological and social processes. We mention this issue at this stage merely in order to emphasize the complexities and ramifications of the processes at work. We hope to deal with them in detail in a subsequent publication.

From what we have said so far, it appears that impression formation, that is learning about persons, and the utilization of impressions in interpersonal adjustment, have much in common with the social psychology of beliefs, attitudes, values and opinions. We shall not attempt to spell out the details, but it is worth mentioning a few major similarities. A stimulus person is the focus of systems of beliefs, feelings, evaluations and intentions on the part of other people. We could, if we wished, construct scales to measure attitudes towards the stimulus person; rating scales, after all, are one sort of attitude scale, and the content analysis of free descriptions that we have used is a recognized method for investigating attitudes.

Our beliefs, values and attitudes tend to develop an internal consistency —partly as a consequence of the processes of assimilation and accommodation to which we have already referred. Impressions, like attitudes, have an *instrumental* function in personal adjustment—in the sense that the subject employs them to work out strategies and tactics of interpersonal adjustment and to weigh up the associated costs and benefits. Similarly, impressions have an *ego-defensive* function in that they reinforce and protect the subject's basic patterns of adjustment. For example, in an attempt to externalize (project) anxiety-provoking feelings—say of sex or aggression—the subject may wrongly attribute characteristics to a stimulus person; alternatively, the subject's overwhelming affection may prevent him from making a realistic appraisal of the stimulus person —'Love is blind'.

Impressions, like attitudes, find expression in opinions; and the written descriptions we have obtained could be regarded as statements of opinion by the subjects about the stimulus person. There is one important point to bear in mind here. A written description tends to be a fairly formal and considered statement of beliefs, often backed up by reference to objective evidence and, as we shall see, characterized by a good deal of qualification and internal coherence. Spoken opinions about others in daily life, on the other hand, are, by comparison, short, simple, informal, and either grossly over-inclusive or tied to specific issues. Moreover, such opinions tend to be strongly expressive and tactical; that is to say, they do not necessarily represent a statement of belief at all, but operate like moves in a social game. Expressions of opinion are used to *test out* the reactions of other people, to *display* conformity or deviance, or to *prepare the ground* for subsequent action; they act as *behavioural outlets* for feelings of aggression and affection, and for the *exercise of dispositional states* like humour, dominance, intelligence and dependence. We are not proposing that there is a difference in kind between written opinions and spoken opinions, for it is not too difficult to detect expressive qualities— sarcasm, admiration, anxiety—in written descriptions. But we are saying that written descriptions do not adequately reflect the *affective* qualities associated with basic beliefs, values and attitudes, although they do reflect the cognitive aspects of a personality impression. The written descriptions, in other words, give a better representation of the explicit mental processes associated with personality impressions, whereas spoken opinions, to the sensitive ear anyway, probably reveal more of the associated affective and motivational processes.

Impression formation and change, like attitude formation and change, depend upon a number of conditions. First, there must be some occasions for learning and some contingencies of reinforcement. These may involve the stimulus person directly, as in face-to-face encounters, or they may involve consequences arising directly or indirectly from the actions of the stimulus person. Alternatively, these learning experiences may involve other people who, through their actions and expressive behaviour in relation to a stimulus person exert an influence on the subject's impression of that stimulus person. Second, there must be psychological mechanisms —of the sort to which we have already referred—which enable the subject to achieve a kind of balance or equilibrium between (a) the requirement that the system of values, attitudes and beliefs should be reasonably coherent and stable (otherwise the subject would not be able to establish consistent and efficient responses), and (b) the requirement that the system should change in response to changed conditions (otherwise the subject's responses would eventually become maladaptive).

It is obvious that one of the factors involved in impression formation and change is the credibility of the *informant*, and this is relevant to the social psychology of reputation; another factor is the credibility of the *information*, that is the ease with which it can be incorporated into the subject's existing frame of reference.

Exchange theory would suggest that we are influenced by the expected personal costs and benefits associated with the existence of the stimulus person, and that these subjective considerations are somehow incorporated into the mechanism of impression formation and change. The fact that we make comparisons between ourselves and others, and between the various stimulus persons we know, means that the impressions we hold are not independent of one another. It is well known that judgments of all kinds are affected by the context or frame of reference in which they occur, so it would not be surprising to find that our impression of a person is formed in terms of, and partly in comparison with, the other people we know, particularly those people with whom we feel the stimulus person can be compared. For example, if the comparison persons we know are on average fairly mild in temper, then this average value is one of the reference points we refer to when we are forming an impression of a particular stimulus person.

In practice, the process of judgment is not as rational or as explicit as we have made out. Moreover, as Smith (1966) and others have pointed out, people are likely to differ from one another in their reference levels, and in their ability to discriminate between stimulus persons.

Other factors relevant to the study of both impressions and attitudes include: the order of presentation of information about the stimulus person, qualified versus unqualified communications, commitment and dissonance, the 'sleeper' effect, influence and persuasibility, and the effects of selectivity and distortion in perception and remembering.

At this point we have clearly moved from a cognitive approach to impression formation to a social-psychological approach, and it would take us too far afield to explore these social issues in more detail. What we have done, however, is to prepare the ground for an analysis of the ways in which impressions are organized.

III. A Theory of Impression Formation and Change

The simplest way of describing how the contents of impressions are organized is to identify the main principles of organization and briefly describe their mode of operation.

Selection. It is obvious that a personality impression is by no means a comprehensive account of a person. When judged against all the things that might be said about the stimulus person—or even only things that might be included in a biography or case study—the personality impression constitutes a very small fraction. Moreover, this small fraction is not representative of all the information that is relevant, but is biased by accidents of behaviour sampling, unequal exposure to sources of information, and by subjective factors in perception and retention. We have seen that over two-thirds of the contents are accounted for by categories 1, 2, 9, 10, 20, 27, 28 and 31, and this in itself illustrates a kind of selection effect, but it is a selection effect common to members of the population we were dealing with. Within each category—including these salient ones —one could probably distinguish subcategories, which would in turn illustrate further characteristic differentials—or selection effects—in the contents of impressions.

Naturally, there are quantitative differences between individuals in the extent to which they conform to this average distribution of contents, but there are also qualitative differences between them. For example, 'dark hair' and 'blue eyes' count equally as elements in Appearance; similarly 'aggressive' and 'generous' count equally as General Personality Attributes. But different subjects will select different elements for different stimulus persons on different occasions.

Focus. Some psychologists argue that personality study is concerned with the 'person as a whole', but a dispassionate analysis of what goes on when psychologists carry out personality assessments or case-studies clearly reveals that the study of the 'whole person' is a myth. We do not study the whole person, we study a very small number of psychological issues focused on *one person*. The same kind of focus takes place in every-day life. When we form impressions of other people, there are usually reasons for doing so—otherwise we tend to regard them as ciphers, that is as persons enacting routine roles of no great personal interest to us; we take note of a few of the more obvious features relating to appearance, identity, and so on, sufficient to allow us to fulfil routine social trans-actions. But when we form impressions of people whose existence we regard as having some importance to us personally—that is persons with whom we are *ego-involved*—we are no longer content to regard the person simply in terms of identity and role. Our concern tends to be focused upon : (a) those characteristics which are basic requirements for a well-formed impression, namely, those referred to above, and (b) those characteristics which are relevant to the particular reasons for forming the impression. For example, the impression formed by a pupil of his teacher, or by a patient of his doctor, or by a housewife of her neighbour, is partly focused upon those characteristics which are relevant to the rela-tionship : the teacher's habits and mannerisms, the doctor's competence and concern, the neighbour's friendliness and status. One reason why the subject's attention is focused upon these characteristics rather than others is that they impinge directly upon the subject's personal adjust-ment. That is, they contribute to or detract from his welfare, they form part of the contingencies of reinforcement which shape his behaviour, they figure as costs and benefits in the individual's system of values. Another reason why the subject's attention is focused upon some charac-teristics of the stimulus person rather than others is that they indirectly reveal that person's basic capacities, dispositions, disabilities, motives, and so on. Knowledge of this kind is then used by the subject to influence, explain or anticipate the behaviour of the stimulus person, with consequential benefits to the subject.

Internal coherence. As with other cognitive systems, impressions of persons tend towards : the elimination of contradictions, the establish-ment of confirmatory relationships and the making good of omissions. These are topics which are mentioned in our review of the literature on person perception. In so far as the elements (contents) can be made explicit, and in so far as he has the necessary intellectual capacities and experience, the subject will become aware that some aspects of the impression he has formed do not equate well with others. For example, he may become aware that his own vague dislike of the stimulus person does not square with his knowledge that the stimulus person is well thought of by other people. This awareness will sensitize him to relevant information, and his puzzlement will motivate him to resolve the contradiction. Whether he does this judiciously or by convoluted defensive manoeuvres—like rationalization—is another matter. Conversely, the subject may become aware that one aspect of his impression ties in very well with another, and this will lead him to feel more confidence in the impression as a whole—even though, as psychologists know very well, internal consistency or reliability is no guarantee of validity.

A further contribution to the internal coherence of an impression is made by a process that we can call *recruitment*. Those features of the stimulus person's existence which are of interest to the subject appear to act like informational magnets. That is to say, they attract relevant information and repel irrelevant information. We shall discuss further in Chapter 12 the probability that the subject's impression is not based on an averaging or summating process of *all* his experiences of the stimulus person—see Anderson (1965) and Triandis and Fishbein (1963). Instead, his attention is *selectively* tuned to certain *foci of interest*, so that he can *recruit information* relevant to his *concern*—or ego-involvement—with the stimulus person. Recruitment seems to be particularly strong in relation to information needed to fill gaps in the impression, to eliminate differences and incompatibilities between elements, to establish connections and similarities, and to reinforce those parts of the impression which are of special concern to the subject. The topic of trait implications mentioned in the literature review is also relevant to the issue of recruitment.

One serious flaw in person perception is the biasing effect of first impressions; the early stages of impression formation generate a subjective need for internal coherence which leads the subject to favour compatible information rather than incompatible information. Hence the process of assimilation leads to cumulative errors unless or until the process of accommodation forces the subject to come to terms with the real world—in the form of incontrovertible and insistent facts—by bringing his impression of the stimulus person more into line with the evidence.

In many instances, however, the demands of life are not so insistent, and the subject may continue to hold hopelessly erroneous and irrational impressions about others because those impressions are never required to be tested against rational and empirical criteria which are sufficiently exacting. Moreover, it seems likely that the average subject can engage in a variety of defensive manoeuvres to avoid the sometimes unpleasant task of readjusting his impressions of others, for example, by refusing to listen, by ignoring facts, by putting his own preferred construction on the evidence, and so on.

Crystallization. Under the heading of crystallization we shall include a collection of processes normally associated with the psychology of memory functions, the spread of rumour, and dream interpretation.

It is well known that the long-term recall even of relatively meaningful material is characterized by various sorts of distortions and omissions. The most familiar of these perhaps are sharpening and levelling, transposition, elaboration, assimilation, omission and false inclusion. That is to say, when we have undergone learning experiences of the sort required for the formation of an impression, the information subsequently recalled is usually considerably less than the original information. Many minor details, or even substantial parts, are forgotten. Other details are retained and achieve greater prominence than they had originally. Where the original information was structured, for example, sequentially or in terms of its own internal logic, elements in the information subsequently recalled may be transposed, with consequential changes in the meaning and functional effectiveness of the impression.

Further distortions of the impression take place because the subject attempts to actively *reconstruct* the information he is attempting to recall, since much of it may not be so familiar or so well rehearsed as to permit a more passive kind of recollection. As a consequence, the subject appears to 'recall', but actually invents, information which was not present originally, he elaborates on some aspects of the information and neglects others, he incorporates material which properly belongs elsewhere in his experience, he assimilates material into personally convenient frames of reference, such as typological or explanatory categories with which he is familiar. His own implicit assumptions about human behaviour lead him to certain implications which he cannot always easily distinguish from his memory of first-hand experience.

The effects upon impression formation of the distortion induced by memory processes in retention and recall are fairly obvious. Our impression of another person will tend to lose content elements; other elements will become relatively more prominent; information relating to biographical sequences will become transposed; the 'internal logic' of the contents—their order of presentation, their relationships with each other—will also become transposed and oversimplified; information relating to other people or to prior experience may get incorporated with the subject's impression of the stimulus person; the subject will tend to 'make good' deficiencies in his impression by introducing false suppositions; and he will tend to distort the information by fitting it into a preconceived, and possibly quite inadequate, frame of reference.

We explained in a previous section that our impressions of others are not independent of each other even for one and the same subject. Considerable benefits are achieved—in the form of speed and economy of effort—if the subject adopts a standard frame of reference and a standard procedure (albeit implicit) for forming impressions of people. Obviously, however, the subject is constrained by the varieties of persons he encounters to adapt his frame of reference to deal with different *sorts* of people.

This situation is further complicated by the fact that our impression of a stimulus person is not independent of the impressions formed of him by other people. This is the phenomenon of reputation to which we have already referred. Among the effects operating here, perhaps the most prominent are those of conformity, and the distortion brought about by the transmission of information from one person to another. The latter distortions have been dealt with in the social psychology of rumour and communication, and are similar to those to which we have already referred. The conformity effect is a well-known phenomenon in social psychology. In the case of impression formation, information about the stimulus person is passed from one person to another during social interaction, and people's attitudes towards to a stimulus person are revealed in their actions and in their expressive behaviour. As a consequence of these shared experiences, there is a convergence of views about the stimulus person. In other words, there is more agreement between people in the contents of their impression and even in the way these contents are organized. This form of majority conformity, however, is only one sort of effect. In addition, we find that persons who are high in esteem or prestige within their social group act as reference points, so that the impressions held by other members of the group tend to converge on those held by these influential people. Furthermore, impressions are susceptible to the effects of propaganda—as revealed by the now common and often successful attempts by experts in public relations to manipulate the public image—or reputation—of a person, such as an entertainer or politician.

In more mundane affairs, gossip, rumour, and self-advertisement produce analogous effects. The term 'reputation' refers to the personality impression shared by, or common to, the members of a given social group. The social psychology of reputation is too large a topic to take up in this book, but it is worth mentioning in passing that, contrary to expectation, our research shows that the extent to which information and opinion about a person is common to people within a social group is surprisingly small, and the information which is *not* widely shared is correspondingly large.

Persons, perhaps more so than anything else in our experience, are the focus of intense and complex feelings and motives. These *affective* processes must be regarded as the main determinants of impression formation, except where relationships with the stimulus person are relatively routine and emotionally neutral. Impressions of the latter type are not very interesting from the point of view of psychological research. Impressions of the former type, on the other hand, are difficult to investigate scientifically. The research we have described has, however, found a middle way between these two extremes, in so far as the subjects' selection of liked and disliked stimulus persons enabled us to sample impressions laden with moderate degrees of affect. Even so, as we have already admitted, the free description method of eliciting personality impressions seems to have the effect of inhibiting emotional expression, in comparison with, say, impressions elicited in casual conversation, or during counselling. For this reason, we have little or no empirical data on the emotional and motivational features of impression formation.

Lack of empirical data, however, is an open invitation to speculation, and we wonder whether the affective determinants in impression formation might operate in a manner comparable with those described in dream theory. Briefly, this would mean that the impression we have of a stimulus person with whom we are emotionally involved is a compromise product. The compromise is required because we cannot construe the stimulus person to be exactly what we *wish* him (or her) to be, and we may be prevented by emotional factors from construing him as he *really* is. The compromise is not static; it shifts with our circumstances and states of mind, it changes in relation to memories of and comparisons with other people, real or imaginary, it shifts in response to our successive experiences with the other person. Impression formation, in other words, produces not a fixed image but a kaleidoscope of changing effects as the individual strives, perhaps intuitively, to balance, or to bring into some sort of equilibrium, those constraints arising from within his own nature and those arising from the environment.

Various facets of the subject's impression of the stimulus person could be focal points for the convergence or *condensation* of latent thoughts, feelings and wishes. For example, a subject who has the impression, among other things, that the stimulus person loves him, may thereby achieve, albeit implicitly, a sense of security and relief from anxiety, a sense of superiority and achievement, opportunities to be aggressive without fear of retaliation, and the revival or continuation of an emotionally satisfying dependency relationship. Also, there may be *contamination* or *displacement* of affect from one impression to another, especially in the heat of an ongoing emotional encounter.

It is convenient, therefore, to assume that the *manifest contents* of a personality impression are the explicit account of the much more extensive *latent contents*—of thoughts, feelings, wishes, and so on—which tend to remain implicit.

The manifest contents operate at various levels of awareness and disclosure : there are those which are unreservedly public, there are those which are for restricted circulation among the subject's friends, confidants or therapist, there are those confined to the subject's private world; and—if we go the whole way with psychodynamic theory—there are latent contents which the subject cannot reveal even to himself.

Even at a relatively commonsense level, it is clear that large parts of the latent contents are nonverbal and noncognitive (to the extent that they can be distinguished as motivational or emotional states). We often struggle to 'find words' to express our impression of the stimulus person; and, having done so, we frequently find that we have somehow failed to convey it.

The manifest contents of the impression are related to the latent contents by the process of *impression formation* which we have analysed in somewhat speculative and approximate terms. In the sections that follow we move away from a broad theoretical approach to a narrower empirical approach which is interesting in its own right—in that it deals with some of the organization factors in impression formation—but by no means provides all the substantial evidence needed to support the speculative theoretical framework we have just outlined. The sections that follow particularly illustrate the 'effort after meaning' so characteristic of rationality.

IV. Qualifying and Organizing Terms

A. Introduction

The analyses reported so far have examined the statements (elements or descriptive units) that make up the *contents* of personality impressions. But most impressions have some semblance of structure or *organization,* in that the elements are selected and arranged so as to form a system, which has its own kind of 'grammar', as it were, and conforms to certain rules (not necessarily known explicitly by the user). A number of investigators, starting with the pioneering studies of Asch (1946), have described the organized and unified nature of impressions. It has become apparent, however, that Asch exaggerated the degree to which this occurs—see Luchins (1948) and Gollin (1954). It was suggested in Chapter 2 that there are two sets of organizing processes : (a) implicit theories (of trait implications) which help the perceiver to generate new associations and close the gaps in his knowledge thus rounding out his impression and achieving consistency and comprehensiveness; (b) the use of words and phrases which modify the meaning of the psychological terms applied to the person, or specify the relationship between actions, attributes and circumstances. These processes are connected with those that we have already referred to as 'recruitment'; they organize the elements in an impression and relate them to one another, give shape to the subject's ideas, give these ideas greater internal coherence, and enable the subject to communicate the information more effectively. Although trait implications have been studied in detail, the organizational aspects of impression formation have been largely ignored.

The aims of the analysis reported in this chapter are to isolate some of the qualifying and organizing processes found in personality descriptions, and to explore developmental changes in the ability of children to organize their impressions. The categories in the present analysis, therefore, are additional to, and serve to integrate and refine, the categories numbered 1 to 33.

B. A Classification of Qualifying and Organizing Terms

Prior to the development of an explicit system for describing the organization of impressions, we had supposed that at least two basic processes were at work. One had the effect of *qualifying* the elements in a description; the other had the effect of *organizing* them. Subsequent examination, however, revealed a larger number of processes. The procedure used to define and classify these organizing and qualifying processes was similar to that used in developing categories for the second content analysis—see Chapter 8. All the words and phrases deemed to qualify and organize the other contents were printed on separate cards, and then sorted into one exhaustive and exclusive set of categories. The number of different statements that were used was 103. An exhaustive set was achieved by using a category for unclassifiable and miscellaneous statements; these statements could have been coded if the system had been extended, but the data would have been so thinly spread that statistical analysis would have been impossible.

Nine categories were developed: two for qualifiers, six for organizers, and one for miscellaneous statements. These categories are listed in Table 14.

The reliability of the coding for the organizing and qualifying terms was assessed by one investigator and one judge analysing 128 descriptions representing all Age, Sex, Intelligence and Stimulus Person factors. There was 78.3 per cent agreement for the qualifying categories and 72.5 per cent agreement for the organizing categories. These levels of reliability

Table 14. Classification of qualifying and organizing terms

A. *Qualifying Terms*

    i. *Modal Qualification* indicates the probability of occurrence of a particular quality, or its intensity if it occurs. These terms say something about the likelihood of occurrence, frequency, intensity, and duration of personal characteristics, for example, 'very', 'mostly', 'sometimes', 'usually', 'always', 'can be', 'scarcely ever', 'quite', 'often', and various combinations of these.

    ii. *Obscurity of Impression* indicates that the writer is not too sure of the impression he has formed, and finds it difficult to decide whether or not the person possesses a given quality, for example, 'seems to be', 'sort of', 'I suppose . . .'

B. *Organizing Terms*

    Note: *Quasi-causal explanations* are statements which attempt to explain *why* a person possesses a particular psychological characteristic, either in terms of the other qualities he possesses, or because of the circumstances he is in. This category divides into two sub categories:

    iii. The *explicit* use of 'because', for example, 'He is . . . because . . .'

    iv. The *implicit* use of 'because', as in: (*a*) the interdependency of psychological processes and qualities, for example, 'He is nervous and this makes him shy at times', 'He is only kind if he is in a good temper'; (*b*) the effects of circumstances on psychological processes, for example, 'He is cheerful considering the difficulties he is in', 'He is quiet when in company'.

    v. *Exclusion of the Usual Trait or Situational Implication.* This is indicated by a statement which, in effect, instructs the reader (or listener) not to make the usual inferences from a particular quality the stimulus person is said to possess. The effect is to modify the operation of the implicit theory of trait implications held by the reader (or listener), for example, 'She is always being kind *but* she is nosy', 'She is very nice *but* keeps breaking friends with me', 'She is quite modern *although* sensible', 'He is very good at work *but* very slow'.

    vi. *Specificity of Trait Expression.* Trait names are highly generalized terms for describing behaviour and behavioural tendencies. When applied to a particular individual, however, additional information may have to be provided so as to specify in greater detail *how* the trait is expressed by that person, for example, 'She does not always argue, if she does, she does not get aggressive', 'She is greedy because she never shares things although others offer her things'. Note, in this last example that the term ' because' is used to make an 'evidential' rather than a 'causal' statement.

    vii. *Distinction between: Qualities which are Real rather than Apparent, Actual rather than Possible, or Past rather than Present,* for example, 'Although she professes to be your friend, when you are ill she doesn't visit you', 'He is not really . . .', 'She used to be . . . , now, she is . . .'

    viii. *Metaphor, Simile, and Analogy.* These are statements which might be assimilated to category vi above, since they are rarely used, for example, 'He flares up easily', 'He's a pig'.

C. *Miscellaneous*

    ix. *Miscellaneous* items are those which do not fall clearly into one or the other of the above categories of organizing and qualifying terms.

---

are lower than in our other content analyses, possibly because the statements are complex. Nevertheless, they represent workable levels of agreement for statistical purposes, although the likelihood of failing to find an association or difference when one exists, rather than the opposite error, is increased. A content analysis of eight descriptions from a single subject is given below.

A boy aged 15,8 describes eight stimulus persons:

A man he likes

Statement	Category
He is *very* understanding and will listen to your problems	i. Modal Qualifier
and is *always* ready with helpful advice. He is a meditative man and likes to think things over. He is	i. Modal Qualifier
very much a family man and	i. Modal Qualifier
likes children. He is *very*	i. Modal Qualifier
forthright *and says what he means even if it hurts the person he is speaking to.*	vi. Specificity of Trait Expression
He boasts *quite a lot*	i. Modal Qualifier
about his son's progress in school	vi. Specificity of Trait Expression

A woman he likes

Statement	Category
She is *always* kind to strangers. She is not old-fashioned and stodgy but is *fairly* modern.	i. Modal Qualifier
She *always seems* calm	ii. Obscurity of Impression
and *yet* she *always seems* to be doing something or going somewhere.	v. Exclude Trait Implication
She is a *very* jovial person, good tempered and	i. Modal Qualifier
good humoured and *very* easy going and lively.	i. Modal Qualifier
She is *fairly* intelligent	i. Modal Qualifier
but does not boast.	v. Exclude Trait Implication

A boy he likes

Statement	Category
Phil is *very* modest. *He is*	i. Modal Qualifier
even shyer than I am with	iv. Quasi-causal Explanation Implicit
strangers and yet is very	i. Modal Qualifier
talkative with people he knows	
and likes. He *always* seems	i. Modal Qualifier
good tempered and I have	
never seen him in a bad	
temper. He *tends to degrade*	i. Modal Qualifier
other people's achievements and	v. Exclude Trait Implication
yet never praises his own.	
He does not *seem* to voice	ii. Obscurity of Impression
his own opinions to anyone.	
He *easily* gets nervous.	i. Modal Qualifier

A girl he likes

Statement	Category
She has the same interests	
as me, and likes reading a	
lot. She *always does well*	i. Modal Qualifier
at school and yet does	
not boast about it.	v. Exclude Trait Implication
She is *very* shy indeed	i. Modal Qualifier
even with people she	
knows very well. She is	
easily upset and yet never	i. Modal Qualifier
gets in a really bad temper.	v. Exclude Trait Implication

A man he dislikes

Statement	Category
He is a bully. He	
expects you to have	
consideration for his	vii. Distinction between Real and Apparent Qualities
feelings and yet he has	
none for yours. He is	
rather thick, as he	i. Modal Qualifier

brings his wife home	vi. Specificity of Trait Expression
from the bus stop in	
his car. He is *always*	i. Modal Qualifier
showing off his car and	
he pretends he knows	vii. Distinction between Real and
	Apparent Qualities
all about them. He is	
inclined to be easily bossed	i. Modal Qualifier
about by his wife.	
He hates children	iii. Quasi-causal Explanation
	Explicit
only because he has none of his own.	

A woman he dislikes

Statement	Category
She will not stand up for	
her own opinion. She is	
very old-fashioned. She	i. Modal Qualifier
never seems to laugh or	ii. Obscurity of Impression
enjoy herself. She is a	
person who in an argument	
will *always* stand and watch	i. Modal Qualifier
cheering both sides on at the	
same time. She *always*	ii. Obscurity of Impression
seems to have a grudge	
against something or	
someone. She *never* enjoys	i. Modal Qualifier
herself and *seems*	ii. Obscurity of Impression
determined to stop anyone	
else from enjoying	
themselves. She is *always*	i. Modal Qualifier
boasting *about her*	
relations' success.	vi. Specificity of Trait Expression

A boy he dislikes

Statement	Category
He is *a big head yet*	v. Exclude Trait Implication
he does not belittle other	
people. He is *inclined* to	i. Modal Qualifier
throw his weight about	iii. Quasi-causal Explanation
	Explicit

as he is rather tall. He
is good mannered and
generally good tempered.

He *always boasts about*	i. Modal Qualifier
his ability as an athlete	vi. Specificity of Trait Expression
and a gymnast. He *always seems*	ii. Obscurity of Impression

too smug and self confident.

A girl he dislikes

Statement	Category
She is *always* talking and	i. Modal Qualifier
boasting when she is with	iv. Quasi-causal Explanation Implicit
her friends and yet is very	i. Modal Qualifier
quiet in the company of	
adults. She is *very definitely*	i. Modal Qualifier
not modest. She is a *very*	i. Modal Qualifier
shallow person and will	
always follow the crowd. She	i. Modal Qualifier
is big headed and thinks	
she knows everything	
and belittles other people's	
successes. She is *inclined*	i. Modal Qualifier
to sulk easily *if she*	iv. Quasi-causal Explanation Implicit

does not get her own way.

C. Results

The frequency of use of the categories of organization and qualification were examined in relation to the now familiar variables of Age, Sex, Intelligence and Stimulus Person. In view of the extremely skewed distributions of responses associated with the low incidence of qualifying and organizing material, nonparametric tests of significance were used. For Age, Sex and Intelligence, the distributions were dichotomized at the median, and the resulting contingency tables were analysed by means of chi-squared. In order to control for fluency, the number of qualifying and organizing statements made about all eight stimulus persons by each subject was expressed as a proportion of his total number of central statements. Note that only those qualifiers and organizers associated with *central* statements were analysed.

There were significant age differences for all categories as shown in Table 15. Clear-cut increases with age in frequency of use were found in all categories except category i (Modal Qualification) where the relationship with age was somewhat erratic. A significant sex difference was found only for category v (Exclusion of the Usual Trait or Situational Implications) ($\chi^2 = 9.24$, $p < 0.01$); girls used this category more than boys. The higher intelligence group (as compared with the lower) made significantly greater use of : category i (Modal Qualification) ($p < 0.001$), category iv (Implicit Quasi-causal Explanations) ($p < 0.05$), category v (Exclusion of the Usual Trait of Situational Implications) ($p < 0.001$), category vi (Specificity of Trait Expression) ($p < 0.01$), and category vii (Distinction between Real and Apparent Qualities, etc.) ($p < 0.02$).

Table 15. Effects of age, sex and intelligence of subject on the use of qualifying and organizing terms

Content categories		Chi-squared values		
				Intelli-
		Age	Sex	gence
Main	Subsidiary	(d.f.=7)	(d.f.=1)	(d.f.=1)
Qualification	i. Modal qualification	14·40	3·20	12·10 §
	ii. Obscurity of impression	8·24 ‖	0·18	1·62
Organization	iii. Quasi-causal explanations explicit	39·56 §	2·74	2·74
	iv. Quasi-causal explanations implicit	24·61 §	3·22	5·17 *
	v. Exclusion of the usual trait implications	42·99 §	9·24 ‡	13·81 §
	vi. Specificity of trait expression	30·38 §	0·01	7·13 ‡
	vii. Distinctions (various)	54·49 §	0·63	5·70 †
	viii. Metaphor and analogy	18·16 §‖	2·50	0·16
Miscellaneous	ix. Unclassifiable	NA	NA	NA

* $p < 0.05$
† $p < 0.02$
‡ $p < 0.01$
§ $p < 0.001$
NA—not analysed, insufficient data
‖—d.f. = 3 (age groups combined in pairs)
Age: increase with age
Sex: girls greater than boys
Intelligence: higher intelligence children greater than lower intelligence children

The category totals associated with the stimulus person variables were expressed as proportions of the number of central statements used to describe the four stimulus persons constituting that level of the variable, that is adult versus child, liked versus disliked. These proportions were converted to ordinal values and analysed by the Friedman Analysis of Variance by Ranks—see Siegel (1956). In view of the infrequent use of organizing material, the categories were not analysed separately; instead, the subsidiary categories were summed and the two broad categories (qualification and organization) were analysed. Only one of the analyses proved to be statistically significant; more qualifiers were used to describe liked stimulus persons than to describe disliked stimulus persons ($p < 0.001$).

D. Discussion

The increase with age in organizing and qualifying statements was reflected in two marked changes in performance. The first occurred between the ages of 7 and 8 years, the second between 12 and 13 years. Only in adolescence were these categories used by half the subjects. The differences in performance between the ages of 7 and 8 years have been reported in previous analyses, but those between the ages of 12 and 13 years have not. It is interesting to observe that, while the frequency of central statements (including traits) tends to level out in adolescence, the use of organizing and qualifying material continues to increase. There must be a ceiling to the number of terms that are normally used to describe other people, and it may be that such a limit is reached either just before or soon after the onset of adolescence. In brief, then, psychological growth means an increased ability to organize and integrate impressions plus a larger and a more useful set of descriptive categories including more specific trait names.

The use of Modal Qualifiers, such as 'very', 'often', 'always', did not increase linearly with age although the effect of age was significant. Young children made frequent use of a few qualifiers such as 'very' and 'always' as part of a general tendency to make extreme judgments. They tended to regard people as either 'very good' or 'very bad' and used qualifiers to polarize their impressions in this manner. It will be remembered that Modal Qualifiers attach rough subjective estimates of frequency and intensity to the attributes of the stimulus person. Older subjects, especially those over 13 years, used a greater variety of qualifiers and were more discerning in their use. They used qualifiers to modify the relative importance of traits and to focus attention on certain qualities —making them more salient than others; so, frequently, qualifiers were applied to only one personal quality in the description.

Modal Qualifiers such as 'very, very', 'very', 'not very' and 'never' increase the range of individual differences over which traits can be applied and considerably increase discrimination between attributes;

for example, a child who uses these four qualifiers and one trait—'kind'
—can make four discriminations in degree of 'kindness', and so extend
the usefulness of the term. Many different qualifiers are used separately
or in combination, thus making possible fine discriminations within
traits. Cliff (1959) has demonstrated that some qualifiers used in combination have a multiplicative and not an additive effect. These findings
illustrate the close connections between impression formation and
language. The dearth of research data on this topic raises the possibility
that trait ratings may do violence to natural usage in the attribution of
traits.

The use of organizing and qualifying statements not only represents
an attempt to make the communication (of information about the
stimulus person) as effective as possible, but also shows that a person's
behaviour can be subjected to causal analysis at a commonsense level.
The incidence of Quasi-causal Explanations (categories iii and iv) in
older children's descriptions showed that children were beginning to
understand that a 'person' is not the absolute cause of his own behaviour,
but merely part of a larger causal nexus, namely, the person in an
environment. That is to say, some of the determining factors of a
person's behaviour are seen to belong in his environment and in biological
factors outside that person's control. Coming to understand this concept
is a major advance, for now the child is able not only to conceptualize
others in terms of psychological qualities, but also to see how these
qualities function in relation to other attributes, and in relation to
situational factors. Instead of perceiving a person in terms of a set of
independent and somewhat unrelated qualities, he perceives a 'gestalt'
or, more realistically, fragments of a gestalt. In effect, the child has
begun to grasp two of the concepts emphasized by Allport (1961) in
this theory of personality: (a) traits interact with one another (see also
Asch, 1946), and (b) behaviour is a function of a person in a particular
situation $(P_i \times E_j \rightarrow B_{ij})$. For example, older children wrote, 'She has an
inferiority complex and wants to hide it', 'She is friendly to you when
she wants something', 'He is nervous and this makes him shy.'

It is interesting to observe that, although asked only to *describe* the
stimulus person, many older children offered *explanations* for his actions.
Presumably, they felt that a mere description of his behaviour was
misleading, in the sense that its causal origins would probably be
misconstrued unless made explicit (not that children need be fully 'aware'
of all this). Some children were aware that their descriptions were
often not so much factual reports as expressions of their feelings and
opinions. They appreciated that other observers might have different
feelings and opinions about the stimulus person; hence the attempt to

justify their beliefs by giving supporting evidence and explanation. Thus, quasi-causal statements have an organizing and integrating function as well as serving to explain and justify the perceiver's impressions; they connect different parts (elements) of the description, thus enhancing the meaningfulness of the whole and its parts.

The use of category v (Instruction to Exclude the Usual Trait or Situational Implications) shows that a subject's system of constructs or beliefs has become structured and organized, since he is somehow aware of his own implicit theory of trait implications. Otherwise, why should he qualify his assertion? He appreciates that trait implications are not absolute, invariant relationships, but flexible and selectively modifiable according to the nature of the stimulus person. The older child seems to possess an implicit understanding that trait implications are convenient and simple social rules and stereotypes that are valuable in achieving internal coherence in impressions, but are liable to frequent exceptions —for example, he writes, 'She is very clever but doesn't boast', 'He is shy and quiet but you can turn to him if in trouble', 'She is very sensible but very jolly.' The existence of such statements in older children's descriptions suggests that the usual studies of trait implications are too simple. This may help to explain the results of a study by Gross (1961) which showed that the effects of implicit theories (of trait implications) are small compared with the effects of stimulus person factors. It also casts doubt on the validity of the Repertory Grid Method (see Kelly, 1955), which seems to assume an invariant relationship between traits regardless of the stimulus person and therefore seems unable to account for how impression formation accommodates to exceptions to the rules (of usage and implication). We need to discover the average directions and strengths of trait implications in a given population, but we also need to know how flexibly they are used in practice, how they are modified through experience to take into account situational factors and the uniqueness of the particular stimulus person. A modification of the Repertory Grid Method along these lines could prove to be an important contribution to the study of cognitive structure and person perception.

The use of qualifying words and phrases like 'but' and 'although' places constraints on trait implications and helps the perceiver to produce a balanced account by counteracting the primacy effect in communication. Such terms serve as a reminder to attach equal importance to particular parts of a statement (and not to attach too much weight to the first, or last, parts). So far we have not considered the problems of salience and serial order in the use of traits and other sorts of content. One would expect salient traits (or other features) to occur early in the description, except that commonly used traits (which by definition carry relatively little information), being familiar, will also tend to occur early in the description. Proximity of items could indicate strength of association, and salience can be indicated by emphasis, repetition, and so on.

The use of category vi (Specificity of Trait Expression) is like that of category v (Instruction to Exclude the Usual Trait or Situational Implications) in so far as it indicates that the subject is aware of the need to accommodate his psychological concepts to the facts of the particular person. The child who uses statements like, 'He does not mind sharing his sweets but is careful not to be over-generous' or 'She is clever in one sense, she comes top of the form' is aware that although traits are generalized descriptions, they need to be particularized if the stimulus person's qualities are to be stated accurately and if the reader (or listener) is to receive the right impression. The child has become aware that 'generosity' is not a physical characteristic, but refers to a common factor in a wide variety of actions, in that 'generosity' can be expressed in different ways, by different people, at different times. This is a substantial intellectual achievement.

It should be noted that subjects in the higher intelligence groups make greater use of organizing terms than subjects of lower intelligence. This result may shed light on the finding described in Chapter 7 that children of higher intelligence use more central statements but not more trait names than children of lower intelligence. The ability to distinguish between different expressions of the 'same' trait adds a qualitative dimension to the quantitative dimension referred to above: Modal Qualification. These dimensions increase the discriminating power of trait concepts because a child need possess only a few traits, and yet differentiate satisfactorily between a great variety of people. The ability to attribute different traits, varying in degree and in mode of expression, to different people provides a covering definition for the attainment of formal cognitive operations (in the Piagetian sense) in the developmental psychology of person perception.

Metaphor and Analogy were rarely used. They probably serve a rhetorical function by drawing attention to a trait (or its specific mode of expression) or by subverting the facts for some ulterior aim such as ridicule, hostility, or admiration one example from a young adult was, 'She is known around here as the town crier.' Note that terms like 'highly strung' or 'open' would be classified as traits.

Equal or greater psychological sophistication is shown in the use of category ii (Obscurity of Impression) and category vii (Distinction between Real and Apparent Qualities, etc). The awareness that one's impressions and interpretations may not be correct is a marked improvement on the self-centredness of early childhood when we implicitly assume that the view we hold is the only one possible and that it is correct. One does not have to look far among adults, even, to find evidence of the same self-centredness in person perception and in social perception generally (the inability to consider that one could be wrong or that others, who think differently, could be right). Self-centredness in social perception has been studied in connection with dogmatism and authoritarianism. Being able to distinguish between 'real' and 'apparent' qualities reveals insight and sensitivity in the subject's understanding of others; it shows a realization that people present a front or façade, which masks their 'true' personality. The concept of 'persona' is a familiar one in the psychology of personality and this illustrates, again, the common-sense roots of psychological theory. The use of statements distinguishing 'real' from 'apparent', 'past' from 'present' and 'actual' from 'possible' shows that the subject can, as it were, stand apart from the evidence and consider alternative interpretations of it. Within a description, these interpretations integrate the facts of observation and achieve internal coherence by showing relationships between disparate (or apparently conflicting) statements, by introducing contextual considerations relating to time and circumstances, by uncovering the 'reality' beneath mere appearances and by showing the 'theme' running through the variations.

Children who can use qualifying and organizing material display considerable understanding of the laws governing human action—albeit at a lay or commonsense level. They are able to formulate and reformu-late systems of psychological concepts and apply them in actual inter-personal judgments. They are able to coordinate observations of people with reasoning about people, and their thinking is flexible, reversible and capable of self-correction. It is not surprising, therefore, that the use of qualifying and organizing terms is associated with intelligence. In fact, the effect of intelligence on the *organization* of impressions was greater than that of any other aspect of impressions analysed in this study. Other variables had more limited effects : girls used more Instructions to Exclude the Usual Trait or Situational Implications than did boys, and more Qualifiers were applied to liked persons than to disliked persons. Thus, more extreme judgments were made about liked persons than about disliked persons, presumably because positive judgments are more socially acceptable than negative judgments. In general, however, the number of qualifying and organizing terms in an impression is a fairly constant proportion of the number of central statements and is relatively unaffected by the type of person described (unlike some other elements in impressions, except that more qualifiers are used to describe liked persons than to describe disliked persons. The qualifying and organizing statements are the products, amongst other things, of the child's 'implicit theory of personality' and the meaning of this term needs to be stretched to include not merely normative trait implications, but also the rules he uses to 'explain' human behaviour generally and the behaviour of particular individuals. These rules, for example, specify dynamic relationships between personal qualities, such as motive and ability, and they show how action depends upon situational factors.

Perhaps the final stage in impression formation is reached when the subject talks about his 'impressions of others' as 'impressions', and sees that they can be critically evaluated in terms of validity, internal coherence, organization, and so on. Hopefully, this advanced 'professional' or 'semiprofessional' level of perceiving and understanding others is achieved by people engaged in counselling (in its widest sense), clinical psychology and personality research; it is achieved in a different manner by writers and in a different manner again by persons who are shrewd in their assessment and management of others, without being able to put their ideas into words.

CHAPTER 11

Cognitive Theory and the Developmental Psychology of Impression Formation

I. Preview

This chapter deals with some further qualitative and theoretical aspects of the developmental psychology of person perception in relation to the cognitive processes underlying the complex and subtle changes in conceptualization and language. Section III is concerned with the fundamental characteristics of pre-operational thinking in so far as they influence impression formation. We do not pretend to develop a rigorous and highly structured theory of development—complete with axioms and corollaries. Instead, we have formulated a 'proto-theory'—see Bromley (1970). It will be recalled that the same approach was adopted in Chapter 10 where we proposed a general theory of impression formation and change.

II. Trait Clusters

Watts (1944) suggested that qualitatively different descriptions of persons are found at four developmental stages: (1) below the age of 7 years children refer to external attributes and rarely use traits or other personality terms; (2) psychological terms (those referring to covert processes) are first used between 7 and 10 years—at first only one personal quality is mentioned; but later (3) several terms similar in evaluation (a univalent

209

trait cluster) are used; (4) descriptions containing both positively and negatively evaluated terms (divalent trait clusters) do not appear until adolescence is reached. The 2560 descriptions were classified under these four headings. The results—see Table 16—provided only partial support for Watts's suggestion. Nearly 50 per cent of descriptions by 7-year-old children contained no reference to psychological qualities despite the investigator's instructions. This percentage declined rapidly with age, although, even in 15-year-olds, 6 per cent of the descriptions lacked psychological content. The next most frequently occurring type of description in 7-year-olds was that referring to one trait, this made up 28 per cent of the total : the univalent trait cluster descriptions made up 21 per cent. In 8-year-olds, 30 per cent of the descriptions were of the single trait variety, and 42 per cent were of the univalent trait cluster type. In all other age groups this latter type of description occurred most frequently.

Table 16. Percentage of descriptions in each age and sex group classified by the four categories suggested by Watts (1944)

| | | Type of description | | | |
Age	Sex	External qualities	Single trait	Univalent trait cluster	Divalent trait cluster
7,10	Boys	55·6	26·9	16·9	0·6
	Girls	43·1	28·8	25·0	3·1
8,10	Boys	23·8	26·9	38·1	11·3
	Girls	8·8	32·5	45·6	13·1
9,10	Boys	12·5	33·8	46·2	7·5
	Girls	6·9	26·9	55·0	11·3
10,10	Boys	11·9	27·5	50·6	10·0
	Girls	5·6	20·0	55·0	19·4
12,4	Boys	17·5	31·9	48·1	2·5
	Girls	6·9	18·8	64·4	10·0
13,2	Boys	4·4	17·5	69·4	8·8
	Girls	1·2	6·9	67·5	24·3
14,3	Boys	7·5	19·4	62·5	10·6
	Girls	2·5	6·9	76·3	14·4
15,3	Boys	6·9	8·1	80·0	5·0
	Girls	5·0	16·9	71·9	6·3
Mean		13·8	21·8	54·5	9·9

The data in Table 16 show that both single traits and univalent trait clusters are well established by the age of 7 years; so the suggestion by Watts that single trait descriptions appear earlier in development than do trait cluster descriptions is neither confirmed nor refuted. It seems likely, however, that both single traits and univalent trait clusters occur before the age of 7. Moreover, in language development, the young child is likely to learn a *class* of words (rather than a single word in a class); in which case the interval of time during which he is restricted to one trait name (or to a few trait names applied singly) is likely to be trivial. In other words, univalent trait clusters are likely to emerge before the age of 7. The main developmental difficulty encountered by the child is when he attempts to conceptualize or describe persons with divalent trait clusters; but even this difficulty is largely overcome by 10 per cent or so of children at the age of 8. There is surprisingly little further improvement with age, apparently, in the proportion of descriptions containing both positive and negative personality attributes, but the age trend is not consistent.

The low incidence of descriptions containing *both* positively and negatively evaluated terms was probably due to the method of investigation which would tend to exclude the use of both types of evaluation in the same description. The incidence of divalent trait clusters increased considerably from age 7 to age 8 (from 2 to 12 per cent, respectively), after which the proportion remained higher, if somewhat erratic, until age 15. As we have seen, however, whereas younger subjects were content merely to *mention* that a person possessed positive and negative attributes, older subjects sought also to *explain* and *relate* the apparent inconsistencies.

III. Invariance and Egocentrism

One of the major achievements of middle childhood is the grasp of the principle of constancy or invariance. This means the child learns that the external world is stable and permanent, that objects do not change with his angle of regard, that the volume of a liquid does not change as it is poured from one sort of vessel to another and that the mass of a body does not vary as its shape changes. Similarly, in his dealings with people, he learns that there are constant and invariant features in human behaviour and personality.

The younger child's ability to comprehend invariance is limited by a strongly egocentric orientation—as shown by studies of the development of concepts pertaining to the physical world. From a social point of view, however, the effects of egocentrism seem to be less detrimental, since, initially at least, egocentrism leads the child to attribute to others psychological processes similar to those he himself experiences. Subsequently, when his egocentrism is no longer dominant, he comes to regard others as having an inner life of their own, independent of him, to which he has no 'privileged access'. The young child's error lies in attributing his psychological states to objects and processes in the physical world. The assumption that other people experience things as we do is an important feature of our social development and its existence probably helps to explain some peculiarities of language development, thinking and inter-personal relationships in childhood. Although egocentrism initially facili-tates our social development, it hinders the realization that people have thoughts, wants and feelings *different* from those that we have, and thus makes it difficult for us to understand people who behave differently, or who are in very different circumstances.

The egocentric child tends to concern himself not with the other person as such, but with the implications that the other person's actions seem to have for himself. These implications may be felt to be either desirable or undesirable, hence his primitive categorization of people as either good or bad (nice or nasty), hence his difficulty in coping when one and the same person exhibits both desirable and undesirable behaviour, and hence the ambivalence he feels towards parents and other figures of love and authority. The child has attempted to find constant or invariant features in the behaviour of persons just as he has attempted to find them in the physical world, for example, good to eat versus bad to eat. The child's simplicity and egocentrism lead him to apply his categories rigidly and absolutely (but temporarily), so that he regards the other person as either absolutely good or absolutely bad (for the moment at least). The salient features of the other person's current behaviour (in so far as they are regarded by the child as affecting his welfare)—rather than its contextual or remote features—dominate the child's impressions. This stage can be regarded as one of *absolute invariance*.

The young child is not only egocentric, he also lacks the ability to 'decentre' (Piaget's term) and consequently focuses upon one isolated dimension of a problem; it may be a material or logical problem of the sort described by Piaget, or it may be an interpersonal problem—such as having to understand another person's behaviour. Affective responses are prominent in children's behaviour, so that the inability to decentre gives rise to impressions which are either strongly positive or strongly negative. The stimulus person may be described by a particular set of categories—good, bad, nice, kind. Changes in the person's behaviour do not lead to minor adjustments in the child's impression. Instead, the impression as a whole is changed, because the child's narrow focus of attention has shifted. This aspect of impression formation in children may account for the finding reported by McHenry (1971) that, when presented with a film showing a person behaving in one way in one situation and in an opposing way in another situation, children aged 3 to 4 years tended to see two different people. It seems that the inability to decentre retards the development of understanding of invariance or constancy in matters associated with human behaviour and psychological processes. In the same way, it has been shown to retard the development of the idea of 'conservation' in relation to number and quantity.

Thus, variations in the stimulus person's behaviour may lead to fundamental (although temporary) changes in a young child's impressions. When he is older, the child will be able to see these variations in the context of the rest of the individual's behaviour, and possibly also in the context of his circumstances. Therefore, these variations have less effect; they are, phenomenologically, less disparate, hence they are more readily assimilated without major revisions in the impression. The achievement of something akin to conservation or invariance in the development of understanding others is a matter of degree, however, because in older children and even in adults there may be an underlying instability in impression formation such that the sensing of a change in the stimulus person's behaviour brings about not a minor revision of the impression but a complete revaluation; the underlying instability seems to be associated with affective processes rather than with cognitive processes.

Although 7-year-old children can make categorical classifications of persons, frequently they fail to do so and produce descriptions which contain no reference to personal qualities—descriptions which are extremely stereotyped, consisting of a string of physical characteristics together with statements about personal identity and family relationships. Consider the following examples.

A Boy aged 7,10 describes a boy he dislikes:

He is very tall. He has dark brown hair, he goes to our school. I don't think he has any brothers or sisters. He is in our class. Today he has a dark orange jumper and grey trousers and brown shoes.

A Girl aged 7,6 describes a boy she likes:

Max sits next to me, his eyes are hazel and he is tall. He hasn't got a very big head, he's got a big pointed nose.

A Girl aged 7,8 describes a man she dislikes:

He is six feet tall. He isn't very well dressed. He has two sons, Peter and William. They can afford a car. Peter and William got a tractor each for Christmas. William has two bicycles. Their dad has blue eyes, black trousers, green jumper. They have hens and a cat and dog and a budgie. Their telephone is . . .

A girl aged 7,11 describes a woman she likes:

She is very nice because she gives my friends and me toffee. She lives by the main road. She has fair hair and she wears glasses. She is 47 years old. She has an anniversary today. She has been married since she was 21 years old. She sometimes gives us flowers. She has a very nice garden and house. We only go in the weekend and have a talk with her.

The child's concept of the other incorporates his family, physical surroundings and even his possessions, so much so that the person is held responsible for the actions of his family and pets. A good example of this is given by a boy who wrote, 'I used to like her but I don't now because her dog bit me.' Thus in some respects the 7- or 8-year-old child's concept of personality is not unlike that of primitive man as described by Werner (1948), who thinks of another person in concrete or literal terms and fails to differentiate between the person and his possessions. This gives rise, perhaps, to a belief in the magical properties of personal belongings and body materials.

The young child's concept of another person is diffuse, that is, fragmented, unstable and lacking focus. This is to be understood in part as a consequence of his egocentrism, his inability to decentre, his simplicity and the syncretic nature of his reasoning, as described by Piaget—see Flavell (1963). In syncretic thinking, a multitude of diverse things are chaotically but intimately related within a global scheme; thus, everything the child knows about a person becomes relevant, and no logical framework exists by means of which he can systematize his knowledge. Instead, items are juxtaposed by simple 'and' connections rather than by causal and organizing statements. The resulting description is, as we have seen, a string of unrelated statements lacking coherence and organization.

Gradually, egocentrism declines as cognitive and social skills develop. The child learns to take into account things other than a person's appearance, identity and possessions. He applies his growing powers of abstraction and generalization and goes beyond the immediate stimulus situation to infer stable and constant features in a person's behaviour, referring to them in terms of trait names and general habits. At about the age of 7 or 8, the child's attempts to conceptualize persons and their behaviour are influenced by another characteristic of pre-operational thinking, traces of which remain. This is the process of identification (via mimicry and role playing) or vicarious learning whereby he 'goes through the motions' of being the other person and in this way experiences something of what it might be like (psychologically) to be the other person. Naturally, he can describe peers better than he can describe adults because he finds it easier to identify with peers than with adults.

A similar natural process of learning—a kind of empathy—may possibly be used throughout life to solve problems in personal relationships since, in contrast to our dealings with the physical world, we lack any detailed understanding of the laws governing human behaviour which would be necessary in order to use a more analytic approach. But perhaps this point of view could be expressed differently; it could be argued that by the time we reach adult life we have acquired, albeit implicitly, all or most of the concepts and rules needed to make sense of the normal behaviour of people in everyday life, and our knowledge of these concepts and rules enables us to relate effectively to other people, to understand why people behave as they do and, if necessary, to imagine how we would behave were we in their position—colloquially, 'in their shoes'. The person who deals with psychological problems at a professional level of competence, however, has at his or her disposal a further set of rules and concepts (hopefully, scientific ones) for dealing with persons whose behaviour—for example, intellectual subnormality, neurosis, backwardness in reading, senile confusion, paranoia, psychopathy, marital conflict, or attempted suicide—falls outside the normal range.

We need not dwell on the scientific merits or demerits of the concepts used by professional workers to cope with such issues, except to say that, as in other disciplines, there must be some firm points of contact between commonsense levels of experience and scientific knowledge. One possible advantage gained by the professional worker is that of being able to study his subject more objectively and with less personal involvement, thus escaping the limits set by egocentrism. It is our hope that, in pursuing a detached scientific investigation into everyday notions about persons and their behaviour, we shall have done something to provide firm points of contact between commonsense and the scientific study of personality and adjustment.

When some of the 7-year-olds used personality terms they usually referred to one quality which was strongly evaluative and diffuse in nature, as in the examples which follow.

A boy aged 7,9 describes a man he dislikes:

He lives down Sandringham Road and his number is 571. He has a little beard and a moustache. I do not like his quite big boy who is 11 and called Percy Carstairs and Bob does not like him either. He is very old and lives just where the old part of Sandringham Road starts. He is usually bad and he has a wife I do not like either. Percy Carstairs has got a racer for a bike and I think he is . . .

A girl aged 7,6 describes a woman she likes:

She has long hair. She wears it in a bun, it is blond hair. She is very kind. She has two children. One is a boy and one is a girl. The boy is called Eric and the girl is called Kathleen. Kathleen wears glasses.

On other occasions several traits were listed, but these were strung together in much the same way as other children strung together a number of physical characteristics. The child made no attempt to interrelate the different elements in the description, and there was no suggestion that some parts of the description were more important than others. Equal weight was placed upon background details and appearance as upon stable aspects of personality, as in the following example.

A boy aged 7,8 describes a girl he dislikes:

I dislike Nancy Middleton because she is very dirty. She is not at all clever. She is always quarrelling. She is not at all pretty. She is very naughty. She has to stay in at playtime a lot. She does not like very many people. She likes Sylvia Evans and Pauline Morris.

The incidence of descriptions referring to personal qualities increased considerably from the age of 7 to the age of 8 years; in fact, this change is almost as great as that between 8 and 15 years. The relative emphasis on physical characteristics and concrete situational factors in descriptions given by 7-year-olds, as compared with the relative emphasis on personal qualities by 8-year-olds and older, is in line with some of Bruner's ideas about development, for example, the decrease with age in the extent to which cognition depends upon stimulus control and the corresponding increase in the ability to perceive without being dominated by the proximal, concrete, stimulus situation—see Bruner (1957) and Bruner et al. (1966).

The concepts used by young children to refer to personal qualities seemed to be vague, diffuse and at a low level of abstraction; even so, they mark a considerable advance in cognitive development, since they reveal some ability to abstract a common feature from a number of positive instances, and they reveal some ability to combine or group together a variety of stimuli into a single class. The organization of experience in terms of conceptual categories like 'traits' and 'habits' means that the subject can construe the stimulus person separately, as it were, from specific stimulus situations; and this enables him to make predictions based on his general impressions. Note that the tendency to organize information about persons into convenient conceptual classes is merely one aspect of a more general tendency to 'encode' stimulus information so as to reduce the demands made upon the storing and processing mechanisms.

Although egocentrism declines from about the age of 7, it continues to colour the child's impressions for several years. Most of the terms used by 7-, 8- or 9-year-old children indicated that the child was not so much describing the stimulus person as describing his own reaction to the stimulus person and the way that person's behaviour affected him. The child describes the other person as 'kind' because 'he gives me sweets', or 'bad tempered' because 'he shouts at me'. Egocentrism is never completely outgrown; even as adults it colours our perceptions of other people and shapes our reactions to their behaviour. The adolescent's developmental achievement is to recognize the limitations of one's personal point of view.

Descriptions containing a string of personality terms intermingled with details of appearance and other concrete details occurred quite frequently up to the age of 10, as in the following example.

A boy aged 9,11 describes a boy he dislikes:

> He smells very much and is very nasty. He has no sense of humour and is very dull He is always fighting and he is cruel. He does silly things and is very stupid. He has brown hair and cruel eyes. He is sulky and 11 years old and has lots of sisters. I think he is the most horrible boy in the class. He has a croaky voice and always chews his pencil and picks his teeth and I think he is disgusting.

Descriptions such as this are considerably more sophisticated in content than those of 7-year-old children but are little better organized. Almost no attempt is made to 'sharpen' the information through the use of qualifying and organizing words and phrases, thus making some items more precise or salient than others. One exception is the use of qualifiers that intensify the impression, such as 'very'. This is undoubtedly a product of the child's tendency to emphasize personally relevant features of his social environment; not that the child is sure about what features are relevant or irrelevant—equal emphasis is often placed upon details of behaviour, mannerisms and appearance.

The list of charcteristics frequently contains opposites; the child apparently is unaware of the conflict and inconsistency in his account. Descriptions of this sort make up approximately 10 per cent of the total in children between the ages of 8 and 10 years which suggests that the univalent impressions of early childhood are giving way to more realistic and complex impressions. Thus *absolute invariance* gives way to an *intermediate stage,* in that the child begins to take into account more than one feature of a person's behaviour and to integrate experience over longer intervals of time. He becomes aware that the same person may exhibit both positive and negative qualities. He notices that a person can be kind on some occasions but mean on others, sometimes good tempered and sometimes bad tempered. Thus a person may be described as both 'nice' and 'not nice', 'good' and 'bad', 'good tempered' and 'bad tempered', as in the following examples.

A boy aged 8,8 describes a boy he likes:

He is tall and a bit bossy and when he leaves this school he is going to try to get into Grammar School and sometimes he is good and sometimes he is bad and that's why I like him. . . .

A girl aged 9,8 describes a boy she likes:

Charles is a sort of cousin of mine. He likes watching television and riding his bicycle. He lives in Preston. His behaviour is sometimes good and sometimes it is bad. He likes watching television and eating sweets. . . .

A boy aged 10,2 describes a girl he likes:

She is quite a kind girl. . . . Her behaviour is quite good most of the time but sometimes she is quite naughty and silly most of the time. . . .

It is probable that at first the child is not aware of the conflict in his impressions, since his beliefs about people are too chaotic or syncretic. At the same time he lacks the intellectual maturity, concepts and experiences needed to integrate his impressions. He cannot discern the common intention underlying diverse actions; to him the actions appear inconsistent and puzzling. The concept of intention is not one that he has so far acquired. Piaget (1932) in his study of children's moral judgments described a parallel effect—the failure to take account of a person's intentions when deciding the punishment deserved for doing wrong.

Another reason why the child in middle childhood cannot resolve apparent inconsistencies in the behaviour of the stimulus person is that he is unable to take account of the way human action is influenced by the stimulus situation and by the residues of past experience. Between 8 and 12 years of age the child's concept of personality is more narrowly defined (focused) than that of the younger child; he makes less frequent reference to concrete situational factors, possessions and family. The descriptive material tends to be confined to the 'person himself', and this is an important developmental advance leading the child to focus on invariances 'within the person' or in his behaviour, that is he focuses on stable inner-personal processes and regularities in behaviour. But in one sense the child goes too far, in that he neglects important environmental influences and historical factors. This leaves him at a temporary disadvantage in that he cannot resolve the inconsistencies he observes in a person's action, and hence cannot predict his behaviour very accurately. Nevertheless, the older child's emphasis on the 'person himself' paves the way for insights and a better understanding of personality and behaviour. Subsequently, his concept of personality is extended so as to embrace more than mere coincidental and contiguous situational factors, to include more pertinent circumstantial determinants.

In some respects, the errors in impression formation at this age are similar to the growth errors described by Bruner *et al.* (1966): as the child grows older he develops mistaken ideas about some matters because he now tries to understand them (having previously been unaware of his ignorance); but eventually by correcting his mistakes he gradually comes to understand those now prominent features of his social environment, such as the rules of games, kinship relations and role sets.

The transition from one mode of conceptualization to another can be described in terms of Piaget's concept of *equilibration*—see Flavell (1963) and Baldwin (1967). As the individual acquires more and more separate beliefs, as his knowledge about a person increases, a point will be reached at which this mass of relatively unorganized material becomes unwieldy; it develops internal contradictions, and contains errors of omission and commission. According to Piaget, these defects in the belief system lead the subject to try to harmonize or resolve the contradictions and errors, that is to achieve *equilibrium*. In this respect, the concept of equilibration is not unlike that of cognitive dissonance—see Festinger (1957). A belief system which permits the child to assign incompatible attributes to a person without attempting to explain or relate them thereby exhibits its own relatively chaotic internal state.

As the system becomes better organized—through the development of networks of trait implications and through the development of beliefs about the connections between a person's actions and his past and present circumstances—the individual reaches the final stage of *integrated invariance*. Before this stage, the child can identify and isolate some invariances—internal dispositions and regular patterns of behaviour—but he is unable to relate them to one another or to see that the various dispositions and behavioural regularities are parts of an overall system (an achievement marking the final stage of the development of the concept of psychological invariance). There are, of course, occasions when older subjects are unable to deal with puzzles and inconsistencies in their beliefs about others, either because they lack ability or experience or because the information about the stimulus person is in fact inadequate or 'inexplicable'. At a commonsense level, when this happens one uses a variety of terms like 'strange', 'peculiar', and 'funny', which have the effect of excluding the stimulus person from the normal range of convenience of everyday concepts of human behaviour (as in the play, *Uncle Vanya*). When this happens at a professional level, one is likely to find that the abnormal behaviour of the stimulus person is assimilated to technical concepts such as: psychopathic, conversion hysteria, schizophrenic.

The final stage is reached when the child grasps the idea that the behaviour of persons, like the behaviour of things, is 'lawful', and recognizes that many of the laws, or rules, are complex and far from explicit—not that everyone admits the lawfulness of the material world. Prediction and explanation are not only possible but also reasonably successful much of the time. If they were not, interpersonal relationships would be far less satisfactory, and social interactions would be much less smooth and effective. Social relationships are facilitated, not only by the processes of person perception already described, but also by an understanding of the 'generalized other'—a term used by Mead (1934)—revealed in the consistency of prescribed patterns of behaviour in social roles.

IV. The Transition to an Adult Level of Impression Formation

A. Adolescence

The changes that take place in personality descriptions after the age of 13 years are clearly demonstrated by the following examples.

A girl aged 14,3 describes a boy she dislikes:

I dislike this boy because he is very rude, ignorant, cheeky and thinks he is the best. Although he can sometimes be very nice, his poorer qualities outnumber his better qualities which are not very good to start with. He is very rude to his friend who is nice and this leads to an argument.

I think he is very ignorant by the way he ignores things when he wants to.

He is exceptionally cheeky to his mother when his friends are there especially.

A girl aged 14,1 describes a girl she likes:

This girl is not in my form she is just in the same division as me. She is very quiet and only talks when she knows a person very well. She is clever in one sense, she comes top of her form. She is very reserved but once you get to know her she is exactly the opposite. It is very unusual to see her not attending the lessons. At sometime or other all our minds wander but hers never seems to do so. One of the things I admire in her is she is very tidy.

A boy aged 15,8 describes a boy he likes:

Andy is very modest. He is even shyer than I am when near strangers and yet is very talkative with people he knows and likes. He always seems good tempered and I have never seen him in a bad temper. He tends to degrade other people's achievements, and yet never praises his own. He does not seem to voice his opinions to anyone. He easily gets nervous.

These descriptions amply illustrate the 'qualitative' difference between younger children and those over 13 years of age. There is a considerable increase and shift in the range of ideas, and in the qualities assigned to the other person; there is greater flexibility in selecting from and dealing with these ideas. The older child is not so greatly misled by irrelevant detail; he attempts to show how the person's behaviour and inner personal states can be related to historical, biological and social factors. He is aware (implicitly) that behaviour is a function of the total situation. Older subjects select some of the more salient or interesting aspects of the stimulus person and present the relevant evidence in a fairly organized way. Integration and organization are achieved through the use of the qualifying and organizing statements described in the previous chapter. The qualifying statements are not used in the simple way that young children use terms like 'very', but in a more constructive way to integrate one quality with another or with the rest of the impression, or to suggest that one quality is more salient or important than another, as in the following examples.

A girl aged 14,4 describes a girl she likes:

... She is very kind and friendly. She is always very sensible and willing to help people. Sometimes she gets a bit cross but that doesn't last long and soon she is her normal self. . . .

Integration is also achieved through the use of organizing words and phrases, for example, in distinguishing between real and apparent qualities.

A girl aged 14,3 describes a girl she dislikes:

... Although she professes to be your friend when you are ill she does not come to visit you. . . .

A girl aged 14,1 describes a girl she likes:

... She is very reserved but once you get to know her she is exactly the opposite. . . .

Some of the older subjects attempted to explain a person's actions and personal qualities by searching for underlying motives, dispositions, or situational factors.

A boy aged 15,5 describes a man he dislikes:

He is very shy. He does not know how to answer snap questions. He does not talk very much. He always obeys his wife to the letter and never thinks for himself. He fusses over his wife but does not stay in all the time he is off work. There is a greater pull on him from his mother who is a hypochondriac. He very often visits her.

This adolescent is probably no longer relying only only personal observation and experience as the sources of his ideas about people. Instead, he is making use of indirect evidence, and information supplied by others; he is using more advanced concepts about behaviour and psychological processes, and he is capable of relating evidence and inference in order to read stability and organization into a person's actions and qualities; thus the descriptions tend to become focused and hierarchically organized through selection, differential emphasis and interconnection. Subjects producing these organized and integrated descriptions usually need to make the important distinction between observation and inference. They must realize that information about a person is to some extent ambiguous in the sense that it can be construed in several ways; hence they try to justify their interpretation or construction by introducing supporting evidence and by illustrative examples. They go to some lengths to verify and amplify the internal consistency of their argument. These subjects have become capable of dealing rationally with systems of psychological ideas; their thinking about other people has become flexible and capable of self-correction; their ideas about other people are functional in the sense that they are connected with the facts of observation and with the demands of personal adjustment.

B. Early Adulthood

Several hundred free descriptions have been written as class exercises by day students and evening students taking courses in psychology. It was assumed that their accounts would approach the upper limits of conceptual development, and provide a sort of 'baseline' for the measurement of developmental level. Surprisingly, perhaps, their reports show little evidence of technical, that is 'professional' or 'scientific', psychological concepts; but we have not speculated on the reasons why their naive interpretations seem so little affected by their psychological studies.

The conditions under which the young adults' free descriptions were collected were too diverse to justify exact quantitative analysis, or to justify exact comparisons with the children's descriptions. They were written as class exercises, and were used to obtain clinical impressions about the content and organization of *adult* conceptions of personality. The systems of classification used in the main developmental study took account of the sorts of ideas produced by those adults. This section and other parts of this Chapter are based on earlier work—see Livesley and Bromley (1967).

The main content categories have been listed. Some of the categories frequently used by young adults overlap considerably with the categories used by the children. Category 9 (General Personality Attributes) and category 10 (Specific Behavioural Consistencies) are frequently used by both young adults and children. Category 1 (Appearance) is prominent in the reports of the young adults and occurs in the children's reports in spite of the instructions to exclude such information. Appearance, evidently, plays an important role in our impressions of other people in spite of the fact that appearance is often quite unrelated to psychological qualities. Statements about appearance serve to introduce and identify the person.

Items in category 11 (Motivation and Arousal) occurred with moderate frequency in the young adult reports but were largely absent from the children's descriptions. Items in category 12 (Orientation) were also largely absent from the children's descriptions but figured quite prominently in the descriptions given by the more sophisticated young adults. An explanation for these apparent differences has already been given (ese p. 150). Intelligent young adults with an interest in human behaviour can be expected to have the abilities needed to handle motivational concepts. Children, in contrast, can do little more than report what they observe or believe; hence their descriptions are usually unorganized collections of items of information about overt behaviour or circumstances.

The difference, between the children and the young adults, is not merely one of vocabulary or experience but also one of conceptual level or 'attitude'. For example, category 2 (General Information and Identity) is used by both children and adults, but whereas the children are usually content simply to *mention* facts, the young adults are usually concerned to *relate* the facts to other items of information and interpretation.

One obvious and important developmental change is a vast increase in the range of available ideas coupled with a much greater flexibility in selecting from and dealing with these ideas. The descriptions given by children are, by and large, limited in content and in focus of interest, so that an investigator can easily compile a 'typical' description. The descriptions given by young adults however, are diverse—they range freely over all the categories and introduce all kinds of foci of interest. Young adults select some of the more salient or interesting aspects of their case and present the relevant evidence in a fairly organized way, whereas younger children soon exhaust their limited ideas and are not greatly concerned with the organization of the material.

Another obvious developmental change is the appearance of a variety of words and phrases which young adults use to 'shape' the material to get greater coherence in, and more effective presentation of, the information. These have been dealt with already under the general heading of 'organizing and qualifying terms'. As we have seen, there are terms which say something about the intensity, frequency, duration and variety of the stimulus person's characteristics, for example, terms like 'very', 'occasionally', 'persistently'. Examples or definitions of the characteristic may be given. Then there are ways of selecting and emphasizing, that is sharpening, the stimulus person's characteristics—even to the point of caricature. In contrast, there are ways of counteracting the primacy effect in communication and presenting a 'balanced account' of the person's qualities by introducing further information beginning with terms like, 'on the other hand', 'but' or 'although'. Adults frequently make distinctions between the real and the apparent characteristics of the stimulus person and between earlier and later impressions, for example, 'Outwardly he seems easy going, but he is really very aggressive', or 'At first he's shy, but when you get to know him he's great fun.' Adults sense that particular psychological characteristics are a function of circumstances or of other psychological factors. Hence some statements in adult personality descriptions are particularly important because they seem to operate rather like logical propositions—see Bromley (1968). Sometimes, quite elaborate quasi-logical forms are used, linking together several parts of the description. They act as foci of interest and give relevance, coherence and meaning to the various parts of the description, for example, 'He is moody and irresponsible most of the time but in a real emergency he always behaves calmly and sensibly.' Other quasi-logical propositions referring to causal connexions and psychological interpretations are common, even though subjects are asked only to *describe* a person and not to *explain* his behaviour. Consider the following example : 'She is curious about people but naive, and this leads her to ask too many questions so that people become irritated with her and withhold information, although she is not sensitive enough to notice it.' More often than not, in the descriptions, the arguments are incomplete. Nevertheless, the 'quasi-logical' arguments found in adult impressions of persons could be subjected to the sort of analysis proposed by Toulmin (1958) and cited in Bromley (1970). Bromley (1968) has described how Toulmin's methods of analysing arguments might be used to advantage in clinical psychology.

The use of terms referring to socially desirable and common personal qualities is widespread among adults and children alike. So that although the descriptions may be fairly accurate, they are often not very informative, since important information deals with *salient* characteristics, that is those which distinguish the person from other people with whom he is usually compared. In practice, we select only a few salient facts and characteristics. These enable us to develop and maintain simple and highly organized concepts of other persons, since all we need to do is to select and interpret the available information so that it fits in with this basic framework. We formulate rules which describe and explain the other person's actions, and these enable us to predict and influence him. The rules, however, are usually implicit.

Adults, more so than children, recognize that their descriptions are personal viewpoints liable to differ from the viewpoints of other observers and liable to be modified. It seemed likely, too, as we have seen, that our opinions of others provide useful outlets for, and are distorted by, our personal feelings. Terms expressing ethical evaluation are commonly found in descriptions by adults.

Unlike the descriptions of younger children, adult descriptions tend not to be confined to statements about the concrete here-and-now situation. They contain statements pointing to the past and others pointing to the future, as well as to the present; they contain statements about what is probable or possible, as well as to what is actually the case. Naturally, descriptions contain many faults and inadequacies which cannot be detailed now.

The following complete examples, from young adult descriptions, illustrate some aspects of the above analysis, namely, the use of qualifiers, selection and emphasis, balancing, real versus apparent characteristics, the effects of circumstances, and psychodynamic explanation.

Julia

On first acquaintance Julia is a quiet and rather nondescript looking person with pale colouring and fair hair. She is not very pretty, taken feature by feature, but she can look attractive when she is happy. She is the only child of wealthy parents and has everything she wants in the way of clothes, personal belongings and spending money. Her parents are very fond of her and she is very fond of them.

Julia's main trouble is that she has no self-assurance socially. In mixed company, she regards herself as utterly unattractive. Following one or two dances when she has not enjoyed herself much, she absolutely refuses to go to another. She can be witty and humorous in company, but with boys she often seems to overdo this and never gets beyond a teasing slanging relationship.

She seems to have reached a stage now, through her feelings of inferiority, that she will not go anywhere or plan anything where she may be the odd girl out and not enjoy herself. She retires more into her shell with periods of depression and harbours romantic illusions about various inaccessible men. She recently cancelled her birthday party because she did not want to invite her friends from home in case the party was not a success. Her real trouble seems to be that she admires some inaccessible man who does not notice her at all, and then assumes that no one likes her, although she has plenty of female friends.

Enid

Enid is all right really, although most people think she is very bad tempered because she goes around looking as if everyone and everything irritates her. In fact, she is quite easily irritated and does not get on very well with people she does not know well. She expects people to adapt themselves to her ways.

Her natural expression is, however, often very deceiving and may arise from the fact that she easily detaches herself from everyday life and is often thinking of things quite different from those which occupy other people's attention. She has a very great love of animals especially horses, and often attributes human characteristics to them that few others would think of.

She is remarkably indifferent to her parents or to any other authority. The only adult she seems to respect is her brother. Nevertheless she enjoys arguing with him—'Just to show we are still alive' as she says. Once she knows you well and feels you are 'on her wavelength', she is a very generous person and willing to help. Her vagueness is a source of great amusement to others which she finds difficult to understand.

Briefly, then, the more obvious developmental changes in the way we conceptualize persons include the following:
(a) An increase in the number of descriptive categories. (b) Greater flexibility and precision in the use of these categories. (c) An increase in the selectivity, coherence, complexity and organization of information and ideas. (d) An increase in the use of subtle qualifying and connecting terms. (e) An increased ability to analyse and interpret the person's behaviour. (f) An increased concern with the presentation of the material, to make it a convincing communication.

By the time we have reached adulthood, we have become capable of formal operations with systems of psychological ideas. We understand the 'grammar' of human behaviour. We are capable of coordinating observation with reason, and our thinking about other people has become flexible and capable of self-correction.

It must be stated clearly, however, that not *all* adults are as capable as this; individual differences are considerable. Adult life, moreover, is associated with further 'developmental' or 'ageing' effects which can be expected to influence impression formation. Individual differences among adults and the effects of ageing on impression formation are topics that will be dealt with in a subsequent publication.

CHAPTER 12

Subsidiary Investigations into the Developmental Psychology of Person Perception

I. Preview

In this chapter we outline some findings which are related to the main inquiry but largely independent of it as regards empirical data. It will be remembered that the 320 subjects in the main inquiry were required to write a number of personality descriptions. One of these was a description of 'Myself' preceding the eight stimulus persons presented in random order. The results for the self-description are presented separately in Section II. Some preliminary studies of the relationships between the perception of persons and the perception of behaviour are described in Section III. This section includes an analysis of impression formation in very young children. Section IV comprises a brief comment on the role of cultural comparisons in relation to person perception, together with some examples of personality impressions obtained from schoolgirls in Gambia. Section V represents an attempt to explore some of the implications of the research results obtained by means of the film, with special reference to the relationships between behaviour perception and person perception, and to the cognitive and linguistic aspects of impression formation.

II. The Self-Concept

The impression a person forms of himself is an important aspect of person perception that appears to be amenable to description and analysis by means of the methods already described in detail. It will be remembered that the subjects in the present study were asked to write a description of 'Myself' before describing the eight stimulus persons. This provided a practice or 'buffer' item that familiarized them with the task. We thought it inappropriate, therefore, to analyse these self-descriptions in conjunction with the descriptions of 'other' stimulus persons. The data are of interest independently of the main inquiry, but they can be analysed by means of the 33 content categories used previously—see Chapter 8.

The content categories proved to be adequate to describe the contents of children's self-descriptions. Three categories, however, were clearly not relevant, and were therefore omitted. These were two categories dealing with Subject-Other Relationships, that is category 27 (Mutual Interaction), category 28 (Subject's Opinion of and Behaviour towards the Stimulus Person) and category 29 (Comparison with Self). Two categories were changed slightly: category 19 (Stimulus Person's Attitude towards Himself) became 'Subject's Attitudes towards Himself', and category 25 (Other People's Behaviour towards the Stimulus Person) became 'Other People's Behaviour towards the Subject'.

A. Results

The effects of the between-subject variables (Age, Sex and Intelligence) on the proportions of statements in the content categories were examined by means of chi-squared; the method employed was the same as that described in Chapter 8. A more stringent level of significance of $p < 0.01$ was specified before the analyses were attempted because of the number of analyses carried out.

1. *Effects of Age of Subject.* The number of statements in each category is given in Table 17 and the proportion of statements in each category is given in Table 18. Table 19 gives the results of analyses using chi-squared on the proportion of statements used.

Chronological age had a significant effect on 16 out of the 30 content categories. The relationships between age and the proportions of the various categories used are summarized below. As in Chapter 8, some categories decrease in frequency with age, some increase in frequency with age, and in others the relationship tends to be curvilinear.

Categories showing a decrease with age:

  1. Appearance
  2. General Information and Identity
  5. Possessions
 23. Friendships and Playmates
 31. Family and Kinship

Categories showing an increase with age:

  9. General Personality Attributes
 10. Specific Behavioural Consistencies
 12. Orientation
 17. Interests and Hobbies
 18. Beliefs, Attitudes and Values
 19. Attitudes towards Self
 26. Relations with Opposite Sex
 30. Comparisons with Others
 32. Collateral Facts and Ideas

Categories showing a curvilinear relationship:

 13. Expressive Behaviour
 20. Evaluations

A *decrease* with age occurred in the use of statements referring to objective information about the self. The age effect was significant in the case of Appearance (1), General Information and Identity (2), and Possessions (5). Objective information accounted for 39 per cent of the statements made by 7-year-olds about themselves but only for 6 per cent in the case of 14-year-old subjects. Greater use of objective information —mainly statements about Appearance—was made by subjects aged 15 years (16 per cent). This seems to reflect the adolescent's concern with his impact upon others, and more particularly with his 'body image' and his attractiveness to members of the opposite sex. Increased age also led

Table 17. Frequency of occurrence of each content category for each age level when describing self

Content category*	Age								Total
	7,10	8,10	9,10	10,10	12,4	13,2	14,3	15,3	
1. Appearance	48	8	19	2	35	8	9	35	164
2. General information and identity	76	16	19	5	49	16	8	22	211
3. Routine habits and activities	10	5	7	10	14	3	0	2	51
4. Actual incidents	34	18	24	14	11	12	11	8	132
5. Possessions	48	6	14	6	12	2	0	3	91
6. Life history	12	1	1	0	2	0	6	0	22
7. Contemporary social circumstances	0	1	1	2	0	1	0	0	5
8. Physical condition	9	4	1	2	0	4	1	1	22
9. General personality attributes	14	37	22	79	39	75	83	51	400
10. Specific behavioural consistencies	7	34	29	61	36	75	61	55	358
11. Motivation and arousal	14	9	11	3	12	22	12	20	103
12. Orientation	0	0	0	6	5	10	14	17	52
13. Expressive behaviour	2	7	5	26	4	3	9	0	56
14. Intellectual aptitudes and abilities	32	35	27	11	16	5	6	8	140
15. Achievements and skills	10	29	32	17	19	10	7	8	132
16. Preferences and aversions	117	137	141	126	136	84	82	89	912
17. Interests and hobbies	40	37	38	14	47	41	28	45	290
18. Beliefs, attitudes and values	1	4	2	5	8	13	28	15	76
19. Attitudes towards self	0	0	1	1	2	2	5	3	14
20. Evaluations	19	57	44	25	13	25	14	6	203
21. Social roles	2	7	1	3	4	3	4	5	29
22. Reputation	1	1	2	4	3	3	3	2	19
23. Friendships and playmates	17	6	7	2	9	6	3	4	54
24. Effect upon, and relations with, others	0	0	0	2	1	2	8	0	13
25. Other people's behaviour towards the self	4	6	3	1	10	4	6	7	41
26. Relations with opposite sex	0	1	1	1	9	2	15	4	33

Table 17. — *Continued*

Content category	Age 7,10	8,10	9,10	10,10	12,4	13,2	14,3	15,3	Total
27. Mutual interactions	0	0	0	0	0	0	0	0	0
28. Subject's opinion of, and behaviour towards, the stimulus person	0	0	0	0	0	0	0	0	0
29. Comparison with self	0	0	0	0	0	0	0	0	0
30. Comparison with others	0	1	1	3	3	3	8	6	25
31. Family and kinship	49	11	11	3	9	7	4	0	94
32. Collateral facts and ideas	3	4	2	1	10	13	10	13	56
33. Irrelevant and unclassifiable facts and ideas	1	2	5	1	3	0	0	0	12
Total	570	484	471	436	521	454	445	429	3810

* Note that categories 19 and 25 have been adapted for the analysis of self-descriptions; three categories (27, 28, 29) are not applicable.

Table 18. Percentage frequency of occurrence of each content category for each age level when describing self

Content category*	Age 7,10	8,10	9,10	10,10	12,4	13,2	14,3	15,3	Mean
1. Appearance	8·42	1·65	4·03	0·46	6·72	1·76	2·02	8·16	4·30
2. General information and identity	13·33	3·31	4·03	1·15	9·40	3·52	1·80	5·13	5·54
3. Routine habits and activities	1·75	1·03	1·49	2·29	2·69	0·66	0·00	0·47	1·34
4. Actual incidents	5·96	3·72	5·09	3·21	2·11	2·64	2·47	1·86	3·46
5. Possessions	8·42	1·24	2·97	1·38	2·30	0·44	0·00	0·70	2·39
6. Life history	2·11	0·21	0·21	0·00	0·38	0·00	1·35	0·00	0·58
7. Contemporary social circumstances	0·00	0·21	0·21	0·46	0·00	0·22	0·00	0·00	0·13
8. Physical condition	1·58	0·83	0·21	0·46	0·00	0·88	0·22	0·23	0·58
9. General personality attributes	2·46	7·64	4·67	18·12	7·47	16·50	18·65	11·89	10·50
10. Specific behavioural consistencies	1·23	7·02	6·16	13·99	6·91	16·50	13·71	12·82	9·40
11. Motivation and arousal	2·46	1·86	2·34	0·69	2·30	4·85	2·70	4·66	2·70
12. Orientation	0·00	0·00	0·00	1·38	0·96	2·20	3·15	3·96	1·36

Table 18. — *Continued*

Content category*	Age 7,10	8,10	9,10	10,10	12,4	13,2	14,3	15,3	Mean
13. Expressive behaviour	0·35	1·45	1·06	5·96	0·77	0·66	2·02	0·00	1·50
14. Intellectual aptitudes and abilities	5·61	7·23	5·73	2·52	3·07	1·10	1·35	1·86	3·67
15. Achievements and skills	1·75	5·99	6·79	3·90	3·65	2·20	1·57	1·86	3·46
16. Preferences and aversions	20·53	28·31	29·94	28·90	26·10	18·50	18·43	20·75	23·93
17. Interests and hobbies	7·02	7·64	8·07	3·21	9·02	9·03	6·29	10·49	7·61
18. Beliefs, attitudes and values	0·18	0·83	0·42	1·15	1·54	2·86	6·29	3·50	1·99
19. Attitudes towards self	0·00	0·00	0·21	0·23	0·38	0·44	1·12	0·70	0·37
20. Evaluations	3·33	11·78	9·34	5·73	2·50	5·51	3·15	1·40	5·33
21. Social roles	0·35	1·45	0·21	0·69	0·77	0·66	0·90	1·17	0·76
22. Reputation	0·18	0·21	0·42	0·92	0·58	0·66	0·67	0·47	0·50
23. Friendships and playmates	2·98	1·24	1·49	0·46	1·73	1·32	0·67	0·93	1·41
24. Effect upon, and relations with, others	0·00	0·00	0·00	0·46	0·19	0·44	1·80	0·00	0·34
25. Other people's behaviour towards the self	0·71	1·24	0·64	0·23	1·92	0·88	1·35	1·63	1·08
26. Relations with opposite sex	0·00	0·21	0·21	0·23	1·73	0·44	3·37	0·93	0·87
27. Mutual interactions	0·00	0·00	0·00	0·00	0·00	0·00	0·00	0·00	0·00
28. Subject's opinion of, and behaviour towards, the stimulus person	0·00	0·00	0·00	0·00	0·00	0·00	0·00	0·00	0·00
29. Comparison with self	0·00	0·00	0·00	0·00	0·00	0·00	0·00	0·00	0·00
30. Comparison with others	0·00	0·21	0·21	0·69	0·58	0·66	1·80	1·40	0·66
31. Family and kinship	8·60	2·27	2·34	0·69	1·73	1·54	0·90	0·00	2·47
32. Collateral facts and ideas	0·53	0·83	0·42	0·23	1·92	2·86	2·25	3·03	1·47
33. Irrelevant and unclassifiable facts and ideas	0·18	0·41	1·06	0·23	0·58	0·00	0·00	0·00	0·31
Total	99·99	100·02	99·97	100·02	100·00	99·93	100·00	100·00	100·01

* Note that categories 19 and 25 have been adapted for the analysis of self-descriptions; three categories (27, 28, 29) are not applicable.

Table 19. Effects of age, sex and intelligence of subject on the proportion of statements in thirty-three content categories when describing self

Category‡	Age	d.f.	Chi-squared values Sex (d.f. = 1)	Intelligence (d.f. = 1)
1. Appearance	35·31†	7	0·07	7·30*
2. General information and identity	72·44†	7	0·22	19·54†
3. Routine habits and activities	5·14	3	1·25	0·14
4. Actual incidents	6·67	7	0·02	0·02
5. Possessions	51·08†	7	2·82	5·25
6. Life history	6·58	1	1·05	0·25
7. Contemporary social circumstances	2·72	1	0·00	0·00
8. Physical condition	3·04	1	1·55	1·55
9. General personality attributes	64·96†	7	3·21	8·47*
10. Specific behavioural consistencies	67·89†	7	2·81	5·51
11. Motivation and arousal	14·62	7	0·29	1·79
12. Orientation	29·67†	3	0·03	13·48†
13. Expressive behaviour	22·34	7	0·00	7·64*
14. Intellectual aptitudes and abilities	8·68	7	6·17	2·89
15. Achievements and skills	10·62	7	7·41	0·15
16. Preferences and aversions	7·08	7	5·03	0·45
17. Interests and hobbies	21·09*	7	7·82*	3·61
18. Beliefs, attitudes and values	30·59*	7	5·28	0·02
19. Attitudes towards self	7·63	1	0·09	2·35
20. Evaluations	39·63*	7	1·96	0·87
21. Social roles	2·52	3	0·72	0·18
22. Reputation	0·24	1	0·24	0·24
23. Friendships and playmates	19·34*	7	1·18	15·83†
24. Effect upon, and relations with, others	3·72	1	1·65	1·65
25. Other people's behaviour towards the self	4·95	3	4·32	0·04
26. Relations with opposite sex	11·80†	3	9·57*	9·57*
27. Mutual interactions	—		—	—
28. Subject's opinion of, and behaviour towards, stimulus person	—		—	—
29. Comparison with self	—		—	—
30. Comparison with others	12·45*	3	0·39	5·29
31. Family and kinship	53·42†	7	6·74*	1·41
32. Collateral facts and ideas	23·92*	7	0·70	3·38
33. Irrelevant and unclassifiable facts and ideas	NA	1	NA	NA

* = p < 0·01.
† = p < 0·001.
NA = not analysed, insufficient data.

‡ Note that categories 19 and 25 have been adapted for the analysis of self-descriptions; three categories (27, 28, 29) are not applicable.

to a decreased use of category 23 (Friendship and Playmates) and category 31 (Family and Kinship).

Increased age led to the *greater* use of categories relating to General Personality Attributes (9), Specific Behavioural Consistencies (10) and Orientation (12). These categories accounted for 4 per cent of statements in 7-year-olds, 35 per cent in 14-year-olds, and 28 per cent in 15-year-olds. References to Interests and Hobbies (17) and Beliefs, Attitudes and Values (18) figured more prominently in descriptions by older subjects. Statements describing Attitudes towards the Self (19) also increased, suggesting that older subjects have become more detached and dispassionate in their assessment of themselves. This suggestion is supported by an increase in Comparisons with Others (30), and the use of Collateral Facts and Ideas (32), which are used to substantiate their assertions about themselves· Not surprisingly, older subjects tended to make more frequent reference to relations with the Opposite Sex (25), statements of this kind were less frequent than one would have expected.

Some categories showed an increased use with age followed by a decrease in older age groups; category 13 (Expressive Behaviour) was of this type. This category was used infrequently by 7-year-olds and not at all by 15-year-olds but accounted for nearly 6 per cent of statements in 10-year-olds. It was surprising how much insight these children had into their own mannerisms and idiosyncrasies. Evaluations (20) increased from 3 per cent at the age of 7 years to 12 per cent at the age of 8, and then decreased to just over 1 per cent at 15 years. Self-evaluations by young children were often unashamedly egotistical, whereas older children often referred to negative qualities, and some actually said they despised themselves.

The most frequently used category was Preferences and Aversions (16) which accounted for 24 per cent of all statements. This category was the one most frequently used by all age groups, and in 9-year-olds it accounted for nearly 30 per cent of all statements.

2. *Effects of Sex of Subject.* The sex of the subject had few effects on the variety of statement used. Only three categories showed significant effects —see Table 19. Boys referred more frequently than did girls to their Interests and Hobbies (17). Girls were more concerned with Relations with the Opposite Sex (26) and with Family and Kinship (31). These effects, and those described elsewhere, may be explained by the different rates of maturation in girls and boys.

3. *Effects of Intelligence of Subject.* Children of higher intelligence made

greater use of statements referring to General Personality Attributes (9), Orientation (12) and Expressive Behaviour (13). Subjects of lower intelligence referred more to Friendships and Playmates (23), Relations with the Opposite Sex (26), Appearance (1), and Identity (2). In general, subjects of lower intelligence formed self-impressions that were at a conceptually lower level—more concrete and more superficial—in comparison with subjects of higher intelligence.

B. A Comparison of Self-Descriptions and Descriptions of Others

The relatively marked developmental trends found in the contents of the self-descriptions are similar to those obtained for descriptions of others. The main differences between descriptions of the self and descriptions of others lies in the larger number of references to Preferences and Aversions (category 16) when a child describes himself.

Descriptions of the self were on average about 34 per cent longer than the average description of another stimulus person. This comparison, however, is not very meaningful since there were considerable within-subject differences in the lengths of descriptions of others. Descriptions of the self were longer than the longest description of another person in 38 per cent of subjects. This was mainly due to the performance of the youngest age group. Seventy-eight per cent of the self-descriptions of 7-year-old children were longer than any description they wrote of another stimulus person. Unless this effect was produced by the fact that the self-description was the first in the series, it could reflect the egocentrism of the younger subjects. Self-descriptions of 15-year-olds tended to be shorter than their descriptions of others and only 20 per cent of their self-descriptions were longer than their longest description behaviour of another person.

When the percentages of self-statements in the various categories (see Table 18) are compared with the percentages used to describe others (see Table 7), the results are strikingly similar.

Young children referred infrequently to personal qualities both when describing the self and when describing others. It was suggested in Chapter 11 that the limiting factors which place constraints upon the child's ability to describe others are his cognitive level, his egocentrism and his inability to decentre. But egocentrism also places constraints on those aspects of the self-concept which are defined by reference to the behaviour of other persons.

The following examples illustrate the concreteness of typical self-descriptions written by 7-year-old children.

A boy aged 7,0 describes himself:

I am 7 and I have hazel brown hair and my hobby is stamp collecting. I am good at football and I am quite good at sums and my favourite game is football and I love school and I like reading books and my favourite car is an Austin.

A girl aged 7,0 describes herself:

I am 7 years old. I have one sister. Next year I will be 8. I like colouring. The game I like is hide the thimble. I go riding every Wednesday. I have lots of toys. My flowers is a rose, and a buttercup and a daisy. I like milk to drink and lemon. I like meat to eat and potatoes as well as meat. Sometimes I like jelly and soup as well.

There are several differences between descriptions of self and descriptions of others among the 7-year-olds. Preferences and Aversions (16) was by far the most frequently used category in self-descriptions but it played only a minor role in descriptions of others. This result suggests that affective factors are even more important in conceptualizing the self than in conceptualizing others. More reference was made in self-description to Interests and Hobbies (17) and Intellectual Aptitudes and Abilities (14). These results indicate two important dimensions in the child's experience. Children's hobbies are usually highly valued and ego-involved activities that form a central part of their personal identity. The emphasis on aptitudes and abilities suggests that competence and excellence are important values for the schoolchild, and probably involve implicit comparisons with others as he attempts to define his self-concept in the context of school activities. Other sorts of self–other comparisons can be found at most stages of the human life-cycle.

Categories 16, 17 and 14 were used more frequently to describe the self than to describe others—they were also used more frequently to describe children and liked persons than to describe adults and disliked persons. It was suggested earlier that understanding others develops more rapidly in connection with persons similar to the self. The self-descriptions tend to support this contention; there are marked similarities in content between self-descriptions and descriptions of liked children. The child's understanding of himself and his understanding of others are reciprocal processes in development; they facilitate each other. The explicit comparisons are small in absolute terms; they comprise 0·65 per cent of all statements when the child is describing others, as compared with 0·56 per cent when he is describing himself. The difference, however, is that the former remains fairly constant from one age group to the next, whereas the latter increases with age fairly systematically.

During middle childhood, developments in self-description are similar to those described earlier in connection with descriptions of others. Development leads to increased abstractness and sophistication of content. Psychological qualities of all kinds are referred to: General Personality Attributes (9) and Specific Behavioural Consistencies (10) are used with increasing frequency and the child begins to show some understanding of his personal Motivation and Arousal (11). Descriptions are not, however, better articulated or better organized. The description usually consists of a list of qualities without any attempt to relate and organize them. For example,

A boy aged 9,0 describes himself:

> I am quite good tempered when I get going. I like other children. I like to play practical jokes on people and I am in the habit of forgetting things. I like rough games especially rugby. I am hurt easily and my brother always picks on me. I am a scouser. I always try to make friends with other children. I dislike jokes that are meant to be funny but aren't.

Descriptions like the previous example reveal a detailed understanding of some aspects of the self. But although some of the observations are quite sensitive there is no overall framework or structure to the impression. The self is perceived not as a unity but as a series of discrete elements. The same applies to the following description which contains references to both positively and negatively evaluated features, and is an interesting illustration of the child's response to adult values.

A boy aged 9,0 describes himself:

> I have dark brown hair, brown eyes and a fair face. I am a quick worker but am often lazy. I am good but often cheeky and naughty. My character is sometimes funny and sometimes serious. My behaviour is sometimes silly and stupid and often good it is often funny my daddy thinks.

Adolescence brings further changes in the contents of self-descriptions that make them somewhat different from descriptions of other stimulus persons. References to Motivation and Arousal (11) and Orientation (12) account for between 6 and 9 per cent of all statements about the self in three adolescent age groups (13 years, 14 years, 15 years) but only for about 1 per cent in descriptions of others. Motivation and orientation are covert psychological processes that are often difficult to infer in others but figure more prominently in our experience of ourselves. This is a particularly interesting finding because it illustrates the subjective origins of motivational concepts and supports our argument that an analysis of the developmental origins of psychological concepts could make a useful contributions to the epistemology of psychology.

Statements about Beliefs, Attitudes and Values (18) are also made more frequently by adolescents than by younger age groups; this seems to be a reflection of the adolescent's attempts to understand himself, and to achieve a stable and enduring sense of identity incorporating a set of basic values. Many adolescents seem to be concerned with political and religious views. Adolescent attempts at self-understanding and self-definition are also illustrated in Comparisons with Others (30) and the use of Collateral Facts and Ideas (31). References to Relations with the Opposite Sex (26) reflect the obvious increase in sexual motivation at this stage.

The older subject's self-descriptions were better organized than those of younger subjects, and attempts were made to structure the information and to make it consistent and coherent.

A girl aged 12,10 describes herself:

I have a fairly quick temper and it doesn't take much to rouse me. I can be a little bit sympathetic to the people I like, but to the poor people I dislike my temper can be shown quite easily. I'm not thoroughly honest, I can tell a white lie here and there when it's nessersary, but I am trying my hardest to redeem myself, as after experience I have found it's not worth it. If I cannot get my way with various people I walk away and most likley never talk to that person again. I take an interest in other people and I like to hear about their problems as more than likley they can help mesolve my own. My friends are used to me now and I don't realy worry them. I worry a bit after I have just yelled somebody out and more than likely I am the first to appologise.

A girl aged 14,2 describes herself:

I am a very temperamental person, sometimes, well *most* of the time, I am happy. Then now and again I just go moody for no reason at all. I enjoy being diferrent from everybody else, and like to think of myself as being fairly modern. Up till I was about 11, I was a pretty regular churchgoer (R.C.), but since then I have been thinking about religion and sometimes I do not believe in God. When I am nervous I talk a lot, and this gives some important new acquaintances a bad impression, when I am trying to make a good one. I worry a lot about getting married and having a family, because I am frightened that I will make a mess of it.

It is interesting to note the social awareness of adolescents as revealed by their self-impressions. They are concerned with how other people see them and what other people think about them, and they are often concerned with the effects they have on others. Most adolescents appear to be aware that they are moody and irritable, and they wish to minimize the effect that this has on other people, although many seem to feel that these are feelings they cannot control.

Adolescents are also concerned, as the last example illustrates, with being *different* from other people. Yet most are ambivalent about this. They like to be thought of as 'modern', 'with it', 'one of the crowd'; but at the same time they do not want their identity to become lost and submerged with that of their peers. Often they attempt to be different from the rest, usually in rather simple ways—like wearing different clothes or behaving in an odd manner, and they are quite pleased when other people react strongly to it. While wanting to be thought different from the rest, most adolescents also take account of group stability and cohesion. Many adolescents, especially the girls, mention their dislike of group arguments and disagreements, and state that they always try to stop them.

As mentioned earlier, a major difference between descriptions of self and descriptions of others is found in statements about Preferences and Aversions (16). This was the most frequently used category when describing the self and accounted for 24 per cent of all statements. For descriptions of others, it ranked tenth in frequency of usage and accounted for less than 4 per cent of all statements. This discrepancy is partly due to children using this category less frequently to describe adults than to describe children. Likes and dislikes seem to be individualized attitudes; they are aspects of personal experience rather than overt actions, so they have much less impact on impressions of others than on impressions of self. In other words, we tend to be relatively unaware of other people's preferences and aversions, but sharply aware of our own. Expressions of like or dislike, of course, are functions of our attitudes, beliefs and values—these are central parts of our self-concept; so it follows that they should figure prominently in self-descriptions. Children with limited vocabulary and language skills are obliged to describe their attitudes and opinions rather simply in terms of the *things* they like or dislike. Like/dislike becomes an important dimension that helps us to construe and order our personal world. Strong preferences and aversions are also ways of differentiating between 'self' and 'not-self'; they support and maintain our sense of personal identity and autonomy. Such statements serve expressive and instrumental purposes as well as fulfilling a descriptive function; they are probably not as superficial or as concrete as they appear.

When we engage in an interaction with another person we usually feel constrained to try to understand him. The most obvious and most easily observed features of another person are those connected with external appearance and overt behaviour. Hence, we tend to form an impression of him which 'centres' on these attributes and on attributes that can be readily inferred from them. The same does *not* apply when we try to understand ourselves. One's impressions of oneself—the self-concept or personal identity—operates on a variety of levels ranging from simple and explicit ideas, such as memories and perceptions, to deep-seated feelings and desires. Perhaps the most salient feature of our experience of ourselves is not what we *know* of our behaviour but rather what we *feel*.

We have not attempted to give an exhaustive account of the developmental psychology of the self-concept. What we have tried to do is to give the bare outline of a content analysis approach to the study of this important aspect of person perception.

III. The Perception of Human Behaviour

A. Introduction

In Chapter 2, under the heading of 'Coping Behaviour', we used the expression, 'stream of behaviour'. Behaviour is continuous; to make sense of it, an observer must both distinguish and connect separate actions. This involves a twofold cognitive function : the observer must be able to discriminate the component parts of a behavioural episode; also he must be able to construct a behavioural episode from a number of component parts. As we pointed out in Chapter 2, Dickman (1963) investigated differences between observers in their natural inclination to divide the 'stream of behaviour' into larger or smaller behavioural episodes.

It is obvious that, from quite an early age, we are able to make sense of perceptual information, that is, we can impose a pattern of meaning on to it. A stream of human behaviour provides such a source of perceptual information and we make sense of it by identifying the various elements and grouping them into orderly structures and sequences—rather like we read a page of print. It seems likely that human action, like other aspects of the physical world, exhibits a number of forms which are perceptually—and perhaps behaviourally—irreducible. Otherwise it is difficult to see how behaviour, perception and cognition ever get started on their developmental course.

As the child acquires intelligence, experience and language, he moves on to increasingly sophisticated modes of perception and understanding in relation to human behaviour. For example, he can anticipate the outcome of a behavioural sequence; he can construe relationships between actions which are widely separated in time; he can attribute intentions, abilities, dispositions and other kinds of subjective states to the stimulus person; he can construe relationships between situational factors and individual action; he can analyse a large segment of the stream of behaviour into its molecular or elementary parts or synthesize a number of such elementary parts into a larger or molar behavioural structure.

The developmental psychology of 'behaviour perception' is, to our way of thinking, a research topic which is even more fundamental than that of 'person perception'. The reason for this is not that children cannot begin to talk sensibly about persons and psychological processes until they have mastered the language of behaviour—a child may very well assert, 'Uncle Jack is angry' without being able to specify Jack's personal qualities or to describe his angry behaviour. The reason is, rather, that a deep analysis of the processes of perceiving and understanding others reveals that human action is a kind of language. We have to learn to 'read' the language; we have to learn the words and the phrases, the grammar and the style; and only in so far as we have mastered the language can we interpret the meaning or significance of its more complex forms as exhibited in the behaviour of individual persons. Each person is the origin of numerous behavioural 'statements'; and it is by reading meanings into his behaviour that we gradually learn to understand him. Observers, however, may differ considerably from one another not only in how they read the other person's behaviour but also in what they 'read into' a particular behavioural 'statement'—apart from having access to different samples of behaviour. It is as if the 'other person' were an unfinished book; we, the readers, wish to read what is 'in' the book; but we are not able to read very much of it, and we are usually prevented from reading some of the more interesting and revealing parts. The book, moreover, is in code, and not always easy to decipher. Matters are made more difficult because we can verify our interpretation of what the book says only by asking some other person what he thinks, or by turning to other parts of the book. But then we find that the other person may not have access to that part of the book. Most puzzling of all, we find that our behaviour as 'readers' affects what appears in the book.

The following sections illustrate some of the ways in which psychological research into this fundamental problem can be pursued.

B. The Research Film

1. *The Analysis of Adult Behaviour Narratives.* In 1968, the Nuffield Foundation awarded a grant for the production of a film to be used for research in person perception and human behavioural ecology. This research indicates some of the ways in which the concepts and methods of the main inquiry can be extended. It was originally conceived as a near-replication of a study by Dickman (1963). Dickman presented subjects with two 8-minute sound films—excerpts from *Our Vines Have Tender Grapes*—each followed by a series of statements printed on cards —constituting a sort of film script. Dickman analysed the way subjects grouped smaller segments of behaviour into larger, more inclusive, segments. His subjects, having viewed the film, were required to refer to the numbered statements (describing the action), to record which statements they felt belonged in the same episode-set, and to group the longer series of actions into a smaller number of behaviour episodes. Briefly, his results indicated that whereas subjects differed considerably in the number of episodes they discriminated, they tended to agree on the transition points between episodes.

With the help of Mr G. A. Kay, a special 12-minute film (silent, 16 mm, colour) was produced. It is essentially a documentary film in that it portrays the naturally occurring behaviour of one main character and two subsidiary characters during a short period of time in their natural surroundings. This was achieved by Dr Livesley re-enacting some routine activities in his normal domestic surroundings, and Mr Kay filming with *minimum* recourse to editing and dramatic film technique. The intention was to test whether subjects would perceive such naturally occurring behaviour differently from the way they would perceive a dramatic story sequence, such as those in the excerpts from *Our Vines Have Tender Grapes.*

We expected that normal behaviour would be perceived as less episodic than behaviour staged for dramatic effect, since in dramatic films the pace of the action is fast and effects are deliberately introduced to shape audience reaction—by providing cues which signal character or changes in the story. Thus, by contrast, the normal stream of routine behaviour should appear undramatic, slower, more detailed, more continuous, more predictable, and so on. Barker (1963) demonstrated a similar contrast between the normal stream of behaviour and the stream of behaviour depicted in children's books of fiction.

The film was first shown to a group of 34 second-year university students who were required to dictate a running commentary on the events in the film. The transcripts of these commentaries (behaviour narratives) were collated and with the aid of a cine-editor a detailed list of all the behaviour episodes was compiled· This was necessary in order to construct a set of statements similar to those used in Dickman's study. It was only at this point that we realized some of the weaknesses in Dickman's method, for example, the indeterminancy and arbitrariness of the 'behaviour units', so-called, purporting to be 'elements' in the stream of behaviour. A 'fine grain' analysis yielded 567 behavioural elements, while a 'coarse grain' analysis, more akin to the sorts of unit used by Dickman, yielded 142 behavioural elements. Naturally, we were not interested in the finer levels of analysis that can be made in studies of the kinesics of interpersonal perception (facial expressions, eye contacts, gestures, and so on) or in studies of mere movement, as in motion and time study. We were interested only in 'commonsense' levels of analysis, that is in the behaviour elements and episodes describable in the ordinary language of everyday life. The results, based on the subjects' running commentaries, showed that on average only 21 per cent (range : 15 to 29 per cent) of the 'fine grain' of behaviour was recorded as compared with 63 per cent (range : 46 to 71 per cent) of the 'coarse grain'. It is not known to what extent this represents the amount of behaviour actually *perceived.*

In terms of the fine-grain analysis there were no significant differences, although the women achieved a mean of 123 compared with 112 for men; similarly there was no significant difference between subjects who acted as observer first and recorder second (mean = 114) as compared with those who acted as recorder first and observer second (mean = 122). Naturally, under different experimental conditions, for example, using practised subjects and tape recorders, fuller and faster commentaries could have been achieved. It is of interest to note that young children tested over short sections of the film seemed to achieve comparable rates of recording, although a few required occasional reminders and prompts to prevent them from lapsing into silence (visual but nonverbal monitoring). This work is described in a later section.

As a matter of interest, it was calculated that the average rate of behaviour of the main character in the film was 47 'fine grain' behavioural units per minute and equivalent to 12 'coarse-grain' behavioural units per minute. These rates compare with estimates of 18 per minute and 13 per minute for the relatively 'coarse-grain' units in the two film excerpts used by Dickman. Thus, it was only after an intensive analysis of the empirical data—the behaviour narratives or 'running commentaries' provided by competent observers—that we were able to construct a series of descriptive behavioural units comparable with those used by Dickman; and even now it is impossible to say whether the same method —if applied to Dickman's film excerpts—would result in just those behavioural items that he listed. Dickman gives the impression that his descriptive units are basic, but it seems obvious to us that the 'stream of behaviour' can be perceptually 'segmented' at *various* levels of analysis —this is really the assumption in both studies. These levels range all the way from fine-grain units, through coarse-grain units and molar episodes, to summary accounts—the categories at higher levels include more behavioural elements than categories lower in the hierarchy; and there is, no doubt, in natural language, a system of conventions which governs the construction of a behaviour narrative. We have already drawn the analogy between language and behaviour. The 'language' of human behaviour and person perception has received little or no attention from psycholinguists, probably because the study of language behaviour itself is of recent origin. Some psychologists and philosophers, however, have contributed analytical accounts of some of the problems, for example, Heider (1958), From (1971), Mischel (1969).

Table 20 gives the list of 142 'coarse-grain' behavioural elements in the film. Figures 9 and 10 show the extent to which a sample of 34 university students agree in assimilating these behavioural elements to more inclusive behavioural episodes. It should be noted that, unlike the Dickman investigation in which subjects grouped statements printed on cards, the present investigation involved an analysis of the contents of running commentaries (behaviour narratives) given by subjects.

Table 20. A standardized behaviour narrative of the events portrayed in the research film

View of the bungalow

1. Through an open window a man is seen sitting on a bed.

2. He puts his hands to his face, scratches the back of his head and yawns.

3. He picks up a sweater and puts it on.

4. He stands up, opens the bedroom door and walks out closing the door behind him.

5. In the kitchen, a woman working at the cooker plugs in an electric kettle.

6. The man enters the kitchen, watches the woman for a moment and puts his hands on her shoulders. She turns to face him.

7. They kiss each other.

8. The man looks out of the window.

9. He takes a biscuit out of the biscuit barrel and eats it.

10. He turns and picks up the coal scuttle, hooking it over his arm.

11. He opens the kitchen door, turns and waves to the woman and goes outside.

12. He walks out through the door of the glass porch and across the yard to a gate, where he looks over the top.

13. He walks away and puts the coal scuttle down near the door of an outhouse or shed.

14. He returns to the gate and puts his hand through it.

15. He strolls along the path with his hands in his pockets taking a hand out once to stroke his head.

16. When he reaches the front door he bends down to pick up the milk and collect the paper from the letter-box.

17. He walks back along the path reading the paper until he reaches the kitchen window.

18. He knocks on the window and the woman opens it.

19. He hands her the paper and milk and she passes him a bowl, a piece of bread and a carrot, and closes the window.

20. The man walks to the gate, opens it and puts the bowl down. A dog comes out and eats from the bowl.

21. The man walks away past the shed and across the garden, looking back once at the dog.

22. He reaches a small cage with a rabbit in it and bends down to feed the rabbit with the carrot.

23. As he feeds the rabbit, the dog comes up to him and he gets hold of it.

24. He puts the bread into the rabbit's cage.

25. He plays with the dog and continues to play with it as he walks back to the dog's pen.

26. When he reaches the gate he opens it and tells the dog to go inside.

27. He puts the dog's bowl inside and closes the gate.

28. He walks towards the porch.

29. In the kitchen, the woman is sitting at the breakfast table as the man enters.

30. He walks across the kitchen, puts his hand on her shoulders and sits down at the table.

31. He helps himself to cereals and the woman pours out the tea.

32. He sprinkles sugar on to his cereals and puts sugar into his tea—stirring it while the woman sips her tea.

33. He reaches for the paper and opens it, while the woman is eating a piece of toast.

34. He reads the paper and drinks his tea; at the same time they talk to each other.

35. He continues to read as he eats his cereal.

36. He is wearing boots as he walks out of the porch into the yard.

37. He walks to the shed and with some difficulty unlocks the door.

38. He enters the shed and emerges moments later with a basket and a saw.

39. He goes to the gate of the dog's pen and opens it to let out the dog.

40. He walks around the shed and into the garden with the dog following him.

41. He places the basket down on the ground and puts the saw inside the basket.

42. He walks over to a heap of grass and after kicking it about picks up a handful, feels it and then throws it down.

43. He picks up some more grass, feels it and throws it down.

44. He then picks up the basket and saw and walks towards a pile of wood.

45. He puts down the basket and saw by the wood pile.

46. He picks up a stick and throws it for the dog who at first runs after it but then stops and turns back.

47. He walks away with the dog following him.

48. He walks back to the shed and enters it.

49. He comes out carrying a fork and a bottle.

50. He runs back to the pile of grass.

51. He begins forking the grass together while the dog plays around him.

52. He puts his hand into his pocket and then bends down to pick up the bottle.

53. He pours some of the contents of the bottle on to the grass.

54. He replaces the top of the bottle and puts it down.

55. He takes a box of matches from his pocket and tries without success to strike a match.

56. He takes another match and again fails to get a light.

57. He stands up and throws the match-box down.

58. He walks away turning back once to look at the dog.

59. When he reaches a wall which separates him from the kitchen he shouts and waves.

60. He climbs the wall and walks round the house to the porch and enters it.

61. He backs quickly out of the porch followed by the woman.

62. She points to his dirty boots, says something and then goes back into the kitchen.

63. The man stands outside waiting.

64. The woman comes out and hands him a box of matches.

65. He turns and walks back around the house tossing the matches in the air.

66. He climbs the wall but drops the matches as he does so.

67. He picks up the matches and walks back to the pile of grass.

68. He picks up the bottle again and empties it on the grass.

69. He replaces the cap on the bottle and puts it down. The dog comes up to him.

70. He stoops to strike a match and sets fire to the grass which burns rapidly.

71. He piles more grass on to the fire and then stands back. The dog runs off.

72. He forks more grass on to the pile.

73. He sticks the fork into the ground and stands back again.

74. He bends down to pick up the bottle and the matches, putting the matches into his pocket.

75. He walks away throwing the bottle from hand to hand.

76. He looks up at the sky shielding his eyes with his hand. An aeroplane flies overhead.

77. He continues walking towards the wood pile.

78. When he reaches the wood pile he throws down the bottle.

79. He picks up a large branch and knocks a small branch to one side.

80. He rests the large branch on a box and makes it steady.

81. He looks up at the sky again.

82. He takes the saw from the basket and begins to saw the branch.

83. He saws a pile of logs.

84. After sawing the last log he stands up and rubs his back.

85. He puts a log into the basket.

86. He moves the saw and puts his hand to his back.

87. He puts all the logs into the basket except one which he throws away.

88. He picks up the saw.

89. He straightens up and again rubs his back.

90. He puts the saw over his shoulder.

91. He picks up the basket of logs.

92. He walks away with the dog chasing after him.

93. He puts the basket down by the fire but it falls over.

94. He readjusts the saw on his shoulder.

95. He picks up the fork.

96. As he forks more grass on to the fire the saw falls on to his wrist.

97. He turns from the fire towards the basket and stands the basket upright.

98. He puts down the fork and the saw.

99. He replaces the logs in the basket.

100. He picks up the saw, fork and basket.

101. He walks past the fire and around the corner of the shed with the dog running after him.

102. As he reaches the door of the shed the woman comes out carrying the coal scuttle.

103. He puts down the basket, saw and fork and the woman puts down the coal scuttle.

104. She points to her watch and he looks at his own watch.

105. She picks up the coal scuttle and he moves to help her but she walks off.

106. He rubs his hands together and looks across the garden.

107. He walks across the garden towards some daffodils; as he does so, the dog bites the sleeve of his sweater.

108. He turns towards the dog, rubs his hands together and scratches his head.

109. He bends down and begins to pick daffodils.

110. A car comes along the road, pulls over to the side and stops.

111. The driver looks over his shoulder and opens the door to get out.

112. The driver walks around the back of the car and looks into the garden.

113. The driver walks up to the fence, leans over it to wave and call to the man picking the daffodils.

114. He looks up and then stands up.

115. He walks towards the driver who points his arm in one direction.

116. As he reaches the fence, he puts his hand into his pocket, then takes it out to brush his hair from his eyes.

117. He speaks to the driver pointing and giving directions.

118. The driver waves his hand, goes back to the car and then turns and waves again.

119. The first man moves about a little fingering the daffodils and then leans on the fence.

120. He waves to the driver and watches him drive away.

121. He pushes his hair back, puts his hand to his mouth and turns towards the house to see the woman walking towards him.

122. She points towards the car and also leans upon the fence.

123. They talk, the man pointing and the woman nodding.

124. The man shows the woman the daffodils.

125. They turn from the fence and he hands the daffodils to the woman.

126. As they walk towards the house, he puts his arm around her shoulders and she puts her arm around his waist.

127. The man takes his arm from her shoulders and points to the daffodils. The dog meanwhile runs behind them.

128. The man walks towards the daffodils.

129. He bends down and picks some more. The woman stands by watching and stroking the dog.

130. The man stands up and gives more daffodils to the woman.

131. The man looks at his watch.

132. He grabs the woman by the hand and they run towards the house—the dog following them.

133. When they reach the porch the woman enters while the man leans against the wall and unlaces his boots before entering.

View of house, view of porch, view of daffodils

134. After a time, the woman comes out of the porch and runs towards the gate.

135. The man, wearing an overcoat and carrying a brief-case runs out of the porch towards the car.

136. He opens the car door and throws the brief-case inside.

137. He gets into the car and shuts the door.

138. He reverses the car and turns it towards the gate.

139. The woman opens the gate.

140. The man waves through the open window as he drives through the gate.

141. The woman closes the gate after him.

142. She stands by the fence waving.

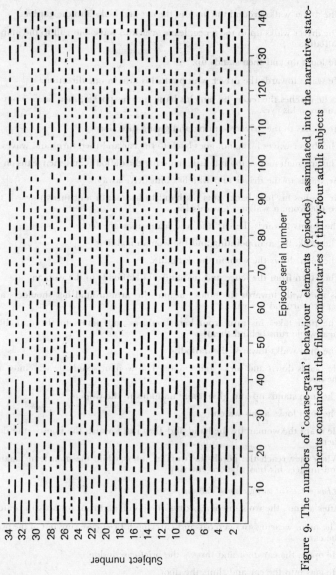

Figure 9. The numbers of 'coarse-grain' behaviour elements (episodes) assimilated into the narrative statements contained in the film commentaries of thirty-four adult subjects

The analysis of the running commentaries confirmed the essential conclusion reached by Dickman that whereas subjects differ considerably in the number of episodes they discriminate, they largely agree about transition points between episodes. This analysis was achieved by matching items, or groups of items, from the running commentaries with items, or groups of items, from the standard list of 142 behaviour units. The

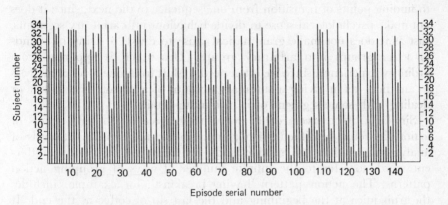

Figure 10. The numbers of subjects ($N = 34$) assimilating each of 142 'coarse-grain' behaviour elements (episodes) into their film commentary

results were also similar in other respects to those obtained by Dickman.

One problem, as formulated by Dickman, is to establish the extent to which independent observers agree that certain actions 'belong to' one functional unit rather than another. The analogous problem in language perception would be that of grouping and punctuating a string of sounds or letter groups so as to construct phrases and sentences. The behaviour of another person, for example, might be perceived, or rather described, as follows—and even at this level, interpretation is called for:

1. She noticed me.
2. She waved her hand.
3. She walked down the steps and crossed the road.
4. She walked up to me and started to talk.

A more perceptive observer, say a private detective or a motion and time study expert, could no doubt give a more detailed (finely grained) or a more valid account of the 'same' behaviour. On the other hand, the entire sequence can be grouped together as one unit in summary form, although much of the information is lost:

She came over and spoke to me.

There are, therefore, different levels of analysis and different kinds of interpretation in the perception and description of human action. To some extent, observers are free to operate at a level they find convenient or appropriate. They are much less free, however, when it comes to finding points of transition from one sequence to the next, since it does not make psychological sense to divide behaviour into arbitrary segments, just as it does not make grammatical sense to divide a string of sounds or letter groups into arbitrary groups. This much is apparent from ordinary experience, since we often need to shift from one level of analysis to another—as in giving a summary account of a person's behaviour or dealing with some segment of it in minute detail.

Similarly, if observers could not usually agree on the end points of actions it would be difficult if not impossible to talk sensibly at levels of analysis higher than the 'motion study' level, and we should need different words to refer to the infinite number of ways of grouping action patterns. The action pattern 'having breakfast', for example, includes the fruit juice at the beginning and the last sip of coffee at the end. It ought not to include walking to or from the breakfast table, though it might or might not include 'sitting down waiting' or 'reading the news-paper'. In general, such fine distinctions are unimportant in everyday life. They become important, perhaps, in legal disputes about what a person was doing at such and such a time, and they become important too in person perception when departures from customary patterns of behaviour lead the observer to make some inference about the person—not eating the food, for example, is perceived and construed not only as a departure from the expected pattern but also as a 'sign' of something, such as an upset stomach, moodiness, attention-seeking, or dislike of the food. Thus by the time we are adults we have acquired a host of shared language forms and rules of inferences for use in social interaction.

In Dickman's investigation, it was found that most subjects were agreed that some points in the film marked the end of one happening or episode and the beginning of another. There were other points in the film, how-ever, which marked transitions for some subjects but not for others. In general, there seemed to be relatively little absolute agreement on the size of the behavioural unit, that is on what were to be regarded as 'happenings' or 'episodes'. The evidence for this was the wide range of differences between individuals in the number of 'happenings' distin-guished, and consequently in the levels of analysis employed. In other words, subjects differed with regard to their 'behaviour perspective'; some used more general, inclusive categories, others used more concrete, limited categories; the same phenomenon was observed in the present series of investigations when the contents of the behaviour narratives were analysed.

In theory, one would expect the different levels of analysis to be compatible, following a hierarchical or tree-like pattern, as in Figure 11. Naturally, if different observers construe the sequence of events differently, then one could expect less agreement between them in the way the elements are grouped and related at higher levels than would be the case if different observers construe the sequence of events in the same way, so that Figure 11 would differ from one subject to another. Subjects might shift from one level to another throughout the behaviour sequence. In Dickman's investigation, not all the evidence relevant to this problem was collected. It would have involved making *successive* groupings of the behaviour elements (statements), giving a description or title to each episode or happening, until the subject had reached the point where he was unable to achieve larger groupings. Alternatively, commencing with the total set of statements, subjects could be required to subdivide them into the smallest number of subsets (major episodes), then into the next larger number, and so on, until single statements were reached. It seems likely that, under these experimental conditions, different groupings might occur, and different parts of the 'story' might be differentially susceptible to subdivision.

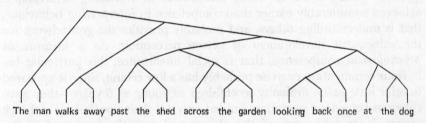

The man walks away past the shed across the garden looking back once at the dog

Figure 11. Sequential order and hierarchical organization of words in a natural language statement describing one 'coarse-grain' behaviour element from the standardized narrative account of the research film

2. *Very Young Children's Responses to the Film.* We were interested in finding the lowest age at which children could construct a reasonably coherent behaviour narrative.

Short excerpts from the film, taken more or less at random, were shown individually to 22 children aged 4 to 8 years who were asked to give a running commentary on what they saw. The children were told: 'You are going to see a film—a silent film—there is no sound or music and you cannot hear the people talking. It is about a man doing ordinary things. Pretend I cannot see the film (or: I am sitting with my back to the film, so I cannot see it) and tell me what is happening. Tell me as much as you can, and keep on telling me. I might interrupt you now and again to ask a question.' Their running commentaries were recorded on tape, transcribed and subsequently analysed for content.

We were surprised to discover that children as young as 5 or 6 years could perform very competently even though probably none had previous experience of such a task. The task was accepted as natural and the performance of it was competent, that is the children's narratives compared favourably with those of young adults. Presumably, transfer from related verbal and conceptual skills was considerable, since the children adopted a type and level of behavioural analysis without further instruction. There were, of course, individual differences and we found many interesting leads worth following up, for example the development of concepts and language forms pertaining to the description and analysis of behaviour, including the description of psychological processes and surrounding circumstances. The young child's understanding of the stream of behaviour stands in marked contrast with his lack of understanding of personal(ity) qualities and psychological processes—revealed in the same investigation and independently corroborated in separate studies using content analysis methods applied to descriptions of persons given by young children. Thus, competence in *describing* behaviour is achieved considerably earlier than competence in *interpreting* behaviour, that is understanding others, and probably provides the groundwork for the subsequent development of person perception. As a measure of *psychological* competence, that is social intelligence, this particular behaviour commentary exercise probably has a low ceiling, since it appeared to offer little or no difficulty to children as young as 6 years—they gave coherent behaviour narratives limited only by their vocabulary and lack of familiarity with some of the objects and activities portrayed in the film. The young child's competence in formulating a behaviour narrative may give a false impression. What he is good at is giving a literal description of the concrete action he is presently observing. This does not necessarily mean that he can give a summary account of several such actions, or see the connections between related actions. We have not yet investigated the different 'levels' at which behaviour can be conceptualized, although this is an obvious and an important problem in cognitive development.

The following interconnected points of interest emerged and can be illustrated by excerpts from the behaviour narratives.

Implicit versus explicit knowledge. With these very young children, aged 4 to 8, the manifest or explicit commentary is small relative to the actual content—the 'fine grain' of the behaviour they are watching, and relative to the latent or implicit content of the child's impression. As explained previously, a standard list of contents was drawn up by reference to the pooled narratives of superior young adults supplemented and adjusted by items contributed by an investigator (Mr T. T. Stallard) using a viewer-editor to give a step-by-step analysis at a micro-behavioural level. The latent or implicit content of the child's impression of the behaviour of the person in the film was apparent from the fact that children could say more in response to probing questions than they spontaneously chose to say by way of commentary on the film.

Jonathan, aged 4,6.
J : He is raking some hay.
J : He is getting something out of his pocket.
Pause
E : Do you know what it is?
J : Matches.
J : Oh, he is going to make a fire.
. . . . .
J : He is waving.
J : He is climbing over the wall.
J : He has gone in a house.
J : He has come out again.
Pause
E : Why is that?
J : He has got mud on his shoes.

It must be assumed that a good deal of what is observed in behaviour may not, or cannot, be made explicit—'we know more than we can say'. The manifest verbal content of the behaviour narrative represents a considerable reduction of the actual behaviour sequence, and leaves much of the experience latent or implicit.

There are obviously limits to the amount of information about the stream of behaviour that subjects can process. Thus, at times, the rate of information exceeds the subject's channel capacity and he is forced to omit, and perhaps subsequently to reconstruct, some behaviour elements. The effect is more pronounced when the stimulus person is carrying out several activities in parallel and when there are several ongoing 'streams of circumstances' relevant to each of these activities. Human actions take place within a set of overlapping and interlocking situations, and a proper account of the stimulus person's behaviour requires some understanding of the 'total situation' in which that behaviour is embedded. Such awareness may make the problem of monitoring the subject's behaviour easier or more difficult. Similarly, the observer's awareness of the stimulus person's state of mind, his motives, and the like, are bound to affect the ease with which he can keep track of what the subject is doing.

An interesting aspect of the task of observing behaviour is that of detecting and reporting behaviour which *does not* occur (when such behaviour was expected). In real life, it is often important to observe what a person did *not* do and did *not* say, because not behaving, somewhat paradoxically, is a kind of behaving. Such behavioural omissions may be especially important in legal disputes and in impression formation. In the film, the dog starts but does not continue to run after the stick which is thrown for him. The fact that we frequently anticipate the behaviour of other people, and could scarcely interact with others if this were not the case, means that, through experience, we learn the 'grammar' of human behaviour, that is we learn its elements and the way these elements are organized into patterns. In language, there are 'transitional probabilities' that certain words will follow other words or groups of words—as in approximations to English. For example, there is a certain probability that 'of' will follow the phrase 'Perhaps one . . .'. Similarly, when we observe the behaviour of another person, there are implicit transitional probabilities which lead us to expect one behavioural element or episode rather than another to follow an antecedent segment of behaviour, as in the film narrative, for example. Perhaps one of the outstanding features of schizophrenic breakdown is that the stream of schizophrenic behaviour, like the speech of a few schizophrenics (see Maher 1966), no longer obeys the 'grammar' of normal behaviour, and so appears meaningless to someone who is trying to construe it in terms of the rules governing normal behaviour.

Some sort of implicit, nonverbal monitoring of the other person's behaviour must precede the development of an explicit verbal commentary, otherwise preverbal social interaction would be impossible. Behaviour narratives are competent from about the age of 6 years, or earlier, and one must assume that the words and language forms have been learned in the course of the child's everyday activities, including, of course, reading and listening to stories. The habit of visual, nonverbal, monitoring is clearly revealed in the tendency of some of the younger children to lapse into silent observation. They need to be reminded to, 'say what is happening'. We conclude that young children can actively scrutinize and report normal behaviour—provided it lies within the range of their conceptual level and vocabulary.

One obvious limitation in the film exercise was the relative lack of more complex patterns of social interaction, and of expressive behaviour or other indications of inner psychological processes. Hence, the developmental aspects of person perception in relation to covert states were not conspicuous, although some of the precursors of later developmental achievements in person perception seemed to be revealed in the young children's narratives and responses to questions:

Caroline, aged 5,3.
C : He is going out of his bedroom.
E : Where do you think he is going?
C : To the kitchen to have his breakfast.
E : Who is that?
C : The wife.
E : What is she doing?
C : Making coffee.
E : Why did he give her a kiss?
C : Because he liked her.

Thomas, aged 7,3.
E : What sort of man was he?
T : I think he has lots of pets and he had a dog and a rabbit and he was a little careless dropping his matches and he left his fire burning.
E : Was he nice or horrible?
T : He was nice because he fed his animals before he eats his breakfast, and he showed the man the way. But he read the paper.... Daddy does it because Mummy is busy and hasn't the time. She works all the time.

Fiona, aged 4,9.
A house.
A man scratching his hair.
He's tired because he woke up early.
He's putting his jumper on because it's cold.
He's going to work.
He's shutting the door.
He's going out to see his wife.

Overall, the developmental trends point towards: (a) an increase in, or elaboration of, the manifest content to give more details, greater exactitude, greater continuity and coherence, (b) some decrease or condensation in manifest content made possible by selective attention and by the assimilation of relatively unimportant actions to a theme or outcome, (c) greater flexibility in the rate of commentary made possible by an improved command of language and a better sense of what is or is not relevant or worth saying, that is knowing what can be taken for granted.

Perception of environmental objects and circumstances. Perhaps because the film portrayed very ordinary events in very ordinary settings, references to objects and physical features of the environment were fairly numerous. For example, in the film, the man's actions had to be linked with clothes, a biscuit tin, animals, tools, buildings, trees, and so on. Very rarely were environmental and situational details mentioned if not directly relevant to the behaviour being reported. Although the man's actions were invariably the focus of the children's attention, they made explicit references to circumstances, for example 'The basket is full', 'The basket has fallen over.' The existence of such statements shows that the young children have learned to analyse the environment (its objects, constraints and opportunities) as well as to analyse behaviour (its actions, organization and direction). Younger children probably define activity cycles or behaviour episodes more simply and holistically than do older children and adults; but global and concrete impressions of behaviour eventually give way to differentiated and integrated impressions.

In very young children, action patterns and objects are more often misconstrued than in older children. The younger children are not perturbed by what we see as errors or incongruities, for example watering can (for coal hod), dressing up (for dressing), but older children tend to avoid or correct such mistakes. Role titles like 'lady' and 'mummy' change to precise ones like 'wife'. Object names follow a similar trend, for example, from 'stuff', 'thing', 'something', 'water', to 'hay', 'fork', 'coal hod', 'paraffin'. Behaviour terms of a more general and nonspecific sort, too, seem to be used by very young children in lieu of specifically named achievements, goals or activities, for example, 'doing something' for 'striking a match', 'drops' for 'throws down irritably', 'talking' for 'asking directions', 'walking' for 'strolling and looking at the weather'. In very young children, long sections of adult behaviour must appear meaningless—or perhaps only nameless. The word 'and', for example, is probably used syncretically in younger children to link small consecutive segments of behaviour; later on, however, the same word can be used more analytically to distinguish parallel activities and to link episodes and events which are not contiguous.

Cognitive schemata. Many notions associated with Bartlett's classic work on remembering (see Bartlett, 1932) can be used to account for the contents and organization of the young children's behaviour narratives. For example, there are many errors of omission when the narratives are compared with a 'fine-grain' or even a 'coarse-grain' account of the same events. The children's descriptions are therefore shorter; some features become sharper (more salient); distortions and transpositions occur, for example, 'He [rather than she] plugs in the kettle', 'He opens [rather than taps on] the window'; there are errors of commission : 'He comes downstairs' (The dwelling is a bungalow!).

A variety of verbal forms are used to refer to the *same* behaviour, for example, 'He gives . . .' and 'The dog takes . . .', 'He rolls the dog over' and 'The dog rolls over', 'Getting up' and 'Sitting on the bed', 'Climbs' and 'Jumps over'. The function of such verbal forms in describing behaviour is to allow the observer almost unlimited flexibility in making sense of what is going on; in particular, it allows him to give rough approximations where nothing more precise and detailed is called for.

Research possibilities. The film could be used for research in connection with the effects of dialogue, commentary and music; it could also be used to investigate person perception in special groups, such as deaf children, maladjusted children, and the like. Written exercises based on the film or similar materials could be profitably used in schools to enlarge the child's awareness of individual and social psychology. This is not to say that the film is an adequate stimulus for simulating impression formation in real life—we have been at pains to explain that this is not the case. Nevertheless, the film can be used as instructional material, provided the distortions induced by the mode of presenting the film person are taken into account. Comparable distortions could no doubt be observed if the stimulus person were presented in other ways, for example, in a story, in a tape/slide sequence or in a projective test.

Even by about the age of 4 or 5 years, the average child has some conception of inner psychological states like need and intention, for example, 'He needs . . .', 'He wants . . .', 'He wants to know . . .', 'He is trying to . . .', 'He is going to . . .'. His vocabulary and experience are the limiting factors in his development, and it must be remembered that the conceptualization and verbalization of such inner psychological states helps the observer to see meaning in, that is make sense of, the behaviour and circumstances of the other person—see de Charms (1968).

One research issue here is : Do a child's 'Why?' questions about another person's actions operate as exploratory mechanisms eliciting information about covert psychological and environmental factors? For example, are questions such as, 'Why is he doing that?', 'What does he need that for?' and 'What is he going to do?', designed to elicit information relevant to the elaboration of the child's conceptions of persons and their behaviour? Is he using such information about another person's actions and states of mind to enlarge his own self-awareness and self-understanding? Note the possibly important fact that although the young child is strongly egocentric, his 'Why?' questions are not often questions about his own behaviour and states of mind. The child's egocentricity must hinder such reflective thinking. Even so, a child might be able to use the information he receives about his own inner-personal states to make sense of another person's behaviour. It is also of interest and somewhat surprising to find that children's spontaneous 'Why?' questions appear to be directed rather infrequently to the topic of human behaviour—in marked contrast to their curiosity about the physical world—although professional opinions on this issue vary. What is happening when a very young child asks, 'What you doing, daddy?' (Adrian aged $2\frac{1}{2}$ years), or 'Doing daddy?' (Nigel, aged 22 months). Consider also in response to the film:

> *Damian, aged 4,6.*
> D : The mummy is making the breakfast. I am hungry.
> D : He's turning a lock.
> D : He's bringing out a basket. What does he need it for?
> E : What do you think he is going to do?
> D : He's going to put grass in it.
>
> D : He's going to light a bonfire.
> D : Getting some matches.
> D : He climbed over the wall.
> D : Why did he climb over the wall?
> D : What did he go back for?

Time-binding, behavioural themes and the attribution of intention. By about the age of 7, behaviour statements can be spoken in the past, present and future tenses. In response to the film, obviously, the present tense was most often used. The awareness of intention or goal-orientation was frequently revealed.

The precision with which the goal (or orientation, action, covert state or consequence) is stated can be expected to vary with such factors as the child's vocabulary, experience and intelligence. Interest and attention too will help to determine whether a brief or slight cue is perceived and properly interpreted. Time-binding is reflected in the ability to shift tense and to relate antecedents to consequences.

> *Neil, aged 7,0.*
> He has lit the match and he has put it to the straw and it's burst into flame quickly.

I think the contents of the bottle was petrol or it wouldn't burst into flames so quickly.
He has put down the fork and he is using it to put the straw away.

Thomas, aged 7,0.
I can see a man just waking up.
He is going to get dressed.
He is getting dressed.
I think he is going to . . .
He is going to have breakfast.

It is interesting to consider how linguistic and intellectual developments are related to person perception. The child's grasp of more complex patterns of behaviour can probably be regarded as a natural precursor of 'person' perception. By the age of 7 years, segmentation, serialization, environmental analysis, causal linkage, interpretation, and parallel themes, are all present—behaviour appears as a serial branching process, related to surrounding objects, circumstances, and events, and is so reported.

Causal connections are perceived at first implicitly, and then explicitly as illustrated by the use of phrases like 'because', 'and so', '(in order) to'. The term 'because', however, may sometimes be used syncretically to link quite disparate statements; we found no evidence of syncretic thought in the behaviour commentaries of the very young children. Later on in development, children begin to use the word in a more adult way to introduce an explanatory clause or an evidential clause —see Section IV in Chapter 10. References to causes, motives and reasons for action, are probably part of a systematic developmental trend towards more integrated and meaningful impressions of behaviour and personality. It is as if particular events, circumstances, objects and actions were assimilated to a common theme, such as feeding the pets or lighting a fire, their interrelations form a temporal pattern. At younger ages the patterns are short and simple; fragments of behaviour are reported and linked by 'and'; there is little or no cohesion, therefore little of person perception proper in very young children. Subsequent development makes it possible for the child to construe the other person's behaviour explicitly and thematically, for example, 'Calling to get a light', 'She's sent him out because he has got dirty boots on.'

At earlier age levels, some of the briefer and less obvious patterns are missed unless the child's attention is focused on them by nondirective questioning. Occasionally, of course, at the younger ages, the pattern is misconstrued, for example, 'She gives him something to wipe his boots on', '. . . pours water on the hay'.

Statements giving an interpretation linking two or more distinguishable episodes can be elicited even from very young children, although usually only in response to a request to explain what is happening, for example, 'His wife has said he is late.' Such statements connect an antecedent episode with a consequence, and thus give meaning to the combined actions.

Some actions, especially those we have defined as 'fine grain', must be regarded as self-evident or uninterpretable. These might include actones (Barker's term), which are embedded in larger segments of behaviour, and the behavioural elements of expressive behaviour; they could also include the very familiar or obvious things that can be taken for granted, such as continuing to hold things which have been picked up, the wearing of clothes, or the changes in bodily posture required for familiar actions.

Usually, one's experience of another person's actions makes sense only when they can be assimilated to a common goal or theme. Very young children, however, may link them syncretically or be unperturbed by their lack of sense or connection. Alternatively, they will assimilate events to themes with which *they* are familiar, for example 'He is pouring water [from the bottle]'—the bottle contained paraffin; 'They are (He is) running away from the dog'—he is playing with the dog; 'He is breaking the plants'—he is picking flowers.

The importance of interpretation in behaviour perception is apparent from an early age. The commentaries remain fragmentary until perspective, relevance and coherence are made possible by 'thematic' statements, such as 'He is getting up', 'He has a sore back', 'He is showing him the way to go with his hands', 'He has come down for breakfast.' Subjects sometimes indicate that they are unsure of the validity of their inferences or the themes they are using. This is revealed by doubt, misinterpretation and correction, for example, 'I think . . .', 'seems', 'I would say . . .', 'might', 'sort of'. Effort after meaning is assisted by perceiving or anticipating an action as terminal, that is as marking the end of a cycle or theme. Naturally, experience and mental age are likely to be important factors in this kind of 'social intelligence'.

Social intelligence. It might be possible to construct a 'social intelligence' scale based on the perception and analysis of behavioural data—as already suggested by Guilford (1967). It is of some historical interest to note that the idea of 'social intelligence' was first formulated by Thorndike (1920) in an article entitled, 'Intelligence and its Uses'. After a short and unproductive life, the idea was put into cold storage following an article by Thorndike and Stein (1937). As we have already seen, the rebirth of this idea in terms of 'person perception' also proved relatively unproductive with regard to the problems of accuracy and validity—hence our present concern with the developmental aspects of the *processes* involved in the way we 'experience' other people.

Unusual responses. Only a few unusual forms of response were observed. They included the following : Attending to very fine detail; Externalization, for example, 'The camera is going closer to . . .', 'The picture has changed', 'Now we see . . .'; Filling in gaps in the story, for example, 'The dog has found a hole somewhere—in the hedge—to get into the field'; Searching for evidence or likely consequences, for example, 'It seems to be petrol or . . .', 'The tree might catch fire . . .'. One child, aged 4,0 gave what appeared to be an abnormal pattern of responses. His narrative was erratic, and he formulated stylized sentences :

> And he's going to break the trees down.
> And he's going to break the car down.
> And he's going to break the garage down.

Perhaps not unnaturally for such a young child, he misconstrued much of what was going on in the film.

Impressions of the person in the film. We have already remarked on the fact that it is not feasible to get very young children to *write* descriptions of persons. Nondirective interviewing or some form of individual testing is required. The children's impressions of the person in the film were typically simple and stereotyped. He is regarded as nice and kind—but the children can give actual incidents as evidential support. Some of his belongings are listed—a dog, a car. Other qualities, such as 'careless' or 'ordinary', are mentioned together with supporting evidence. He is compared with known others. Otherwise the children's impressions are vague and implicit and require non directive questioning to elicit them. Some children (more often girls?) are aware of the social roles of wife, mother, and so on.

> *Betty, aged 5,0.*
> E : What did you think of the man in the film?
> B : He was nice.
> E : You liked him. Why do you say he was nice?
> B : Because he had a nice dog and a nice wife.
> E : Suppose Mummy asked what sort of man was in the film, what would you say about him?

B : He is a man who was married and he had a dog and a car.

3. *Very Young Children's Impressions of Others in Real Life.* In real life, very young children appear to conceptualize others mainly in terms of Physical Appearance (category 1), for example, 'He's little', and Mutual Interactions (category 27), for example, 'He plays with me.' Reflective thought and verbal elucidation are at a minimum. The problems encountered when using subjects below the age of about 5 years need not be discussed in detail, but they include simple facts like such children's inability to read and write, their disinclination to take things seriously, their inability to concentrate for long, their tendency to romance and perseverate in response to questions. Piaget and others have dealt at length with the problems encountered in observing and questioning very young children. In spite of the very young child's limitations, the overall pattern of the contents of his impressions of others shows that already, in the pre-school years, he is adopting the vocabulary and the frames of reference (content categories) used by older children and adults.

Preliminary investigations show that in real-life situations the commonest kinds of content of personality impressions among pre-school children reflect adult values, for example, comparisons of physical size, and associated age comparisons—'She is a big girl', 'He is in my class'. Given adequate opportunity and stimulation, the average 3- to 5-year-old will give about four 'statements' per description, in about 25 words. Some of the more sophisticated and 'deeper' kinds of content, such as trait names and expressive behaviour, appear rarely if at all. The 'other' child's characteristics are reported in behavioural rather than in psychological terms, that is they are construed more concretely and literally than at later ages. Emphasis and intensity are conveyed by repetition and urgency of expression. The impression, however, although simple, is organized; it may contain simple explanatory or evidential material, for example, 'I don't like Jane; she's naughty because she snatches my doll.' The descriptions given by very young children frequently include statements about : General Information and Identity (category 2), for example, 'He lives near me'; Evaluations (category 20), for example, 'He's horrible'; Subject's Opinion of, and Behaviour towards, the Stimulus Person (category 28), for example, 'I don't like him'. Statements from many other categories may be observed—but much less frequently.

Very young girls seem more likely to refer to details of physical appearance than do boys. But, in the impressions formed by very young children, even physical characteristics seem to take second place to the child's behaviour towards the stimulus person, illustrating the young child's egocentric attitudes towards others.

Examples of personality impressions elicited from very young children by means of non-directive questioning are:

> I don't like Billy because he's naughty. He's a big boy and he hits me.
> John is my best friend. We play in the street. He has a big sister. I like him because I play with his toys.

As might be expected, descriptions by very young children lack the detail, the systematic coverage and the coherence (internal consistency) characteristic of descriptions given by older children.

4. *Older Children's Impressions of the Person in the Film.* The research idea underlying the production of the film was that the central character, John Smith, would not be a 'dramatic character'; he would be neutral or ordinary, and lack conspicuous personality traits portrayed by expressive behaviour and psychologically significant actions. He was intended to be an ambiguous 'stimulus person'. In terms of the theory of projective testing, this should reduce the constraints imposed by the external stimulus and increase the extent to which the subject's impressions are directed by inner-personal factors—such as his motivation and attitudes. It was thought that, as compared with definite real persons, a neutral (ambiguous) stimulus person would give rise to impressions, that is descriptions, which would more clearly reflect some of the social and psychological factors affecting person perception, for example, age, sex and intelligence as in the main inquiry, as well as introversion/extraversion, neuroticism, social class, and so on. It seemed reasonable to suppose that, faced with a genuinely neutral stimulus person, and having to form an impression fairly quickly on the basis of relatively formless data, subjects would have to fall back on their implicit personality theory—using this notion in its widest sense. That is to say, the pattern of meaning imposed upon the unstructured behavioural events in the film would be largely determined by the psychological characteristics of the subject—but see Kenny (1964).

The subjects for the inquiry were selected from a pool of 100 children in four classes of one Comprehensive School on Merseyside. From this pool, 80 children were selected as follows:

Group I	:	20 boys aged 14–15 years
Group II	:	20 girls aged 14–15 years
Group III	:	20 boys aged 12–13 years
Group IV	:	20 girls aged 11–12 years

The school records indicated that the children were of average ability.

The film was shown in a normal classroom and preceded by the following verbal instructions :

> We are going to show you a short silent film. It has to do with an ordinary morning's activities in the life of a man we shall call John Smith. He will be the first person you see in the film, and it is to this person that we want you to pay attention. Watch him carefully and try to form an impression of him as a person. After you have seen the film, you will be asked to write down your own opinions of what John Smith is like.
>
> We do not want you to describe his appearance or to say what he did in the film. Rather, we want you to describe the *sort* of person he is, what you think about him—as if you were talking to someone who did not know him.

The second paragraph, above, was repeated. The children were asked if they had any questions, and if so, these were answered in a non-directive manner.

After the children had watched the film, the second paragraph was again repeated, and they were instructed to write down their impressions of John Smith on one side of the paper provided. No time limit was imposed; the reports were collected when a child had either filled one side or indicated that he had written all he could.

The children's written descriptions of the 'film person' were subsequently analysed for content and organization in the same way as for the main inquiry. The percentage frequency of occurrence for each content category is given in Table 21 and compared with the frequency for a 'person in real life' calculated from figures obtained in the main inquiry. These comparison frequencies were achieved by averaging the values observed for ages 12,4, 13,2 and 14,3 and adjusting for number of subjects (80/120) and number of descriptions (1/8), which means, in effect, dividing the figures in the main inquiry by 12. The relative differences can be calculated by means of the formula :

$$\text{Relative Difference} = (A-B)/\tfrac{1}{2}(A+B)$$

As the inquiry was exploratory and the sample small, no prior hypotheses were subjected to statistical test. *Post hoc* examination, however, suggested that the observed differences between a 'real person' and the 'film person' in the contents of impressions are as follows :

Table 21. Similarities and differences in the contents of personality impressions for persons in real life and a person in a film

| | Frequency | | Percentage | | Relative Difference |
| | Main sample (adjusted) | Film sample | Main sample (adjusted) A | Film sample B | |
Content category	Main sample (adjusted)	Film sample	Main sample (adjusted) A	Film sample B	$(A-B)/\frac{1}{2}(A+B)$
1	47·8	11	6·27	0·77	+ 1·56
2	56·8	44	7·45	3·07	+ 0·83
3	2·3	30	0·30	2·09	− 1·50
4	33·0	119	4·33	8·30	− 0·63
5	8·7	26	1·14	1·81	− 0·45
6	2·8	2	0·37	0·14	+ 0·89
7	3·6	8	0·47	0·56	− 0·17
8	4·6	4	0·60	0·28	+ 0·73
9	116·4	339	15·27	23·64	− 0·43
10	129·3	195	16·97	13·60	+ 0·22
11	3·2	10	0·42	0·70	− 0·50
12	3·1	10	0·41	0·70	− 0·52
13	17·2	2	2·27	0·14	+ 1·77
14	8·1	9	1·06	0·63	+ 0·51
15	8·7	10	1·14	0·70	+ 0·48
16	23·8	73	3·12	5·09	− 0·48
17	10·0	24	1·31	1·67	− 0·24
18	6·2	—	0·81	0·00	+ 2·00
19	11·3	1	1·48	0·07	+ 1·82
20	53·8	174	7·06	12·13	− 0·53
21	10·8	13	1·42	0·91	+ 0·44
22	10·0	2	1·31	0·14	+ 1·61
23	5·3	1	0·70	0·07	+ 1·64
24	7·7	2	1·01	0·14	+ 1·51
25	5·0	2	0·66	0·14	+ 1·30
26	8·8	36	1·16	2·51	− 0·74
27	52·0	—	6·82	0·00	+ 2·00
28	52·9	4	6·94	0·28	+ 1·84
29	6·2	1	0·81	0·07	+ 1·68
30	6·6	13	0·87	0·91	− 0·04
31	27·9	8	3·66	0·56	+ 1·47
32	17·5	251	2·30	17·50	− 1·54
33	0·7	10	0·09	0·70	− 1·54

Substantially greater frequency for a 'film person' for categories:

3. Routine Habits and Activities.
32. Collateral Facts and Ideas.
33. Irrelevant and Unclassifiable Material.

Substantially greater frequency for the 'real person' for categories:

1. Appearance.

13. Expressive Behaviour.
18. Beliefs, Attitudes and Values.
19. Stimulus Person's Attitudes towards Himself.
22. Reputation.
23. Friendships and Playmates.
24. Effect upon, and Relations with, Others.
27. Mutual Interaction.
28. Subject's Opinion of, and Behaviour towards, the Stimulus Person.
29. Comparisons between Subject and Stimulus Person.
31. Family and Kinship.

Although the basic idea was to portray a 'neutral' character in the film, the profile obtained on a set of personality ratings shows that the children tended to see him as a 'liked' person but were to some extent ambivalent. The comparison figures from the main inquiry relating to the content analysis of descriptions are based on four liked plus four disliked stimulus persons. Thus the observed differences ought not to be affected unduly by the effect of the 'stimulus person', but ought to be affected by the mode of presentation, that is real-life versus films. The observed differences fit this supposition reasonably well. Another way of emphasizing the contrast between the two types of impression is to say that, whereas 67 per cent of the total contents of a personality impression in real life are composed of categories 1, 2, 9, 10, 20, 27 and 28, for the film person, 67 per cent of the total contents are composed of categories 9, 10, 20 and 32. For the film person, 80 per cent of the total contents are composed of categories 4, 9, 10, 16, 20 and 32.

Some of the observed differences, of course, must be attributed to the special qualities of the particular film actually used: it was silent, the main character was engaged in routine, relatively undramatic activities, and so on. Nevertheless, the results offer *prima facie* evidence that observers do not form exactly the same sorts of impressions of a person in a film as they do of a person in real life. Therefore results derived from personality research employing film stimuli, for ratings and checklists, etc., do not necessarily reflect effects operating in real life. On the other hand, it could be argued that the differences between the results for the person in the film and those for the person in real life are the sorts of differences one would expect, considering the different stimulus situations, and that the similarities between them are more impressive than the differences. In this sense, the descriptions of the film person validate the method used in the main inquiry, because the differences are in the expected directions, and the impressions of the film person are much more highly structured—in terms of general personality attributes, specific behavioural consistencies, evaluations and explanatory or supportive material. But this is not to say that the two methods are interchangeable; rather, the comparisons add further weight to the argument that the 'stimulus person' variable is a potent determinant of impression formation.

Whilst it would be wrong to assert that the impressions formed of the person in the film are entirely different from the impressions formed of persons in real life, since we have already seen that they share much in the way of contents and organization, we must recognize that there are some differences and these can be regarded as artefacts arising from the stimulus properties of the film. This confirms arguments advanced in Chapters 2 and 3 that more attention should be paid to the manner in which the stimulus information is presented in studies of impression formation.

Four specimens drawn randomly from the children's descriptions of the person in the film are shown below. They illustrate many of the features of impression formation described elsewhere in this book—varieties of content, selective perception, effort after meaning, and the organization of ideas—and they further illustrate something of the range of individual differences in impression formation. Note that John Smith's physical characteristics are hardly mentioned, but the children found it impossible to convey their impression of him without frequent references to what he actually did in the film—in spite of instructions to the contrary. References to Routine Habits and Activities (category 3) were significantly more frequent than for persons in real life. The spelling, punctuation, style and grammar of the original descriptions have been retained, since they are indicative of the child's ability.

Ian, aged 14,0.
John Smith is an affectionate man and shows this towards his wife. He is sentimental towards animals and he prefers the country to the town. Also John Smith is an agreeable man at times but he is quick tempered. He is a man of reasonable intelligence but has an uncareful nature. He also likes to help other people and does not hesitate to give a helping hand. He is also a self respecting man who takes pride in his belongings. He is also a man who likes to know what is happening in the world around him. He is a more country minded man who prefers a log fire to a coal fire. He is proud of the appearance of his property and especially the house and farm and

also his car. He is a clean man and probably comes from a good background.

Ben, aged 14,0.
John Smith is a friendly person who likes animals. When he gets up in the morning he goes out and feeds his dog and his rabbit and then goes in and has his breakfast. Then he goes out and cuts some logs up for the fire and burns all the grass which has been cut.

He is sometimes forgetful and forgets to do things. Like take off his boot when they are full of mud and forgets to bring the coal in from the shed when he goes out for it. He always seems to be happy and does not lose his temper. He also likes his wife.

Doreen, aged 11,0.
The film we just sore was about a man named John Smith. This man looks kind, hard working gets up as soon as he wakes up. does what a man should do of a morning if he lives in the country, and uses coal. John Smith is a Peron who likes Pets alot and loves Playing with them even if he has got work to do. Many People who live in the country doent get up so early so they don't have to do the work before they go to the city, But Mr. John Smith gets up very early so he has time to help his wife and then go to work. Every were he went the dog would go with him, so he must like dogs. And also rabbits. I think he likes working so early in the mornings. Works till the job is done. For gets to take of muddy or dirty things before he goes into the house and gets very angry so quickly. Must love the country side. As soon as he gets his breakfast he does'ent sit round and be lazy he is active. Loves hobbys that are different to others, comon hobbys. I think Mr. Smith is sort of lasy. Some things he doesent like doing he just looks as if he would'ent do them at all.

Karen, aged 11,0.
John Smith is a very helpful and kind man. He helps in the morning before he goes to work. If he met someone who he did not know I think he would be very helpful to that person. If they started to argue I think he would try a lot to keep his temper. He is kind, if any body had lost their way in the night when it was raining he mite even say come on in and have a drink while I get a macanic on the phone to say come and fix your car, and if he could not get the man to come he would have asked them to stay the night till the morning. He mite even say take my car tow yours behind it and you

can return my car in the morning. I think that he is very helpful
indeed because he his very good for his wife and he plays withe the
dog and feeds them as well every morning before he gose to work
and he does a good job of it as well. He has a good wife and he leeds
a happy life. He is helthy because he chops the wood every morning
for the fire. John Smith is clean excepted for when he forgets to
wipe his feet after he has been in the field. Other wise he is very
clean.

5. *Older Children's Attribution of Traits to the Person in the Film.*
Written descriptions of the 'film person'. As in the main inquiry, the
traits spontaneously attributed to the person in the film follow a well-
known type of frequency distribution referred to in Zipf's law (Zipf,
1949) in which a few trait names are used by many subjects, and many
trait-names are used by a few or only one subject. The numbers of
subjects employing various trait names to characterize the person in the
film are given in Table 22. They are compared with the adjusted values
for ages 12,4, 13,2 and 14,3 in the main inquiry. Table 12 gives details
of frequencies based on eight stimulus persons.

It will be observed that there are similarities and differences in the
trait names used to characterize the person in the film and persons in
real life. Some traits which were observed in the main inquiry were not
observed in the film study, and vice versa. For example, *careless, clumsy*
has a frequency of 1/562 in the main inquiry and 47/471 in the film
study; *generous* has a frequency of 36/562 in the main inquiry and
1/471 in the film study. There is no doubt that other sorts of film would
have produced other sorts of differences. If we consider only those traits
which the two studies have in common, we find slight, although statistically significant, agreement in their frequency of usage ($\rho = +0.36$). This
suggests that children are predisposed to attribute certain qualities to
people in general, but their actual responses are to some extent modified
to fit the particular stimulus person.

In response to the film, the typical description comprised an
evaluation, one main personality trait or behavioural consistency, possibly
qualified, together with supporting evidence based on behaviour episodes
in the film. But, as we shall see, it is not clear whether the film was
relatively successful in portraying a neutral stimulus person and in
demonstrating the effects (and lack of effects) to be described, or whether
it was *not* successful and so failed to reveal true effects.

Trait ratings of the 'film person'. After the subjects had completed
their written description of the person in the film, they were given a copy
of a specially designed seven-point rating scale. The way in which the

Table 22. Number of subjects attributing various traits to the stimulus person in the research film and to persons in real life

	Trait frequencies	
	Film sample N = 80 K = 1	Main sample Ages: 12,4, 13,2 and 14,3 N = 120 K = 8
Nice/good/pleasant	34	81
Kind/loving	83	73
Helpful/capable	25	43
Generous	1	36
Quiet/shy	5	34
Bad-tempered	23	31
Friendly	27	23
Happy/content	30	22
Bossy	1	21
Clever	16	17
Good-tempered/even-tempered	8	15
Selfish	4	14
Thoughtful	6	13
Energetic/active	6	12
Polite	3	11
Stupid/foolish	6	10
Impolite/rude	5	10
Honest	2	9
Lazy	8	9
Dirty	12	8
Hardworking/works hard	16	8
Clean	2	7
Easygoing	1	7
Not shy	5	6
Not clever	11	6
Rough	1	5
Patient	1	5
Untidy	6	4
Not rough	4	4
Playful	8	4
Unhelpful/not helpful	1	4
Impatient	8	3
Forgetful	13	2
Not bossy	1	2
Cruel	1	2
Careless/clumsy	47	1
Country loving	4	1
Status/wealthy/rich	11	0
Loner	3	0
Busy/hurried	6	0
Dreamy/distracted	4	0
Optimistic	2	0
Planespotter	1	0
Homeloving	2	0
Not greedy	1	0

	Trait frequencies	
	Film sample N = 80 K = 1	Main sample Ages: 12,4, 13,2 and 14,3 N = 120 K = 8
Nervous	1	o
Worried	1	o
Half-hearted	2	o
Healthy	1	o
Normal	1	o
Passionate	1	o
Wasteful	1	o
Not strict	1	o
Not lazy	1	o
Odd	1	o
Total	471	562

person in the film was to be described by means of the rating scale was explained to them. The instructions were also printed at the top of the rating scale. The scales themselves were derived from the main study, and consisted of terms known to be familiar to the children in our sample. In our review of the literature on impression formation, we suggested that one could not rely upon simple antonyms to act as polar opposites to trait names. Hence, the polar opposite of each trait used in the present study was its negation, that is gentle versus not gentle rather than gentle versus rough, selfish versus not selfish rather than selfish versus generous. Most, if not all personality traits have a greater or lesser degree of social desirability, and the scales were arranged so that sometimes the socially desirable end of the scale was associated with low ratings, and at other times with high ratings. In the analysis, however, the directions have been made consistent—for ease of understanding—by reversing the values of some of the scales.

Table 23 gives the median ratings, on a seven-point scale, for sixteen personal attributes derived from the responses of the eighty children after they had seen the film and written their description of the person.

The general conclusions which seem to be implied by the results obtained when children are asked to rate the personal qualities of a relatively neutral 'film person' are as follows. First, many children aged from 11 to 15 years understand human behaviour and personality well enough to make ratings—such understanding seems to have been taken for granted rather than conclusively demonstrated in previous research.

Table 23.* Frequency distribution and median ratings on sixteen specified attributes of the stimulus person in the research film

Rating	1	2	3	4	5	6	7	
A: Not good tempered	9	8	11	*16*	11	11	14	Good tempered
B: Not gentle	3	1	3	12	7	*23*	31	Gentle
C: Bossy	2	2	1	15	9	*16*	35	Not bossy
D: Not happy	4	1	0	7	13	14	*41*	Happy
E: Not clever	1	4	5	27	*12*	13	18	Clever
F: Shy	4	3	8	13	*13*	11	28	Not shy
G: Not talkative	12	11	22	20	7	6	2	Talkative
H: Not friendly	1	2	0	2	6	17	*52*	Friendly
I: Clumsy	24	*18*	7	8	9	6	8	Not clumsy
J: Not kind	0	2	2	9	6	21	*40*	Kind
K: Strict	2	0	2	27	*11*	16	22	Not strict
L: Rough	4	4	4	21	*10*	14	23	Not rough
M: Worries	7	7	2	19	*16*	9	20	Does not worry
N: Not nice	3	1	1	8	15	*21*	31	Nice
O: Selfish	3	2	3	16	8	*13*	35	Not selfish
P: Bad	1	0	1	13	10	15	*40*	Not bad

* The figures in italics indicate the median rating for each attribute.

If this were not the case, the results would have been much less consistent than they were. John Smith had a characteristic personality profile which varied little from subgroup to subgroup and even the frequencies with which each of the ratings from 1 to 7 were used by each subgroup were fairly constant. Second, the experimental presentation of an effectively 'neutral' stimulus person is difficult and may be a contradiction in terms. It would seem to require a stimulus person who is given an average rating of 4 on a seven-point scale for each of a representative set of characteristics.

As already explained, the investigations using the film were exploratory extensions of the main inquiry. No prior hypotheses were formulated and the *post hoc* analyses do no more than illustrate some additional research problems and methods. The *post hoc* examination of age and sex differences revealed a few items of interest, although most of the comparisons yielded nonsignificant statistical differences. The absence of age differences is not altogether unexpected since the main inquiry had shown that developmental differences between 12 and 15 years are relatively small.

A comment on 'personality' variables in attribution. Measurements of personality differences within the normal range as measured by the Eysenck Junior Personality Inventory (see Eysenck, 1965) revealed little or nothing of statistical significance. In the sample of eighty children, median tests indicated that there were no significant differences between introverted and extraverted subjects or between the neurotic and stable subjects in their tendency to mention specific traits to a greater or lesser degree in their descriptions of John Smith. Although some statistically significant differences were detected in the smaller Age × Sex subgroups (twenty subjects in each), no consistent pattern emerged.

Similarly, although a few statistically significant results were obtained when the personality variables were looked at in relation to the rating scales, they were not consistent and seemed not to fall into any meaningful pattern. Hence, the results are not presented in detail.

Assuming that the film person was a reasonable approximation to a neutral stimulus person, it is difficult to escape the conclusion that the organismic variables of sex and age (at least in the three years between 11 + and 14 +) have little, if any, effect on the process of attribution. Similarly, introversion/extraversion and neuroticism/stability appear to have negligible differential effects. Some caution is called for here, however, since the range of individual differences in these psychological characteristics may have been too narrow. Alternatively, the Eysenck Junior Personality Inventory may not have discriminated reliably or validly between the subjects. Another possibility is that the effects of organismic and psychological variables on the process of attribution are complex and interactive. We have tended to regard some apparently significant results obtained within subgroups as spurious, since they were obtained in a *post hoc* fashion, they were inconsistent, and could have arisen as a consequence of making multiple comparisons. Obviously, further research into the processes of attribution along these lines demands a more sophisticated statistical design as well as a more thoroughgoing theoretical framework.

Sentence completion as a method of studying relational thinking in impression formation. The third part of the exercise using the research film required the children to complete a series of sentences, of the form:

I think John Smith is . . . because . . .

The aim of this exercise was to examine the sorts of evidence and explanation that children use in forming impressions of persons. The most common responses were as follows:

John Smith is *kind and happy* because
    he is kind to his animals.
    he is kind to his wife.
    he doesn't argue.
    he likes people.
John Smith is *careless and clumsy* because

he does not complete his chores.
he is inattentive.
he is impatient.
he enters his house in muddy boots.
he stumbled and knocked over his basket.
he neglected the fire.
John Smith is *friendly* because
he talks to strangers.
John Smith is *contented and happy* because
he has a nice home.
he leads an outdoor life.
he is easygoing.

The results of the main inquiry showed that, as compared with younger children, older children and adults are better able to formulate and organize their ideas about other people and better able to explain certain features of the person's behaviour or psychological qualities. They are better able, that is, to go beyond the behavioural data to the underlying psychological themes and to justify their inferences by reference to behavioural evidence. As we have explained in the main inquiry, the older children and adults make more use of qualifying and organizing statements (categories i to viii). It is of interest to ask, therefore, what kinds of cues children use in forming impressions of people. Thirteen schoolboys aged 12 were shown the research film and asked to watch carefully and form an impression of the main character in the film. Afterwards they were given an eight-item, forced-choice, open-ended sentence completion test. This consisted of items like the following:

I think Mr Smith is QUIET/LIVELY because . . .
I think Mr Smith is CHEERFUL/SERIOUS because . . .

They were asked to select one of the two alternatives in each item that they considered best fitted Mr Smith, and then to explain their reasons for their choice. There was considerable agreement between the boys on the scales for: Honest versus Dishonest, Friendly versus Unfriendly, Cheerful versus Serious, Lively versus Quiet, Gentle versus Rough, Intelligent versus Not Intelligent, Irritable versus Calm, Unusual versus Ordinary.

The responses to the open-ended part of this sentence completion test were analysed for content by reference to the existing categories of personality impressions. The most frequently used category, not surprisingly, was Actual Incidents (category 4) which accounted for 53 per cent of all responses to all the items. Two other frequently used categories were Specific Behavioural Consistencies (category 10) which accounted for nearly 12 per cent and Expressive Behaviour (category 13) which accounted for nearly 11 per cent. Almost all the responses could be accounted for in terms of information which could be categorized in one or other of 11 of the 33 content categories. Examples are as follows:

I think Mr Smith is LIVELY because '... of the things he does early in the morning like chopping up the firewood. I think he did this so he would be better off (in his house).'

I think Mr Smith is INTELLIGENT because '... he likes the work he is doing.'

I think Mr Smith is CALM because '... he was not bad tempered at all, he just got on with his work calmly.'

I think Mr Smith is UNUSUAL because '... when he got up he went strat out to put the bucket out for the coal.'

I think Mr Smith is FRIENDLY because '... he talked nicely to the man and when he had just had a small row with his wife he offered her flowers from the garden to show he was sorry.'

It is clear from these few examples that even though these 12-year-old children may be able to make some kinds of inference about people from the behaviour they exhibit, they nevertheless have a long way to go before they could be regarded as competent observers and judges of human behaviour—partly because the facts they use are sometimes irrelevant to the judgments they have made, partly because they do not use the 'best evidence' available, partly because some of them are disposed to concrete and literal modes of cognition.

It is an interesting aspect of the way we form impressions of other people that we disregard the bulk of the stimulus person's behaviour and focus our attention on a few facts which literally 'make an impression on us'. These facts may be from any of the areas listed in our content categories; the point is that our impression is strongly shaped by what we can call 'critical episodes' in the behaviour of the other person— episodes that we find 'revealing', for example, remarks which reveal basic beliefs or values, reactions which reveal instability or lack of insight, and so on. Most readers will be able to think of many examples from their own experience of such critically revealing behaviour episodes. Such revelations can be contrasted with the 'privileged access' we have to our own states of mind, which enable us to construe our own behaviour differently from, and usually more realistically than, an outside observer.

10—PP * *

For this small group of schoolboys, the critical episodes in the film which revealed Mr Smith's character were as follows:

> Playing with and feeding his animals.
> Giving directions to the motorist.
> Lighting the fire.
> Performing early morning tasks.

But, as in real life probably, the same behaviour did not create the same impression in all the subjects. For example, Mr Smith's behaviour in relation to the animals creates a variety of different impressions: gentle, cheerful, lively, rough, friendly, calm. His reactions to the motorist lead some children to regard him as friendly, whereas others regard him, on the same evidential basis, as honest.

An attempt to assign marks on the basis of the adequacy of the evidence cited in support of a judgment was successful in discriminating fairly reliably between the children. The group was too small, however, to enable one to make definite statements about the usefulness of the device as a measure of 'social intelligence', but the initial results looked promising in this respect, especially when taken in conjunction with other features of children's responses, for example, their ability (or inability) to operate with abstract and general ideas in qualifying and organizing their impressions of people.

IV. Cultural Comparisons

There is little doubt that the contents and organization of personality impressions are strongly influenced by cultural factors. What we mean by cultural factors in this context is the wide range of social influences brought to bear upon the individual member of a community as a consequence of his interactions with other people and of his exposure to communications and pressures from other sources, for example, newspapers, films and television.

These influences start at birth and persist throughout life. They lead the individual to adopt certain frames of reference rather than others in selectively perceiving and construing (making sense of) the behaviour of people. For example, in one sort of social environment people may see each other in terms of religious affiliation and its associated values, roles and statuses; in another sort of environment people may see each other in terms of socio-economic differences—occupation, wealth, life-style and manners.

Large urban industrial societies comprise a number of 'subcultures', for example, social classes, regional populations and political groupings, as well as a myriad of primary (face-to-face) groups. These groups have much in common with each other; but at the same time they bring to bear upon the individual member their own particular sorts of influence. They inculcate certain attitudes, values, beliefs and other personal qualities. He is led to feel more 'at home' with some people than with others, and he is taught that certain personal qualities and forms of behaviour are more socially desirable than others.

In the main study, we examined only organismic and psychological variables; sex, age and intelligence, and type of stimulus person. In the subsidary study, using a film, we also examined introversion/extra-version and stability/neuroticism as factors likely to affect the process of person perception. Probably for a number of reasons, however, these psychological variables appeared to have little or no connection with the contents of personality impressions in older children or with the differential attribution of traits to a relatively neutral film person. But cutting across any effects of organismic and psychological variables are the effects of sociological variables : socio-economic class, ethnic or religious membership, regional location, political affiliation, and the like. It has not yet been possible to examine the relationships between these sociological variables and the contents and organization of personality impressions. Nevertheless, it would be surprising if one failed to find marked social class differences in person perception, even if the associated influences of intelligence and education were to be experimentally controlled. It is known that, on average, working-class children, as compared with middle-class children, suffer a retardation in linguistic competence which—because of the requirements of vocabulary and sentence structure—must put them at a disadvantage when it comes to formulating and expressing complex ideas about the behaviour and psychological characteristics of other people.

A disability in cognitive complexity and verbal expression may have little practical effect on psychological skill in understanding and dealing with people. In some persons, the ability to 'read' the psychological significance of certain kinds of actions or expressive behaviour in others may operate in a largely nonverbal way—as a kind of native shrewdness in handling people or judging character. The only things lacking in such people are the inclination to reflect on the process of impression formation and the ability to render an intelligible account, that is a rational verbal account, of how they form their impressions.

It is a rather sad reflection on psychology—if the results of the relevant investigations are to be believed—that its practitioners seem to be no better at making judgments and predictions about people in real-life situations than are relatively untutored subjects. Becoming a psychologist is, in one sense, a kind of 'acculturation'. One is selectively exposed to a variety of social influences which have the effect of shaping one's beliefs, attitudes, values and actions—especially, of course, in relation to human behaviour. In this way, one psychologist's frames of reference for perceiving and understanding other people gradually become more like those of other psychologists (or at least more like other subgroups of psychologists), and less like those of people in relatively unrelated occupations—businessmen, engineers, politicans—who in their turn tend to conform to the frames of reference prevailing in their subcultures.

These brief remarks do no more than hint at the scope for research into the cultural determinants of impression formation. But two other important areas of social research deserve to be mentioned, namely, cross-cultural comparisons and anthropological studies of impression formation in 'primitive' peoples. For example, little or nothing is known about national differences in the content and organization of personality impressions, although it should not be difficult to examine such differences—for example, by analysing the contents of comparable newspaper items or children's books. The ideal method, of course, would be to carry out parallel research investigations in which comparable data—like those in the main inquiry—are collected under identical conditions. Again, it would be surprising if there were no systematic differences between, say, Eastern and Western societies, or between capitalist and socialist societies. Similarly, it would be surprising if beliefs in sorcery and the supernatural and the special conditions of life and upbringing in 'primitive communities' did not profoundly affect the individual's understanding of human behaviour in general and his impressions of other persons.

The following personality impressions are examples from the descriptions of their teachers written by schoolgirls in West Africa. The reader is invited to speculate on the way cultural factors may have contributed to their contents and organization. Note that the word 'Tubab' means white or European : the names and other details have been changed in the interests of anonymity, as in all previous examples.

Ann, aged 13 years.
Miss T. teaches us science. she is short and likes to wear short clothes which is dyed. She has curly hair, long nose and a very small mouth. Her finger nails are white and nice. She looks very prietty when she walks quickly with a bag hanging over her shoulder.
Miss F. teaches us Geography She is nice but she talks too much.

She has some black sports on her body. Her hair is long. I do not like her because she O C upon us

Mary, aged 13 years.
Miss T. is one of our Tubab teachers. She teach us Science. She is short with a curl hair. She is a good Teacher and I like her very much. She is full of life and fun. And she always wear a short dress. She os Good in teaching She never shouto to people. She wear chain and ear-rings. She walk quickly and lifely. She is the beautiful of our Tubab Teahers.

Miss F. is another teacher. She teach us Geography. She is tall but not too tall with a long hair. She is not a good teacher. She is not lifely. She always wear a short dress she is not quite good in teaching, and shout a lot that is why I do not like her. She has a black and white eyes with a blue colour on his eyes.

Lena, aged 14 years.
Miss F. teach us Geography. She looks like a good teacher. I like her. she is short. She will explain me until I understand.

She is a kind teacher. She is very kind to children. She is a Tubab teacher. She likes me. She is a nice teacher. She never beat us in class. The children will talked and she didnot mind about it.

She will just said less your noise please. She explain us well in class. She is a clean and tidy teacher. She looks nice. I liked her because she is very kind and beautiful. I wish if I could kiss her one day.

Miss P. teach us art lesson. She is a very kind teacher, because she did not do anything to us. We will taked and she did not mind anything.

Betty, aged 13 years.
Miss P. teaches us Art. She is very fat and plum. Her hair is black and long. She is a kind teacher and wants to joke with people. Her height is 6ft. 6 in. She looks quiet pretty when her smile broadens and two lovely rows of white teeth are seen. Beneath her heavy eye brown are two big innocent eyes which adds to her beauty. She wore African dresses, and everyday she styles her hair beautiful. She put on slippers everyday when coming to school. In all the Tubab teachers she is the one I like most. Miss P. teaches us Geography and RK. She is a young girl under 20 years old. She is a short girl and likes to wore mini skirt. Miss P. is the beautiful Tubab Teachers in the School. Her nose is very long and her hair is black.

Sometimes Miss P. gave me bad mark and sometimes she gave me good mark. She is also a kind teacher. She likes me very well. Even when we went for R.K. she joke with the pupils, but she likes to talk very much. As for me I like her very much.

The sample of descriptions from which the above examples have been drawn have not been subjected to rigorous analysis because they were not collected systematically and under controlled conditions, but they illustrate a variety of similarities and differences when compared with the sorts of impressions written by English schoolchildren.

V. The Foundations of Person Perception—A Commentary on the Developmental Psychology of Perceiving and Understanding Human Behaviour

The problem of how we perceive and interpret normal human action is not often raised in psychological research—perhaps because there appears to be common agreement about how behaviour is to be described. Even if difficulties arise regarding such description, they can usually be resolved by clarification of terminology and frames of reference. On reflection, however, it is likely that, at times, different observers will construe, and therefore describe, the 'same' behaviour differently. Children, moreover, have to *learn* to observe and interpret the behaviour of others —it is not an instinctively given function. Psychopathological conditions, such as paranoia, and other, less obvious factors, seem to affect the way a stimulus person's behaviour is perceived (or construed). In addition, mental set and context can be expected to play a part in the perception of overt behaviour, as they do in the attribution of psychological states, dispositions and capacities.

Warr and Knapper (1968) have dealt with the issue of whether the perception of persons conforms to the normal rules governing the perception of physical events—see also From (1971), and we shall not deal with this issue again. But this is not to affirm that we really 'understand' the processes of behaviour perception and person perception. We need to look at them as closely as other workers have looked at, say, space perception or perceptual-motor skills.

The cognitive processes engaged when we 'construe' or impose a pattern of meaning upon a person's behaviour must be closely linked with the perceptual and verbal processes reflected in the opinions, judgments and descriptions we give about that person. Training in psychiatric and psychological nomenclature and concepts can provide a new 'frame of reference' for an individual, for example, a teacher or a psychiatric nurse, sensitizing him to behavioural cues, situational constraints and psychological factors, and thus enabling him to make a different sort of sense of what he observes than he would have done before training. Smith (1966) has considered some other basic issues in the study of sensitivity to others.

The transition from 'statements about behaviour (or movements)' to 'statements about actions' is by no means simple—see Mischel (1969). Sometimes it is not even recognized as a problem. But obviously one 'action' can take many different forms, and this raises the problem of how different behaviour patterns come to be regarded as equivalent or not equivalent.

It seems sensible to regard the problem of 'behaviour perception' as more fundamental than that of 'person perception' since it is only by first attending to, and making sense of, an individual's behaviour that we can form an impression of him as a person. We recognize, of course, that a prior impression of a person may subtly affect the perception and interpretation of his behaviour. There is also the correlated problem of how a person's experience of his own subjective states leads him to understand or misunderstand the behaviour and inner-personal states of other people. This topic has been dealt with at length by philosophers and psychologists (see Mischel, 1969, and de Charms, 1968, for more recent analyses) but still remains an area of confusion and ignorance.

We assume that the cognitive processes required for comprehending behaviour and forming impressions of persons will be reflected in the verbal descriptions and judgments we make. That is to say, we assume that the analysis of cognitive 'products' will enable us to formulate and test theories about cognitive 'processes'. The notion that adults, at least, develop implicit theories about people and their behaviour is nowadays quite familiar, Kelly's (1955) work having given rise to considerable research into 'personal constructs'. Presumably, in the process of forming impressions about people, the use of a personal construct like 'aggressive' or 'intelligent' has the effect of rendering many morphologically different action patterns functionally equivalent, since the behaviour which leads me to attribute the trait 'aggressive' to one person may be different, at least in part, from the behaviour which leads me to attribute the 'same' trait to another person. Similarly, the form of words that I use to refer to one behavioural episode can also be used to refer to other, morphologically different, but functionally equivalent activities. The activities referred to as 'telling a joke', 'buying a loaf', or 'kissing' are, then, *classes* of functionally equivalent actions. If, on the other hand, we regard two behavioural episodes as nonequivalent or wish to make some distinction between them, then two different forms of words must be employed. Similarly, two 'constructs' will be needed to distinguish between two functionally nonequivalent behavioural dispositions or personal characteristics, such as 'jealous' and 'dependent', even though, to the uninformed or insensitive person, the morphology (structure) of the two behavioural patterns appears to be the same. Again, it is not unusual for a person to be unwilling to apply a socially undesirable term, such as lazy or jealous, to himself, even if impartial observers construe his behaviour in that way. Such a person may construe his own behaviour as 'preoccupied' or as 'protective' respectively.

In connection with the study of how people observe and interpret behaviour and personal qualities, it is interesting to observe that the study of animal behaviour advanced considerably when ethologists, through painstaking observation and analysis, managed to identify significant 'action patterns' and to show their relationships with other action patterns and with gentic factors, physiological states and stimulus conditions. We are not proposing that human behaviour in all its complexity, and with its important and correlated subjective states, can be construed by means of the concepts and methods developed in animal ethology. On the contrary, we believe that psychologists have a long way to go in analysing the way *human* action is organized, and that the concepts and methods of animal ethology will have little direct or immediate relevance to this problem. It seems to us more likely that a better understanding of complex human action will be achieved through the following approaches : (a) behavioural ecology (see Barker, 1963), (b) social learning (see Tharp and Wetzel, 1969; Bandura and Walters, 1963), (c) quasi-judicial methodolgy (see Bromley, 1968), and (d) the logico-philosophical analysis of psychological issues (see Mischel, 1969; de Charms, 1968; and Bromley, 1970).

In the normal adult, the perceptual field is articulated or structured— as in the perception of figure and ground, or in the grouping of temporal events like notes in a melody. Similarly, in the perception of human behaviour, perceptual organization takes place so that some features of the other person's actions and circumstances stand out against a background of other actions and circumstances which may go unnoticed (or unremarked at the time) but help to provide a context contributing to the 'meaning' of the salient features. In virtue of their gestalt properties, and as a consequence of learning, some behavioural events which are separated in time will be seen as belonging together—for example, they will be seen as parts of a larger action, or as causes and effects.

The ease with which behaviour can be perceived depends not only upon its complexity and its rate of occurrence, but also upon the intelligence, experience and state of mind of the observer. In order to impose a pattern of meaning upon a continuous 'stream of behaviour', the observer must selectively identify component parts of the behaviour, group them into episodes (segmented parts of the stream of behaviour), relate them to relevant events in the environment, and serialize them in narrative form or story form. The difference between these two forms is that the first implies a relatively unconnected episode-by-episode description of the events in question, of the sort that even young children can give, whereas the second implies an attempt to go beyond the particular facts of observation to reach higher-order grouping, sequences and interpretations. For example, in the attribution of traits or motives, or in causal analysis, the individual episodes become organized into themes or patterns—the behaviour is experienced as having structure, coherence, direction and meaning.

At some stage in the perceptual process, behavioural *elements* of some sort must be identified, but a behavioural *episode* consists of a temporal and structural pattern or organization of several such elements. In addition, the perceptual process enables the observer to identify or recognize transitions from one episode to another, otherwise it would be difficult to explain why the subjects in Dickman's research felt able to group the behavioural statements into episodes (sets of behavioural statements), or even to explain how the behavioural statements could have been compiled in the first place. So, even though human behaviour, like the physical environment, is fundamentally continuous, nevertheless it must be regarded as having morphological characteristics which change over time and give rise to structured impressions in observers.

A useful analogy, probably worth closer study, is that which holds between language perception and behaviour perception. When literate observers attend to printed or spoken language, they can detect individual letters, letter groups (or syllables), words and spaces (or pauses). Normally, these elements—lower in the hierarchy of language—are not salient, and we readily organize them into phrases, sentences and themes. Obviously, understanding language is an acquired skill, and we need not, at this stage, consider the recent arguments about the extent to which language depends upon innate characteristics on the one hand and experience on the other. Similarly, understanding human actions is an acquired skill— no doubt similarly liable to be a focus for disputes about its genetic and environmental determinants. The letters in written language, or the syllables in spoken language, could be regarded as analogous to the as yet undeciphered 'actones'—Barker's term (1963)—in behaviour. An 'actone' is a term referring to hypothetical segments of the stream of behaviour which constitute the smallest unit of action; specification at a finer level of analysis would entail a shift into a different language and frame of reference, namely, the psychophysiology of perceptual-motor activities.

It is possible that 'kinesics'—the study of the fine details of normal behaviour (usually in connection with social interaction and expressive behaviour)—may eventually enable us to decipher the behaviour code and to make explicit what we have come to know implicitly through a combination of innate ability and experience, namely, the 'meaning' of another person's behaviour. Thus, letters or syllables are analogous to actones, words and phrases are analogous to actions, longer or multiple phrases and sentences are analogous to behavioural episodes, and so on. In this way, we can refer, quite sensibly, to the 'grammar' of human behaviour, that is to the structural relationships between the elements in an action; we can refer to the 'vocabulary' of human behaviour, that is to the different behavioural acts and their relationships; we can refer to the 'semantics' of human behaviour, that is to the meaning or significance of actions and patterns of action.

Naturally, the meaning of any one action is determined in part by its behavioural and situational context, just as the meaning of a word or sentence is determined by its wider context. At present, the analogy is difficult to spell out in more detail, but, for example, punctuation marks, or pauses and speech inflections, could be regarded as analogous to pauses, changes in tempo, and expressive 'inflections' in behaviour. It is with good reason, therefore, that we often use figures of speech like : 'His actions *tell* you that. . .', '*Reading* the expression on his face . . .', 'I find his behaviour *incomprehensible* . . .'. After all, language is a kind of behaviour, and an analysis of how human behaviour is organized—at levels of analysis higher than those attempted in psychophysiology—must include an analysis of language behaviour. Indeed, it may be that the study of natural language behaviour will prove to be the key to understanding how human behaviour in general is organized. The present enterprise, however, is complementary to that of studying language behaviour, since what we are aiming to do is analyse the langauge *of* behaviour and experience. That is to say, we are taking language as given, and systematically studying the natural forms it takes when it is used to describe and analyse actions and persons. In this way, we hope to improve our understanding of the language of behaviour and impression formation and thereby improve our understanding of the facts to which the language refers.

CHAPTER 13

Retrospect and Prospect

I. Retrospect

The main aim of this study has been to apply a developmental descriptive analysis to the process of impression formation. Developmental changes in personality impressions were investigated in the hope that they would provide a basis for, and a guide to, the study of impression formation in adults We examined some of the processes underlying the child's understanding of himself and his social environment. Methods were developed for describing the contents and organization of impressions formed by adults and children. The work was seen to have implications for the scientific and professional study of personality and adjustment—implications which we have noted and commented upon without working them out in detail.

The research strategy and the theoretical considerations which guided this research were derived from a critical examination of part of the extensive literature on person perception in adults, and the more limited literature on person perception in children. For various reasons, theoretical as well as practical, the main method in our developmental studies has been the analysis of the contents and organization of free descriptions. This method reveals the subject's normal, everyday ways of conceptualizing others, and has the additional advantage of being similar to other traditional techniques of developmental psychology. Particular attention was paid to the effects that different sorts of stimulus person might have on the contents and organization of impressions.

Apart from providing normative data on the size, contents and organization of personality impressions, and data which can be used in clinical and educational settings, the investigations we have described have made a contribution to the methodology of research in psychological development. We have confirmed that the free description method is useful for studying developmental trends in impressions of self and others, and for studying group and individual differences. The procedures developed for analysing the contents of personality impressions were relevant to some previous investigations by others, and helped to clarify some of the issues they raised. The procedures for analysing the qualifying and organizing aspects of personality impressions have added a new dimension to the content analysis of impression formation.

Our studies have demonstrated the advantages of using moderately complicated statistical designs which make it possible to examine the relative contributions of several main independent variables and their numerous interactions Even where the results are not definitive, but merely indicative, such methods are valuable for showing which variables deserve more systematic investigation. Repeated measures designs, moreover, are particularly useful where individual differences are considerable and where one wishes to examine interactions between subject variables and stimulus person variables.

Quantitative analyses revealed a number of systematic changes in the content and organization of the descriptions over the age range studied. In general, the change in *content* was greatest between the ages of 7 and 8 years. It is not clear whether we have discovered a *special* sort of developmental sequence, namely, that associated with impression formation, or whether we have simply demonstrated that the development of impression formation follows a sequence comparable to that of other sorts of cognitive development. We have offered our theories to account for the data, but no doubt others will wish to put a different construction on the evidence.

As expected, the 'psychological' contents of impressions, that is the central statements, were more pronounced in the older children's descriptions. The increase in the use of terms referring to personal qualities and behavioural regularities did not arise merely because there is an increase in fluency, since the *proportion* of central statements (and of traits) in each description also increased with age. Thus, development brings a change in attitude and orientation, and the acquisition of more refined concepts of personality and behaviour. The increase in organizing and qualifying statements supported this finding.

Children under the age of 7 or 8 years described people in terms of external, readily observable attributes. Their concept of a person was too inclusive—it embraced not only the person proper, but his family, possessions and physical circumstances. At this age, children categorized people in a simple, absolute, moralistic manner and used vague, global terms, such as good, bad, horrible, nice. Between the ages of 8 and 12 years there was a rapid growth in psychological vocabulary; the words and phrases became more precise, as if the global evaluative concepts were becoming differentiated into more specific and precise terms. By this age the child has discovered a number of invariant features in behaviour—internal dispositions and behavioural regularities—that seem to him to summarize and account for the observed behaviour of the stimulus person. He has become aware that people sometimes exhibit apparently incompatible qualities, but he lacks the ability to resolve the contradictions in his impressions by seeing them as parts of a coherent system. The descriptions written by adolescent subjects showed that they had developed the ability to organize impressions and to see behaviour in its context of personal qualities, historical links, biological factors and other surounding circumstances.

It may be convenient to think of the products of cognitive development in impression formation as the outcome of a search for useful, predictive psychological concepts. This development can be described in terms of Werner's concepts of differentiation and integration. In general, one can describe children's judgments as becoming more differentiated with age, in that there is a considerable increase in the number of descriptive dimensions; the earlier-appearing terms seem to subdivide into more specific later-appearing terms which give a better fit to experience and predict the other person's actions more exactly. The increase in integration was shown by the development of abstract and general psychological constructs and of various organizing and qualifying words and phrases which integrated and related the diverse elements of a personality impression.

Our investigations have added to our knowledge of sex differences in impression formation. Girls used more central statements than did boys because of their greater fluency—they did not use a higher *proportion* of central statements. Their descriptions, however, were more abstract and generalized than those of boys because they used more traits and a higher *proportion* of traits. The more frequent use of traits by girls could be explained by their larger vocabulary of trait names and by their more frequent use of each term. Girls appeared to be more interested in people than did boys, and more sensitive to the range of qualities people possess, thus highlighting an important psychosocial sex difference.

Intelligence was included mainly as a control variable since subjects exercised a verbal skill rather than a strictly interpersonal skill in which temperament might have been a more relevant variable. The expected effects of intelligence were supported. Children of higher intelligence used more central statements and a higher *proportion* of them than did children of lower intelligence; but intelligence did not affect the number or proportion of traits used even though the children of higher intelligence possessed a larger vocabulary of traits. Intelligence had its greatest influence on the organization of descriptions—the brighter children made much greater use of organizing statements.

The different sorts of stimulus person gave rise to considerable differences in the contents of impressions, often greater in fact than differences associated with age, sex or intelligence Person perception, apparently, first develops in response to the repeated behaviour of familiar persons in familiar situations, and gradually extends to cover a wider range of people and a wider range of behavioural and psychological processes. The children found it easier to describe other children than to describe adults, perhaps because of their greater similarity, or their higher frequency of interaction, or their greater interest in other children. Children used a larger number and a higher *proportion* of central statements and traits to describe other children than to describe adults. In the case of central statements this difference increased with age.

Children used more central statements to describe males than to describe females, although a higher *proportion* of central statements was used to describe females than to describe males. Children used more traits and a higher proportion of traits to describe males than to describe females. Thus interpersonal similarity or frequency of interaction cannot account for these effects of the sex of the stimulus person. In general, the sex of the stimulus person had little effect on descriptions written by younger subjects, but the differences increased slightly in older groups, possibly because of cultural factors; on average, males were seen as more interesting and more active than females. Children found most difficulty in describing adult females, that is people who are different from them (in being adults) and who are members of the less preferred sex (females).

Liking or disliking the stimulus person did not affect the number of central statements or trait names. Liking or disliking the stimulus person, however, did have a considerable effect on other types of statement. Descriptions of liked persons were less factual than those of disliked persons, and subjects were better informed about, and more interested in, people they liked; more explanatory and supportive statements were made about disliked people, partly because subjects were trying to justify and explain their feelings.

Our results showed that although the effects of some stimulus person variables were considerable, these effects were limited to the *elements* in the descriptions—they had relatively little effect on organizing and qualifying statements. The organization of a personality description was mostly determined by the subject's chronological age and intelligence, and by the number of central or psychological concepts he had acquired.

II. Prospect

The value of the research we have reported lies in the answers it provides to specific questions and in the additional problems and issues it raises. Additional research data and more diverse research methods are called for, however, in order to confirm and enlarge our general conclusions. There are advantages to be gained from using a multiplicity of techniques. For example, Piagetian interviews and naturalistic methods of observation would be useful in exploring the pre-school child's concept of 'person' and his understanding of human behaviour; other methods might be developed from existing psychometric procedures.

We are currently employing the methods and concepts we have described in a new series of investigations into person perception in adult life and old age. Preliminary results show that the major development after the age of 15 is a further increase in the 'psychological' content of impressions arising mainly from an increased awareness of the more covert determinants of behaviour. Much greater use is made of the categories dealing with motivation and orientation. It may be necessary to develop subsets of content categories to deal with the many sorts of psychological (central) qualities, and to deal with the many sorts of interpersonal relationships referred to, for example, submission, generosity and aggression.

The developmental psychology of person perception can be explained in part as the growth of an ability to assign invariances (dispositions and behavioural regularities) to the behaviour of individual people. The attribution of traits depends partly on the ability to discern motives and intentions in behaviour, thereby segmenting or organizing the stream of behaviour into meaningful acts. In a sense, the ability to observe and make sense of *behaviour* is basic to person perception; as illustrated by studies using the research film. It is a remarkably neglected topic in developmental psychology and deserves much more attention. The investigations we have described at least provide a start, and these methods can be further adapted for use with children and adults. Correlational studies might reveal relationships between various aspects of impression formation, and perhaps reveal something of the relationship between impression formation and general intelligence, temperament and personal adjustment.

Hitherto, the importance of trait implications in impression formation seems to have been exaggerated, partly because trait implications have been studied artificially—out of their natural context, as it were, and without the benefit of normative data on trait vocabulary. Techniques which are more refined and valid are needed in order to study cognitive structures since there is considerable uncertainty about the way trait implications get established and the way they affect impression formation. For example, it might be possible to use cluster analysis to examine patterns of trait implications at different developmental stages. Furthermore, a sequential analysis of the differentiation of trait names may clarify some of the issues in the study of trait implications.

Considerable individual differences in performance are found among children and adults in the way they describe and conceptualize others, and it is tempting to relate these differences to personality variables. It is our belief that this sort of research diverts attention from two basic problems : (a) that of delineating the processes involved in impression formation, and (b) that of examining whether the psychology of person perception constitutes a sort of 'infrastructure' to the psychology of personality and adjustment.

Practical and theoretical considerations demand that attention be paid to the psychopathology of impression formation. A number of psychological disorders in childhood and adult life appear to be associated with disturbances in impression formation. So far, we have stressed the *cognitive* aspects of person perception, but it is obvious that cognition is merely a part of the total process, and emotional factors play a crucial role. A person's *feelings* about others help to determine how he perceives and reacts towards them. Preliminary observations suggest that maladjusted girls use fewer central statements and a lower *proportion* of central statements than do normal girls, and they do not adequately differentiate between different stimulus persons.

If we are to have an adequate developmental psychology of person perception, we need a description of developmental changes in the way children 'explain' behaviour. Even very young children can explain simple and familiar forms of behaviour, but it is not until about the age of 9 or 10 years that they are able to use motivational concepts with any facility. Some young adults, however, can make surprisingly insightful inferences about people. The explanation of human behaviour is a topic that continues to baffle psychologists and philosophers alike—partly for conceptual reasons, partly for empirical reasons.

It seems to us that the developmental psychology of person perception can hardly fail to be a fertile area of research. The theoretical value of such research may well be considerable because an adequate conceptualization of the development of person perception would be of value in understanding impression formation in clinical situations. The practical value of the research lies in the possibilities it offers for more soundly based systems of education and training in psychological skills.

Our studies in the general area of person perception are based on the assumption that it is possible to develop a true 'science of the individual', and that such a body of knowledge is a necessary basis for psychology as it is applied to individual cases.

Bibliography

Allport, G. W. (1937), *Personality*, London: Constable and Co.

Allport, G. W. (1961), *Pattern and Growth in Personality*, London: Holt, Rinehart and Winston Inc.

Allport, G. W., and Odbert, H. S. (1936), 'Trait names: a psycholexical study', *Psychological Monographs*, **41**, (1 Whole 211).

Altrocchi, J. (1961), 'Interpersonal perceptions of repressors and sensitizers and component analysis of assumed similarity scores', *Journal of Abnormal and Social Psychology*, **62**, 528–34.

Anderson, N. H. (1965), 'Primacy effects in personality impression formation using a generalised order effect paradigm', *Journal of Personality and Social Psychology*, **2**, 1–9.

Anderson, N. H., and Barrios, A. A. (1961), 'Primacy effects in personality impression formation', *Journal of Abnormal and Social Psychology*, **63**, 346–50.

Anderson, N. H., and Hubert, S. (1963), 'Effects of concomitant verbal recall on order effects in personality impression formation', *Journal of Verbal Learning and Verbal Behaviour*, **2**, 379–91.

Anderson, N. H., and Lampel, A. K. (1965), 'Effect of context on ratings of personality traits', *Psychonomic Science*, **3**, 433–4.

Anderson, N. H., and Norman, A. (1964), 'Order effects in impression formation in four classes of stimuli', *Journal of Abnormal and Social Psychology*, **69**, 467–71.

Argyle, M. (1967), '*The Psychology of Interpersonal Behaviour*', Harmondsworth, England: Penguin Books.

Argyle, M., and McHenry, R. (1971), 'Do spectacles really affect judgments of intelligence?', *British Journal of Social and Clinical Psychology*, **10**, 27–9.

Asch, S. E. (1946), 'Forming impressions of personality', *Journal of Abnormal and Social Psychology*, **41**, 258–90.

Asch, S. E. (1952), *Social Psychology*, Englewood Cliffs: Prentice Hall.

Asch, S. E. (1958), 'The metaphor: a psychological inquiry', in Taguiri, R. & Petrullo, L. (Eds.), *Person Perception and Interpersonal Behaviour*, Stanford: Stanford University Press.

Ayer, A. J. (1964), 'One's knowledge of others' minds', in Gustafson D. F. (Ed.), *Essays in Philosophical Psychology*. New York: Doubleday and Company Inc.

Baer, D. J. (1964), 'Trait judgments of military pilots from photographs', *Journal of Psychology*, **58**, 257–60.

Baldwin, A. L. (1967), *Theories of Child Development*, New York: John Wiley and Sons.

Baldwin, C. P., and Baldwin, A. L. (1970), 'Children's judgements of kindness', *Child Development*, **41**, 29–47.

Bandura, A., and Walters, R. H. (1963), *Social Learning and Personality Development*. New York: Holt, Rinehart and Winston Inc.

Bannister, D., and Fransella, F. (1971), *Inquiring Man*, Harmondsworth, England: Penguin Books.

Bannister, D., and Mair, J. M. M. (1968), *The Evaluation of Personal Constructs*, London: Academic Press.

Barker, R. G. (Ed.) (1963), *The Stream of Behaviour*, New York: Appleton-Century-Crofts, Meredith Pub. Co.

Bartlett, F. C. (1932), *Remembering*, Cambridge: Cambridge University Press.

Beach, L., and Wertheimer, H. (1961), 'A free response approach to the study of person cognition', *Journal of Abnormal and Social Psychology*, **62**, 367–74.

Benedetti, D. T., and Hill, J. C. (1960), 'A determiner of the centrality of a trait in impression formation', *Journal of Abnormal and Social Psychology*, **60**, 278–80.

Bieri, J. (1955), 'Cognitive complexity—simplicity and predictive behaviour', *Journal of Abnormal and Social Psychology*, **51**, 263–8.

Bieri, J., Atkins, A. L., Briar, S., Leaman, L., Miller, H., and Tripodi, T. (1966), *Clinical and Social Judgment*, New York: John Wiley and Sons.

Bieri, J., Bradburn, W. M., and Galinsky, M. D. (1958), 'Sex differences in perceptual behaviour', *Journal of Personality*, **26**, 1–12.

Birdwhistell, R. F. (1971), *Kinesics and Context*, London: Allen Lane.

Bonarius, J. C. J. (1965), 'Research in the personal construct theory of G. A. Kelly: role construct repertory test and basic theory', in Maher, B.A., *Progress in Experimental Personality Research*, Vol. 2, New York: Academic Press.

Boucher, J., and Osgood, C. E., (1969), 'The Pollyanna Hypothesis', *Journal of Verbal Learning and Verbal Behaviour*, **8**, 1–8.

Brierley, D. W. (1966), 'Children's use of personality constructs', *Bulletin of British Psychological Society*, **19**, no. 65, 72.

Bromley, D. B. (1966a), 'The social psychology of reputation', *Bulletin of British Psychological Society*, **19**, no. 65, 73.

Bromley, D. B. (1966b), 'Rank-order cluster analysis', *British Journal of Mathematical and Statistical Psychology*, **19**, 105–23.

Bromley, D. B. (1968), 'Conceptual analysis in the study of personality and adjustment', *Bulletin of British Psychological Society*, **21**, 155–60.

Bromley, D. B. (1970), 'An approach to theory construction in the psychology of development and aging, in Goulet, L. R., and Baltes, P. B. (Eds.), *Life-Span Developmental Psychology*, New York: Academic Press.

Bruner, J. S. (1957), 'Going beyond the information', in Bruner, J. S. *et al. Contemporary Approaches to Cognition*, Cambridge, Mass.: Harvard University Press.

Bruner, J. S., Olver, R. R., and Greenfield, P. M. *et al.* (1966), *Studies in Cognitive Growth*, New York: John Wiley and Sons.

Bruner, J. S., Shapiro, D., and Tagiuri, R. (1958), 'The meaning of traits in isolation and in combination', in Tagiuri, R. and Petrullo, L. (Eds.), *Person Perception and Interpersonal Behavior*, Stanford: Stanford University Press.

Bruner, J. S., and Tagiuri, R. (1954), 'The perception of people', in Lindzey, G. (Ed.), *Handbook of Social Psychology*, Cambridge, Mass.: Addison-Wesley Pub. Co. Inc.

Brunswik, E., and Reiter, L. (1937), Eindrucks-Charakters schematisierter Gesichter, *Zeitschrift für Psychologie*, **142**, 67–134.

Burke, C. J. (1953), 'Additive scales and statistics', *Psychological Review*, **60**, 73–5.

Buzby, D. E. (1924), 'The interpretation of facial expressions', *American Journal of Psychology*, **35**, 602–4.

Cattell, R. B. (1965), *Scientific Analysis of Personality*, Harmondsworth, England: Penguin Books.

Clark, K. B., and Clark, M. P. (1947), 'Racial identification and preference in Negro children', in Newcomb, T. M., and Hartley, E. L. (Eds.), *Readings in Social Psychology*, New York: Holt, Rinehart and Winston Inc.

Cliff, N. (1959), 'Adverbs as multipliers', *Psychological Review*, **66**, 27–44.

Cline, M. G. (1956), 'The influence of social context on the perception of faces', *Journal of Personality*, **25**, 142–58.

Cline, V. B. (1964), 'Interpersonal perception', in Maher, B. A. (Ed.), *Progress in Experimental Personality Research*, Vol. I, New York: Academic Press.

Cohen, J. (1965), 'Some statistical issues in psychological research', in Wolman, B. B. (Ed.), *Handbook of Clinical Psychology*, New York: McGraw Hill.

Cook, S. W. (1939), 'The judgment of intelligence from photographs', *Journal of Abnormal and Social Psychology*, **34**, 384–9.

Crandall, J. E. (1970), 'Predictive value and confirmability of traits as determinants of judged trait importance', *Journal of Personality*, **38**, 75–90.

Crockett, W. H. (1965), 'Cognitive complexity and impression formation', in Maher, B. A. (Ed.), *Progress in Experimental Personality Research*, Vol. 2, New York: Academic Press.

Crockett, W. H., and Meidinger, T. (1956), 'Authoritarianism and interpersonal perception', *Journal of Abnormal and Social Psychology*, **53**, 378–80.

Cronbach, L. J. (1955), 'Processes affecting scores on "understanding others" and "assumed similarity" ', *Psychological Bulletin*, **52**, 177–93.

Cronbach, L. J. (1958), 'Proposals leading to the analytic treatment of social perception scores', in Tagiuri, R., and Petrullo, L. (Eds.), *Person Perception and Interpersonal Behavior*, Stanford: Stanford University Press.

Dahlem, W. (1970), 'Young Americans' reported perception of their parents', *Journal of Psychology*, **74**, 187–94.

De Charms, R. (1968), *Personal Causation*, New York: Academic Press.

De Charms, R., Carpenter, V., and Kuperman, A. (1965), 'The "origin-pawn" variable in person perception', *Sociometry*, **28**, 241–58.

DeSoto, C., Kuethe, J. L., and Wunderlich, R. (1960), 'Social perception and self perception of high and low authoritarians', *Journal of Social Psychology*, **52**, 149–55.

Dickman, H. R. (1963), 'The perception of behavioural units', in Barker, R. G. (Ed.), *The Stream of Behavior*, New York: Appleton-Century-Crofts, Meredith Pub. Co.

Dittman, A. T. (1962), 'The relationship between body movements and moods in interviews', *Journal of Consulting Psychology*, **28**, 480.

Dornbusch, S. M., Hastorf, A. H., Richardson, S. A., Muzzy, R. E., and Vreeland, R. S. (1965), 'The perceiver and the perceived: their relative influence on the categories of interpersonal cognition', *Journal of Personality and Social Psychology*, **1**, 434–40.

Dubin, R., and Dubin, E. R. (1965), 'Children's social perceptions: a review of research', *Child Development*, **36**, 809–38.

Dunlap, K. (1927), 'The role of the eye-muscles and mouth-muscles in expression of emotions', *Genetic Psychology Monographs*, **2**, 199–233.

Edwards, A. L. (1965), *Experimental Design in Psychological Research*, New York: Holt, Rinehart and Winston.

Ekman, P. (1964), 'Body position, facial expression and verbal behaviour during interviews', *Journal of Abnormal and Social Psychology*, **68**, 295–301.

Emmerich, W. (1961), 'Family role concepts of children ages six to ten', *Child Development*, **32**, 609–24.

Engen, T., and Levy, N. (1956), 'Constant-sum judgments of facial expressions', *Journal of Experimental Psychology*, **51**, 396–8.

Engen, T., Levy, N., and Schlosberg, H. (1957), 'A new series of facial expressions', *American Psychologist*, **12**, 264–6.

Erikson, E. (1950), *Childhood and Society*, New York: W. W. Norton.

Eysenck, S. B. O. (1965), *Manual of the Junior Eysenck Personality Inventory*, London: University of London Press.

Fancher, R. E. (1966), 'Explicit personality theories and accuracy in person perception', *Journal of Personality*, **34**, 252–61.

Farrell, B. A. (1964), 'The criteria for a psycho-analytic interpretation', in Gustafson, D. F. (Ed.), *Essays in Philosophical Psychology*, New York: Doubleday and Company.

Fay, P. J., and Middleton, W. C. (1936), 'Judgments of stranger personality types from voice as transmitted over a public address system', *Character and Personality*, **8**, 144–55.

Fay, P. J., and Middleton, W. C. (1941), 'The ability to judge sociability from voice as transmitted over a public address system', *Character and Personality*, **13**, 303–9.

Feffer, M. H., (1959), 'The cognitive implications of role-taking behaviour', *Journal of Personality*, **27**, 152–68.

Feffer, M. H. (1970), 'Developmental analysis of interpersonal behaviour', *Psychological Review*, **77**, 193–214.

Feffer, M. H., and Gourevitch, V. (1960), 'Cognitive aspects of role-taking in children', *Journal of Personality*, **28**, 383–96.

Fensterheim, H., and Tresselt, M. E. (1953), 'The influence of value systems on the perception of people', *Journal of Abnormal and Social Psychology*, **48**, 93–8.

Festinger, L. (1957), *A Theory of Cognitive Dissonance*, Evanston, Illinois: Row, Peterson.

Fiedler, F. E., and Hoffman, E. L. (1962), 'Age, sex and religious background as determinants of interpersonal perception among Dutch children: a cross cultural validation', *Acta Psychologica*, **20**, 185–95.

Fisher, G. H., and Cox, R. L. (1971), 'Development and initial application of the facial attribute differential', *Bulletin of the British Psychological Society*, **24**, 84, 259.

Flavell, J. H. (1963), *The Developmental Psychology of Jean Piaget*, Princeton, New Jersey: Van Nostrand Co. Inc.

From, F. (1960), 'Perception of human action', in David, H. P., and Brengelman, J. C. (Eds.), *Perspectives in Personality Research*, London: Crosby Lockwood.

From, F. (1971), *Perception of Other People*, New York: Columbia University Press.

Gergen, K. J. (1971), *The Concept of Self*, New York: Holt, Rinehart and Winston, Inc.

Gollin, E. S. (1954), 'Forming impressions of personality', *Journal of Personality*, **23**, 65–76.

Gollin, E. S. (1958), 'Organizational characteristics of social judgment: a developmental investigation', *Journal of Personality*, **26**, 139–54.

Goodenough, E. W. (1957), 'Interest in persons as an aspect of sex difference in the early years', *Genetic Psychology Monographs*, **55**, 287–323.

Gottschalk, L. A., and Gleser, G. C. (1969), *The Measurement of Psychological States through the Content Analysis of Verbal Behavior*, Berkeley and Los Angeles: University of California Press.

Gross, C. F. (1961), 'Intrajudge consistency in ratings of heterogeneous persons', *Journal of Abnormal and Social Psychology*, **62**, 605–10.

Guildford, J. P. (1967), *The Nature of Human Intelligence*. New York: McGraw Hill.

Haire, M., and Grunes, W. F. (1950), 'Perceptual defences: processes protecting an organized perception of another personality', *Human Relations*, **3**, 403–12.

Hall, C. S., and van der Castle, R. L. (1966), *The Content Analysis of Dreams*, New York: Appleton-Century-Crofts, Meredith Co. Inc.

Hall, E. T. (1969), *Hidden Dimension*, London: Bodley Head.

Hallworth, H. J., Davies, H., and Gamston, C. (1965), 'Some adolescent perceptions of adolescent personality', *British Journal of Social and Clinical Psychology*, **4**, 81–91.

Hammond, K. R., Wilkins, M. M., and Todd, F. J. (1966), 'A research paradigm for the study of interpersonal learning', *Psychological Bulletin*, **65**, 221–32.

Hartley, R. E., and Hardesty, F. P. (1964), 'Children's perception of sex roles in childhood', *Journal of Genetic Psychology*, **105**, 43–51.

Hastorf, A. H., Richardson, S. A., and Dornbusch, S. M. (1958), 'The problem of relevance in the study of person perception', in Tagiuri, R., and Petrullo, L. (Eds.), *Person Perception and Interpersonal Behavior*, Stanford: Stanford University Press.

Haycock, V. G. (1969), 'An investigation in person perception in children using a free response approach', *Bulletin of the British Psychological Society*, **22**, 140.

Hays, W. L. (1958), 'An approach to the study of trait implication and trait similarity', in Tagiuri, R., and Petrullo, L. (Eds.), *Person Perception and Interpersonal Behavior*, Stanford: Stanford University Press.

Heider, F. (1958), *The Psychology of Interpersonal Relations*, New York: John Wiley and Sons.

Heider, F., and Simmel, M. (1944), 'An experimental study of apparent behaviour', *American Journal of Psychology*, **57**, 243–58.

Hempel, C. G. (1965), *Aspects of Scientific Explanation, and other essays in the Philosophy of Science*, New York: The Free Press.

Hinkle, D. N. (1965), The change of personal constructs as determined by the implication grid technique'. Unpublished doctoral dissertation, Ohio State University.

Holmes, D., and Berkowitz, L. (1961), 'Some contrast effects in social perception', *Journal of Abnormal and Social Psychology*, **62**, 150–2.

Holsti, O. R. (1969), *Content Analysis for the Social Sciences and Humanities*, Reading, Massachusetts: Addison-Wesley.

Ichheiser, C. (1949), 'Misunderstandings in human relations', *American Journal of Sociology*, **55**, Part 2.

Ittelson, W. H. (1960), *Visual Space Perception*, New York: Springer.

Ittelson, W. H., and Slack, C. W. (1958), 'The perception of persons as visual objects', in Tagiuri, R., and Petrullo, L. (Eds.), *Person Perception and Interpersonal Behavior*, Stanford: Stanford University Press.

Jackson, D. N. (1962), 'The measurement of perceived personality trait relationships', in Washburne, N. F. (Ed.), *Decisions, Values and Groups*, Vol. 2. Oxford: Pergamon.

Jahoda, G. (1959), 'Development of the perception of social differences in children from 6 to 10', *British Journal of Psychology*, **50**, 159–75.

Jones, E. E. (1954), 'Authoritarianism as a determination of first impression formation', *Journal of Personality*, **23**, 106–27.

Jones, E. E., and Davies, K. E. (1965), 'From acts to dispositions: the attribution process in person perception', in Berkowitz, L. (Ed.), *Advances in Experimental Social Psychology*, New York: Academic Press.

Jones, E. E., Davies, K. E., and Gergen, K. J. (1961), 'Role playing variations and their informational value in person perception', *Journal of Abnormal and Social Psychology*, **63**, 302–10.

Jones, E. E., and De Charms, R. (1958), 'The organizing function of interaction roles in person perception', *Journal of Abnormal and Social Psychology*, **57**, 155–64.

Jones, E. E., and Thibaut, J. W. (1958), 'Interaction goals as bases of inference in interpersonal perception', in Tagiuri R., and Petrullo, L. (Eds.), *Person Perception and Interpersonal Behavior*, Stanford: Stanford University Press.

Kagan, J. (1956), 'The child's perception of the parent', *Journal of Abnormal and Social Psychology*, **53**, 257–8.

Kagan, J. (1958), 'Socialization of aggression and the perception of parents in fantasy', *Child Development*, **29**, 311–20.

Kagan, J. (1961), 'Child's symbolic conceptualisation of parents', *Child Development*, **32**, 625–6.

Kagan, J., and Lemkin, J. (1963), 'The child's differential perception of parental attributes', *Journal of Abnormal and Social Psychology*, **61**, 440–7.

Kates, S. L. (1959), 'First impression formation and authoritarianism', *Human Relations*, **12**, 277–86.

Kelley, N. H. (1950), 'The warm-cold variable in first impressions of persons', *Journal of Personality*, **18**, 431–9.

Kelly, G. A. (1955), *The Psychology of Personal Constructs*, New York: W. W. Norton.

Kenny, D. T. (1964), 'Stimulus functions in projective techniques', in Maher, B.A. (Ed.), *Progress in Experimental Personality Research*, Vol. 1, New York: Academic Press.

Kogan, N., Stevens, J. W., and Shelton, F. C. (1961), 'Age differences: a developmental study of discriminability and affective response', *Journal of Abnormal and Social Psychology*, **62**, 221–30.

Koltuv, B. B. (1962), 'Some characteristics of intrajudge trait inter-correlations', *Psychological Monographs*, **76**, No. 33, Whole No. 552.

Kramer, E. (1964), 'Elimination of verbal cues in judgments of emotion from voice', *Journal of Abnormal and Social Psychology*, **68**, 390–6.

Krech, D. and Crutchfield, R. S. (1948), *Theory and Problems of Social Psychology*, New York, McGraw-Hill.

Kretschmer, E. (1936), *Physique and Character*, 2nd Edn., London: Kegan Paul, Trench, Trubner.

Laing, R. D., Phillipson, H., and Lee, A. R. (1966), *Interpersonal Perception*, London: Tavistock.

Lalljee, M. G. (1971), cited by Argyle M., 1971. Research project on non-verbal communication. Final report to Social Science Research Council, for period 1 October 1967–30 September 1971.

Lay, C. H., and Jackson, D. N. (1969), 'Analysis of the generality of trait-inferential relationships', *Journal of Personality and Social Psychology*, **12**, 12–21.

Leventhal, H., and Singer, D. (1964), 'Cognitive complexity, impression formation and impression change', *Journal of Personality*, **32**, 210–26.

Levy, L. H. (1960), 'Context effects in social perception', *Journal of Abnormal and Social Psychology*, **61**, 295–7.

Levy, L. H. (1967), 'The effects of variance on personality impression formation', *Journal of Personality*, **35**, 179–93.

Levy-Schoen, A. (1964), '*L'image d'autrici chez l'enfant*', Paris: Presses Universitaires de France.

Lipetz, M. E. (1960), 'The effects of information on the assessment of attitudes by authoritarians and non-authoritarians', *Journal of Abnormal and Social Psychology*, **60**, 95–9.

Little, B. R. (1968), 'Age and sex differences in the use of psychological, role and physicalistic constructs', *Bulletin of the British Psychological Society*, **21**, 34.

Livesley, W. J. (1969), 'The developmental psychology of person perception', Ph.D. Thesis, University of Liverpool, England.

Livesley, W. J., and Bromley, D. B. (1967), 'Studies in the developmental psychology of person perception', *Bulletin of British Psychological Society*, **20**, 67, 21A.

Lord, F. M. (1953), 'On the statistical treatment of football numbers', *American Psychologist*, **8**, 750–1.

Lott, A. J., Lott, B. E., Reed, T., and Crow, T. (1970), 'Personality-trait descriptions of differentially liked persons', *Journal of Personality and Social Psychology*, **16**, 284–90.

Lovie, A. D., and Davies, A. D. M. (1970), 'An application of Bayes' theorem to person perception: the effect of rate of revision and initial revision on the perception of another's age', *Acta Psychologica*, **34**, 322–7.

Luchins, A. S. (1948), 'Forming impressions of personality: a critique', *Journal of Abnormal and Social Psychology*, **43**, 318–25.

Luchins, A. S. (1957a) 'Primacy—recency in impression formation', in Hovland, C. I. (Ed.), *The Order of Presentation in Persuasion*, New Haven: Yale University Press.

Luchins, A. S. (1957b), 'Experimental attempts to minimize the impact of first impressions', in Hovland, C. I. (Ed.), *The Order of Presentation in Persuasion*, New Haven: Yale University Press.

Lyons, J. (1956), 'The perception of human action', *Journal of General Psychology*, **54**, 45–55.

McHenry R. (1971), Cited by Argyle M., 1971. 'Project on non-verbal communication'. Final report to Social Science Research Council, for period 1 October 1967–30 September 1971.

McKeachie, W. J. (1952), 'Lipstick as a determiner of first impressions of personality', *Journal of Social Psychology*, **36**, 241–4.

McLeod, R. N. (1960), 'Person perception: a commentary', in David, H. P., and Brengelmann, J. C. (Eds.), *Perspectives in Personality Research*, London: Crosby Lockwood.

Maher, B. A. (1957), 'Personality, problem-solving, and the Einstellung effect', *Journal of Abnormal and Social Psychology*, **54**, 70–3.

Maher, B. A. (1966), *Principles of Psychopathology*, New York: McGraw-Hill.

Manz, W., and Lueck, H. E. (1968), 'Influence of wearing glasses on personality ratings: cross cultural validation of an old experiment', *Perceptual and Motor Skills*, **27**, 704.

Matkom, A. J. (1963), 'Impression formation as a function of adjustment', *Psychological Monographs*, **77**, 5, Whole No. 568.

Mayo, C., and Crockett, W. H. (1964), 'Cognitive complexity and primacy-recency effects in impression formation', *Journal of Abnormal and Social Psychology*, **68**, 335–8.

Mead, G. H. (1934), *Mind, Self, and Society*, Chicago: University of Chicago Press.

Meehl, P. E. (1954), *Clinical Versus Statistical Prediction*, Minneapolis: University of Minnesota Press.

Mehrabian, A. (1969), 'Significance of posture and position in the communication of attitude and status relationships', *Psychological Bulletin*, **71**, 359–72.

Meili, R. (1960), 'Research in personality assessment: a commentary', in David, H. P., and Brengelmann, J. C. (Eds.), *Perspectives in Personality Research*, London: Crosby, Lockwood.

Mensh, I. M., and Wishner, J. (1947), 'Asch on "Forming impressions of personality": further evidence', *Journal of Personality*, **16**, 188–91.

Miller, A. G. (1969), 'Amount of information and stimulus valence as determinants of cognitive complexity', *Journal of Personality*, **37**, 141–57.

Miller, H., and Bieri, J. (1965), 'Cognitive complexity as a function of the significance of the stimulus objects being judged', *Psychological Reports*, **16**, 1203–4.

Mink, N. D. and Briggs, F. F. (1965), 'Content and order in the formation determinants of cognitive complexity', *Perceptual and Motor Skills*, **20**, 765–70.

Mischel, T. (Ed.), (1969), *Human Action—Conceptual and Empirical Issues*, New York: Academic Press.

Mischel, W. (1968), *Personality and Assessment*, New York: John Wiley and Sons.

Morrison, A., and Hallworth, H. J. (1966), 'The perception of peer personality by adolescent girls', *British Journal of Educational Psychology*, **36**, 241–7.

Mott, S. N. (1954), 'Concept of mother—a study of four- and five-year-old children', *Child Development*, **25**, 99–106.

Murray, H. A. (1933), 'The effect of fear upon estimates of the maliciousness of other personalities', *Journal of Social Psychology*, **4**, 310–29.

Newcomb, T. M., Turner, N. H., and Converse, P. E. (1966), *Social Psychology*, London: Tavistock.

Nidorf, H. J., and Crockett, W. H. (1965), 'Cognitive complexity and the integration of conflicting information in written impressions', *Journal of Social Psychology*, **69**, 98–101.

Norman, W. T. (1963), 'Towards an adequate taxonomy of personality attributes', *Journal of Abnormal and Social Psychology*, **66**, 574–83.

Oldfield, R. C. (1941), *The Psychology of the Interview*, London: Methuen.

Osgood, C. E. (1953), *Method and Theory in Experimental Psychology*, New York: Oxford University Press.

Osgood, C. E. (1962), 'Studies on the generality of affective meaning systems', *American Psychologist*, **17**, 10–28.

Osgood, C. E. (1966), 'Dimensionality of the semantic space for communication via facial expressions', *Scandinavian Journal of Psychology*, **7**, 1–30.

Osgood, C. E., and Luria, Z. (1954), 'A blind analysis of a case of multiple personality using the semantic differential', *Journal of Abnormal and Social Psychology*, **49**, 579–91.

Osgood, C. E., Suci, G. J., and Tannenbaum, P. H. (1957), *The Measurement of Meaning*, Urbana, Illinois: University of Illinois Press.

Passini, F. T., and Norman, W. T. (1966), 'A universal conception of personality structure', *Journal of Personality and Social Psychology*, **4**, 44–9.

Pastore, N. (1960a), 'Attributed characteristics of liked and disliked persons', *Journal of Social Psychology*, **52**, 157–63.

Pastore, N. (1960b), 'A note on changing toward liked and disliked persons', *Journal of Social Psychology*, **52**, 173–5.

Peabody, D. (1967), 'Trait inferences: evaluative and descriptive aspects', *Journal of Personality and Social Psychology Monographs*, **7**, 4, Whole No. 644.

Peabody, D. (1970), 'Evaluative and descriptive aspects in personality impression formation: a reappraisal', *Journal of Personality and Social Psychology*, **16**, 639–46.

Pear, T. H. (1957), *Personality, Appearance and Speech*, London: Allen and Unwin.

Pepitone, A. (1958), 'Attributions of causality, social attitudes and cognitive matching processes', in Tagiuri, R., and Petrullo, L. (Eds.), *Person Perception and Interpersonal Behavior*, Stanford: Stanford University Press.

Pepitone, A., and Hayden, R. C. (1955), 'Some evidence for conflict resolution in impression formation', *Journal of Abnormal and Social Psychology*, **51**, 302–7.

Peters, R. S. (1960), *The Concept of Motivation*, 2nd Edn. London: Routledge and Kegan Paul.

Piaget, J. (1926), *The Language and Thought of the Child*, New York: Harcourt Brace.

Piaget, J. (1932), *The Moral Judgment of the Child*, London: Kegan Paul.

Podell, J. E. (1961), 'A comparison of generalisation and adaptation level theories of connotation', *Journal of Abnormal and Social Psychology*, **62**, 594–7.

Rabin, H. M. (1962), 'Perception of others by adjusted and maladjusted subjects as reflected in measures of perceptual space', *Journal of Social Psychology*, **56**, 149–58.

Rabkin, L. Y. (1964), 'The disturbed child's perception of his pranks', *Journal of Individual Psychology*, **20**, 172–8.

Raven, J. C. (1948), *Guide to using the Mill Hill Vocabulary Scale with Progressive Matrices*, London: H. K. Lewis & Co. Ltd.

Raven, J. C. (1958), *Extended Guide to using the Mill Hill Vocabulary Scale with Progressive Matrices Scales*, London: H. K. Lewis & Co. Ltd.

Raven, J. C. (1960), *Guide to the Standard Progressive Matrices Sets ABCD&E*, London: H. K. Lewis & Co. Ltd.

Richardson, S. A., Dornbusch, S. M., and Hastorf, A. H. (1961), Children's categories of interpersonal perception. Final report June 1961, National Institute of Mental Health Research, Grant 7–2480.

Rosenbaum, M. E., and Levin, I. P. (1968), 'Impression formation as a function of source credibility and order of presentation of contradictory information', *Journal of Personality and Social Psychology*, **10**, 167–74.

Rosenbaum, M. E., and Levin, I. P. (1969), 'Impression formation as a function of source credibility and the polarity of information', *Journal of Personality and Social Psychology*, **12**, 34–7.

Rosenkrantz, P. S. and Crockett, W. H. (1965), 'Some factors influencing the assimilation of disparate information in impression formation', *Journal of Personality and Social Psychology*, **2**, 397–402.

Samuels, M. R. (1939), 'Judgments of faces', *Character and Personality*, **8**, 18–27.

Sarbin, T. R. (1954), 'Role theory', in Lindzey, G. (Ed.), *Handbook of Social Psychology*, Cambridge, Massassuetts: Addison-Wesley.

Sarbin, T. R. (1968), 'Ontology Recapitulates Philology: the mythic nature of anxiety', *American Psychologist*, **23**, 6, 411–18.

Sarbin, T. R., Taft, R., and Bailey, D. E. (1960), *Clinical Inference and Cognitive Theory*, New York: Holt, Rinehart and Winston.

Scarlett, H. H., Press, A. N., and Crockett, W. H. (1971), 'Children's descriptions of peers: A Wernerian developmental analysis', *Child Development*, **42**, 439–53.

Schonell, F. J., and Adams, R. H. (1940–9), *The Essential Intelligence Test*, Edinburgh: Oliver and Boyd Limited.

Schlosberg, H. (1954), 'Three dimensions of emotion', *Psychological Review*, **61**, 81–8.

Schulberg, M. C. (1961), 'Authoritarianism, tendency to agree, and interpersonal perception', *Journal of Abnormal and Social Psychology*, **63**, 101–8.

Scodel, A., and Friedman, M. L. (1956), 'Additional observations on the social perception of authoritarians and non-authoritarians', *Journal of Abnormal and Social Psychology*, **52**, 92–5.

Sechrest, L. (1962), 'Biographical similarity and similarity in personal construction'. Unpublished manuscript. Cited by Sechrest (1964), 'The psychology of personal constructs: George Kelly', in Wepman, N. M., and Heine, R. W. (Eds.), *Concepts of Personality*, London: Methuen and Co. Ltd.

Sechrest, L. and Jackson, D. N. (1961), 'Social intelligence and accuracy of interpersonal predictions', *Journal of Personality*, **29**, 167–82.

Secord, P. F. (1958), 'Facial features and inference processes in interpersonal perception', in Tagiuri, R., and Petrullo, L. (Eds.), *Person Perception and Interpersonal Behavior*, Stanford: Stanford University Press.

Secord, P. F., and Backman, C. W. (1964), *Social Psychology*, New York: McGraw Hill.

Secord, P. F., Dukes, W. F., and Bevan, W. (1954), 'Personalities in faces: I. An experiment in social perceiving', *Genetic Psychology Monographs*, **49**, 231–79.

Secord, P. F., and Muthard, J. E. (1955a), 'Personalities in faces: II. Individual differences in the perception of women's faces', *Journal of Abnormal and Social Psychology*, **50**, 238–42.

Secord, P. F., and Muthard, J. E. (1955b), 'Personalities in faces: IV. A descriptive analysis of the perception of women's faces and the identification of some physiognomic determinants', *Journal of Psychology*, **39**, 269–78.

Secord, P. F., Stritch, T. H., and Johnson, L. (1960), 'The role of metaphorical generalisation and congruency in the perception of facial characteristics', *Journal of Social Psychology*, **52**, 329–37.

Sheldon, W. H. (with the collaboration of S. S. Stevens and W. B. Tucker) (1940), *The Varieties of Human Physique*, New York: Harper.

Sheldon, W. H. (with the collaboration of S. S. Stevens) (1942) *The Varieties of Temperament*, New York: Harper.

Sherwood, M. (1969), '*The Logic of Explanation in Psychoanalysis*', New York: Academic Press.

Shrauger, S. (1967), 'Cognitive differentiation and the impression formation process', *Journal of Personality*, **35**, 402–14.

Shrauger, S., and Altrocchi, J. (1964), 'The personality of the perceiver as a factor in person perception', *Psychological Bulletin*, **62**, (5), 289–308.

Siegel, S. (1956), *Nonparametric Statistics for the Behavioral Sciences*, New York: McGraw Hill.

Siegelman, M. (1965), 'Evaluation of Bronfenbrenner's questionnaire for children concerning parental behaviour', *Child Development*, **36**, (1), 163–74.

Slater, P. (1964), *The Principal Components of a Repertory Grid*, London: The Maudsley Hospital.

Smith, H. C. (1966), *Sensitivity to People*, New York: McGraw-Hill.

Smith, M. B., Bruner, J. S., and White, R. W. (1956), *Opinions and Personality*, New York: Wiley and Sons.

Steiner, I. D., and Johnson, H. H. (1963), 'Authoritarianism and "tolerance of trait inconsistency" ', *Journal of Abnormal and Social Psychology*, **67**, 388–91.

Stone, G. P. (1962), 'Appearance and the self', in Rose A. M. (Ed.), *Human Behaviour and Social Processes*, Boston: Houghton Mifflin Co.

Stone, P. J., Dunphy, D. C., Smith, M. S., Ogilvie, D. M., and associates (1966),

The General Inquirer: A Computer Approach to Content Analysis, Cambridge, Massachusetts. MIT Press.

Strawson, P. F. (1964), 'Persons', in Gustafson, D. F. (Ed.), *Essays in Philosophical Psychology*, New York: Doubleday & Company Inc.

Stritch, T. M., and Secord, P. F. (1956), 'Personality in faces: VI. Interaction effects in the perception of faces', *Journal of Personality*, **24**, 270–84.

Supnick, J. (1964), Unpublished Senior Honours Thesis: Clark University, Worcester, Massachussetts. Cited by Crockett, W. H. (1965).

Taft, R. (1955), 'The ability to judge people', *Psychological Bulletin*, **52**, 1–23.

Tagiuri, R. (1957), 'The perception of feelings among members of small groups', *Journal of Social Psychology*, **46**, 219–27.

Tagiuri, R. (1958), 'Social preference and its perception', in Tagiuri, R. and Petrullo, L. (Eds.), *Person Perception and Interpersonal Behavior*, Stanford: Stanford University Press.

Tagiuri, R. (1960), 'Movement as a cue in person perception', David, H. P., and Brengelman, J. C. (Eds.), *Perspectives in Personality Research*, London: Crosby Lockwood & Son Ltd.

Tagiuri, R. (1969), 'Person Perception', in Lindzey, G., and Aronson, E. (Eds.), *The Handbook of Social Psychology*, Vol. 2, 2nd Edn., Reading, Massachussetts: Addison-Wesley.

Tankard, J. W. (1970), 'Effects of eye position on person perception', *Perceptual and Motor Skills*, **31**, 883–93.

Taylor, H. C. (1934), 'Social agreement in personality traits judged from speech', *Journal of Social Psychology*, **5**, 244–8.

Tharp, R. G., and Wetzel, R. J. (1969), *Behavior Modification in the Natural Environment*, New York: Academic Press.

Thibaut, R. J. W., and Riecken, H. W. (1955), 'Some determinants and consequences of the perception of social causality', *Journal of Personality*, **24**, 113–33.

Thorndike, E. L. (1920), 'Intelligence and its Uses', *Harper's Magazine*, 140.

Thorndike, R. L., and Stein, S. (1937), 'An evaluation of attempts to measure social intelligence', *Psychological Bulletin*, **34**, 5.

Thornton, G. R. (1943), 'The effect upon judgments of personality traits of varying a single factor in a photograph', *Journal of Social Psychology*, **18**, 127–48.

Thornton, G. R. (1944), 'The effects of wearing glasses upon judgments of personality traits of persons seen briefly', *Journal of Applied Psychology*, **28**, 203–7.

Todd, F. J., and Rappoport, L. (1964), 'A cognitive structure approach to person perception: a comparison of two models', *Journal of Abnormal and Social Psychology*, **68**, 469–78.

Toulmin, S. E. (1958), *The Uses of Argument*, London: Cambridge University Press.

Triandis, H. C., and Fishbein, M. (1963), 'Cognitive interaction in person perception', *Journal of Abnormal and Social Psychology*, **67**, 446–53.

Triandis, H. C., and Lambert, W. W. (1958), 'A re-statement and test of Schlosberg's theory of emotion with two kinds of subjects from Greece', *Journal of Abnormal and Social Psychology*, **56**, 321–8.

Turner, M. B. (1965), *Philosophy and the Science of Behavior*, New York: Appleton-Century-Crofts, Meredith Co. Inc.

Vannoy, J. S. (1965), 'Generality of cognitive complexity—simplicity as a personality construct', *Journal of Personality and Social Psychology*, **2**, 385–96.

Veness, T., and Brierley, D. W. (1963), 'Forming impressions of personality', *British Journal of Social and Clinical Psychology*, **2**, 11–9.

Vernon, P. E. (1964), *Personality Assessment: A Critical Survey*, London: Methuen.

Vogel, W., and Lauterbach, C. G. (1963), 'Relationships between normal and disturbed sons' percepts of their parents' behavior and personality attributes of the parents and sons', *Journal of Clinical Psychology*, **19**, 52–6.

Warr, P. B. (1968), 'Trends and terminology in person perception research', *Bulletin of the British Psychological Society*, **21**, 94.

Warr, P. B., and Knapper, C. (1966a), 'The relative importance of verbal and visual, information in indirect person perception', *British Journal of Social and Clinical Psychology*, **5**, 118–27.

Warr, P. B., and Knapper, C. (1966b), 'The role of expectancy and communication content in indirect person perception', *British Journal of Social and Clinical Psychology*, **5**, 244–53.

Warr, P. B., and Knapper, C. (1968), *The Perception of People and Events*, London: John Wiley and Sons.

Warr, P. B., and Sims, A. (1965), 'A study of cojudgment processes', *Journal of Personality*, **33**, 598–604.

Watts, A. F. (1944), *The Language and Mental Development of Children*, London: Harrap & Co. Ltd.

Werner, H. (1948), *The Comparative Psychology of Mental Development*, New York: International Universities Press.

Werner, H. (1957), 'The concept of development from a comparative and organismic point of view', in Harris, D., *The Concept of Development: An Issue in the Study of Human Behavior*, Minneapolis: University of Minnesota Press. Quoted by Baldwin, A. L. *Theories of Child Development*, New York: Wiley and Sons.

Wilkins, E. J., and DeCharms, R. (1962), 'Authoritarianism and the response to power cues', *Journal of Personality*, **30**, 439–57.

Williams, B. A. O. (1964), 'Personal identity and individuation', in Gustafson, D. F., (Ed.), *Essays in Philosophical Psychology*, New York: Doubleday and Co. Inc.

Winer, J. (1962), *Statistical Principles in Experimental Design*, New York: McGraw-Hill.

Wishner, J. (1960), 'Reanalysis of "impressions of personality" ', *Psychological Review*, **67**, 96–112.

Wyer, R. S. Jr. (1970), 'Information redundancy, inconsistency and novelty and their role in impression formation', *Journal of Experimental Social Psychology*, **6** (1), 111–27.

Wyer, R. S., Jr., and Watson, S. F. (1969), 'Context effects in impression formation', *Journal of Personality and Social Psychology*, **12**, 22–33.

Wylie, R. C. (1961), *The Self Concept*, Lincoln: University of Nebraska Press.

Yarrow, M. R., and Campbell, J. D. (1963), 'Person perception in children', *Merrill-Palmer Quarterly*. **9**, 57–72.

Zajonc, R. D. (1960), 'The process of cognitive tuning in communication', *Journal of Abnormal and Social Psychology*, **61**, 159–67.

Zipf, G. K. (1949), *Human Behavior and the Principle of Least Effort*, Cambridge, Massachusetts: Addison-Wesley.

Author Index

Adams, R. H., 93
Allport, G. W., 45, 73, 157, 159, 166, 167, 204
Alltrocchi, J., 47, 50
Anderson, N. H., 30, 191
Argyle, M., 23, 24
Asch, S. E., 14, 18–20, 29–31, 33, 36–38, 67, 74, 182, 195, 204
Atkins, A. L., 34, 39
Ayer, A. J., 4

Backman, C. W., 23
Baer, D. J., 23
Bailey, D. E., 8
Baldwin, A. L., 75, 179, 219
Baldwin, C. P., 179
Bandura, A., 284
Bannister, D., 10, 15, 40
Barker, R. G., 26, 71, 243, 262, 284, 285
Barrios, A. A., 30
Bartlett, F. C., 18, 258
Beach, L., 33, 45, 70, 98, 123
Benedetti, D. T., 50
Berkowitz, L., 29
Bevan, W., 22
Bieri, J., 34, 39, 45, 48, 49, 106
Birdwhistell, R. A., 25
Bonarius, J. C. J., 40
Boucher, J., 43
Bradburn, W. M., 34, 46, 106
Briar, S., 34, 39
Brierley, D. W., 25, 37, 62, 65, 66, 70, 73, 109, 123
Briggs, F. F., 31
Bromley, D. B., 10, 20, 43, 46, 52, 60, 61, 64–66, 77, 153, 168, 209, 223, 225, 284
Bruner, J. S., 6, 7, 14, 17, 35, 37, 41, 53, 69, 73, 75, 216, 219

Brunswik, E., 22
Burke, C. J., 84
Buzby, D. E., 25

Campbell, J. D., 59, 61, 63–66, 70, 77, 98, 123, 147
Carpenter, V., 29
Cattell, R. B., 157, 179
Clark, K. B., 65
Clark, M. P., 65
Cliff, N., 204
Cline, M. G., 29
Cline, V. B., 14, 50
Cohen, J., 84, 99
Converse, P. E., 6
Cook, S. W., 22
Cox, R. L., 23
Crandell, J. E., 157
Crockett, W. H., 33, 48, 49, 61, 65, 66
Cronbach, L. J., 14, 17, 37, 39, 40, 44, 50, 67
Crow, T., 51, 74
Crutchfield, R. S., 182

Dahlem, W., 56
Davies, A. D. M., 30
Davies, H., 66
Davies, K. E., 28, 51
De Charms, R., 4, 6, 29, 49, 51, 259, 283, 284
De Soto, C., 49
Dickman, H. R., 26, 27, 241, 243–245, 250–253
Dittman, A. T., 25
Dornbusch, S. M., 33, 44, 45, 58, 59, 68, 70, 71, 98, 123, 153
Dubin, E. R., 55
Dubin, R., 55
Dukes, W. F., 22

307

Subject Index

Abstraction: sex differences in, 152; mentioned, 214, 216–217,

Abstract-concrete dimension: describing others, 34; as in constructs, 61–62; in central versus peripheral terms, 106; in development, 149–150

Achievements and Skills (category 15): effects of age on, 142; effects of age of stimulus person on, 146, 154; effects of like/dislike on, 146, 154

Actones: in behaviour perception, 262, 285–286

Actual Incidents (category 4): effects of age on, 140; effects of age of stimulus person on, 145, 153; effects of like/dislike on, 146, 155; in descriptions of film person, 276–277

Affect: in person perception, 43, 78, 139, 152, 186–187, 193–194, 212–213; in self-descriptions, 237

Age differences: in concepts of personality, 57; in use of content categories, 60–62, 65; in organization of impressions, 60, 66; in personal constructs, 62–63; in integration of conflicting information, 64; in pilot studies, 86–87; in statement fluency, 101; in central statements, 110, 112, 117–118; in trait statements, 159, 161, 163, 165, 166; trend analysis of, for trait statements, 161, 163; in trait vocabulary, 167, 179–183; in differential use of traits, 169, 170–171

Age of stimulus person: effects of, on statement fluency, 103, 104; effects of, on central statements, 116, 119, 120–121; effects of, on trait statements, 163, 164, 166

Ambivalence: towards parents, 212

Analysis of variance design: method of, 81–83, 114; illustrated in Figure 1, 83

Animism: mentioned, 182

Appearance (category 1): effects of age on, 140, 151; effects of intelligence on, 143; effects of like/dislike on, 146, 155; used by young adults, 223; in self-descriptions, 230, 231, 236, used by very young children, 264; in descriptions of film person, 267

Assumed similarity: effects of, on attribution, 49–50

Assumptions: implicit, in psychology, 3–4, 12

Attributes: projection of, 49, 265; of parents, 55–56

Authoritarianism: in person perception, 49

Behaviour elements: in stream of behaviour, 244; 'grain' of, 244–245, 254–255, 262; at different levels of analysis, 251–255; transitional probabilities between, 256

Behaviour episodes: functional equivalence of, 283–284

Behaviour narrative: see Film

Behaviour perception: mentioned, 27–28; perspectives in, 27, 252; in relation to schizophrenia, 27, 256; decentring in, 28; invariances in, 149–150; as fundamental to person perception, 242, 261, 283–284; children's literal descriptions in, 254; contrasted with person perception, 254; implicit versus explicit

BOSTON PUBLIC LIBRARY

3 9999 00409 358 7

WITHDRAWN
No longer the property of the
Boston Public Library.
Sale of this material benefits the Library.

Boston Public Library

Copley Square

General Library

HM132
.L58

1351410376

The Date Due Card in the pocket indicates the date on or before which this
book should be returned to the Library.
Please do not remove cards from this
pocket.